MIDDLE ENGLISH ROMANCE
An Annotated Bibliography, 1955–1985

Joanne A. Rice

GARLAND PUBLISHING, INC. • NEW YORK & LONDON
1987

Library of Congress Cataloging-in-Publication Data

Rice, Joanne A., 1950–
Middle English romance.

(Garland reference library of the humanities ; v. 545)
Bibliography: p.
Includes index.
1. Romances, English—Bibliography. 2. English
literature—Middle English, 1100–1500—Bibliography.
3. Romances, English—History and criticism—Bibliography.
4. English literature—Middle English, 1100–1500—
History and criticism—Bibliography. I. Title.
II. Series.
Z2014.R6R5   1987   [PR321]   016.82′08′001   84-45377
ISBN 0-8240-8830-1 (alk. paper)

Printed on acid-free, 250-year-life paper
Manufactured in the United States of America

For Jack and Richard,

who introduced me to romance

CONTENTS

VERSE ROMANCES

Preface   xi
Acknowledgment.   xv
Introduction.   xvii
Abbreviations   xxv
General and Background.   3-37
Definition and Genre. 39-63
Alexander Romances: General Studies. 65-69
Alliterative Poetry 71-84
Arthurian Literature. 85-114
Breton Lay. .115-119
Chivalry and Knighthood 121-126
Conventionality and Popular Nature of ME Romance. .127-133
Influence Studies 135-139
Manuscripts and Editors 141-151
Thebes and Troy Studies 153-160
Thematic Studies. 161-165
Women 161-171
Other Studies 173-183
Collections of Romances 185-193
Alliterative Alexander Fragments. 195-199
Amis and Amiloun. 201-204
Amoryus and Cleopes   205
Apollonius of Tyre. 207-208
Arthour and Merlin. 209-212
Arthur.   213
Athelston 215-217
Avowynge of King Arthur 219-220
Awnytyrs off Arthure. 221-226
Bevis of Hampton. 227-229
Bone Florence of Rome 231-232
Buik of King Alexander.   233
Cambridge Alexander-Cassamus Fragment   235
Carle off Carlile   237
Chevalere Assigne 239-240
Clariodus   241
Destruction of Troy 243-245
Duke Roland and Sir Otuel of Spain.   247
Earl of Toulous 249-250
Eger and Grime. 251-252

Emare. 253-254
Floris and Blauncheflur. 255-258
Gamelyn. 259-262
Generides. 263-264
Gest of Robin Hood 265-271
Golagrus and Gawain. 273-274
Grene Knight 275
Guy of Warwick 277-280
Havelok. 281-289
Here Begynneth the Lyfe of Joseph. 291
History of the Holy Grail. 293
Horn Child 295
Ipomadon and Lyfe of Ipomydon. 297-299
Jeaste of Sir Gawayne. 301
Joseph of Arimathie. 303-304
King Alexander (See Lyfe of Alisaunder). 305
King Horn. 307-314
King of Tars 315-316
Knight of Curtesy. 317
Lai le Freine. 319-320
Lancelot of the Laik 321-322
Laud Troy-Book 323
Libeaus Desconus 325-327
Lyfe of Alisaunder 329-331
Merlin 333-334
Le Morte Arthur. 335-340
Morte Arthure. 341-364
Octavian 365-366
Otuel A Knight 367
Otuel and Roland 369
Partonope of Blois 371-372
Richard Coer de Lyon 373-375
Roberd of Cisyle 377-380
Roland and Vernagu 381
Romauns of Partenay. 383
Roswall and Lillian. 385
Scottish Alexander Book. 387
Scottish Troy fragments. 389
Seege of Troye 391-392
Sege of Melayne. 393
Siege of Jerusalem 395-396
Siege of Thebes. 397-403
Sir Amadace. 405-406
Sir Cleges 407-408
Sir Degare 409-412
Sir Degrevant. 413-414
Sir Eglamour of Artois 415-416
Sir Firumbras. 417
Sir Gawain and the Green Knight. 419-466

Sir Gowther. 467-468
Sir Isumbras 469-471
Sir Landeval 473
Sir Launfal. 475-480
Sir Orfeo. 481-501
Sir Perceval of Galles 503-506
Sir Torrent of Portyngale. 507
Sir Triamour 509-510
Sir Tristrem 511-517
The Song of Roland 519
The Sowdon of Babylon. 521-522
The Squyr of Lowe Degre. 523-525
Syr Gawene and the Carle of Carelyle 527
The Taill of Rauf Coilyear 529-530
Titus and Vespasian. 531-532
Troy-Book. 533-536
The Turke and Gowin. 537-538
The Weddynge of Sir Gawen and Dame Ragnell 539-541
William of Palerne 543-546
Ywain and Gawain 547-552

PROSE ROMANCES

General and Background 555-561
Caxton Studies 563-566
Collections. 567
Arthur of Little Britain 569-571
Boke of Duke Huon of Burdeux 573
Charles the Grete. 575
Dublin Alexander Epitome 577
Foure Sonnes of Aymon. 579
Helyas, The Knight of the Swan 581
Ipomedon 583
King Ponthus and the Fair Sidone 585
Melusine 587-588
Paris and Vienne 589-590
Prose Alexander. 591
Prose Lyfe of Joseph and De Sancto Joseph. 593
Prose Merlin 595
Prose Siege of Jerusalem 597
Prose Siege of Thebes. 599
Prose Siege of Troy. 601
Robert the Deuyll. 603
Three Kings' Sons. 605
Valentine and Orson. 607
William of Palerne 609

Index. 611-626

PREFACE

I had originally intended that my entire preface be condensed into the epigraph "I did what I did because I am what I am." Although certainly true, this may not say everything that needs to be said about this bibliography, which evolved from research I began for my doctoral dissertation. That work was made more difficult because there were few bibliographic aids or books dedicated to the genre of Middle English romance. No one had ever tried to bring together in a single volume an annotated bibliography of all primary and secondary sources for this large body of medieval literature. J. Burke Severs, however, did publish an indispensable volume, although it is not annotated and not particularly easy to use. In Fascicule 1 of *A Manual of the Writings in Middle English 1050-1500*, Severs includes all manuscripts and editions as well as published secondary material complete through 1955 and selective to 1967 for over ninety Middle English romances. My annotated bibliography is intended to fill the gap since the publication of Severs' volume. For thirty years, research has continued, but no one until now has tried to update the scholarship in any systematic way for the works recognized as Middle English romance.

I have followed Severs in including all of what he labeled as verse and prose romances—with a few discrepancies. I have omitted ballads, which Severs does include, because these short works, found mainly in the Percy Folio, do not belong to the same tradition as other Middle English works generally classified as romances; ballads are a related, but separate genre. I have included, however, a work that Severs omitted: *A Gest of Robin Hood*, because it provides interesting links to romance in its mix of history, folklore, and conventionality. In fact, some recent scholars have labeled it a Middle English romance. Also included are two Lydgate works: *Siege of Thebes* and *Troy-Book*. Both, though historically based, share the same concerns as romance and are illuminated by an understanding of romance contexts and generic similarities. I have excluded Malory

and Chaucer, both major figures who have received extensive
critical attention elsewhere; they would have overshadowed
the works already considered and added more bulk to an
already bulky book. For *Sir Gawain and the Green Knight*, I
have included all editions but only secondary material published since 1977, the *terminus ad quem* of Malcolm Andrews'
annotated bibliography. It seemed unnecessary to duplicate
entries that are available elsewhere, but appropriate to
include information on that poem through 1985 with the other
romances.

   This volume is separated into two major parts: Verse
Romances and Prose Romances. Under Verse Romances, there
are fourteen broad categories that provide an introduction
to various aspects of ME romance study: General and background studies, Definition and genre, Alexander, Alliterative, Arthurian, Breton lays, Chivalric, Conventionality,
Influence, Manuscript, Thebes and Troy, Thematic, Women, and
Other. These categories were established in order to group
research that had a broad scope instead of a close focus on
a single romance and to provide the reader contexts within
which ME romances have been studied. After these general
sections but before the specific romances, there is a Collections section, which lists alphabetically all those
editions that include more than one ME romance. I did not
want to duplicate the bibliographic information under each
relevant romance, but I did want to have all the major
collections of romance in one place in this bibliography.
This decision has created potential confusion for the reader
who is not aware of the way this was handled. The editions
in Collections—items 579-622—recur throughout this bibliography under the appropriate romances, and as a result, an
"Editions" section may not have sequential numbering.
Whenever an editor occurs with page numbers only, the full
bibliographic information is supplied under the original
entry in Collections.

   After the general and collections sections, each romance, arranged alphabetically by the spelling used by
Severs, has its own section. On each title page, the name
of the romance is followed by a number in square brackets,
which corresponds to the number given by Severs, so that the
reader will be able to go directly to the appropriate bibliographic section there.

   Each romance section has two parts: Editions and Criticism. The editions, which are not restricted to 1955-1985
as is criticism, are intended to be comprehensive; however,

I have included no modern translations or renderings—only those in Middle English. Anyone working on a romance must know what kind of edition was intended, when it was published, and whether textual or critical commentary is included. Many of the editions were published in the late 19th or early 20th century with reprinted editions containing no revisions. This kind of information is essential. The secondary material—gathered in a section loosely called Criticism—includes articles, notes, published abstracts of papers delivered, essays in collections, and dissertations. I felt it was important to include dissertations, which are often the genesis of later editions and sometimes represent the best texts available. Also, dissertations, which provide an idea of future trends and the kinds of scholarly approaches to the romances, can give beginning doctoral candidates a sense of what has been done, what is being done, and what needs to be done.

Articles are annotated without judgment or evaluation. I tried to summarize the main points or suggest the scope or focus of the article. Books were handled in a different way. Because a title could be misleading or so general as to be useless, I included a complete table of contents along with annotations only of specific or relevant chapters. In this way, a reader is able to determine the scope of the book, its approach, and the relative amount of space devoted to the pertinent material. Because of this editorial decision, I have included at times material that might seem peripheral or irrelevant to some; nonetheless, this supplementary information provides a context for the relevant material and seems important enough to include.

Each entry contains complete bibliographical information and an annotation, except in cases where the title was self-explanatory. In a few cases, I have not seen the work and therefore could not annotate it; most of these were Japanese articles or very early editions.

The prose section has only two general categories at its beginning: one on background and one on Caxton. Because Caxton studies have appeared in many other places recently, I have included only those works directly related to his production of prose romances or to relevant background material that sheds light on his selections of material or his publishing decisions; I do not intend this section to be a comprehensive Caxton bibliography.

Each section is followed by cross-reference citations,

noted by SEE ALSO. The entry numbers are listed with page numbers in parentheses. Many books have scattered refer- ences to individual romances, but I have included only those with at least two consecutive pages. The general sections, intended as background, are not always cross-referenced directly to every possible romance. They may be of interest to different kinds of readers and are accessible without cumbersome cross-referencing.

The index includes only authors and editors. Since the romances are arranged alphabetically and the general files already order relevant articles under general rubrics, titles of romances or general categories like "Alliterative romance" do not occur in the index. The Table of Contents indicates the pages devoted to each category and romance.

I have aimed for completeness with all American publi- cations and have included as many foreign publications as I could. Given the scope of this bibliography, I am sure that some articles, books, and dissertations have been omitted unintentionally. For those omissions and any errors, I apologize and welcome additions and corrections to keep my computer files as accurate and complete as possible. I have tried to organize this book in a manner most convenient for the user. Verse and prose romances are separate, individual romances have their own sections, and general or background material is included. The whole book is organized alphabet- ically under each section, with the index providing refer- ences to all authors.

Joanne A. Rice
Butler University

ACKNOWLEDGMENTS

First of all, I would like to thank Professor John A. Yunck for setting me on the road that led to this work. For many years, he has been a guiding force and an inspiration to me in my work on medieval romance. To him, I owe an un-calculable debt. For this particular undertaking, I place some blame on John A. Alford, who thought this would be a nice undertaking while I was recuperating from my doctoral dissertation. My thanks to him.

In working on this bibliography, I have had the assis-tance of many librarians, and I especially thank Tony Shipps, Louis Jordan, Linda Horvath, Sharon Lewis, and Janice Lauzon. I have frequented the Library of Congress, Widener Library, the university libraries at Johns Hopkins, Indiana, Notre Dame, and Butler, which have all provided invaluable services and help.

Dave Andrews and Paul van der Heijde performed some computer tricks to transfer files from my Kaypro to IBM diskettes, which were then fed into the System 6, on which the final draft of this manuscript was printed.

For translation of articles from German, Italian, and Spanish, the following people generously gave their time and expertise: my friends Linda Conrad, Peter Sauer, and Karl Hornberger, and my colleagues Katharina Dulckeit, Irving and Serine Fine, and especially Willi Schwoebel.

For the final typing of the book, I thank Vicki Town-send, who begin the work, but left it to Shirley Copple, who has earned a special place in heaven for taking over *in media res* while thinking we were "almost there" nine months ago. Her many evenings and weekends, filled with patience and determination to finish this book, were essential to me. Butler University provided financial assistance and a summer fellowship to help me finish this project; I am grateful to my colleagues, Dean Patricia Meszaros, and the university for their support and encouragement.

Finally, and most importantly, I thank my husband, who sacrificed many of his weekends and vacation days to work with me. His scientific passion for accuracy and detail prevented many errors from creeping into the work, and his moral and intellectual support helped me complete this task.

INTRODUCTION

Middle English Romances constitute a peculiar, even problematic genre. They encompass prose as well as vastly different metrical forms ranging from the four-stress couplet and tail-rhyme stanza to the alliterative long line; they cover subject matter not usually considered suitable for "romantic" fiction such as Charlemagne, Joseph of Aramathia, and Havelok the Dane; they vary in length from 370 lines to over 700 pages; they span hundreds of years from the early thirteenth-century *King Horn* to the sixteenth-century *Carle off Carlile* and *Arthur of Little Britain*. Because of this diversity, scholars have looked in many places for grounds of commonality, but metrical patterns, subject matter, length, dating, basic story types, structure, and theme have all failed to provide the distinguishing criteria by which these diverse narratives may legitimately be called "romance."

From the very start, the word "romance" itself has had a certain vagueness about it, an unspecified generic sense. Originally, it meant simply a work written in a Romance language, nothing more. In the early years of modern scholarship, however, the works constituting the genre of romance were defined by their differences from works in other established genres, rather than by shared similarities. This critical perspective is perhaps best represented by W.P. Ker's early and influential study *Epic and Romance*, which approaches romance as a story form that is antithetical and inferior to epic. Scholars have never agreed on a single approach to romance, nor has there emerged a standard or satisfactory definition for romance.

The narratives themselves provide little help in pointing to specific generic groupings. In fact, the ambiguities inherent in the romance genre are reflected by the very labels the Middle English romance writers attached to their works. A single work like *Amis and Amiloun* calls itself a "geste," "romance," "tale," and "vita" at different stages in its story. This is not unusual. It is virtually impos-

sible to determine generic classification from clues provided by the texts themselves. Critics then have moved beyond
the texts for generic criticism. Northrop Frye has called
romance both the "mythos of summer" and "secular Scripture."
Other critics have focused, not on generic definition, but
on the essential attributes of this genre. Many have drawn
attention to the importance of fantasy, magic, and the
supernatural; of the love element, of the quest or perilous
journey of a lone knight; of chivalric idealism; of the
knight's adventures; of the testing of the individual or his
moving through *rites de passage*. Using one or more of these
characteristics as the basis for a loose system of classification, critics have been able to label certain Middle
English narratives "romances," partly because they are not
exactly chronicles, epics, saints' lives, histories, or any
other readily recognizable literary type.

The early 1800s marked the emergence of this label
"romance" for certain Middle English metrical works. The
word first appeared in the title of a collection in three
volumes published in 1802 by Joseph Ritson and entitled
Ancient English Metrical Romances; George Ellis followed in
1805 with his three volumes called *Specimens of Early English Metrical Romances*. Since then, the word "romance" has
been continually applied to the group of approximately 100
Middle English metrical works. Just as the production of
prose romances lagged behind the verse ones in medieval
England, the publishing of prose romance texts came later.
About 50 years after Ritson and Ellis, William J. Thoms
first published a collection called *Early English Prose
Romances*. These early editions marked the outpouring of the
great age of manuscript collecting and editing, sparked
perhaps by Thomas Percy's *Reliques of Ancient English Poetry*
in 1765.

The famous figures—Thomas Warton, George Ellis, Joseph
Ritson, Sir Walter Scott, and Sir Frederic Madden— remain
legendary today because they set out to illuminate the Dark
Ages and to evoke a lost romantic and chivalric age. The
early scholars established the Roxburghe, Bannatyne, and
Abbotsford clubs, the Camden Society and the Early English
Text Society (EETS) which were all influential in promoting
a systematic and scholarly study of Middle English romance.
The EETS was responsible for an extensive and impressive
collection of editions of ME romances, beginning as early as
1867. By the turn of the century, approximately thirty ME
romances were already in print, many of which remain the
only available editions today. Interest in the Middle Ages

was strong not only in England, but also in Germany during this time. Scholars such as Julius Zupitza, F. Hülsman, and Eugen Kölbing set the standards for modern scholarship with their editions and textual studies.

Once the texts were printed, the stage was set for investigations into the nature of these works. Early 20th century scholars focused their attention on specific numbers or types of ME romances, with study of the genre itself postponed until more texts were available. Anna Hunt Billings published one of the first book-length studies of Middle English Romance: *A Guide to Middle English Metrical Romance* in 1901, which dealt specifically with thirty-seven verse romances under three general headings: English and Germanic Legends, Charlemagne Legends, and Arthurian Legends. Many of these early studies began with an explicit or implicit rejection of the traditional grouping of romance by matter, first propounded by Ellis in 1805. His classification, in turn, was based on Jean Bodel's twelfth-century classification for medieval French romances into the now-famous three matières: "De France et de Bretaign et de Rome la grant." The Middle English romances fit this scheme so poorly that a fourth matière—the Matter of England—had to be invented to salvage the system. This too proved inadequate, and scholars soon turned away from these four subject matters to pursue other directions in their study of romance. The Matter of England, however, is still occasionally used, especially as a convenient label.

In the 1920s Laura Hibbard Loomis devoted *Medieval Romance in England* to thirty-nine of these verse narratives, which she then subdivided into three broad categories: "Romances of Trial and Faith," "Romances of Legendary English Heroes," and "Romances of Love and Adventure." This is a valuable work in studying analogues and giving useful information on the works. Sara Barrow came out with her work on the courtly romances of France in the twelfth and thirteenth centuries, which peripherally applies to some Middle English works, especially those based on French originals. This work, *The Medieval Society Romances*, appeared in 1924. In 1929, Dorothy Everett published her important study "A Characterization of the English Medieval Romance," a work still considered a classic for its insights into this troublesome genre. Shortly thereafter in the 1930s, A. McI. Trounce tackled the tail-rhyme romances in three long articles in *Medium Aevum* (1932-34), and J.P. Oakden analyzed the alliterative romances in his two-volume study (1930-35). At this time too, Walter Hoyt French and

Charles Brockway Hale came out with their edition of *Middle English Metrical Romances* (1930), which included the romances that had not been published in the Early English Text Society series. By the end of the 1930s Middle English Romances had been covered in the literary histories, by J.W.H. Atkins in *The Cambridge History of English Literature* and by Charles Sears Baldwin in his *Three Centuries of Literature in England, 1100-1400.*

The next productive period of published research in this field—the beginning of a new era, in which Middle English romance came into their own as legitimate and worthwhile narratives began in the 1950s. Research began to move away from the earlier negative response to Middle English Romance as incompetent handling and bad imitation of the great French romances. Many early critics felt that English hacks were still churning out bad romances long after the period of the great flowering of romance associated with writers like Chrétien de Troyes. The underlying assumption behind much of this negative criticism was that Middle English writers had attempted to write French romances, but had failed miserably in their imitation. An example of this kind of study focusing on these works as failures and mediocre narratives is George Kane's *Middle English Literature: A Critical Study of the Romances, the Religious Lyrics, Piers Plowman* (1951). Fortunately, critics in the last thirty years have begun to re-examine the Middle English narratives without some of the early preconceptions and prejudices. A great deal of credit for this belongs to Albert C. Baugh's important work on authorship, improvisation, creation, and convention and individuality in Middle English Romance, work first published in 1950 and continuing until 1971.

By 1952, most of the Middle English romances had already appeared in print; however, some important texts did not appear in modern editions until the 1960s and 1970s: *Ywain and Gawain* in 1964, *Sir Orfeo* in 1966, *Libeaus Desconus* in 1969, *Le Bone Florence of Rome* in 1976, and the Southern version of *Octavian* in 1979. New editions, which have been appearing regularly during the past thirty years, are a welcome and essential tool for the serious researcher, since many of the Middle English romances were printed in the nineteenth century, often with no critical apparatus.

The 1960s and 1970s reflected an ever increasing interest in the Middle English verse romances. During this time, Eugène Vinaver published his famous work on romance,

culminating in *The Rise of Romance* in 1971. Perhaps most
important was the rewriting and expansion of John Edwin
Well's *A Manual of the Writings in Middle English 1050-1400*
with its nine supplements. This work, spearheaded by J.
Burke Severs, updated scholarship through 1955, with selected important studies up to 1967. This volume is an invaluable tool for any serious student of Middle English romance,
although it does retain a somewhat oudated organization,
broken into eight major groupings plus a general study and
one on miscellaneous romances. These subdivision include:
Romances derived from English legends, Arthurian legends,
Charlemagne legends, Legends of Godfrey of Bouillon, Legends
of Alexander the Great, Legends of Troy, Legends of Thebes,
Eustace-Constance-Florence-Griselda Legends, and Breton
Lays. This work was followed two years later by one of the
best studies of Middle English romance, Dieter Mehl's *The
Middle English Romances of the Thirteenth and Fourteenth
Centuries*. In this detailed and thoughtful study, Mehl
re-evaluates the Middle English romances and considers their
historical context, their authors and audiences, their
narrative techniques, and definitions of Romance. He deals
with the problematic question of classification by subdivid-
ing the works into Shorter Romances, Homiletic Romances,
Longer Romances, and Novels in Verse.

Like Mehl in perceiving the didactic nature of many of
these works, Hanspeter Schelp focused his critical attention
on *Exemplarische Romanzen in Mittelenglischen* in 1967, and
thus pointed to one of the major distinctions between French
and English romances, which have a decidedly pietistic or
didactic intention, lacking in their French counterparts.
John Stevens, in 1973, published his study of *Medieval
Romance: Themes and Approaches*, which became an important
work for all students of romance literature since he included traditional themes of man and women, man and society, man
and superman, man and God. In 1974 two important collections of essays were published: Larry Benson's *The Learned
and the Lewed* and Peter Haidus's *Approaches to Medieval
Romance*. These were followed by Urs Dürmüller's detailed
study of a metrical type: *Narrative Possibilities of Tail-
Rhyme Romances* as well as Velma Richmond's broader view,
which treats romances like modern detective stories in *The
Popularity of Middle English Romances* (1975). Two more
book-length studies treating ME romances appeared within a
few years: Anne Wilson's *Traditional Romance and Tale: How
Stories Mean* (1976) and Susan Wittig's *Stylistic and Narrative Structures in the Middle English Romances* (1978). The
most recent work has been Derek Brewer's *Symbolic Stories:*

Traditional Narrative of the Family Drama in English Literature (1980).

Individual romances also began attracting critical attention during these important years. Much work has been done on the *Awntyrs off Arthure at the Terne Wathelyne*, *Havelok*, *King Horn*, the alliterative *Morte Arthure*, *Sir Gawain and the Green Knight*, and *Sir Orfeo*. Arthurian studies are growing every year. There is a new periodical *Arthurian Literature* in it fifth volume in 1985, a new *Arthurian Encyclopedia* edited by Norris J. Lacy, and *Arthurian Legend and Literature: An Annotated Bibliography* recently edited by Edmund Reiss, Louise Horner Reiss, and Beverly Taylor.

Since 1955, there have been numerous studies of Middle English romance pursuing generic questions and offering new definitions, from Gillian Beer's *The Romance* in 1970 to Derek Brewer's "The Nature of Romance" in *Poetica* in 1978, with many insightful studies by Derek Pearsall. Questions of audience, intention, connections to historical events and real geography have also been addressed. Gerald Bordman and William A. Quinn have treated questions of folklore and oral formulaic techniques, and David C. Fowler has investigated connections between romances and ballads. Chivalric literature and the nature of knighthood have been of great interest to scholars such as Larry Benson, Diane Bornstein, John Leyerle, W.H. Jackson, and Arthur B. Ferguson. Caroline D. Eckhardt and Shirley Marchalonis have examined the role of women in Middle English romance. John Ganim has investigated style and consciousness in Middle English romance, and C. David Benson has done a full-length book treatment of the history of Troy.

Recently scholars have also been working on manuscript studies. The most famous collection of Middle English romance, the Auchinleck Manuscript, has received attention, including a facsimile edition by Derek Pearsall and I.E. Cunningham, which was published in 1979. Interest in the Thornton Manuscript has also burgeoned in the past ten years, and articles on Middle English romance are beginning to appear with some regularity in journals such as *Scriptorium*, *Studies in Bibliography*, and *Manuscripta*. This recent scholarship has done much to provide a context within which these works can be better understood and evaluated. It is significant, for example, that none of these works appears in collections with Chaucer, Gower, or other romance literature. They are instead often placed in collections of devotional and didactic literature. *Joseph of Arimathie*, *King of Tars*, and *Robert of Cisyle* all appear in the MS Bodleian 3938, a manuscript containing chiefly religious pieces. The Cambridge University Manuscript ff.2.38, a similar collection of didactic and religious work, contains nine Middle English romances. *Sir Isumbras* is interestingly positioned between *Chevalere Assigne* and two devotional poems: "Quinque Vulnera" and "Quinque Gaudia." Likewise, some of the historical Middle English Romances are placed in specifically historical manuscripts. For example, a fragment of *Arthour and Merlin* is inserted into a prose chronicle in the Harley MS 6223, and *Arthur* is similarly found in a Latin chronicle of the kings of England. Future studies may well center on the difficult problems of purpose and audience, perhaps most objectively approached through a re-examination of manuscripts.

Prose romances are another matter. Except for Malory's *Morte Darthur*, few of these works have received any critical attention at all. *Arthur of Little Britain* is the only exception. Lack of interest has been demonstrated both by the small number of published articles and by a lack of modern editions. Even dissertation writers have not been attracted to these works, as George Keiser has noted in the only essay devoted exclusively to prose romances [1654]. In fact, Tony Edwards and George Keiser are among the only scholars publishing in this field, with N.F. Blake concentrating on Caxton. Maurice Keen is interested in chivalry in the 15th century, and Diane Bornstein in late chivalric romances as mirrors of courtesy. Otherwise, the field is open.

Like many other fields of research, Middle English romance provides fertile ground for anyone interested in a certain kind of scholarly work. The past thirty years have been especially rich in stimulating discussions and in opening new directions for future study. Much work remains to be done, however, especially on individual romances. I hope that this annotated bibliography may provide new impetus to the novice as well as to the seasoned scholar by delineating the kind of work, type of approach, and the nature of the research already completed on this diverse body of works known as Middle English Romance.

ABBREVIATIONS FOR PERIODICALS AND SERIES

ABR	American Benedictine Review
AI	American Imago: A Psychoanalytic Journal for Culture, Science, and the Arts
AJP	American Journal of Philology
AN&Q	American Notes and Queries
Anglia	Anglia: Zeitschrift für englische Philologie
AnM	Annuale Mediaevale
Archiv	Archiv für das Studium der neueren Sprachen und Literaturen
ArL	Archivum Linguisticum: A Review of Comparative Philology and General Linguistics
ArlingtonQ	Arlington Quarterly
ArthurL	Arthurian Literature
Atlantis	Atlantis: A Women's Studies Journal
AUMLA	Journal of the Australasian Universities Language and Literature Association: A Journal of Literary Criticism, Philology & Linguistics
AvC	Avalon to Camelot
BB	Bulletin of Bibliography
BBSIA	Bulletin Bibliographique de la Société Internationale Arthurienne
BC	Book Collector
Bibliotheck	The Bibliotheck: A Scottish Journal of Bibliography and Allied Topics

BJRL	Bulletin of the John Rylands University Library of Manchester
BNYPL	Bulletin of the New York Public Library
BodLibR	Bodleian Library Review
BSUF	Ball State University Forum
BUSE	Boston University Studies in English
C&M	Classica et Medievalia
CahiersE	Cahiers Elisabéthains: Etude sur la Pré-Renaissance et la Renaissance Anglaises
CE	College English
Centrum	Centrum: Working Papers of the Minnesota Center for Advanced Studies in Language, Style, and Literary Theory
CF	Classica Folio
ChauR	The Chaucer Review: A Journal of Medieval Studies and Literary Criticism
ChildL	Children's Literature
CL	Comparative Literature
CLS	Comparative Literature Studies
CMCS	Cambridge Medieval Celtic Studies
Comitatus	Comitatus: A Journal of Medieval and Renaissance Studies
CP	Concerning Poetry
DA	Dissertation Abstracts
DAI	Dissertation Abstracts International
DQR	Dutch Quarterly Review of Anglo- American Letters
DR	Dalhousie Review
DVLG	Deutsche Vierteljahrsschrift für Literaturwissenschaft und Geistesgeschichte
E&S	Essays and Studies
EA	Etudes Anglaises: Grande-Bretagne, Etats-Unis
EETSES	Early English Text Society Extra Series

EETSOS	Early English Text Society Original Series
EHR	English Historical Review
ELH	[Formerly Journal of English Literary History]
ELN	English Language Notes
ELR	English Literary Renaissance
EM	English Miscellany: A Symposium of History, Literature and the Arts
ES	English Studies: A Journal of English Language and Literature
ESA	English Studies in Africa: A Journal of the Humanities
ESC	English Studies in Canada
ESELL	Tohoku Gakuin University Review: Essays and Studies in English Language and Literature
ESRS	Emporia State Research Studies
ESt	Erlanger Studien
EStn	Englische Studien
Expl	Explicator
Fabula	Fabula: Zeitschrift für Erzählforschung/ Journal of Folklore Studies/Revue d'Etudes sur le Conte Populaire
FCS	Fifteenth Century Studies
FFC	Folklore Fellows' Communications
FForum	Folklore Forum
FMLS	Forum for Modern Language Studies
FN	Filologicheskie Nauki
GJ	Gutenberg-Jahrbuch
GRM	Germanisch-Romanische Monatsschrift
HJAS	Harvard Journal of Asiatic Studies
HLQ	Huntington Library Quarterly
ISSQ	Indiana Social Studies Quarterly

Interpretations	Interpretations: A Journal of Ideas, Analysis, and Criticism
JAAC	Journal of Aesthetics and Art Criticism
JAF	Journal of American Folklore
JEGP	Journal of English and Germanic Philology
JEH	Journal of Ecclesiastical History
JES	Journal of European Studies
JHI	Journal of the History of Ideas
JMH	Journal of Medieval History
JMRS	Journal of Medieval and Renaissance Studies
JNT	Journal of Narrative Technique
JPC	Journal of Popular Culture
JRMMRA	Journal of the Rocky Mountain Medieval and Renaissance Association
JWCI	Journal of the Warburg and Courauld Institutes
JWSL	Journal of Women's Studies in Literature
KN	Kwartalnik Neofilologiczny (Warsaw, Poland)
KPAB	Bulletin of the Kentucky Philological Society
KRQ	Kentucky Romance Quarterly
L&H	Literature and History: A New Journal for the Humanities
L&P	Literature and Psychology
Lang&S	Language and Style: An International Journal
LangQ	The USF Language Quarterly (Tampa, FL)
LeedsSE	Leeds Studies in English
Library	The Library: A Quarterly Journal of Bibliography
LitR	Literary Review: An International Journal of Contemporary Writing
Lore&L	Lore & Language

LOS	Literary Onomastic Studies
LM	Letterature Moderne
MAE	Medium AEvum
M&H	Medievalia et Humanistica: Studies in Medieval and Renaissance Culture
Manuscriptum	Manuscriptum: Revista Trimestriala Editata de Muzeul Literaturii Române
MCR	Melbourne Critical Review
Mediaevalia	Mediaevalia: A Journal of Mediaeval Studies
MFS	Modern Fiction Studies
MichA	Michigan Academician: Papers of the Michigan Academy of Science, Arts, and Letters
MidwestQ	Midwest Quarterly
MissFR	Mississippi Folklore Register
MLN	Modern Language Notes
MLQ	Modern Language Quarterly
MLR	Modern Language Review
Mosaic	Mosaic: A Journal for the Interdisciplinary Study of Literature
MP	Modern Philology: A Journal Devoted to Research in Medieval and Modern Literature
MQR	Michigan Quarterly Review
MS	Mediaeval Studies (Toronto, Canada)
N&Q	Notes and Queries
Neophil	Neophilologus (Groningen, Netherlands)
NLH	New Literary History: A Journal of Theory and Interpretation
NM	Néuphilologische Mitteilungen: Bulletin de la Société Néophilologique
NMS	Nottingham Medieval Studies
NYFQ	New York Folklore Quarterly
P&P	Past and Present

PAPS	Proceedings of the American Philosophical Society
Parergon	Parergon: Bulletin of the Australian and New Zealand Association for Medieval and Renaissance Studies
PBA	Proceedings of the British Academy
PBSA	Papers of the Bibliographical Society of America
PCP	Pacific Coast Philology
Peritia	Peritia: Journal of the Medieval Academy of Ireland
PLL	Papers on Language and Literature: A Journal for Scholars and Critics of Language and Literature
PMASAL	Proceedings of the Michigan Academy of Science, Arts, and Letters
PMLA	Publications of the Modern Language Association of America
PoetT	Poetics Today
PPMRC	Proceedings of the PMR Conference: Annual Publication of the International Patristic, Mediaeval and Renaissance Conference
PQ	Philological Quarterly
PSTS	Publications of the Scottish Text Society
QFG	Quaderni di Filologia Germanica della Facolta di Lettere e Filosofia dell' Universita di Bologna
QJS	Quarterly Journal of Speech
RBPH	Revue Belge de Philologie et d'Histoire
RES	Review of English Studies: A Quarterly Journal of English Literature and the English Language
RITL	Revista de Istorie şi Teorie Literara
Romania	Romania: Revue Consacrée à l'Etude des Langues et des Litératures Romanes
RomJ	Romanistiches Jahrbuch
RomN	Romance Notes

RPh	Romance Philology
RSC	Rivista di Studi Classici
RUO	Revue de l'Université d'Ottawa/ University of Ottawa Quarterly
SAB	South Atlantic Review
SAC	Studies in the Age of Chaucer
SAQ	South Atlantic Quarterly
SB	Studies in Bibliography: Papers of the Bibliographical Society of the University of Virginia
ScLJ	Scottish Literary Journal
ScS	Scottish Studies
Scriptorium	Scriptorium: Revue Internationale des Etudes Relatives aux Manuscrits/International Review of Manuscript Studies
SELit	Studies in English Literature (Tokyo, Japan)
SFQ	Southern Folklore Quarterly
SIcon	Studies in Iconography
SLit	Studies in Literature (Kyushu University, Fukuoka, Japan)
SMC	Studies in Medieval Culture
SML	Statistical Methods in Linguistics
SN	Studia Neophilologica: A Journal of Germanic and Romance Languages and Literature
SoQ	The Southern Quarterly: A Journal of the Arts in the South
SP	Studies in Philology
Speculum	Speculum: A Journal of Medieval Studies
SSF	Studies in Short Fiction
SSL	Studies in Scottish Literature
StG	Studi Germanici
STS	Scottish Text Society
StudH	Studies in the Humanities (Indiana, PA)

TCBS	Transactions of the Cambridge Bibliographical Society
TGB	Index to Theses Accepted for Higher Degrees in the Universities of Great Britain and Ireland.
Traditio	Traditio: Studies in Ancient and Medieval History, Thought, and Religion
Tristania	Tristania: A Journal Devoted to Tristan Studies
TSL	Tennessee Studies in Literature
TSLL	Texas Studies in Literature and Language: A Journal of the Humanities
UCTSE	University of Cape Town Studies in English
UES	Unisa English Studies: Journal of the Department of English
UMSE	University of Mississippi Studies in English
Viator	Viator: Medieval and Renaissance Studies
WS	Women's Studies
WW	Wirkendes Wort: Deutsche Sprache in Forschung und Lehre
YES	Yearbook of English Studies
YWES	Year's Work in English Studies
ZAA	Zeitschrift für Anglistik und Amerikanistik
ZDMG	Zeitschrift für deutschen morgenländischen Gesellschaft
ZFSL	Zeitschrift für französische Sprache und Literatur

VERSE ROMANCES

BACKGROUND AND GENERAL

1. Ackerman, Robert W. *Backgrounds to Medieval English Literature.* New York: Random House, 1966.

    Chapter: 1. Social and religious backgrounds: Old English period, 3-20.
    2. Social and religious backgrounds: Middle English period, 21-53.
    3. The English language in the Middle Ages, 54-79.
    4. Popular Christian doctrine, 80-102.
    5. The world view of the Middle Ages, 103-126.
    Appendix: Critical approaches, 127-142.
    Notes, bibliography, and index, 143-171.

2. ------. "Middle English Literature to 1400." *The Medieval Literature of Western Europe: A Review of Research, Mainly 1930-1960.* Ed. John H. Fisher. New York: NYU P, 1966. 73-123.

    Section VIII, 'The Romance' (94-101), includes lists of works in three categories: general, non-Arthurian romances, and Arthuriana.

3. Auden, W.H. "The Quest Hero." *Tolkien and the Critics: Essays on J.R.R. Tolkien's The Lord of the Rings.* Ed. Neil D. Isaacs and Rose A. Zimbardo. Notre Dame: U of Notre Dame P, 1968. 40-61.

    Defines six essential elements of the quest: the finding of a precious object or person, the undertaking of a journey, the hero, the testing of the hero, the overcoming or winning over of the guardians of the object, and helpers who assist the hero.

4. Baird, Lorrayne Yates. "The Status of the Poet in
    the Middle Ages and the Problem of Anonymity." *DAI* -
    30 (1970): 3422A-3423A. U of Kentucky.

    Argues that factors in anonymity and deliberate
    self-effacement were ecclesiastical distrust of
    sensual beauty, the equation of poetic invention with
    lying, and the charge of presumption against those
    inventive and creative. Examines the literary lan-
    guage and poetic style of English writers who, aware
    of their vulnerability, refer to authority, disclaim
    responsibility, and use the claim-for-truth *topos*.

5. Barron, W.R.J. "A propos de quelques cas d'écorche-
    ment dans les romans anglais et français du Moyen
    Age." *Mélanges de Littérature: Du moyen âge au XXe
    siècle*. Offerts à Mademoiselle Jeanne Lods, profes-
    seur honoraire de littérature médiévale à l'Ecole
    Normale Supérieure de Jeunes Filles. 2 vols. Paris:
    Ecole Normale Supérieure de Jeunes Filles, 1978. 1:
    49-68.

    Discusses flaying alive, a penalty for treason in
    the Middle Ages, in such works as *Sir Gawain and the
    Green Knight*, *King Alexander*, *Guy of Warwick*, and
    Havelok.

6. Beatie, Bruce A. "Patterns of Myth in Medieval
    Narrative." *Symposium* 25 (1971): 101-122.

    Investigates the "bride-wooing" pattern and "hus-
    band's return" in *King Horn* and other works to show
    that certain pervasive patterns exist and that they
    are related to myth. Further suggests that medieval
    patterns tend to be bipartite with ritualistic pat-
    terns relating to the personal and societal aspects
    of medieval society.

7. Bennett, Michael J. "Courtly Literature and North-
    west England in the Later Middle Ages." *Court and
    Poet* [20]. 69-78.

    Outlines two possible modes of cultural interpene-
    tration between the courtly world and northwest
    England: either through the role of manor houses and

monastic libraries or through men from the northwest moving to more cosmopolitan settings.

8. Benson, Larry D., ed. *The Learned and the Lewed: Studies in Chaucer and Medieval Literature.* Harvard English Studies 5. Cambridge: Harvard UP, 1974.

    Includes essays on Chaucer and medieval romance [157], *Bone Florence of Rome* [719], *Emare* [754], *Gest of Robin Hood* [798], and *Troy-Book* [1592], and *Arthur of Little Britain* [1685].

9. Bessinger, Jess B., Jr., and Robert R. Raymo, eds. *Medieval Studies in Honor of Lillian Herlands Hornstein.* New York: NYU P, 1976.

    Includes essays on *Bone Florence of Rome* [718] and *Morte Arthure* [989].

10. Bloomfield, Morton W. "The Problem of the Hero in the Later Medieval Period." *Concepts of the Hero in the Middle Ages and the Renaissance.* Ed. Norman T. Burns and Christopher J. Reagan. Albany: SUNY P, 1975. 27-48.

    Discusses the absence of a true charismatic hero in the later Middle Ages and the development of the ambiguous hero noted for his unheroic or self-destructive heroism (as in *Sir Gawain and the Green Knight*). Also notes the rise of the bourgeois hero (in *Squyr of Lowe Degre* and *Guy of Warwick*), which indicates an erosion of the ideal. Suggests causes in the rising sadness of the late Middle Ages, a fatalistic sense that man is the victim of fortune, and the fundamental polarity between fame and conscience.

11. Boitani, Piero. *English Medieval Narrative in the Thirteenth and Fourteenth Centuries.* Trans. Joan Krakover Hall. Cambridge: Cambridge UP, 1982.

    Chapter: 1. Religious tradition, 1-27.
              2. Comic tradition, 28-35.
              3. The world of romance, 36-70.

Investigates the nature of romance; notes two tendencies in its
development: anglicized French works
and indigenous legends. Gives an
overview of the different types,
themes, treatment, and uses of legend in the ME romance.
    4. Dream and vision, 71-113.
    5. Narrative collections and Gower,
       114-132.
    6. Chaucer, 133-272.
Notes, further reading, and index, 273-309.

12. Bolton, W.F. Introduction: "The Conditions of Lit-
    erary Composition in Medieval England." Bolton [13].
    ix-xxxvii.

    Touches on the differences between the medieval and
    modern ages; the meaning of the Middle Ages; medieval
    books (their cost, production, multiple forms in
    different manuscripts); authorship, anonymity, and
    audience; patronage; sources; originality; borrowing
    from debates, dream visions, letters, plays, lyrics,
    epics, and complaints; and special conventions of
    medieval literature.

13. ------, ed. *The Middle Ages*. Vol. 1 of *History of
    Literature in the English Language*. 10 vols. London:
    Barrie & Jenkins, 1970.

    Includes essays on literary composition [12], early
    ME literature [92], popular traditions [108], allit-
    eration [266], and prose [1644].

14. Brahmer, Mieczyslaw, Stanislaw Helsztynski, and
    Julian Krzyzanowski, eds. *Studies in Language and
    Literature in Honour of Margaret Schlauch*. Warsaw:
    PWN—Polish Scientific Publishers, 1966.

    Includes essays on Arthurian romance [268], *Awntyrs
    off Arthure* [703], *Siege of Jerusalem* [1134], and
    Squyr of Lowe Degre [1564].

15. Brewer, Derek S., ed. *Chaucer and Chaucerians: Crit-*

ical *Studies in Middle English Literature*. London: Nelson; University: U of Alabama P, 1966.

Includes chapters on Chaucer and the English tradition [17] and the English Chaucerians [491].

16. ------. *English Gothic Literature*. History of Literature Series. New York: Schocken Books, 1983.

Chapter: 1. Continuities and beginnings, 1-16.
2. The inner life, 17-29.
3. The question of song, 30-39.
4. The question of song—lyrics, short poems, ballads, 40-69.
5. Adventure and love: romances in rhyme, 70-88.
   Highly general discussion of literary trends with brief plot summaries and a few remarks on *King Horn*, *Havelok*, *Floris and Blauncheflur*, *Sir Orfeo*, the Breton lay, audience, and 14th and 15th century romances.
6. Chaucer, 89-127.
7. Chaucer's friends and followers in England and Scotland, 128-141.
8. Alliterative poetry, 142-154.
   Mentions the Alexander romances and discusses *Morte Arthure*.
9. The *Gawain*-poet, 155-180.
   Gives elements of the story, its sources, values, and symbolic meaning.
10. *Piers Plowman*, 181-212.
11. Drama, 213-240.
12. Later religious prose, 241-261.
13. Secular prose: Malory and Caxton, 262-279.
    Discusses ways that Malory and Caxton continued literary trends in their prose works.
14. The re-making of English, 280-299.
Further reading, chronological table, and index, 300-315.

17. ------. "The Relationship of Chaucer to the English

and European Traditions." Brewer [15]. 1-38.

Suggests that the English tradition—the aristocratic northern and western alliterative works, the
secular fiction, the verse romances, the appeal to
middle-class audience—was the root of Chaucer's poetry, but that Chaucer grafted a new more formal diction based on the European literary traditions and
his knowledge of rhetoricians onto the basic English
style of romance.

18.   ------. *Symbolic Stories: Traditional Narratives of
the Family Drama in English Literature*. Cambridge,
Eng.: D.S. Brewer, 1980.

Introduction, 1-14.
Chapter: 1.   Fairy tales, 15-53.
           2.   The stories of David, Judas, and
                some medieval romances, 54-71.
                Connects two motifs, "Twin Broth-
                ers" and the "Fairy Mistress," to
                Eger and Grime; discusses *King Horn*
                as a male Cinderella and *Sir Degare*
                as a story of integrating the mascu-
                line.
           3.   *Sir Gawain and the Green Knight*,
                72-91.
                Views *Sir Gawain and the Green
                Knight* as a story of an individual
                wanting to regress into infancy as
                he deals with mother and father
                figures.
           4.   Chaucer, 92-99.
           5.   The story of Gareth, 100-111.
           6.   Some examples from Shakespeare, 112-
                147.
           7.   Mainly on Jane Austen, 148-167.
           8.   *Great Expectations*, 168-183.
Epilogue and references, 185-190.

19.   Brunner, Karl. "Die Überlieferung der mittelenglischen Versromanzen." *Anglia* 76 (1958): 64-73.

Reviews the secular tradition of the ME romance,
briefly discusses the manuscripts and early editions,
and touches on their purposes or uses.

20. Burgess, Glyn S., A.D. Deyermond, W.H. Jackson, A.D. Mills, and P.T. Ricketts, eds. *Court and Poet.* Selected Proceedings of the Third Congress of the International Courtly Literature Society (Liverpool 1980). ARCA Classical and Medieval Texts, Papers and Monographs 5. Liverpool: Francis Cairns, 1981.

    Includes articles on the literature of northwest England [7], *King Alexander* [950], and the figure of Morgan [1300].

21. Burrow, J.A. *Medieval Writers and Their Work: Middle English Literature and its Background 1100-1500.* Oxford: Oxford UP, 1982.

    Chapter: 1. The period and the literature, 1-23.
               2. Writers, audiences, and readers, 24-55.
               3. Major genres, 56-85.
               4. Modes of meaning, 86-118.
               5. The survival of Middle English literature, 119-133.
    Notes, bibliography, and index, 134-148.

    Intended not as a history or survey, but as an introduction to the literature by focusing on differences between medieval and modern literature that confront a 20th-century reader. No extended discussion of romance, which is briefly mentioned on pp. 8-9, 11, 17, 51-52, 71-72, 76, 78, 79, 81, 82, 84.

22. Clanchy, M.T. *From Memory to Written Record: England, 1066-1307.* Cambridge: Harvard UP, 1979.

    Argues that although the literary mass movement did not occur until the 19th century, it had its origins in the 12th and 13th centuries with the shift from memory to written record, from sacred script to practical literacy, which went along with the practical business of government, politics, and commerce. Divides the book into two parts: I. The Making of Records, 9-147, including memories and myths of the Norman Conquest, the proliferation of documents, types of records, the technology of writing, and the preservation and use of documents; and II. The Literate Mentality, 149-265, including the languages of record, literate and illiterate, hearing and seeing, trusting writing, and practical literacy. Also includes plates and index, 267-330.

23. Clark, Donald Lemen. "Rhetoric and the Literature of the English Middle Ages." *QJS* 45 (1959): 19-28.

Discusses the uses of rhetoric from Priscian, especially *narratio*, *sententia*, *refutatio*, *locus communus*, *laus*, *comparatio*, *allocutio*, *descriptio*, and *legislatio*. Argues that these devices taught both poets and prose writers how to embellish their style.

24. Coleman, Janet. *Medieval Readers and Writers: 1350-1400*. English Literature in History. London: Hutchinson; New York: Columbia UP, 1981.

Chapter: 1. Introduction, 13-15.
           2. Vernacular literacy and lay education, 15-57.
           3. The literature of social unrest, 58-151.
           4. Memory, preaching and the literature of a society in transition, 152-231.
           5. Theology, non-scholastic literature and poetry, 232-270.
           6. Conclusion, 271-280.
Notes, references, and index, 281-337.

25. Colquitt, Betsy Feagan, ed. *Studies in Medieval, Renaissance, American Literature: A Festschrift*. Honoring Troy C. Crenshaw, Lorraine Sherley, Ruth Speer Angell. Fort Worth: Texas Christian UP, 1971.

Includes essays on romance [138] and on *Gamelyn* [780].

26. Cooper, Helen. "Magic That Does Not Work." *M&H* ns 7 (1976): 131-146.

Proposes the theory that the supernatural that fails or the magic that does not work should be seen as a device to measure and define the human, especially emotions and ideals.

27. Davidson, Clifford. "The Love Mythos in the Middle Ages and Renaissance." *BSUF* 16.4 (1975): 3-14.

Outlines an approach to medieval love literature that would illuminate the essentials of the relationships of love and circumvent the problems in courtly love studies. Suggests a need to apply the techniques of phenomenological analysis in rigorous ways to specific works.

28. Dean, Kitty Chen. "'*Maritalis Affectus*': Attitudes Towards Marriage in English and French Medieval Literature." *DAI* 40 (1980): 5044A-5045A. U of California, Davis.

Demonstrates that despite ecclesiastical and antimatrimonial feeling, marriage between a man and woman of comparable status was still portrayed in medieval literature as the ideal love relationship.

29. Doyle, A.I. "English Books In and Out of Court from Edward III to Henry VII." Scattergood and Sherborne [84]. 163-181.

Investigates the role the courts played in the demand for and supply of English books. Finds that no ME manuscript was connected with Edward III, but that in the north and west Midlands, copying and authorship were well established before any metropolitan, court-centered literary center. Concludes with doubts about the influence of the court on the character of book production or creation.

30. Dubois, Marguerite-Marie. *La Littérature Anglaise du Moyen Age (500-1500)*. Paris: Presses Universitaires de France, 1962.

Contains a relatively short section entitled "La littérature romanesque," 133-144, with paragraph subdivisions: le roman moral, le roman sentimental, le roman d'aventures, le roman exotique, le roman merveilleux, le cycle de Troie, le cycle d'Alexandre, le cycle de Thèbes, le cycle de Charlemagne, les romans historiques, la légende Arthurienne, and les romans imprimés.

31. Duncan, Edgar Hill. "Short Fiction in Medieval Eng-
     lish: II. The Middle English Period." *SSF* 11 (1974):
     227-241.

     A brief sampling of some works in the major genres:
     short or multi-episodic romances (*King Horn* and
     Athelston), the Breton lay (*Sir Orfeo*, *Sir Landeval*,
     Sir Launfal), as well as those in the *exemplum* tradi-
     tion, beast tales, fabliaux, and dream visions.

32. Eckhardt, Caroline D., ed. *Essays in the Numerical
     Criticism of Medieval Literature*. Lewisburg: Buck-
     nell UP; London: Associated UP, 1980.

     Includes two essays on *Sir Gawain and the Green
     Knight* [1290, 1317].

33. Evans, W.O. "*Cortaysye* in Middle English." *MS* 29
     (1967): 143-157.

     Examines the semantic range of the word *cortaysye*
     in 13th- and 14th-century English literature and
     cautions against associating it with concepts and
     conventions of courtly love. Argues that its context
     is usually Christian virtue, dealing with acquired
     patterns of correct behavior, polite procedure in
     chivalric matters, or practical charity.

34. Everett, Dorothy. *Essays on Middle English Litera-
     ture*. Ed. Patricia Kean. Oxford: Clarendon P, 1955.

          Chapter: 1. A characterization of the English
                         medieval romances, 1-22.
                            Discusses romance's connections
                         with other genres such as the ballad
                         and saints' lives and points to the
                         idealizing tendencies of romance and
                         the importance of the hero.
                     2. Layamon and the earliest Middle Eng-
                         lish alliterative verse, 23-45.
                     3. The alliterative revival, 46-96.
                            Devotes most of the chapter to the
                         Morte Arthure and *Gawain*-poet, with
                         brief mentions of other works in the
                         tradition.

             4. Chaucer's love visions, with partic-
                 ular reference to the *Parlement of*
                 Foules, 97-114.
             5. *Troilus and Criseyde*, 115-138.
             6. Chaucer's 'good ear,' 139-148.
             7. Some reflections on Chaucer's 'art
                 poetical,' 149-174.
       Index, 177-179.

35. Fisher, John H. "English Literature." *The Present*
     State of Scholarship in Fourteenth-Century Litera-
     ture. Ed. Thomas D. Cooke. Columbia: U of Missouri
     P, 1982. 1-54.

     Includes a discussion of research on the allitera-
     tive revival (7-8), the *Gawain*-poet (16-18), romance
     (23-24), with extensive bibliographies under specific
     headings (26-54).

36. Ford, Boris, ed. *Medieval Literature: Chaucer and*
     the Alliterative Tradition. Vol. 1, Part 1 of *The*
     New Pelican Guide to English Literature. 7 vols.
     Harmondsworth, Eng.: Penguin, 1982.

     Includes a chapter on medieval verse and drama
     [94], a discussion of *Sir Gawain and the Green Knight*
     [1242], the text of *Sir Launfal* [1400], and a study
     of ME prose [1648].

37. Ganim, John M. "History and Consciousness in Middle
     English Romance." *LitR* 23 (1980): 481-496.

     Corrects the negative criticism leveled against the
     ME romance by investigating the entirely different
     literary and rhetorical strategies of these works.
     Argues that the ME romance speaks not to an elite
     audience, but to a larger community, that the narra-
     tive voice includes itself in that world, that the
     crucial scenes are of revelation, discovery, and
     communication, and that the characters are meant to
     embody synthesis, not internal conflict.

38. ------. *Style and Consciousness in Middle English*
     Narrative. Princeton: Princeton UP, 1983.

Includes individual chapters on ME romance [846], *Siege of Thebes* [1148], *Sir Gawain and the Green Knight* [1273], as well as Henryson's *Testament of Cresseid* and Chaucer's *Troilus and Criseyde*.

39. Gradon, Pamela. *Form and Style in Early English Literature*. London: Methuen, 1971.

Introduction, 1-31.
Chapter: 1. The allegorical picture, 32-92.
            2. Literary structures, 93-151.
            3. Daughters of earth, 152-211.
            4. The romance mode, 212-272.
                Distinguishes between two strands of the romantic mode: one from OE poetry and the aristocratic *chansons de geste*, the other from religious chivalry. Further discusses the fluidity and range of these works in terms of their concept of love and remoteness from life and concludes that there is no real genre, but rather a romance mode.
            5. Medieval realism, 273-331.
            6. Mannerism and Renaissance, 332-381.
Conclusion, 382-387.
Bibliographic index and glossary, 388-398.

40. Green, D.H. "Irony and Medieval Romance." *FMLS* 6 (1970): 49-64. Rpt. in Owen [339].

Suggests that the force of medieval irony derives from the discrepancy between what is and what should be in terms of ideal chivalry, and this leads to self-criticism; distinguishes different kinds of irony in romance: verbal, narrative, dramatic, structural, as well as irony of values.

41. ------. *Irony in the Medieval Romance*. Cambridge: Cambridge UP, 1979.

Chapter: 1. Introduction, 1-13.
            2. The possibilities of irony in courtly literature, 14-50.
            3. Irony and chivalry, 51-90.

4. Irony and love, 91-131.
5. Irony and narrative technique, 132-170.
6. Verbal irony, 171-212.
7. Irony of the narrator, 213-249.
8. Dramatic irony, 250-286.
9. The irony of values, 287-325.
10. Structural irony, 326-358.
11. The reasons for irony in the medieval romance, 359-393.
Discusses ways in which the following encourage irony in romance: the poet's status, language of courtesy, the select audience, written composition, patronage and rhetoric, secularism, the critical spirit, literary polemics, narrative features, and didacticism.
Bibliography, 394-418.
Index of passages discussed, 419-424.
General index, 425-431.

41a. Haidu, Peter. "Repetition: Modern Reflections on Medieval Aesthetics." *MLN* 92 (1977): 875-887.

Juxtaposes modern ideas of creativity and authenticity with medieval aesthetics, which found repetition and conventionality validated by both Christian and neoplatonic ideas about the created world as revelations of divine meaning or intention.

42. Hinton, Norman. "Anagogue and Archetype: The Phenomenology of Medieval Literature." *AnM* 7 (1966): 57-73.

Addresses problems of interpretation of medieval literature, especially romance, when the reader comes to it with modern conceptions of form, structure, development, and sense of an ending. Suggests that the unification expected at the literal level is supplied at other levels, with *anagogia* the ultimate structuring principle. Does not claim that all romances are allegories, but rather that the investigation into the similarities of romance to archetype and of archetype to anagogical and allegorical thought is worth undertaking.

43. Hornstein, Lillian Herlands. "Middle English Ro-
     mances." *Recent Middle English Scholarship and
     Criticism: Survey and Desiderata.* Ed. J. Burke
     Severs. Pittsburgh: Duquesne UP, 1971. 55-95.

     A brief overview of bibliographic tools, seminal
     works, and range of scholarship and interest in ME
     romance; with extensive notes.

44. Hunt, Tony. "Irony and the Rise of Courtly Romance."
     GLL ns 35 (1981): 98-104.

     Raises the question of how sensitive to irony the
     medieval writers were and qualifies many of the ideas
     in Green [41].

45. ------. "The Structure of Medieval Narrative." *JES*
     3 (1973): 295-328.

     Analyzes the shortcomings of recent books on narra-
     tive structure (Bulatkin, Dorfman, and Ryding) and
     calls for structural studies that begin with texts
     rather than theories.

46. Jackson, W.T.H.   "The Changing Face of Medieval
     Literature." *Essays on the Reconstruction of Medie-
     val History.* Ed. Vaclav Mudroch and G.S. Couse.
     Montreal: McGill-Queen's UP, 1974. 52-66.

     Reviews the characteristic approaches to medieval
     literature in the 1940s and 1950s as basically tex-
     tual studies and an obsession with the study of ori-
     gins and analogues. Points to changes in attitudes
     and approaches, especially the study of *topoi* and
     allegorical and theological readings. Calls for
     detailed studies of medieval style and of the rela-
     tionship between milieu and subject.

47. ------. *The Literature of the Middle Ages.* New
     York: Columbia UP, 1960.

          Chapter: 1. The survival and influence of the
                          classics, 1-33.
                      2. The reasons for writing literature,

34-44.
3. The audience for medieval literature, 45-61.
4. The literary types, 62-79.
5. The romance, 80-159.
   Concentrates on the Arthurian romances, tracing their development during the 12th and 13th centuries.
6. The chanson de geste, 160-174.
7. The Germanic epic, 175-215.
8. The medieval lyric, 216-275.
9. The drama, 276-327.
10. The beast epic, 328-353.
Conclusion, 354-357.
Chronology, bibliography, and index, 359-432.

48. Jauss, Hans Robert. "Cinq modèles d'identification esthétique: Complèment à la théorie des genres littéraires au moyen âge." *XIV Congresso Internazionale di Linguistica e Filologia Romanza.* Naples, 15-20 April 1974. Vol. I. Ed. Alberto Várvaro. Naples: Gaetano Macchiaroli; Amsterdam: Benjamins, 1978. 145-164.

Proposes and discusses five models of aesthetic identification: associative with reference to play and festivities; admirative with a perfect hero, sage, or saint; sympathetic with an ordinary hero; cathartic with a suffering hero or one in trouble; and ironic with no true hero or even an antihero.

49. Johnston, Arthur. *Enchanted Ground: The Study of Medieval Romance in the Eighteenth Century.* London: Athlone P, 1964.

Chapter:
1. Introduction, 1-59.
2. Epic and romance: Richard Hurd, 60-74.
3. Thomas Percy, 75-99.
4. Thomas Warton, 100-119.
5. Joseph Ritson, 120-147.
6. George Ellis, 148-176.
7. Walter Scott, 177-194.
8. What then was romantic? 195-218.
Appendices, bibliography, and index, 219-249.

50. Kahn Blumstein, Andrée. *Misogyny and Idealization in
     the Courtly Romance*. Studien zur Germanistik,
     Anglistik und Komparatistik 41. Bonn: Bouvier Verlag
     Herbert Grundmann, 1977.

     Discusses the misogynistic tendency even in ideal-
     ized romance, especially in Hartmann von Aue's *Iwein*,
     Gottfried von Strassburg's *Tristan*, and Wolfram von
     Eschenbach's *Parzival*.

51. Kean, P.M. Introduction: "Chaucer and the English
     Tradition." *Love Vision and Debate*. Vol. 1 of
     Chaucer and the Making of English Poetry. 2 vols.
     London: Routledge & Kegan Paul, 1972. 1-30, 179-
     182.

     Claims that Chaucer took elements of the English
     style and the straightforward maintenance of a narra-
     tion from the metrical romances, but then built his
     own poetry with a new kind of organization replacing
     episodic narrative and with a new kind of learned
     subject matter and philosophy.

52. Kellogg, Robert. "Varieties of Tradition in Medieval
     Narrative." *Medieval Narrative*. Proceedings of the
     Third International Symposium Organized by the Centre
     for the Study of Vernacular Literature in the Middle
     Ages. Held at Odense University on 20-21 November
     1978. Ed. Hans Bukker-Neilsen, Peter Foote, Andreas
     Haarder, Preben Meulengracht Sørensen. Odense, Den.:
     Odense UP, 1979. 120-129.

     Distinguishes between traditional art (communal,
     conservative, continuous with the past, rhythmical,
     authorless, and oral) and high art (personal and in-
     novative), with popular art mediating between them
     since it is both communal and innovative. Raises
     difficulties in interpreting traditional art and
     suggests that much medieval literature belongs in the
     movement from traditional to popular art.

53. Kelly, Henry Ansgar. *Love and Marriage in the Age of
     Chaucer*. Ithaca: Cornell UP, 1975.

          Part: I. *Hymenaeus Amorque*: the compatibil-

ity of love and marriage, 31-67.
II.   The age of Ovid, 69-160.
III. Clandestine marriage, 161-242.
IV.   Matrimonial sin and virtuous pas-
      sion, 243-334.
Index, 335-359.

Romances are mentioned on pp. 21-22, 39, 177.

54. Kossick, Shirley. "The Mediaeval Ethos." *UES* 8.1
     (1970): 3-6.

     Dispels the popular view of the Middle Ages as a
     time of darkness, austerity, and conformity and
     touches on the variety and spirit of medieval forms
     from Arthurian romance to the morality play.

55. Lasater, Alice E. *Spain to England: A Comparative
     Study of Arabic, European, and English Literature of
     the Middle Ages.* Jackson: UP of Mississippi, 1974.

     Chapter: 1. Introduction, 3-14.
                2. Medieval Spain, 15-34.
                3. Lyric poetry, 35-55.
                4. Visions of the afterlife, 56-95.
                5. Tales and fables, 96-138.
                6. Romances, 139-196.
                    Discusses English and European
                    romance and the romance tradition in
                    Spain, France, and England; then
                    gives brief synopses of six romances
                    and focuses on the Grail (139-167).
                    The second part of the chapter
                    focuses on *Sir Gawain and the Green
                    Knight*: its prosody and structure,
                    religious and festive elements, Mor-
                    gan la Fee, courtly love, sources
                    and analogues, the Green Knight, and
                    Khadir (168-196).
                7. Spain to England, 197-206.
     Bibliography and index, 207-230.

56. Leach, MacEdward, ed. *Studies in Medieval Literature
     in Honor of Professor Albert Croll Baugh.* Philadel-
     phia: U of Pennsylvania P, 1961.

Includes essays on the audience of ME romance [121], *Sir Orfeo* [1495], and *Sir Tristrem* [1537].

57. Legge, M. Dominica. *Anglo-Norman Literature and its Background*. Oxford: Clarendon P, 1963.

> Chapters: 1. Introduction, 1-6.
> 2. The early twelfth century, 7-26.
> 3. Stephen and the anarchy, 27-43.
> 4. The court of Henry II, 44-73.
> 5. 1170 and after, 74-107.
> 6. The end of the twelfth century, 108-138.
> 7. The 'ancestral' romance, 139-175.
> 8. Religious literature at the turn of the century, 176-205.
> 9. The interdict and the Fourth Lateran Council, 206-242.
> 10. The development of the legends of the saints, 243-275.
> 11. History and chronicles, 276-310.
> 12. The Anglo-Norman drama, 311-331.
> 13. The lyric and its background, 332-361.
> 14. Conclusion, 362-373.
> Index, 375-389.

58. Lipski, John Michael. "Diachronic Hierarchies in Romance." Diss. U of Alberta, 1974.

59. Lock, Richard. *Aspects of Time in Medieval Literature*. Garland Publications in Comparative Literature. New York: Garland, 1985.

Distinguishes style and narrative structure in *Sir Gawain and the Green Knight* and *Yvain*, which are linear and hypotactic, from those in works such as *Song of Roland* with characteristics of oral literature and discontinuous time. Aims at developing a new approach to distinguish between oral and written literature through concepts of time.

60. Lucas, Peter J. "The Growth and Development of English Literary Patronage in the Later Middle Ages

and Early Renaissance." *Library* 6th ser. 4 (1982): 219-248.

Suggests that the development of patronage had its roots in literacy, with mutual benefits to the patron (who increased his personal "magnificence" and reputation at court while exercising some control over written material) and the writer (who needed the patron to reach a larger reading public). Further suggests that this trend peaked in the 15th century when printing made patrons—at least in theory—less necessary.

61. MacLaine, Allan H. *The Beginnings to 1558.* Great Writers Student Library 1. New York: St. Martin's P, 1980.

   Introduction, 1-28.
   The beginnings to 1558, 29-83.
   Notes on contributors, 85-86.

   Each entry includes a brief biography, list of author's published works, select list of bibliography and critical studies, followed by a short signed essay and reading list. Romances mentioned, 9-11.

62. Malone, Kemp, and Albert C. Baugh. *The Middle Ages.* Vol. I of *A Literary History of England.* 2nd ed. 4 vols. Ed. Albert C. Baugh. New York: Appleton-Century-Crofts, 1967.

   Part 2:   The Middle English Period (1100-1500).
   Chapter: 9. The romance I, 173-184.
               Definitions, characteristics, Matter of England and Rome.
            10. The romance II, 185-199.
               Matter of France and Britain, non-cyclical romances, Breton lay and fabliaux.
            14. The alliterative revival, 232-239.
               Verse of the north and west of England, in particular that of the *Gawain*-poet.

63. Mandel, Jerome, and Bruce A. Rosenberg, eds. *Medieval*

*Literature and Folklore Studies: Essays in Honor of
Francis Lee Utley.* New Brunswick: Rutgers UP, 1971.

A collection of twenty-five essays with a variety
of approaches to both OE and ME literature and folklore, including one on conventions in ME romance
[398].

64. Mehl, Dieter.   "'Point of View' in mittelenglischen
Romanzen." *GRM* ns 14 (1964): 35-46.

Defends the ME works against the negative charges
that they are the unoriginal products of hack writers
and suggests an artful use of clichés as a narrative
technique. Finds it remarkable that some of these
neglected works use some of the same techniques as
modern novels in combining the external and internal
through a certain point of view in presenting their
stories.

65. ------. "Weltliche Epik in England: Von Sir Beues
of Hamtoun bis Malorys Morte Arthur." *Europäisches
Spätmittelalter.* Neues Handbuch der Literaturwissen-
schaft 8. Ed. Willi Erzgräber. Wiesbaden: Akademische Verlagsgesellschaft Athenaion, 1978. 205-220.

Includes five sections: Historical context (English works totally different from the French and
German in history and language); Definition and form
of romance (impossibility of a single criterion for
definition of genre); Towards a history (imprecise
knowledge of author and audience and mixing of oral
and learned origins); Lydgate and the Chaucerians
(shows change from popular entertainment to scholarly
productions under the growing influence of literary
patrons and Lydgate's work as characteristic of
changes in 15th-century England); and Malory and
prose romances.

66. Meletinsky, Elizar M. "The Typology of the Medieval
Romance in the West and in the East." *Diogenes* 127
(1984): 1-22.

Contrasts the use of sentimental emotion and role
of love, the connections between epic and romance,

the interiorization and idealizing propensities of romances in the West and those in the Near East, Persia, Japan, and Soviet Georgia.

67. Metlitzki, Dorothee. *The Matter of Araby in Medieval England.* New Haven: Yale UP, 1977.

   Arranges the eight chapters into two equal parts: Scientific and Philosophical Learning and The Literary Heritage.

68. Moore, Arthur K. "Medieval English Literature and the Question of Unity." *MP* 65 (1968): 285-300.

   Attacks unity studies of medieval works for their confusion of opinion and fact; critical intentionalism; abuse of the rules of evidence; qualification by terms such as structural, thematic, artistic, or dramatic; and a preference for the term "unity" over more accurate terms such as "cohesion." Also argues that most claims of unity are pretexts for other, larger claims; i.e., a work gains deeper significance and enhanced value once unity has been attributed to it.

69. Nicastro, Anthony Joseph. "Linguistic Realism in Early Romance Texts." Diss. Columbia U, 1972.

70. Painter, Sidney. "The Family and the Feudal System in Twelfth Century England." *Speculum* 35 (1960): 1-16.

   Discusses the feudal custom of England as embodied in common law that gave the lord effective control over the acquisition of lands by vassal families and marriage alliances between them.

71. Parmisano, S.A. "A Study of the Relationship between the Attitudes towards Love and Marriage in Late Fourteenth- and Early Fifteenth-Century English Poetry and Contemporary Ecclesiastical Teachings on these Topics." *TGB* 19 (1968-69): 349. Ph.D., Cambridge U.

72. Partridge, A.C. *A Companion to Old and Middle Eng-*
     lish Studies. The Language Library. London: André
     Deutsch, 1982.

     Part: 1. To the Conquest, 1-223.
                  2. To the introduction of printing,
                      227-438.
     Chapter: 9. Transition, 227-253.
                      Discusses transitions from OE to
                      ME in language and the historical
                      process by which English asserted
                      itself as a spoken language of the
                      people in the reign of King John.
                 10. Feudalism and life in society, 254-
                      279.
                      Explores life, chivalry, pilgrims,
                      crusades, universities, trade, and
                      Norman French.
                 11. Dialect, literature and language,
                      280-310.
                      Discusses *King Horn*, *Gawain*-poet,
                      Chaucer, and Langland.
                 12. Experiments in verse, 311-329.
                      Points to the rise in accentual
                      verse, alliterative verse, especial-
                      ly in *William of Palerne*, and Chau-
                      cer's technical accomplishments.
                 13. The reigns of Edward III and Richard
                      II, 330-352.
                      Treats feudalism and chivalry and
                      the loss of noun inflections in ME,
                      1372-1399.
                 14. Prose from Mandeville to Malory and
                      medieval drama, 353-381.
                      Explores the beginnings of prose
                      in ME.
                 15. The close of the Middle Ages, 382-
                      417.
                      Treats authors such as Gower, Dun-
                      bar, Hoccleve, Lydgate, and Henry-
                      son.
                 16. The significance of the fifteenth
                      century, 418-438.
                      Discusses the rise of prose and
                      the dissemination of information and
                      newly translated material unavail-
                      able before the printing press.
                      Treats Trevisa, Pecock, and Caxton

as the last medievalists.
Bibliography, 439-452.
Index, 453-462.

73. Patterson, Lee Willing. "Heroism and the Rise of Romance: An Essay in Medieval Literary History." *DAI* 30 (1969): 694A. Yale U.

Discusses the decline of epic heroism, the appearance of the romance hero in the 12th century, and the late medieval loss of values characterized as romantic heroism in works such as Malory's.

73a. Pearsall, D.A., and R.A. Waldron, eds. *Medieval Literature and Civilization: Studies in Memory of G.N. Garmonsway.* London: Athlone P, 1969.

Includes essays on Saracens and Crusaders [104] and *King Alexander* [947].

74. Pettitt, T. "Middle English Social Comment: A Survey of Attitudes to the Peasantry in Certain Types of Fourteenth-Century English Literature." *TGB* 19 (1968-69): 360. M.A., Wales U.

75. Pietrkiewicz, C.F.E.B. "The Use of Metaphor in Some Old French and Middle English Lyrics and Romances." *TGB* 5 (1954-55): 239. Ph.D., London U.

76. Popova, M.K. "Angliiskii rytsarskii roman v stikhakh" ["The English Verse Romance"]. *FN* 5[137] (1983): 23-29 [in Russian].

A reading indebted to the principles of socialist realism, that sees the differences between French and English romances as reflections of ideological, national, and historical differences between the two countries.

77. Reiss, Edmund. "Medieval Irony." *JHI* 42 (1981): 209-226.

Claims that medieval narratives, while lacking in the modern consciousness of irony, are nonetheless deeply ironic in their world view and literary expression. Argues that their irony stems from a recognition of man's place in creation and a sense of *connexio rerum*, the ultimate compatibility of things, so seeming oppositions to the natural order were dismissed as more apparent than real.

78. Richmond, Velma E. Bourgeois. "The Development of the Rhetorical Death Lament from the Late Middle Ages to Marlowe." *DA* 20 (1960): 2807.

Justifies the lament as a minor literary form and discusses examples of it from the Middle Ages, especially in the chronicles and romances, and in Tudor narratives.

79. ------. *Laments for the Dead in Medieval Narrative*. Duquesne Studies Philological Series 8. Pittsburgh: Duquesne UP, 1966.

Chapter: 1. Introduction, 13-28.
          2. General characteristics of laments for the dead, 29-49.
          3. Characteristic ideas in laments for the dead, 51-81.
          4. Elements of style in laments for the dead, 83-100.
          5. Dramatic elements in laments for the dead, 101-131.
Anthology, 132-187.
Bibliography, 188-197.
Index of anthology, 198-199.

Contains laments for the dead from many ME romances.

80. ------. *The Popularity of Middle English Romance*. Bowling Green: Bowling Green U Popular P, 1975.

Chapter: 1. The popularity of Middle English romance, 1-24.
              Considers some of the reasons for the broad appeal of ME romance and

suggests an analogy with modern thrillers and science fiction in their popularity.

2. Fortune's heroes, 25-57.

Discusses *Destruction of Troy*, *King Alexander*, *Prose Alexander*, and *Morte Arthure* as works that deal with classical values and pagan attitudes, which the ME authors transform.

3. Fiendish origins transformed, 58-85.

Examines those romances that use a human-devil to demonstrate the necessity for penance and its importance in man's salvation: *Emare*, *Sir Gowther*, *Robert the Deuyll*, and *Romauns of Partenay*.

4. Friendship and brotherhood, 86-118.

Treats the bonds of friendship in *Athelston*, *Amis and Amiloun*, and *Valentine and Orson*.

5. The delights of love, 119-148.

Examines the exploration of chastity, constancy, and sexual love in *Ywain and Gawain*, *Morte Arthur*, and *Paris and Vienne*, which reject the illicit love of an adulterous relationship.

6. The most popular hero: *Guy of Warwick*, 149-193.

Explores the reasons for the broad appeal of *Guy of Warwick* with its concern for values and moral purpose and the skill of its author.

Conclusion, 194-198.
Notes and index, 199-237.

81. Rowland, Beryl, ed. *Chaucer and Middle English Studies in Honour of Rossell Hope Robbins*. London: Allen & Unwin, 1974.

Includes essays on the alliterative long line [228], medieval romance [281], and the Vernon MS [444].

82. Salter, Elizabeth. *Fourteenth-Century English Poet-*

ry: Contexts and Readings. Oxford: Clarendon P,
1983.

Chapter: 1. Introductory: standards, 1-18.
                Suggests that even works that seem
                inadequate as imaginative literature
                reveal a cultural situation of great
                interest, a fascinating interrela-
                tionship among religious, social,
                and educational forces.
            2. Conditions and status, 19-51.
                Explores the post-Conquest status
                of English literature and its depen-
                dencies on Anglo-French and the
                demand by the middle-class laity for
                English poetry as entertainment and
                instruction.
            3. Mappings, 52-85.
                Evaluates the usual mapping of the
                main literary areas of the 14th
                century and suggests instead a
                highly mobile and interconnected
                English society without the usual
                demarcations between north, south,
                and London areas.
            4. Alliterative verse and *Piers Plow-
                man*, 86-116.
                Questions the usual account of an
                alliterative "revival" (which is
                oversimplistic), explores the larger
                context for alliterative verse, and
                treats in detail *Piers Plowman*.
            5. Chaucer and medieval English tradi-
                tion, 117-140.
                Explores the ways in which Chaucer
                is both allied with and disengaged
                from his English contemporaries.
            6. Chaucer and Boccaccio: *The Knight's
                Tale*, 141-181.
        Notes, bibliography, and index, 182-224.

83. Scattergood, V.J. "Literary Culture at the Court of
     Richard II." Scattergood and Sherborne [84]. 29-43.

     Argues that anyone interested in the development of
     English literature should know the extent of liter-
     acy; the availability of texts; the reading habits of

the public; and the ownership, use, and cost of
books—all aspects of literary culture. Tests the
general assumption that authors like Gower and Chaucer were patronized by the aristocracy against available evidence. Claims their audience most likely
consisted of career diplomats, civil servants, and
other officials attached to the government and court,
not the aristocratic, courtly audience.

84. ------, and J.W. Sherborne, eds. *English Court Culture in the Later Middle Ages*. London: Duckworth,
1983.

Includes essays on the role of the courts in the
demand for English books [29] and on literary culture
at the court of Richard II [83].

85. Schlauch, Margaret. *Antecedents of the English
Novel, 1400-1600 (from Chaucer to Deloney)*. Warsaw:
PWN—Polish Scientific Publishers, 1963.

Chapter: 1. Introductory remarks, 1-10.
2. The heritage of medieval fiction,
11-46.
3. The late phase of medieval romance,
47-81.
Discusses the changing social contexts, survival and adaptations of
simpler types, and Caxton's contributions to the development of a new
prose style; summarizes and evaluates some of the ME prose romances.
4. The rise of popular fiction: its
minor forms, 82-119.
5. Romantic fiction continued and
transformed, 120-163.
6. Courtly romance, Elizabethan style,
164-205.
7. Towards the forms of modern fiction,
206-245.
8. Retrospect and summary, 246-248.
Index, 249-264.

References to medieval romance appear on pp. 9, 11,
14-17, 23-28, 47-51, 110.

86. ------. *English Medieval Literature and its Social*
     Foundations. Warsaw: Panstwowe Wydawnictwo Naukowe,
     1956.

            Part: I.   Old English, 1-96.
                      II.   Early Middle English, 97-172.
                     III.   Later Middle English, 173-280.
                            Includes the chapter "The flour-
                            ishing of romance and didactic lit-
                            erature in English," 175-200, which
                            reviews romances of adventure,
                            classical and Carolingian themes,
                            the Arthurian cycle, miscellaneous
                            romances and lays, and works of
                            instruction.
                      IV.   Towards the New Age, 281-341.
            Index, 343-366.

87. ------. "Realism and Convention in Medieval Litera-
     ture." *KN* 11 (1964): 3-12.

     Argues that too much has been made of the so-called
     realism in many medieval works and calls for a more
     precise literary formulation, perhaps a neutral term
     like "anti-romantic," midway between romantic and
     realistic.

88. Schmolke-Hasselmann, Beate.   "Middle English Lyrics
     and the French Tradition—Some Missing Links." *The*
     Spirit of the Court. Selected Proceedings of the
     Fourth Congress of the International Courtly Litera-
     ture Society. Toronto 1983. Ed. Glyn S. Burgess and
     Robert A. Taylor. Woodbridge, Eng.: D.S. Brewer,
     1985. 298-320.

     Points to the interchangeability of narrative and
     lyrical portraits of beauty and diagrams a network of
     influence and a complex system of interrelationships
     that may have influenced the creation of ME love
     poetry. Argues that both Anglo-French and ME ro-
     mances played a role in this development and gives
     examples from *Guy of Warwick* and *Sir Launfal.*

89. Seaton, Ethel. "Marlowe's Light Reading." *Elizabe-*
     than and Jacobean Studies Presented to Frank Percy

Wilson in Honour of His Seventieth Birthday. Ed.
Herbert Davis and Helen Gardner. Oxford: Clarendon
P, 1959. 17-35.

Suggests that medieval romance was a source of the
references, allusions, and similes in Marlowe's
plays. Claims there are two strata: popular romances
of native heroes such as *Bevis of Hampton*, *Richard
Coer de Lyon*, and *Guy of Warwick*; and more reputable
romances such as Lydgate's and *Arthur of Little Britain*. Finds three kinds of influence: general reminiscences, the Troy legend, and historical material
like Godfrey.

90. Severs, J. Burke, ed. *A Manual of the Writings in
     Middle English 1050-1500.* Fasc. 1. New Haven: Con-
     necticut Academy of Arts and Sciences, 1967.

Includes chapters on romances in general [167],
Alexander [204], Arthurian literature [337], Breton
lays [371], Eustache-Griselda legends [410], Troy and
Thebes [488], English legends [548], miscellaneous
romances [556], Godfrey of Bouillon [563], and Charlemagne legends [574]. Also includes the most comprehensive bibliography on ME romances through 1955
(199-332).

91. ------. "The Tales of Romance." *Companion to Chau-
     cer Studies.* Ed. Beryl Rowland. Rev. ed. New York:
     Oxford UP, 1979. 271-295.

Surveys the scholarship and criticism on Chaucer's
tales of romance.

92. Shepherd, G. "Early Middle English Literature."
     Bolton [13]. 67-106.

Treats animal fables, gnomic material, fabliaux,
debate, religious literature, and romances. Characterizes romance as verse narrative embodying the
life, adventures, and values of aspiring knights.
Distinguishes between the French and the ME versions,
which are less refined, less liberal, and more interested in the physical, popular, and societal or
communal aspects of life.

93. Speirs, John. *Medieval English Poetry: The Non-Chaucerian Tradition.* London: Faber and Faber, 1957.

Chapter: 1. Introduction, 13-41.
          2. Carols and other songs and lyrics, 45-96.
          3. Romances, 99-211.
              Notes different schools, diversity in subject matter and themes, reflecting different social and cultural levels. Describes in detail the story lines, with substantial textual quotation, of *Ywain and Gawain*, *Sir Perceval*, *Sir Orfeo*, *Sir Degare*, *Emare*, *Sir Launfal*, *King Horn*, *Havelok*, *Turke and Gowin*, and *Carle off Carlile*.
          4. Alliterative romances and poems, 215-304.
              Summarizes the plots and story lines of *Sir Gawain and the Green Knight* and *Awntyrs off Arthure*.
          5. The Mystery cycle: certain Towneley plays, 307-375.
          6. The relation between the literature and the painting and sculpture in medieval England, 379-392.
          7. Conclusion, 395-400.
Index, 401-406.

94. ------. "A Survey of Medieval Verse and Drama." Ford [36]. 43-96.

     Includes a brief discussion of alliterative poems (55-65) and metrical romances (65-69).

95. Strohm, Paul. "Chaucer's Audience." *L&H* 5 (1977): 26-41.

     Examines Chaucer's possible audience; his actual audience, which was composed of knights, esquires, civil servants, and women of equal station—all of whom were the most socially mobile people of that time; and his contemporary appeal to those living with uncertainty and change, but most likely to benefit from them.

96. Stugrin, Michael. "Innocence and Suffering in the Middle Ages: An Essay about Popular Taste and Popular Literature." *JPC* 14 (1980): 141-148.

    Suggests that literary texts, prose treatises, and sermons all reflect a perception of the emotional costs of the human experience and all bespeak an urgency to secure a tenable model of experience in the midst of cultural stress.

97. Tarlinskaja, Marina. *English Verse: Theory and History*. The Hague: Mouton, 1976.

    Introduction, 1-16
    Chapter: 1. Verse and syllable, 17-39.
               2. Verse and word stress, 40-59.
               3. Verse and phrasal stress, 60-83.
               4. The formation of English syllabotonic poetry, 84-99.
               5. A typology of English four-ictic verse, 100-137.
               6. The nondramatic iambic pentameter, 138-158.
               7. The dramatic iambic pentameter, 159-182.
               8. The transition from iambics to syllabics, 183-198.
    Appendices, 199-229.
    Conclusion, 230-233.
    References, tables and figures 235-340.
    Bibliography, 341-351.

98. Tuve, Rosemond. *Allegorical Imagery: Some Mediaeval Books and their Posterity*. Ed. Thomas P. Roche, Jr. Princeton: Princeton UP, 1966.

    Chapter: 1. Problems and definitions, 3-55.
               2. Allegory of vices and virtues, 57-143.
               3. Guillaume's pilgrimage, 145-218.
               4. Imposed allegory, 219-333.
               5. Romances, 335-436.
                  Approaches the romance basically as a means of illuminating Spenser, whose temper, tone, and habits all depended on medieval romances.

List of illustrations and sources, appendix, index, 437-461.

99. Utley, Francis Lee. "Folklore, Myth, and Ritual." *Critical Approaches to Medieval Literature.* Selected Papers from the English Institute, 1958-1959. Ed. Dorothy Bethurum. New York: Columbia UP, 1960. 83-109, 163-168.

Points to weaknesses in mythic criticism, which lacks strict logic and methodology, and suggests the possibility and value of extending the comparative and morphological study of folktales and ballads to other kinds of literature.

100. Vitz, Evelyn Birge. "Desire and Causality in Medieval Narrative." *RR* 71 (1980): 213-243.

Suggests that although desire initiates the action and sets off the causal chain in a medieval narrative, it does not have great efficiency, since it is limited by the unforeseeable interactions of human causes, by coincidence, and by the mysterious intervention of God or Providence.

101. Wehrli, Max. "Strukturprobleme des mittelalterlichen Romans." *WW* 10 (1960): 334-345.

Does not provide a detailed structural analysis of medieval romances, but instead gives a highly general and discursive view of the problems of romance in dealing with the combination of Christian, chivalric, and folk motifs and the problems of any author in trying to order such disparate elements and impose a structure.

102. Weiss, Alexander. Introduction: "Chaucer and the Critical Tradition." *Chaucer's Native Heritage.* American U Studies 11, Series 4. New York: Peter Lang, 1985. 1-22.

Reviews critical opinion on the nature and place of Chaucer's poetry in both European and native English traditions, touching on the influence on the metrical

romances and seeing Chaucer not so much as the beginning of a new English poetic tradition, but as the
culmination of an existing native tradition.

103. White, Beatrice. "Cain's Kin." *The Witch Figure:
    Folklore Essays by a Group of Scholars in England
    Honouring the 75th Birthday of Katharine M. Briggs.*
    Ed. Venetia Newall. London: Routledge & Kegan Paul,
    1973. 188-199.

    Suggests that giants replace witches or warlocks as
    evil figures in ME romances in which they are the
    principal malefactors and representative of rampant
    evil on this earth. Further argues that as elemental
    forces of chaos and evil, the giants share some
    features with the medieval churl.

104. ------. "Saracens and Crusaders: from Fact to Alle-
    gory." Pearsall and Waldron [73a]. 170-191.

    Reviews the treatment of the Saracens and Crusaders
    in ME romance and other works aimed at exaggerated
    effects, making both equally ferocious, fanatical,
    and symbolic; further suggests that the transition to
    moral allegory was slow, but easy and inevitable.

105. Wilson, Anne. *Traditional Romance and Tale: How
    Stories Mean.* Ipswich, Eng.: D.S. Brewer, 1976.

    Chapter: 1. Story as festival, 1-8.
             2. Story as dream, 9-19.
             3. Story and fantasy, 20-33.
             4. Disguises, 34-54.
             5. Form, 55-71.
             6. Imagery, 72-83.
             7. Transformation and recognition, 84-
                95.
             8. *Sir Gawain and the Green Knight,*
                96-108.
                Summarizes the story line and
                views storytelling as a creation of
                the protagonist, as thoughts within
                his mind, which are grasped by the
                unconscious of the audience.
    Conclusion, 109-110.

Select bibliography and index, 111-116.

106. Wilson, Richard M. "Romance." *The Lost Literature
      of Medieval England.* New York: Cooper Square, 1969.
      114-132.

      Provides evidence for the assumption that few of
      the works belonging to the three traditional Matters
      have been lost, but many belonging to the Matter of
      England are no longer extant.

107. Wolpers, Theodor. *Die englische Heiligenlegende des
      Mittelalters.* Tübingen: Max Niemeyer, 1964.

      Traces the development of the narrative form and
      structure of the English saints' legends from the
      early to late Middle Ages and tries to explain char-
      acteristics of each development, especially the
      central theme of edification. Discusses the influ-
      ence of contemporary secular forms and the didactic
      and moralizing concerns of the 15th and early 16th
      centuries.

108. Woolf, Rosemary. "Later Poetry: The Popular Tradi-
      tion." Bolton [13]. 263-311.

      Focuses on lyrics, mystery and morality plays, and
      romances. Defines romances as novels in verse with
      remote settings that focus on idealization of conduct
      with love and chivalric adventure as their subject
      matter. Differentiates among romances of trial and
      faith, Breton lays, and Arthurian romances.

109. Yeager, Robert F., ed. *Fifteenth-Century Studies:
      Recent Essays.* Hamden, CT: Archon, 1984.

      Includes essays on romance and form [136], courtly
      love and chivalry [384], 15th-century manuscripts
      [464], Lydgate [484], *Siege of Thebes* [1158], and
      Caxton [1673].

110. Zanco, Aurelio. *La Letteratura del "Middle English."*
      Parte 2. Milan: Goliardica, 1957.

A study of ME romances.

111. Zesmer, David M. *Guide to English Literature from Beowulf through Chaucer and Medieval Drama.* With Bibliographies by Stanley B. Greenfield. College Outline Series 53. New York: Barnes & Noble, 1961.

Includes a brief survey of OE and ME literature, indicating directions in recent scholarship, and selective annotated bibliographies.

DEFINITION AND GENRE

112. Amsler, Mark E. "Literary Theory and the Genres of Middle English Literature." *Genre* 13 (1980): 389-396.

Raises problems with generic theory for ME literature with its mixed forms and overlapping categories. Argues that genre criticism cannot be tied to an inflexible set of categories prescribed by theory or history nor to the generic relationship between texts. Rather it must depend on the precise description of the intrinsic forms of texts, on the articulation of the organizing principles by which elements of a text are conjoined.

113. Beer, Gillian. *The Romance.* Vol. 1 of *The Critical Idiom.* London: Methuen, 1970.

Chapter: 1. History and definition, 1-16.
Discusses the nature of romance and its themes of love and adventure with simplified characters, archetypal patterns, sensuous detail, strongly enforced code of conduct, and its happy ending.
2. Medieval to Renaissance romance: history and myth, 17-38.
3. Cervantes to the Gothic novel: the romance and the rise of the novel, 39-58.
4. Romanticism and post-Romantic romance, 59-77.
5. Conclusion, 78-79.
Bibliography and index, 80-88.

114. Beston, Rose Marie. "C.S. Lewis's Theory of Ro-

mance." *Ariel* 15 (1984): 3-16.

Synthesizes Lewis's views of romance, which focus on the liberating and imaginative world where quest and adventures abound, and which are unsympathetic to the anthropological approach of critics such as Jessie Watson and John Spiers.

115. Bloomfield, Morton W. "Episodic Motivation and Marvels in Epic and Romance." *Essays and Explorations: Studies in Ideas, Language, and Literature.* Cambridge: Harvard UP, 1970. 96-128.

Distinguishes epic and romance on structural grounds and finds that the differentiating quality seems to lie in the *aventure*, which is lacking in epic. The irrational and unmotivated episode is at the heart of romance's adventure.

116. Bordman, Gerald. "Folklore and the Medieval Romance." *Folklore in Action: Essays for Discussion in Honor of MacEdward Leach.* Ed. Horace P. Beck. PAFS Bibliographical and Special Series 14. Philadelphia: American Folklore Society, 1962. Rpt. New York: Kraus, 1970.

Discusses the piecemeal, careless, and perfunctory use of folklore motifs in romances and dispels the idea that romance is more fantastic than epic. Contrasts the looseness of romance with the cohesiveness of epic.

117. Brewer, Derek. "The Interpretation of Dream, Folktale and Romance with Special Reference to *Sir Gawain and the Green Knight*." *NM* 77 (1976): 569-581.

Uses concepts from analyzing dreams and folktales to illuminate the nature of romance as a non-naturalistic and symbolic story of the emergence of an adult from the trials of childhood, including psychological problems dealing with both mother and father figures.

118. ------. "Medieval Literature, Folk Tale and Traditional Literature." *DQR* 11 (1981): 243-256.

Emphasizes the traditional nature of romances and argues for a critical approach that does not denigrate them for the qualities they possess.

119. ------. "The Nature of Romance." *Poetica* 9 (1978): 9-48. ◊ oʰ M

Investigates the nature of romance by examining its structure, literary techniques, subject matter, and literal and symbolic meanings. Gives examples of Western European works generally recognized as romances and then notes similarities in subject matter concerning love and fighting as well as explicit quests or conflicts with the hero seeking personal fulfillment through virtue. Notes romance's interweaving of fact and fiction, appearance and reality; its use of the marvelous; its paradoxical reconciliation of an individual's self-realization with a sense of social responsibility. Views romances as stories about growing to adulthood literally and symbolically, with an absence of "organic form."

120. Brownlee, Kevin, and Marina Scordilis Brownlee, eds. *Romance: Generic Transformation from Chrétien de Troyes to Cervantes.* Hanover, NH: UP of New England, 1985.

Includes introduction and thirteen essays that investigate the nature and function of romance from Chrétien to Cervantes and depend on recent developments in genre theory from Frye and Hirsch to Todorov, Genette, Bakhtin, and Jameson.

121. Brunner, Karl. "Middle English Metrical Romances and Their Audience." Leach [56]. 219-227.

Surveys the manuscripts of the later 14th and 15th centuries that contain the metrical romances and shows that most were destined for readers interested in historic and pietistic material.

122. Campbell, Leslie Jean. "The Matter of England in Middle English Romance." *DAI* 44 (1983): 1785A. U of Mississippi.

Argues against The Matter of England label for
Bevis of Hampton, *Guy of Warwick*, *William of Palerne*,
and *Richard Coeur de Lyon*, which do not share common
origins or content.

123.   Childress, Diana T.   "Between Romance and Legend:
        'Secular Hagiography' in Middle English Literature."
        PQ 57 (1978): 311-322.

        Drawing on Northrop Frye's classification of liter-
        ary types, the author examines the hero's power of
        action, his moral character, and his active or pas-
        sive role within the story as distinguishing traits
        of the secular legends.

124.   Clarke, Marlene Beth.   "Three Periods of Middle
        English Romance." *DAI* 44 (1984): 2467A.   U of Cali-
        fornia, Berkeley.

        Examines thirty non-Chaucerian romances and groups
        them into three periods, with a movement away from
        simple harmony in action and outlook toward a more
        ambiguous hero and an unstable world.

125.   Coffer, Karin Boklund.   "Myth, Code, Order: Trans-
        formations in the Narrative Structure of Courtly Ro-
        mance." *DAI* 36 (1976): 5273A.   U of Colorado.

        Contrasts the socioeconomic and ethical systems
        underlying the French and German romances with those
        in *Sir Gawain and the Green Knight*.

126.   Diekstra, F.N.M.   "Le roman en moyen anglais." *Le*
        Roman. Typologie des Sources du Moyen Age Occidental
        12. Ed. J.Ch. Payen and F.N.M. Diekstra. Turnhout,
        Belg.: Brepols, 1975. 69-127.

        Includes a discussion of the definition of the
        romance genre by examining the English context; the
        romance mode; differences between romance and epic,
        saints' lives, chronicles, ballads, and tales; the
        evolution of the genre; typical problems of interpre-
        tation, especially in terms of authorship, composi-
        tion, and presentation; and ME romances as mirrors of

society, containing chivalric virtues and love and marriage themes.

127. Dunn, Vincent Ambrose, III. "Narrative Modes and Genres in Medieval English, Celtic and French Literature." *DAI* 45 (1985): 2868A. U of California, Berkeley.

Examines the narrative pattern of initiation conflated with the hero's quest for a bride and investigates the syntagmatic and paradigmatic narrative modes that reflect the value structures important to the culture of the audience. Deals with metrical romance, especially *Sir Gawain and the Green Knight*, in the final section of this study.

128. Erdoss, Patricia Klari. "Of Saintly Persuasion: A Study of Saints' Lives as Rhetoric and a Rhetorical Approach to Romance." Diss. U of Chicago, 1973.

129. Ferrante, Joan M. "The Conflict of Lyric Conventions and Romance Form." *In Pursuit of Perfection: Courtly Love in Medieval Literature*. Ed. Joan M. Ferrante and George D. Economou. National University Publications Series in Literary Criticism. New York: Kennikat P, 1975. 135-178.

Argues that once courtly love was taken out of its lyric form and forced into a narrative genre, it began to collapse, since the code was a delicate balance—achieved only in an idealistic and fictive framework—between the higher and lower impulses within man's nature. Once the romance hero acts on his passion, his deeds have serious moral and social consequences, and love's ennobling force becomes a destructive passion that threatens the order of society.

130. Finlayson, John. "Definitions of Middle English Romance." *ChauR* 15 (1980): 44-62, 168-181.

Reviews problems in the unwieldy generic classification; distinguishes between romances and *chansons de geste*; and discusses romances of adventure, courtly romances, and religious romances.

131.   Foster, Robert Alfred. "The Romances of the Medieval
       English Frontier." *DAI* 36 (1975): 272A. U of Penn-
       sylvania.

       Distinguishes the romances of the north and west of
       England from those in the south and east in two ways:
       a greater concern with the nature of chivalry and a
       more serious theme. Studies examples of this fron-
       tier sensibility.

132.   Frakes, Jerold C. "Metaphysical Structure as Narra-
       tive Structure in the Medieval Romance." *Neophil* 69
       (1985): 481-489.

       Describes romance narrative as the *ordo* of *fortuna*,
       a sequence of cycles from an event that causes a
       lack, to a state of insufficiency, to an event that
       eliminates the lack, and finally back to a state of
       sufficiency again. Thus, romance narrative may be
       seen as less arbitrary than earlier supposed, since
       it derives from a rigidly defined structure of the
       order of fortune and is a manifestation of the meta-
       physical structure of romance.

133.   Frye, Northrop. *The Secular Scripture: A Study of
       the Structure of Romance*. Cambridge: Harvard UP,
       1976.

            Chapter: 1. The word and world of man, 1-31.
                         Argues that romance is at the
                         structural heart of all fiction, with
                         man's vision of his own life as a
                         quest.
                     2. The context of romance, 33-61.
                         Suggests two polarized worlds in
                         romance: one above ordinary experi-
                         ence (idyllic world) and the other
                         below it (demonic or night world).
                     3. Our lady of pain: heroes and heroines
                         of romance, 63-93.
                         Argues that because heroism in ro-
                         mance is defined by endurance, suf-
                         fering, and patience, the heroine

often holds on to chastity and virginity or moves into love and marriage at the end. The other type of
romantic heroine is the redemptive
woman.
4. The bottomless dream: themes of descent, 95-120.

Distinguishes between two descent
themes, which both focus on confusion
of identity and enchainment: one is
descent from heaven or Eden into our
human world, and the other is a sub-
terranean descent.
5. *Quis hic locus?* Themes of ascent,
127-157.

Points to the chief themes of ascent as escape, remembrance, discovery of identity, and the breaking of
enchantments.
6. The recovery of myth, 159-188.

Discusses the wish fulfillment of
romance and its union of the past and
future into a vision of the pastoral
and paradisaical.
Notes and index, 191-199.

134. Furrow, Melissa McCleave. "Comic Middle English
Treatments of Romance." *DAI* 41 (1980): 2119A. Yale
U.

Examines changes in the kinds of parodies, from the
13th to 15th centuries, from those that support the
assumptions and conventions of romance by assimilat-
ing idiosyncratic characters (Octavian, Perceval) to
the impossibility in the 15th century of incorporat-
ing parody into serious romance, leading to a split
between quasi-instructional romances and burlesques
or satires.

135. Ganim, John Michael. "Mutable Imagination: Time,
Space and Audience in Medieval English Narrative."
DAI 35 (1974): 2221A. Indiana U.

Studies the ways in which a poet's projection of
time and space influences the meaning of his work.
Specifically examines *Havelok, Floris and Blaunche-*

flur, and *King Horn*, which have utopian time and a
minimal sense of space, as well as *Sir Gawain and the
Green Knight*, which assaults the sensibilities of the
audience through deliberate disorientation of form
and style.

136. Garbáty, Thomas J. "Rhyme, Romance, Ballad, Bur-
      lesque, and the Confluence of Form." Yeager [109].
      283-301.

      Examines existing evidence and theories concerning
      the relationship between romances and ballads and
      concludes on the basis of vocabulary, presentation,
      improvisation, audience and even authorship, that
      there are no clear distinctions between the two
      genres. Uses *Weddynge of Sir Gawen* and its ballad
      analogue as a test case for chronological priority
      and similarities, finding in both a fast-moving
      story, an ironic or wry outlook, a prosaic view of
      life, and a matter-of-factness typical of the angli-
      cizing of literary texts as well as a general 15th-
      century outlook.

137. Green, D.H. "The Pathway to Adventure." *Viator* 8
      (1977): 145-188.

      Examines the narrative methods available to medie-
      val authors for convincingly describing the crucial
      transition from the world of the court or feudal
      society to the realm of adventure and enchantment;
      these include the creation of a deliberately blurred
      transition, the belated widening of the narrative
      dimensions, and the exploitation of verbal ambiguity,
      all dealing with the aesthetics of irony as a rhetor-
      ical strategy for controlling audience response.

138. Gunn, Alan M.F. "The Polylithic Romance: With Pages
      of Illustrations." Colquitt [25]. 1-18, 189-191.

      Offers a tentative taxonomy of medieval romance
      from primary, chivalric romances to proto-romances,
      narratives of love and adventure, with at least
      twenty sub-genres. Explores the polylithic nature of
      romance, a complex and varied genre in which no
      single sub-genre exhibits simplicity, purity of type,

mode, or purpose.

139. Haidu, Peter, ed. *Approaches to Medieval Romance.* Yale French Studies 51. New Haven: Yale French Studies, 1974.

> Introduction and fifteen essays organized under the headings: status of the text, texts and other series, typologies and techniques, meaning as structure, and translocations. Includes essays on the nature of romance [148], Chaucerian romance [151], and spatial form in romance [155].

139a. ------. "Romance: Idealistic Genre of Historical Text?" *The Craft of Fiction: Essays in Medieval Poetics.* Ed. Leigh A. Arrathoon. Rochester, MI: Solaris P, 1984. 1-46.

> Challenges Frye's and Jameson's theories of romance, as a genre characterized by "fantasy" or the textualization of wish-fulfillment; focuses on ideas about a text's historicity and the encounter between a concrete medieval text (Chrétien's *Yvain*) and a socio-historically oriented semiotics. Raises questions about the nature of textuality and the limits of a medieval text, which cannot be defined by its syntagmatic conclusion.

140. Haymes, Edward R. "Chaucer and the English Romance Tradition." *SAB* 37.4 (1972): 35-43.

> Selects twelve formulaic expressions from the romances and quotes lines from Chaucer using the same expressions to establish beyond the possibility of coincidence that Chaucer derived much of his poetic diction from the English romance tradition.

141. Hill, D.M. "Romance as Epic." *ES* 44 (1963): 95-107.

> Critiques the approach of W.P. Ker, N.E. Griffin, and C.S. Baldwin and suggests instead the continuity between epic and romance.

142. Hoeper, Jeffrey David. "The English Verse Tale."
      DAI 39 (1979): 6142A-6143A. Michigan State U.

      Traces the development of this genre—the verse
      tale—which is intermediate between short poetry and
      long narrative verse, from the Breton lay through
      Victorian examples.

143. Hudson, Harriet Elizabeth. "Middle English Popular
      Romances." *DAI* 43 (1983): 2661A-2662A. Ohio State
      U.

      Develops a definition of "popular romance" and sug-
      gests that the composers of such works cultivated an
      aesthetic of familiarity and anonymity in the voice
      of the oral minstrel style and offered the fantasy of
      upward social mobility through marriage with someone
      of higher social class.

144. Hume, Kathryn. "The Composition of a Medieval Ro-
      mance: Walter Map's 'Sadius and Galo.'" *NM* 76
      (1975): 415-423.

      Claims that this work is uniquely able to shed
      light on the creative processes of medieval romance
      writers, since the author's sources and his aims are
      known. Reconstructs his steps in the choice of theme
      (love and virtue), story pattern, and selection of
      motifs from other works (such as the Amis and Amiloun
      story) and then shows how he recast his sources to
      fit the logic of romance.

145. ------. "The Formal Nature of Middle English Ro-
      mance." *PQ* 53 (1974): 158-180.

      Proposes a construct by taking two foci of inter-
      est: the hero and the background against which he
      works out his destiny; then distinguishes three types
      of romance along this spectrum: hero is all, locale
      is unimportant (folktales); events overshadow the
      hero (histories); both variables are significant.

146. ------. "Romance: A Perdurable Pattern." *CE* 36
      (1974): 129-146.

Suggests that romance has three different stages: equilibrium, struggle, and higher harmony. Further suggests that this pattern encompasses six different story types, three with hero as seeker (morally acceptable, at fault initially, or at fault at the end) and three with hero as victim (morally acceptable, at fault initially, or at fault near the end).

147. Hurley, Margaret. "Saints' Legends and Romance Again: Secularization of Structure and Motif." *Genre* 8 (1975): 60-73.

    Concludes that romance, while consciously adopting structure, plot, *topoi*, and verse form from hagiography, remains a separate genre that expresses the value of human activity and aspiration in a secular society.

148. Jackson, W.T.H. "The Nature of Romance." Haidu [139]. 12-25. Rpt. in *The Challenge of the Medieval Text: Studies in Genre and Interpretation.* Ed. Joan M. Ferrante and Robert W. Hanning. New York: Columbia UP, 1985. 172-184.

    Investigates the nature of romance as a genre of the individual with two principal motifs: the pointless combat and love-service. Finds a difference in romance and epic, not in structure, but in milieu, with romance's principle of unreality and literary artifice.

149. Jauss, Hans Robert. "The Alterity and Modernity of Medieval Literature." *NLH* 10 (1979): 181-229.

    Introduces the hermeneutical concept of alterity, poses the question of historicity and a modern reader's perception of medieval literature, and suggests that the reader must reconstruct expectations raised by the texts and value their alterity, the ways they open up new experiences and worlds.

150. Jeffrey, David L. "Literature in an Apocalyptic Age; or, How to End a Romance." *DR* 61 (1981): 426-446.

Suggests that medieval romance had an intensive
preoccupation with prophetic imagination and the
question of meaning in history, which becomes focused
in the endings.

151. Jordan, Robert M.   "Chaucerian Romance?"   Haidu
     [139]. 223-234.

Tries to discover whether structural elements con-
firm or deny a significant literary relationship
among narratives traditionally termed romances. Using Chrétien's *conjointure* and Vinaver's definition
of romance as the linking of *conte* and *conjointure*,
the author points to the inorganic nature of romance
stories, which provides structural justification for
dilation and digression, which in turn disrupt the
linear sequence of the story. Concludes that the
structural principle of inorganic composition also
governs fabliaux, saints' lives, and other genres, so
the term "romance" has little critical value.

152. Ker, W.P.   *Epic and Romance: Essays on Medieval*
     Literature. 1896; rpt. New York: Dover, 1957.

     Chapter: 1. Introduction, 3-61.
                   Includes four sections: the heroic
                   age, 3-15; epic and romance, 16-34;
                   romantic mythology, 35-49; the three
                   schools: Teutonic epic, French epic,
                   and the Icelandic histories, 50-61.
               2. The Teutonic epic, 65-175.
               3. The Icelandic sagas, 179-284.
               4. The Old French epic, 287-317.
               5. Romance and the Old French romantic
                   schools, 321-370.
     Appendix, 373-389.
     Index, 391-398.

153. Kissam, Margaret Denslow.   "The Narrative Structure
     of Middle English Romances." *DAI* 38 (1978): 4811A.
     CUNY.

     Defines the structure of romance as episodic and
     scenic and differentiates the genre from others by
     its emphasis on dramatization and organization of

episodes.

154. Kobayashi, Atsuo. *Chuseiki ni okeru Eikoku Romance.*
      Tokyo: Nan'undo, 1977 [in Japanese].

      On English romance in the Middle Ages.

155. Lacy, Norris J. "Spatial Form in Medieval Romance."
      Haidu [139]. 160-169.

      Discusses three aspects of the aesthetic form of
      romances: their formal, non-sequential techniques,
      the necessity of retrogressive reading, and their
      generic, not organic, unity.

156. Legge, M. Dominica. "Anglo-Norman Hagiography and
      the Romances." *M&H* ns 6 (1975): 41-49.

      Suggests that the early AN *Voyage of St. Brendan*
      may have influenced later romances, especially in
      their standard verse form (octosyllabic couplets),
      but concludes that social conditions can account for
      most resemblances between the AN saints' lives and
      romances.

157. Lenaghan, R.T. "The Clerk of Venus: Chaucer and
      Medieval Romance." Benson [8]. 31-43.

      Suggests that the romance offered Chaucer a liter-
      ary, narrative, and dialectically structured role for
      a clerk who had the authority to speak of morality
      and *fin amour*, as well as the social position and
      administrative role to attend to the formalities and
      ceremonies of the court.

158. Lenz, Joseph Martin. "The Mirror of Finity: A Study
      of Closure in Romance." *DAI* 41 (1981): 4721A. U of
      Illinois at Urbana-Champaign.

      Examines three principles governing audience expec-
      tation of a romance text: narrative fulfillment,
      enclosed space or removal, and revelation (as exem-
      plified in works including Chaucer's *Troilus and*

Criseyde, *Sir Gawain and the Green Knight*, and *Le Morte Darthur*).

159. Long, Clarence Edward. "Shapeshifting and Associated Phenomena as Conventions of the Middle English Metrical Romances." *DA* 17 (1957): 2260. U of New Mexico.

   Examines eighty romances and reports upon the frequency, origins, and suggested symbolism of these motifs, as well as historical and chronological records of philosophers, theologians, and Patristic fathers and scholars to testify that shapeshifting was readily accepted.

160. Macrae, Suzanne Haynes. "A Study of Ideal Kingship in the Middle English Romances." *DAI* 33 (1973): 4353A. U of North Carolina at Chapel Hill.

   Judges the artistic use of kingship in *Morte Arthure*, *King Alexander*, and *Havelok* and discusses ME romance as a genre more exemplary and political than the French.

161. Marino, James Gerard Americus. "Game and Romance [A Discussion of the Game-Like Structure of Certain Middle English Metrical Romances]." *DAI* 37 (1976): 1538A-1539A. U of Pittsburgh.

   Exposes the game-like structure of naive romances such as *Guy of Warwick*, *Bevis of Hampton*, *Havelok*, *King Horn*, and *Emare*, which operate wholly in the ludic sphere, and then examines the double vision in *Sir Gawain and the Green Knight*.

162. Martin, Jeanne Suzette. "History and Truth: Generic Transformations in Three Middle English Genres." *DAI* 36 (1976): 4471A-4472A. U of Virginia.

   Examines the different relationships between history and truth in romance, saints' lives, and the Corpus Christi drama cycle and contrasts the focus of *Sir Isumbras* on the diachronic with the importance of the synchronic in the St. Eustache legend.

163. Mehl, Dieter. *The Middle English Romances of the Thirteenth and Fourteenth Centuries.* London: Routledge & Kegan Paul, 1968.

Chapter: 1. Introduction: the Middle English romances, 1-29.
Explores the historical context, authors, audience, definition, and narrative techniques of ME romance.
2. The problem of classification, 30-38.
Identifies major problems with classifying by matter, content, metrical form, geographical distribution, sociological background. Proposes instead division by length, so distinctive features may be more easily recognized.
3. The shorter romances (I), 39-70.
Considers the Breton lays, the two accounts of *Sir Launfal, King Horn, Horn Child, Reinbrun, Roland and Vernagu, Otuel A Knight*, and both versions of *Ipomadon*.
4. The shorter romances (II), 71-119.
Treats *Libeaus Desconus, Sir Eglamour, Sir Torrent, Earl of Toulous, Sir Degrevant, Sir Perceval, Amis and Amiloun*, and *Octavian*.
5. Homiletic romances, 120-158.
Groups the following romances with similar didactic intentions: *Bone Florence of Rome, Athelston, King of Tars, Roberd of Cisyle, Sir Gowther, Sir Isumbras, Emare, Sege of Melayne*, and *Chevalere Assigne*.
6. The longer romances, 159-206.
Considers some of the likenesses among *Havelok, Sir Tristrem, Ywain and Gawain, Morte Arthur*, and *Sir Gawain and the Green Knight*.
7. Novels in verse, 207-251.
Treats *Bevis of Hampton, Guy of Warwick, King Alexander, Arthour and Merlin, Richard Coer de Lyon*, and *William of Palerne*.
Conclusion, 252-256.
Appendix, notes, select bibliography, and index, 257-300.

164. ------.   "Die kürzeren mittelenglischen 'Romanzen'
      und die Gattungsfrage." *DVLG* 38 (1964): 513-533.

      Discusses the difficulties of labeling as "romance"
      many short works that border between legend and
      popular literature.   Differentiates three subgroups:
      lais (including *Lai le Freine*, *Sir Orfeo*, *Sir Degare*,
      Sir Landeval); short romances or romance-like verse
      novellas (such as *Sir Launfal*, *Octavian*, and *Libeaus
      Desconus*); and homiletic romances, almost legends
      (*Emare*, *Bone Florence of Rome*).

165. Meyer, Robert J.   "Chaucer's Tandem Romances: A
      Generic Approach to the *Wife of Bath's Tale* as Pali-
      node." *ChauR* 18 (1984): 221-238.

      Argues that Chaucer achieves a remarkable experi-
      ment in romance narrative: "back-to-back, or tandem
      romances—mirror images reflecting ironically on each
      other—each of which treats a distinct phase in the
      growth of the bachelor" toward a moment of truth.

166. Moran, Noreen Deane.   "Middle English Romance Narra-
      tive: Length and Structure as Related to the Hero
      and his Adventures." *DAI* 43 (1982): 1966A-1967A.
      U of Notre Dame.

      Investigates whether minstrels had a prescribed
      notion of the shape of the literary product they were
      fashioning, by examining three short romances (*King
      Horn*, *Athelston*, and *Gamelyn*), two longer ones (*Amis
      and Amiloun* and *Havelok*), and one long one (*Bevis of
      Hampton*).

167. Newstead, Helaine.   "Romances: General."   Severs
      [90]. 11-16.

      A brief survey of the genre of romance, which is
      defined as "a narrative about knightly prowess and
      adventure, in verse or in prose, intended primarily
      for the entertainment of a listening audience."
      Lists all the romances chronologically with the dia-
      lect of original composition.

168. Nygard, Holger Olof. "Popular Ballad and Medieval
      Romance." *Folklore International: Essays in Tradi-
      tional Literature, Belief, and Custom in Honor of
      Wayland Debs Hand.* Ed. D.K. Wilgus with the assis-
      tance of Carol Sommer. Hatboro, PA: Folklore Asso-
      ciates, 1967. 161-173.

      Reviews scholarly opinion about the connections
      between ballads and romance from Francis J. Child
      through E.K. Chambers and concludes that the origins
      of ballads are too obscure to assign the ballads to
      degenerate or transformed minstrelsy of medieval
      romance.

169. Patten, Clara Lucille. "A Consideration of *Pearl* as
      a Medieval Romance." *DA* 28 (1968): 4139A-4140A. U
      of Denver.

      Argues that the poem uses not only romance elements
      but also the structural form, narrative patterns, and
      material content of the romance genre.

170. Pearsall, Derek. "The Development of Middle English
      Romance." *MS* 27 (1965): 91-116.

      Offers a tentative outline for the growth and de-
      velopment of ME romance from 1240 to 1400, dividing
      the selected works into two broad groups: nineteen
      epic romances in four-stress couplets and twenty-five
      lyric romances in tail-rhyme stanzas.

171. ------. "The English Romance in the Fifteenth Cen-
      tury." *E&S* ns 29 (1976): 56-83.

      A preliminary study of authorship, audience, and
      contemporary taste in the 15th century, which empha-
      sizes the need to understand the fluid nature of
      popular romance, so they are viewed not as garbled
      versions of an original, but rather as many recompo-
      sitions of a text. Points to trends in the 15th cen-
      tury: a growing reading public, a greater degree of
      sophistication, a continuation of popular traditions
      in recopying and recomposing texts rather than creat-
      ing new works, a more self-conscious literary mode,
      and the beginnings of prose romances as straightfor-

ward redactions of the "matter of antiquity" including the works of Malory and Caxton.

172.   ------. "John Capgrave's *Life of St. Katharine* and
        Popular Romance Style." *M&H* ns 6 (1975): 121-137.

        Explores the deliberately cultivated features of
        romance style that authors of saints' lives used to
        enhance the appeal of their work and absorb the natu-
        rally profane instincts of their audience.

173.   ------. "Middle English Romance and its Audiences."
        *Historical and Editorial Studies in Medieval and
        Early Modern English for Johan Gerritsen.* Ed. Mary-
        Jo Arn and Hanneke Wirtjes, with Hans Jansen. Gron-
        ingen, Neth.: Wolters-Noordhoff, 1985. 37-47.

        Discusses the compositional mode of romances as
        improvisational, the composers best described as
        disours, and the range of possible audiences from the
        sophisticated metropolitan audience to the provincial
        one. Also notes a historical change as audiences
        became more self-conscious concerning their status;
        as the number of individual readers increased, so did
        the literary quality of the texts.

174.   ------. *Old English and Middle English Poetry.* Vol.
        1 of *The Routledge History of English Poetry.* 4
        vols. London: Routledge and Kegan Paul, 1977.

        Chapter: 1. *Beowulf* and the Anglo-Saxon poetic
                     tradition, 1-24.
                  2. Anglo-Saxon religious poems, 25-56.
                  3. Late Old English poetry and the
                     transition, 57-84.
                  4. Poetry in the early Middle English
                     period, 85-118.
                     Treats the relationship between ME
                     and AN, clerical tradition, poetry of
                     popular instruction, Layamon, and
                     13th-century romance and chronicle,
                     especially *King Horn*, *Floris and
                     Blauncheflur*, *Havelok*, *Guy of War-
                     wick*, *Bevis of Hampton*, *Richard Coer
                     de Lyon*, *Arthour and Merlin*, and *King*

Alexander. Discusses the frustrated efforts in classification because romance blurs into history, chronicle, and exempla. Defines romances as secular narratives, with a hero, designed for secular entertainment.
5. Some fourteenth-century books and writers, 119-149.
Discusses MS Harley 2253, Vernon MS, Auchinleck MS, and collections of religious verse. Characterizes the tone of popular romances as pious, exemplary, and didactic with an absence of chivalric idealism and generalizes about 14th-century romances: most are based on French, not AN; most have an "aspirant bourgeoisie" as their audience; and most are based on the matter of France, the Constance legend, or Breton *lais*.
6. Alliterative poetry, 150-188.
Considers the revival, techniques of alliterative verse, *Morte Arthure*, Gawain poems, *Piers Plowman*, and stanzaic alliterative poems. Discusses trends in the 15th century as romances expanded their social range upward and downward, with the lower popular tastes dominating.
7. Court poetry, 189-222.
Treats Chaucer, Gower, and 15th-century courtly traditions.
8. The close of the Middle Ages, 223-281.
Discusses Lydgate, romances, Scots poetry, and other 15th-century works.
9. Conclusion, 282-283.
Appendices, notes, and index, 284-352.

175. ------. "The Story and its Setting." *The Mediaeval World*. Vol. 2 of *Literature and Western Civilization*. Ed. David Daiches and Anthony Thorlby. London: Aldus, 1973. 371-406.

Discusses English romances (401-404) as suppressing the love element; coarsening the chivalric code to bravado; greeting the marvelous with open-mouthed wonder; and adding homely piety and realism to the earlier, more sophisticated, and artful French romances.

176. Puryear, Leslie Cram. "A Structural Approach to the Middle English Metrical Romances." *DA* 29 (1968): 1213A-1214A. Vanderbilt U.

Subdivides the group into romance proper, didactic romances, and Breton lays by using methods developed by Vladimir Propp.

177. Reiss, Edmund. "Romance." Heffernan [408]. 108-130.

Analyzes the nature of romance as a composite and synthesized form, encompassing elements of the folk tale, ballad, exemplum, and saints' lives. Views romance as "at once heroic, historical, erotic, and religious."

178. Rice, Joanne Adrienne. "Middle English Verse Romances: A Problematic Genre." *DAI* 42 (1982): 5115A. Michigan State U.

Tests ME romance against commonly accepted criteria of romance (existence of the supernatural, marvelous, and exotic; interest in courtly love; adherence to a chivalric code; emphasis on the individual; and use of the quest pattern) and argues that the generic label is a misnomer for the majority of the works.

179. Rosenberg, Bruce A. "The Morphology of the Middle English Metrical Romance." *JPC* 1 (1967): 63-77.

Analyzes the works according to methods developed by Propp and separates them into three structural groups: crime and punishment, separation-reunion, and test-reward.

180. Runde, Joseph. "Magic and Meaning: The Poetics of Romance." *DAI* 41 (1980): 2128A. Pennsylvania State U.

Examines five narratives to discover what they have in common to be called romances and finds that the magician defines romance; his magic, the deep understanding of nature, defines both development and plot.

181. Schelp, Hanspeter. *Exemplarische Romanzen im Mittelenglischen.* Palaestra 246. Göttingen: Vandenhoeck & Ruprecht, 1967.

Chapter 1. Einleitung, 11-30.
2. Hauptteil: Exemplarische Züge in der mittelenglischen Romanzendichtung, 31-251.
Havelok the Dane, 31-53.
Sir Ysumbras, 53-69.
Roberd of Cisyle, 69-84.
Sir Gowther und *Sir Cleges*, 84-97.
Emare, 97-113.
Le Bone Florence of Rome und andere Romanzen um tugenhafte Frauen, 114-132.
Guy of Warwick, 133-149.
Alexander und Arthur in der Dichtung der *alliterative revival*: Aufstieg und Untergang des grossen Menschen, 149-181.
Troja und Theben-Grösse und Untergang eines Gemeinwesens, 181-235.
Allgemeiner Teil, 236-251.
3. Schluss, 252-253.
Literaturverzeichnis, 254-263.

182. So, Francis Kei-hong. "The Romantic Structure: A Rhetorical Approach to *Ch'uan Chi'i* and Middle English Tales." *DAI* 40 (1980): 6284A. U of Washington.

Examines the actions and character of the hero, the narrator's handling of time and space, and the rhetorical formalism in terms of the spirit of mystery and idealism characteristic of the romance genre, and then concludes that both the ME tales and the Chinese work share the same surface structure, as well as a deeper level of aesthetic expression and the same structural prototype.

183. Stark, Marilynn Dianne. "Chaucer as Literary Critic:
     The Medieval Romance Genre in *The Canterbury Tales*."
     DAI 39 (1978): 2925A. U of Illinois at Urbana-Champaign.

     Describes the romance genre (with its adventure,
     wonder, didacticism, and love); examines *Sir Thopas*,
     which parodies the content of romance while mastering
     its rhyme and meter; and views *The Knight's Tale* as a
     philosophical romance. Concludes that Chaucer believed romance was capable of dealing with philosophical and aesthetic themes on a high level of sophistication and used the genre as a vehicle to integrate
     narrative, rhetorical, and poetic style with philosophy.

184. Stevens, John. *Medieval Romance: Themes and Approaches*. New York: Norton, 1973.

     Preface and author's note, 9-14.
     Chapter: 1. Introduction: the permanence of romance, 15-28.
              2. Man and woman: idealisms of love, 29-49.
              3. Man and society: the romance of the 'gentil' man, 50-71.
              4. Man and superman: the romance of the self, 72-95.
              5. Man and supernature: the marvellous in romance, 96-118.
              6. Man and God: religion and romance, 119-141.
              7. The images of romance, 142-167.
              8. Realism and romance: 'characters' and types, 168-187.
              9. Realism and romance: discourse of love, 188-207.
             10. The storyteller and the poet, 208-226.
             11. Epilogue: the pervasiveness of romance, 227-237.
     Historical note, booklist, and index, 238-255.

185. Strohm, Paul. "Middle English Narrative Genres."
     Genre 13 (1980): 379-388.

Includes a taxonomy of the following narrative terms: *comedy/tragedy*, *cronicle*, *ensample*, *fable*, *gestes*, *legend*, *lyf*, *myracle*, *passioun*, *pley*, *proces*, *romance*, *spelle*, *storie*, *tale*, *tretys*, *visioun*. Suggests a range of particular generic possibilities shared by author and audience.

186.   ------.   "The Origin and Meaning of Middle English *Romaunce*." *Genre* 10 (1977): 1-28.

A survey of the use of the term from the 12th-century OF *romans* through 15th-century ME *romaunce*, with brief sections on the related terms *storie*, *geste*, and *lay*.

187.   ------.   "*Passioun*, *Lyf*, *Miracle*, *Legende*: Some Generic Terms in Middle English Hagiographical Narrative." *ChauR* 10 (1975): 62-75, 154-171.

Analyzes ME hagiographical terms and suggests that *lyf* is more inclusive than *vita*, that *miracle* is often simply a descriptive term, and that *legende* is used most often as a direct reference to the work of Jacobus Voragine.

188.   Vinaver, Eugène.   *Form and Meaning in Medieval Romance*. The Presidential Address of the Modern Humanistic Research Association. New York: Modern Humanistic Research Association, 1966.

Discusses the patterns of recurring themes and the aesthetic possibilities of digression and interlace, both reflections of medieval techniques of amplification, which, in the romances, became the interweaving of many themes in a linear or horizontal extension.

189.   ------.   "From Epic to Romance." *BJRL* 46 (1964): 476-503.

Cautions against attempts that differentiate romance from epic by subject matter, the spirit of the times, or the nature of the hero. Suggests that the novelty of romance was not in its breaking away from medieval views of literary artistry, but in its

reflecting the deep concern of the medieval mind to
find understanding.

190.   ------. *The Rise of Romance*. New York: Oxford UP,
        1971.

                Chapter: 1. Roland at Roncevaux, 1-14.
                          2. The discovery of meaning, 15-32.
                              Finds the real novelty of romance
                              in its "ordering" quality, its shap-
                              ing and understanding of events and
                              relationships.
                          3. Tradition and design, 33-52.
                              Discusses the romance writers'
                              creative techniques in resolving the
                              incongruities between *conjointure* and
                              the received matter (*conte*).
                          4. The waste land, 53-67.
                              Follows the evolution of this theme
                              in the French and English Grail leg-
                              ends.
                          5. The poetry of interlace, 68-98.
                              Abandons organic unity as a rele-
                              vant idea for many romances and de-
                              velops the idea of interlace, the in-
                              terweaving of narrative threads of
                              the story.
                          6. Analogy as the dominant form, 99-122.
                              Examines the use of parallel scenes
                              and typological reading to shed new
                              light on the meaning of romance
                              texts.
                          7. A new horizon, 123-139.
                              Discusses Malory's unraveling of
                              the interlaced themes he found in his
                              sources.
                Appendix and index, 141-158.

191.   Wilson, A.D. "Medieval Romance Seen as a Story."
        TGB 26 (1975-76): 287. Ph.D., Birmingham U.

192.   Wittig, Susan. "Formulaic Style in the Middle Eng-
        lish Romance." *NM* 78 (1977): 250-255.

        Finding Loomis's bookshop theory and oral transmis-

sion inadequate to account for the formulaic quality
of romance, the author hand counts formulas in
twenty-five selected romances and tabulates the
results, which raise questions about the critical are
one-fourth formulaic and twenty-four are one-third
formulaic, yet there is no uniformity or clear-cut
distinctions among the works.

ALEXANDER ROMANCES: GENERAL STUDIES

194. Arnold, F.E.A. "The Source of the Alexander History in B.M. MS Sloane 289." *MAE* 33 (1964): 195-199.

Points to Ranulph Higden's version of the Alexander story in *Polychronicon* (3.26-30) as the source for the Alexander story in MS Sloane 289, which is not a historical account, but an amalgam of legendary, anecdotal, and quasi-historical material.

195. Boyle, John Andrew. "The Alexander Romance in the East and West." *BJRL* 60 (1977): 13-27.

Discusses the versions of the Pseudo-Callisthenes work.

196. Buck, David Earle. "Studies in Middle English Alexander Literature." *DAI* 34 (1973): 1233A. U of Missouri-Columbia.

Contends that works focusing on Alexander present him unfavorably, emphasizing his *superbia* and his origin from an adulterous relationship; further suggests that this bias is partially explained by his similarity to the Antichrist and by the general medieval antipathy to magic.

197. Cary, George. *The Medieval Alexander.* Ed. D.J.A. Ross. Cambridge: Cambridge UP, 1956.

General introduction, 1-5.
Part A. A Brief Survey of the Sources for Medieval Knowledge of Alexander the Great, and of Their Principal Medieval Derivatives.
Chapter: 1. The primary sources of medieval

knowledge of Alexander the Great, 9-
23.
2. The principal medieval derivatives of
Pseudo-Callisthenes, 24-61.
3. The principal medieval texts derived
from historical sources, 62-70.
4. The principal Latin chronicle accounts of Alexander, 71-74.
Part B.   The Medieval Conception of Alexander the
Great.
Introduction, 77-79.
Chapter: 1. The conception of Alexander in moral-
ists to the fourteenth century with a
prospect of the opinions of later
writers, 80-117.
2. The conception of Alexander in theologians and mystics, 118-142.
3. The conception of Alexander in the
books of 'exempla' and in preachers,
143-162.
4. The conception of Alexander in secular writers to the fourteenth century, with a prospect of the opinion
of later writers, 163-225.
5. The late medieval conception of
Alexander in England, France, and
Germany, 226-259.
6. The conception of Alexander in late
medieval and Renaissance Italy, 260-
272.
7. Summary conclusion, 273-274.
Notes, 275-351.
Appendices, 355-377.
Bibliography, 378-393.
Index, 395-415.

198. Cleaves, Francis Woodman. "An Early Mongolian Version of the Alexander Romance." *HJAS* 22 (1959): 1-
99.

Examines four distinct episodes in introduction:
ascent to the top of Mt. Sumur, descent to the bottom
of the sea, descent into the land of darkness, and
return to the city of Misir. Also compares these
episodes to their counterparts in other versions of
the Alexander romance.

199. Davenport, S.K. "Illustrations Direct and Oblique in the Margins of an Alexander Romance at Oxford." *JWCI* 34 (1971): 83-95.

     Finds that a large proportion of the pictorial margins illustrates specifics in the poem with some deliberate commentaries; points to the need for reconsidering the long-held opinion that marginal illuminations are usually unrelated to the text.

200. Flynn, Elizabeth Ann. "The Marvellous Element in the Middle English Alexander Romances." *DA* 29 (1968): 1866A. U of Wisconsin.

     Examines five Alexander romances in terms of their use of marvels concerning the life of the hero as well as oddities in nature.

201. Hill, Betty. "Alexanderromance: The Egyptian Connection." *LeedsSE* ns 12 (1981): 185-194.

     Sketches the Egyptian background from Greek Pseudo-Callisthenes, summarizes the main points of the narrative from two English histories, and indicates the divergent treatments in four ME poems: *Alexander A*, *King Alexander*, *Wars of Alexander*, and Gower's *Confessio Amantis*.

202. Jones-Lee, Hazel. "The Alexander Tradition and the Middle English Alliterative Alexander Poems." *TGB* 24 (1975): 245. D.Phil., York U.

203. Kitchel, Luann Marie. "A Critical Study of the Middle English Alexander Romances." *DAI* 34 (1973): 3347A. Michigan State U.

     Evaluates five major ME Alexander romances as independent works of literature and concludes that *Alexander A* and *B* are inferior works, that *King Alexander* and the *Prose Alexander* are skillfully constructed stylistically and structurally, and that *Wars of Alexander* conforms to epic, not romance conventions.

204. Lumiansky, R.M. "Legends of Alexander the Great."
      Severs [90]. 104-113.

      Includes a headnote on the medieval conception of
      Alexander as well as individual entries on the six ME
      romances and the four fragments; information such as
      dating, rhyme scheme, sources, and plot summaries is
      included.

205. Poppe, Nikolaus. "Eine mongolische Fassung der Alex-
      andersage." *ZDMG* 107 (1957): 105-129.

      Identifies an anonymous and fragmentary text,
      7r-13v of Turfan document TID 55, a Mongolian version
      of the Alexander romance.

206. Reich, Rosalie. *"Tales of Alexander the Macedonian*:
      A Study of Alexander Tales as Found in a Hitherto
      Unpublished Medieval Hebrew Manuscript and Earlier
      Hebraic Sources and a Comparison with Parallel Alex-
      ander Tales Appearing in Middle English Literature."
      DA 28 (1968): 2655A. NYU.

      Concludes that although there is no direct borrow-
      ing, the Alexander themes and tales found in the
      Hebrew manuscript are "widely diffused" in varied
      works of the ME period.

207. Ross, D.J.A. *Alexander Historiatus: A Guide to
      Medieval Illustrated Alexander Literature.* Warburg
      Institute Surveys 1. London: Warburg Institute, U of
      London, 1963.

          Preface, 1-4.
          Part: I.   Pseudo-Callisthenes and its deriv-
                              atives, 5-65.
                         II.   Historical accounts of Alexander,
                              67-83.
          Notes and appendices, 84-115.
          Index, 117-128.

208. Schmelter, H.U. "Alexander der Grosse in der Dich-
      tung und Bildenden Kunst des Mittelalters. Die Nek-
      tanebus-Sage." *DAI* 40 (1979-80): 1497C. U of Bonn.

209. Southgate, Minoo Sassoonian. "A Study and a Translation of a Persian Romance of Alexander, its Place in the Tradition of Alexander Romances, and its Relation to the English Versions." *DAI* 31 (1971): 6569A-6570A. NYU.

Analyzes episodes and themes found in both the Persian and English Alexander romances, which belong to the same redaction of the Pseudo-Callisthenes.

210. Turville-Petre, Thorlac. "A Lost Alliterative Alexander Romance." *RES* ns 30 (1979): 306-307.

Refers to a 14th-century fragment, translations of two passages from *Les Voeux du Paon* in the Fairhurst MS, which was in the possession of London antiquarian bookseller Alan Keen in 1948, but which has not been traced since.

SEE ALSO items 16 (142-154), 34 (54ff.), 232, 234, 237, and 413 (69-96).

ALLITERATIVE POETRY

211. Anttila, Raimo. "Sound Preference in Alliteration."
      SML 5 (1969): 44-48.

      Tries to determine whether poets preferred certain
      sounds to others or whether they formed alliteration
      in proportion to their vocabulary; using the *Gawain*-
      poet as a test case, the author found that the poet
      was partial to forming alliteration, avoiding vowels
      and h staves as well as fricatives, and favoring
      voiced stops, especially "b" and "g."

212. Barron, W.R.J. "Alliterative Romance and the French
      Tradition." Lawton [237]. 70-87, 140-142.

      Examines the relationship between the ME romances
      and their sources, the nature of the redactive pro-
      cess, and the varying degrees of originality achieved
      by the redactors; specific studies of *William of
      Palerne*, *Chevalere Assigne*, and *Golagrus and Gawain*
      focus on the technical demands of alliterative verse
      and the impossibility of literal translation from the
      originals.

213. Bennett, J.A.W. "Survival and Revivals of Allitera-
      tive Modes." *LeedsSE* ns 14 (1983): 26-43.

      Questions the usefulness of the term "alliterative
      revival" except as it applies to the modern age with
      its wholly deliberate, largely academic revival.
      Reviews the use of the alliterative line from the
      early Harley lyrics through Tolkien's poetry.

214. Blake, N.F. "Chaucer and the Alliterative Romances."
      ChauR 3 (1969): 163-169.

By examining alliterative patterns and vocabulary
in the *Knight's Tale*, 2605-2616 and *Legend of Good
Women*, 635-648, the author concludes that Chaucer did
not borrow from alliterative romances.

215.   ------. "Rhythmical Alliteration." *MP* 67 (1969):
        118-124.

Points to limitations in the theory of the continuity of the alliterative tradition from OE popular
poetry to Layamon's *Brut*. Argues that it is better
to see a close relationship and blurred distinctions
between poetry and prose in the early stages of the
development of the literature. Indicates an intermediate form between verse and prose, called "rhythmical alliteration" or "rhythmical prose."

216.   Borroff, Marie. *Sir Gawain and the Green Knight*: A
        Stylistic and Metrical Study. Yale Studies in Eng-
        lish 152. New Haven: Yale UP, 1962. Rpt. Hamden,
        CT: Archon, 1973.

            Part One: Style.
                      1.   Style and meaning, 3-26.
                      2.   The historical study of style, 27-
                           51.
                      3.   Style and the alliterative tradi-
                           tion, 52-90.
                      4.   The criticism of style, 91-129.
            Part Two: Meter.
                      5.   The phonological evidence, 133-143.
                      6.   The metrical evidence, 144-163.
                      7.   The alliterative long line: the nor-
                           mal form, 164-189.
                      8.   The alliterative long line: the ex-
                           tended form, 190-210.
            Notes, bibliography, and index 211-295.

217.   Brown, W.R.J. "The French Sources of Middle English
        Alliterative Romance." *TGB* 10 (1959-60): 148. Ph.D.,
        St. Andrew's U.

218.   Coffey, Jerome Edward. "The Evolution of an Oral-
        Formulaic Tradition in Old and Middle English Allit-

erative Verse." *DAI* 30 (1969): 2477A. SUNY, Buffalo.

Tests the theories of Parry, Lord, and Magoun
against OE verse, *Morte Arthure*, and *Sir Gawain and
the Green Knight* and concludes from evidence of
traditional diction and meter that an oral tradition
permeated even the late medieval texts.

219. Diamond, Sara Arlyn. "A Study of the Middle English
Alliterative Romances." *DAI* 31 (1971): 3500A-3501A.
U of California, Berkeley.

Concentrates on nine of the works, discusses the
expectations of alliterative romance, and examines
type scenes not found in courtly romances.

220. Doyle, A.I. "The Manuscripts." Lawton [237].
88-100, 142-147.

Investigates the manuscripts containing late alliterative verse and suggests that wherever and whenever
an alliterative work originated, it could have "wide
dissemination, by no means all amateur or provincial,
and lasting beyond the middle of the 15th century,
outside the northern regions."

221. Duggan, Hoyt N. "The Rôle of Formulas in the Dissemination of a Middle English Alliterative Romance."
SB 29 (1976): 265-288.

Using two manuscripts of *Wars of Alexander* as a
test case, the author argues that the tension between
oral and written language as modes of dissemination
best accounts for the kind of variation found in different manuscripts of the same poem.

222. ------. "Strophic Patterns in Middle English Alliterative Poetry." *MP* 74 (1977): 223-247.

Concludes that the evidence does suggest a stanza
structure, the 24-line strophe, in *Wars of Alexander*,
more or less determined by the manuscript divisions
in the Latin source. Further suggests that poets may

have learned to compose stanzas of four unrhymed alliterative long lines from their Norse neighbors between the 10th and mid-12th centuries.

223.   Elliot, R.W.V. "Landscape and Rhetoric in Middle English Alliterative Poetry." *MCR* 4 (1961): 65-76.

Accounts for the artistic failures of description in alliterative poetry in two ways: the popularity of the *Roman de la Rose*, which established a "pattern of poetic landscape to which the medieval worship of 'auctoritee' was only too ready to subscribe," and the claims of high-pressure episodic narrative, which inevitably conflicted with the claims of art.

224.   Field, Rosalind. "The Anglo-Norman Background to Alliterative Romance." Lawton [237]. 54-69, 136-140.

Directly compares the alliterative ME romances with the surviving romances of the AN period and discovers resemblances of literary type and attitude, similarity of audience, and aristocratic, not royal patronage. Suggests that the co-existence of provinciality with courtliness is the most important feature shared by the two groups of romances and that an understanding of the ME romances is heightened by an awareness that they were not created in a vacuum; earlier insular romances treated some of the same material, themes, and the portrayal of the ethics and ideals of feudal society.

225.   Frankis, John. "Word-Formation by Blending in the Vocabulary of Middle English Alliterative Verse." *Five Hundred Years of Words and Sounds: A Festschrift for Eric Dobson*. Ed. E.G. Stanley and Douglas Gray. Cambridge, Eng.: D.S. Brewer, 1983. 29-38.

Gives examples of blending, which seems characteristic of alliterative verse, in the words *clynterand* (*Wars of Alexander* 4863); *maskel* (*Wars of Alexander* 4989, 5138; *Cleanness* 556; and *Pearl* 726, 843); *runisch*, *renish*, and *roynish*; *schinder* (*Sir Gawain and the Green Knight* 424, 1458, 1594; *Joseph of Arimathie* 513; *Awntyrs off Arthure* 501, 503); *skel-*

ten; (*Destruction of Troy* 1089, 6042); *sniteren* (*Sir Gawain and the Green Knight* 2003; *Awntyrs off Arthure* 82); *stryþþe* (*Sir Gawain and the Green Knight* 846, 2305).

226. Hartle, P.N. "Middle English Alliterative Verse and the Formulaic Theory." *TGB* 31 (1982): 288. Ph.D., Cambridge U.

227. Herschel, James Andrew. "The Northern Pageant: Six Late Medieval Alliterative Poems." *DAI* 32 (1972): 4566A. Syracuse U.

Argues that *Awntyrs off Arthure*, *Golagrus and Gawain*, and *Taill of Rauf Coilyear* as well as three didactic alliterative poems share an ontological perspective by depicting reality as a feudal pageant.

228. Hieatt, Constance B. "The Rhythm of the Alliterative Long Line." Rowland [81]. 119-130.

Theorizes that hypermetric verse influenced alliterative patterns, since there is a noticeable tendency to use double, triple, multiple, crossed, transversed, or mixed patterns.

229. Hussey, S.S. "Langland's Reading of Alliterative Poetry." *MLR* 60 (1965): 163-170.

Argues that of the alliterative works composed before the A-text, *Parlement of Thre Ages*, *Somer Soneday*, *William of Palerne*, and *Winner and Waster* are the most likely to have influenced or inspired Langland in his treatment of the poor and in his use of alliteration.

230. Jacobs, Nicolas. "Alliterative Storms: A Topos in Middle English." *Speculum* 47 (1972): 695-719.

Suggests that the storm description may have had the quality of a rhetorical *topos* and examines sources and parallels, origins and developments of the *topos*, especially in *Destruction of Troy* 1983-

2011, 3686-3714, 4625-4636, 7618-7633, 9636-9639, 12469-12474, 12493-12508; *Siege of Jerusalem* 53-70; *Wars of Alexander* 549-568, 4139-4150, 4171-4186; and less importantly, in *Awntyrs off Arthure* 75-82, and *Sir Gawain and the Green Knight* 1998-2005.

231. Joseph, Ruth Fairbanks. "Alliterative Style in *The Awyntyrs off Arthure*, *The Avowing of King Arthur*, *The Turke and Gowin*, and *Golagros and Gawane*." *DAI* 38 (1978): 5496A-5497A. Saint Louis U.

Analyzes the uses of alliteration in these four northern ME romances: to emphasize visual ugliness, to reinforce meaning or bind together speeches, and to act as a structural device.

232. Kossick, Shirley. "Epic and the Middle English Alliterative Revival." *ESA* 22 (1979): 71-82.

Considers the alliterative treatment of the legends of Troy and Alexander as following conventions of the epic, not romance, with close generic bonds to OE verse.

233. Lawrence, R.F. "The Formulaic Theory and Its Application to English Alliterative Poetry." *Essays on Style and Language: Linguistic and Critical Approaches to Literary Style*. Ed. Roger Fowler. New York: Humanities P; London: Routledge and Kegan Paul, 1966. 166-183.

Reviews the origins of the formulaic theory and its application to alliterative verse in which oral composition is unlikely. Critiques the work of Waldron [265] and Finlayson [1002] and argues that formulaic writing is not necessarily mechanical or artistically uninteresting.

234. Lawton, David A. "Form and Style in Middle English Unrhymed Alliterative Verse: Studies in the Formal Corpus." *DAI* 37 (1977): 1/4761C. York U.

Distinguishes between formal and informal unrhymed alliterative poems, discusses theory of meter, and

compares poems. Claims that a close comparison of
the three Alexander poems reveals differences in stylistic procedure that are more significant than the
similarities.

235. ------. "Gaytryge's Sermon, *Dictamen*, and Middle
English Alliterative Verse." *MP* 76 (1979): 329-343.

Offers a model for ME unrhymed alliterative verse,
which may be a conscious attempt to construct a
vernacular high style from the principles of *ars
dictaminis*, and suggests that the sermon is an English imitation of *compositio* and that the Gaytryge
sermon is an antecedent of alliterative verse.

236. ------. "Literary History and Scholarly Fancy: The
Date of Two Middle English Alliterative Poems."
Parergon 18 (1977): 17-25.

Suggests that confusion over the date of *St. Erken-
wald* and *Winner and Waster* may seriously affect the
literary and historical treatment of alliterative
poetry. If the date of *Winner and Waster* is later
than 1352-53, then its style, as well as that of
other late 14th-century aa/ax poems such as *Destruction of Troy*, is a development from the earlier, less
formal alliterative style exemplified in such texts
as *William of Palerne*.

237. ------, ed. *Middle English Alliterative Poetry and
its Literary Background: Seven Essays*. Cambridge,
Eng.: D.S. Brewer, 1982.

Includes an introductory essay [238] as well as
essays on alliterative romance and the French tradition [212], manuscripts [220], AN background to alliterative romance [224], early ME alliterative verse
[245], and the alliterative revival [255].

238. ------. "Middle English Alliterative Poetry: An Introduction." Lawton [237]. 1-19, 125-129.

Discusses important issues concerning problems of
classification; characteristics of formal allitera-

tive verse; questions of source materials, especially
Latin influence; and stylistic concerns. Points to
the importance of distinguishing the history of
composition and that of its reception and points to
areas needing more research.

239.   ------. "Middle English Unrhymed Alliterative Poetry
        and the *South English Legendary.*" *ES* 61 (1980):
        390-396.

        Argues that the *Legendary* is an antecedent of the
        poems of the alliterative revival and that the manu-
        scripts containing it also contain alliterative
        verse, so the popularity of the *Legendary* may be re-
        sponsible for the survival of *William of Palerne*,
        Joseph of Arimathie, and perhaps *Chevalere Assigne*.

240.   ------. "*Scottish Field*: Alliterative Verse and
        Stanley Encomium in the Percy Folio." *LeedsSE* ns 10
        (1978): 42-57.

        Claims that the 16th-century survival of unrhymed
        alliterative verse in the Lancashire and Cheshire
        areas is directly connected with an audience that
        read and enjoyed the poems of Stanley glorification
        and regional patriotism.

241.   Lehman, Anne Kernan. "Thematic Patterning and Narra-
        tive Continuity in Four Middle English Alliterative
        Poems." *DAI* 31 (1971): 6558A. Cornell U.

        Studies the relationship between thematic patterns,
        especially the use of enveloping, and narrative
        continuity in *Parlement of Thre Ages*, *Awntyrs off
        Arthure*, *Morte Arthure*, and *Sir Gawain and the Green
        Knight*.

242.   Levy, Bernard S., and Paul E. Szarmach, eds. *The
        Alliterative Tradition in the Fourteenth Century.*
        Kent: Kent State UP, 1981.

        Includes articles on the origins of the allitera-
        tive revival [256], characterization of women [523],
        Awntyrs off Arthure [700], and *Morte Arthure* [1057].

243. Lupack, Alan C. "Structure and Tradition in the Poems of the Alliterative Revival." *DAI* 36 (1975): 323A. U of Pennsylvania.

Defends the poems in terms of their artistry and structure; examines their experimentation with formal structure, which displays artistry in the diptych principle of organization; gives thematic and critical analyses of *Awntyrs off Arthure, Golagrus and Gawain, Taill of Rauf Coilyear,* and *Sir Gawain and the Green Knight.*

244. MacDonald, Donald. "Verse Satire and Humor in Middle Scots." *DA* 19 (1958): 1387-1388. Northwestern U.

Argues that the satiric and humorous poetry of Middle Scots is essentially derivative, having connections particularly with Northern alliterative romances, with English satirical traditions, and with the common stock of European literature.

245. McIntosh, Angus. "Early Middle English Alliterative Verse." Lawton [237]. 20-33, 129-31.

Presents the basic problems of terminology and taxonomy and proposes two new terms to eliminate the confusions inherent in the old terminology of accentual and syllabic modes. *Heteromorphic* designates rhythmical material in which foot units have a number of different forms and feet proceed in no fixed order, whereas *homomorphic* designates material in which there is only one basic foot unit and lines and larger entities are made up of a continuous succession of examples of this unit.

246. Mackay, M.A. "The Alliterative Tradition in Middle Scots Verse." *TGB* 26 (1977): 290. Ph.D., Edinburgh U.

247. Matonis, A.T.E. "Middle English Alliterative Poetry." Benskin and Samuels [538]. 341-354, 412-413.

Draws attention to the technical aspects of shorter alliterative stanzaic poetry and then points to five

problems that inhibit neat classification of alliterative verse: counting alliterative syllables
carrying secondary metrical stress, accounting for
instances of compound or alternating alliteration,
identifying incidental or supplemental alliteration,
coming to terms with generic alliteration, and distinguishing consonantal correspondences that extend
into the interior of two or more words or across a
line.

248.   ------. "A Reexamination of the Middle English Alliterative Long Line." *MP* 81 (1984): 339-360.

Reviews the occasions and conditions of alliteration in the long-line unrhymed narrative and finds
metrical and dramatic considerations can never be
absent. Discusses the question of whether poets were
more interested in alliterative conventions than
metrical or rhetorical ones.

249.   Milgrom, Robert Lee. "Light against Dark: The Presentation of Heroic Life in Four Medieval English Alliterative Poems: *Beowulf*, *Maldon*, *Morte Arthure*,
and *Gawain and the Green Knight*." *DAI* 40 (1979):
2697A. CUNY.

Deals with the clash between human aspiration and
necessity, which accounts for the narrative strate-
gies of the medieval heroic poem and which distinguishes it from other verse.

250.   Moorman, Charles. "The English Alliterative Revival
and the Literature of Defeat." *ChauR* 16 (1981):
85-100.

Distinguishes loosely between two traditions: poems
from the south and east of England with Christian and
political themes, and those from the north and west
with epic heroism, a pagan ethos, the violence of
nature, and a mythic strain—a natural part of the
"inheritance of any defeated and humiliated people
who have seen their agrarian, individualistic way of
life destroyed by the forces of industrial, urban,
structured society."

251. ------. "The Origins of the Alliterative Revival."
      SoQ 7 (1969): 345-371.

      Evaluates the theories of Hulbert, Salter, and Oak-
      den and summarizes the evidence for a tradition orig-
      inating in OE heroic literature, continuing in an
      oral tradition during the AN period, and re-emerging
      as written verse in the baronial courts of the 14th
      century.

252. Moseley, C.W.R.D. "Chaucer, Sir John Mandeville, and
      the Alliterative Revival: A Hypothesis Concerning
      Relationships." *MP* 72 (1974): 182-184.

      Identifies a possible intellectual link between the
      Gawain-poet and Chaucer through a member of John of
      Gaunt's household by attributing Mandeville's *Travels*
      to a dependent of Humphrey de Bohun, whose work was
      circulated among the cultured circle of John of Gaunt
      and the poets of the alliterative revival.

253. Noble, James Erwin. "Layamon's *Brut* and the Continu-
      ity of the Alliterative Tradition." *DAI* 43 (1983):
      2683A. U of Western Ontario.

      Argues that three-quarters of the half-lines in
      Brut have rhythms similar or identical to ones in OE
      verse, that the repetitions are similar in form and
      function to the two basic types of formulaic repeti-
      tion in OE verse, and that the poet was acquainted
      with rhetorical tropes of his forebears.

254. O'Loughlin, J.L.N. "The English Alliterative Ro-
      mances." Loomis [320]. 520-527.

      Gives a brief sampling of the North Midlands and
      Northern school of alliterative verse to illustrate
      its "masculine force, its fondness for action and
      realistic detail, and its occasional disregard of
      unity."

255. Pearsall, Derek. "The Alliterative Revival: Origins
      and Social Backgrounds." Lawton [237]. 34-53,
      132-136.

Divides the essay into the evidence of formal identity, evidence of regional identity, continuity and transmission, and social background of authors and audiences. Begins with the fact that between 1250 and 1350 there is a blank in the history of alliterative verse, but in the 60-70 years after 1350 there is a flood of both formal and informal alliterative verse, a phenomenon that must be explained. Suggests that poems from the earlier period may very likely have been lost because of their presumably secular subject matter, regional affiliation, and the disadvantaged status of English during that period.

256.   ------.   "The Origins of the Alliterative Revival." Levy and Szarmach [242].   1-24.

Argues that monasteries in the southwest Midlands, possibly at Worcester, with their extensive historical source materials were responsible for the writing, presentation, and dissemination of alliterative verse, and that this context provided continuity for its provenance and a strong directive for its development.

257.   Salter, Elizabeth.   "Alliterative Modes and Affiliations in the Fourteenth Century."   *NM* 79 (1978): 25-35.

Suggests that the alliterative revival was not so much self-conscious literary antiquarianism as it was the transformation and formalization of rougher accentual materials in hybrid prose and in verse texts with unrhymed, semi-alliterative lines.

258.   ------.   "The Alliterative Revival."   *MP* 64 (1966-67): 146-150, 233-237.

Reviews theories concerning alliterative poetry, suggesting that they do not account for the differences in style and tone among works from 1200 to 1350. Further argues that much investigation is still needed on the movement of lords and officials between Westminster and the estates in the west and north.

259. Sapora, Robert William, Jr. *A Theory of Middle English Alliterative Meter with Critical Applications.* Diss. U of Connecticut, 1976. Speculum Anniversary Monographs 1. [Cambridge, MA]: Mediaeval Academy of America, 1977.

     Chapter: 1. Approaches to the study of Middle English alliterative verse, 1-15.
               2. A theory of Middle English alliterative meter, 17-29.
               3. Problems of scansion, 31-45.
               4. The theory applied to various poems in the tradition, 47-62.
               5. Literary style, stylistics, and metrical theory, 63-79.
     Appendices, 81-117.

     Proposes a theory specifying a unique degree of complexity for each metrical form and applies this to *Sir Gawain and the Green Knight* and large parts of *Morte Arthure* and *Destruction of Troy.*

260. Shepherd, Geoffrey. "The Nature of Alliterative Poetry in Late Medieval England." *PBA* 56 (1970): 57-76.

     Argues that many passages in the late medieval alliterative writing become more intelligible when they are considered vestigially mnemonic in form and content.

261. Singh, C. "The Alliterative Tradition in Scottish Poetry." *TGB* 21 (1970-71): 314. Ph.D., Leeds U.

262. Suzuki, Eiichi. "Poetic Synonyms for 'Man' in Middle English Alliterative Poems." *ESELL* 49-50 (1966): 209-227 [in Japanese].

263. Turville-Petre, Thorlac. *The Alliterative Revival.* Cambridge, Eng.: D.S. Brewer, 1977.

     Chapter: 1. The origins of the Alliterative Revival, 1-25.
               2. The revival, 26-47.

3. Metre, 48-68.
4. Poetic diction, 69-92.
5. The art of narrative, 93-114.
6. Epilogue: after the revival, 115-128.

Notes, lists of editions, and index, 129-152.

264. ------. "Two Notes on Words in Alliterative Poems." *N&Q* ns 25 (1978): 295-296.

Suggests that *tried* in *Sir Gawain and the Green Knight* 3439 meant "found out, exposed" and that the *porte* in *Morte Arthure* 2609 referred to the seaport of Alexandria.

265. Waldron, Ronald A. "Oral-Formulaic Technique and Middle English Alliterative Poetry." *Speculum* 32 (1957): 792-804.

Demonstrates that a common formulaic diction runs through 14th-century alliterative poetry; analyzes twenty-five lines of *Morte Arthure*, as well as formulas from fifteen other alliterative poems, for supporting evidence.

266. Williams, D.J. "Alliterative Poetry in the Fourteenth and Fifteenth Centuries." Bolton [13]. 107-158.

Describes the form, background, audience, and history of alliterative verse. Discusses representative works in this tradition, such as *William of Palerne*, *Chevalere Assigne*, *Destruction of Troy*, *Awntyrs off Arthure*, *Morte Arthure*, and the Alexander and Gawain poems.

SEE ALSO items 1 (58-62, 71-72), 16 (142-154), 17, 34 (23-96), 35 (7-8), 62 (232-239), 82 (48-49, 68-83, 86-100), 93 (215-304), 94 (55-65), 111, and 403 (3-4, 33-34).

ARTHURIAN LITERATURE

267. Ackerman, Robert W. "The English Rimed and Prose
      Romances." Loomis [320]. 480-519.

      Organizes the twenty-three heterogeneous English
      Arthurian narratives according to the classification
      of Wells' *Manual* and briefly discusses their literary
      merits and connections to related works.

268. Adolf, Helen. "The Concept of Original Sin as Re-
      flected in Arthurian Romance." Schlauch Essays [14].
      21-29.

      Studies certain recurring themes—incest, nuptial
      fraud, including shameful or blessed births, and
      wounded or blinded knights and kings—as part of the
      symbolic vocabulary dealing with the concept of
      original sin. Discusses *tradux peccati* and the asso-
      ciation of incest with lust or libido, which is then
      related to original sin.

269. Alexander, Flora. "Late Medieval Scottish Attitudes
      to the Figure of King Arthur: A Reassessment."
      Anglia 93 (1975): 17-34.

      Contends that attitudes towards Arthur are not as
      uniform as R. H. Fletcher [*Arthurian Material in the
      Chronicles*, 2nd ed. (New York, 1966)] or Göller [298]
      suggests; instead, in *Lancelot of the Laik* Arthur is
      subjected to criticism, which is not, however, the
      same as that connected with the national fear of Eng-
      lish aggression in the Scottish *Golagrus and Gawain*.

270. App, August J. *Lancelot in English Literature: His
      Rôle and Character*. Diss. Catholic U of America,

1929. Rpt. New York: Haskell House, 1965.

Chapter: 1. Introductory: Lancelot previous to his appearance in English literature, 1-23.
2. Lancelot in English literature before Malory's *Morte Darthur*, 24-52.
3. Lancelot in the first seventeen books of Malory's *Morte Darthur*, 53-73.
4. Lancelot in the last four books of Malory's *Morte Darthur*, 74-90.
5. Lancelot in English literature after Malory to 1600, 91-112.
6. Lancelot in English literature from 1600 to 1800, 113-131.
7. Lancelot in English literature from 1800 to Tennyson, 132-150.
8. Lancelot in the poetry of Tennyson, 151-175.
9. Lancelot in Tennyson's contemporaries, 176-194.
10. Lancelot in English literature from 1875 to 1900, 195-210.
11. Lancelot in English literature since 1900, 211-232.

Summary, 233-239.
Bibliography and index, 240-260.

271. Ashe, Geoffrey. *King Arthur's Avalon: The Story of Glastonbury*. London: Collins, 1957.

Chapter: 1. The glass island, 13-41.
2. Roma Secunda, 42-79.
3. Arthur, 80-121.
4. The Celts, 122-159.
5. The conquerors, 160-202.
6. Double majesty, 203-225.
7. The Grail, 226-279.
8. A golden age 280-306.
9. Dissolution, 307-337.
10. Desolation, 338-362.

Appendix A. The Grail and "Bartholomew," 363-367.
B. Bibliographical note, 368-369.
Bibliography and index, 370-384.

272. Barber, Richard. *Arthur of Albion*: *An Introduction*

to the *Arthurian Literature and Legends of England*. London: Barrie & Rockliff, 1961. Reissued with corrections, London: Boydell P, 1971.

Chapter: 1. The unknown commander, 1-12.
2. From reality to romance, 13-24.
3. Arthur the Emperor, 25-52.
4. Arthur and Avalon, 53-64.
5. The earliest English poems, 64-94.
   Examines the English romances from 1250, characterizing them as inferior to their French parallels, shortened and simplified versions lacking in sophistication and taste.
6. Gawain, 95-121.
   Discusses the main ME Gawain romances, suggesting that except for *Sir Gawain and the Green Knight*, most are uninspired and popular works.
7. The flower of chivalry, 122-135.
   Explores the achievement of Malory.
8. Reaction and revival, 136-164.
9. The modern view, 165-187.

Apendices, 188-198
Notes and index, 199-216.

273. ------. *The Figure of Arthur*. London: Longman, 1972.

Chapter: 1. The Arthurian controversy, 11-20.
2. Arthur of Dalriada, 21-33.
3. Arthur of Dyfed, 34-38.
4. The unknown leader: Badon Hill, 39-53.
5. The bardic image: names and places, 54-79.
6. A political hero, 80-107.
7. The national Messiah, 108-121.
8. Popular beliefs, 122-136.

Bibliography, references, and index, 137-160.

274. ------. *King Arthur in Legend and History*. Ipswich, Eng.: Boydell P, 1973.

Chapter: 1. The unknown commander, 11-24.
2. From reality to romance, 25-34.

3. Arthur the Emperor, 35-56.
4. Arthur and Avalon, 57-67.
5. The Matter of Britain: romances in French, 68-86
6. Tristan and Parzival: the German romances, 87-101.
7. The English poems, 102-120.

Treats *Arthour and Merlin*, *Sir Perceval of Galles*, and the ME romances dealing with the figure of Arthur or Gawain.

8. The flower of chivalry, 121-133.
9. An enduring fame, 134-169.

Notes, 171-174.
Chronological list of Arthurian literature, 175-179.
Select bibliography, and index, 181-192.

Part of this book was originally published as *Arthur of Albion* [272].

275. Barron, W.R.J. "Arthurian Romance: Traces of an English Tradition." *ES* 61 (1980): 2-23.

Analyzes the dominant literary characteristics of Layamon's *Brut*, *Morte Arthure*, *Golagrus and Gawain*, and *Sir Gawain and the Green Knight* in order to investigate similarities or traces of an English tradition.

276. Bergner, Heinz. "Gawain und seine literarischen Realisationen in der englischen Literatur des Spätmittelalters." Wolfzettel [362]. 3-15.

Argues that even when Gawain degenerates into a henpecked husband or womanizer as in *Weddynge of Sir Gawen* and *Jeaste of Syr Gawayne*, he still remains the superman/hero for his audience, who tried to make the chivalric Gawain into one of their own—still a hero, but one who conformed more closely to the everyday realities of their social class.

277. Bernstein, Linda. "Politics and Kingship in the Middle English Arthurian Romance." *DAI* 46 (1985): 147A. Columbia U.

Examines this subgroup and finds a consistent pattern of recasting the Continental sources in order to de-emphasize supernatural elements and illustrate the nature of a good king. Contrasts seven poems with their French analogues and sources (*Ywain and Gawain, Sir Launfal, Libeaus Desconus, Sir Perceval, Lancelot of the Laik, Arthour and Merlin*, and the alliterative *Morte Arthure*.

278. Bliss, A.J. "Celtic Myth and Arthurian Romance." *MAE* 30 (1961): 19-25.

Critically reviews Harward's monograph [301], but also warns against mere speculation and implausible conjecture.

279. Bloomgarden, Ira. "Northern Middle English Arthurian Romance and its Historical Background." *DAI* 31 (1971): 6539A-6540A. CUNY.

Views the ambivalent presentation of Arthur and Gawain's role as his foil as a product of the political outlook of northern barons and then shows that the northern topography influences the use of locale and nature descriptions.

280. Bollard, J.K. "Medieval English Arthurian Romances and their Celtic Analogues: A Comparative Study." *TGB* 28 (1981): 4919. Ph.D., Leeds U.

281. Brewer, D.S. "Chaucer and Chrétien and Arthurian Romance." Rowland [81]. 255-259.

Argues that Chaucer's derision of ME romances was probably based on an earlier knowledge of and youthful fascination with them as well as Chrétien's Arthurian romances; the nature of his mockery suggests a deep engagement with the material.

282. Campbell, Alphonsus M. "The Character of King Arthur in the Middle English Alliterative Poems." *RUO* 45 (1975): 26-41.

Defends Arthur in *Sir Gawain and the Green Knight*, *Morte Arthure*, *Awntyrs off Arthure*, and *Golagrus and Gawain* against much criticism and finds the Christian hero and king as noble and chivalrous, cut off not through his own fault, but by the whim of Fortune.

283. Cosman, Madeleine Pelner. *The Education of the Hero in Arthurian Romance.* Diss. Columbia U, 1964. Chapel Hill: U of North Carolina P, 1966.

Introduction, xiii-xvii.
Chapter: 1. The education of Tristan: music and manners make the man, 3-48.
2. The education of Perceval: a brave man slowly wise, 49-100.
3. The education of Lancelot: altar, bower, and sword, 101-135.
4. The education of the Arthurian hero: prevalence and provenance, 137-196.
Conclusion, 197-202.
Bibliography and index, 203-239.

284. Darrah, John. *The Real Camelot: Paganism and the Arthurian Romances.* London: Thames and Hudson, 1981.

Introduction, 12-22.
Part: I. Sacred kings in the Arthurian romances, 24-70.
II: The historical background of the 'Arthurian' sacred kings, 71-102.
III: The pagan framework underlying the Arthurian legend, 103-140.
Appendices, notes, bibliography, and index, 141-160.

285. Dean, Christopher. "Sir Kay in Medieval English Romances: An Alternative Tradition." *ESC* 9 (1983): 125-135.

Traces the dual portrait of Kay in ME romance. Of the fifteen romances in which Kay appears, six portray him as the mocking, surly, incompetent knight, in accord with the French romance tradition (*Syre Gawene and the Carle of Carelyle*, *Ywain and Gawain*, *Turke and Gowin*, *Grene Knight*, *Sir Perceval*, and

Avowynge of Arthur). In five others, Kay is presented in the chronicle tradition as a valiant fighter,
loyal to Arthur, and highly respected (*Prose Merlin*,
Arthour and Merlin, *Morte Arthure*, *Merlin*, and *Lancelot of the Laik).* In two other works, *Golagrus and
Gawain* and Malory's treatment, there are elements of
both traditions; in the remaining, his appearance is
too brief to characterize.

286. Eckhardt, Caroline Davis. "Arthurian Comedy: Perspectives on the Hero." *DAI* 32 (1972): 6372A. U of
Michigan.

Questions the notion of epic degeneration in a number of medieval Arthurian works and characterizes the
hero in such works as *Sir Perceval* as a *Dümmling*, a
simpleton resembling the wildman or comic *vilain*.

287. Eisner, Sigmund. *The Tristan Legend: A Study in
Sources.* Evanston: Northwestern UP, 1969.

Chapter: 1. King Arthur in history and legend, 3-
21.
2. The tradition of Tristan & Isolt, 23-
37.
3. Celtic monasticism, 39-44.
4. Drust, 45-54.
5. King March, 55-73.
6. North British nomenclature, 75-85.
7. The reluctant lover, 87-113.
8. The tribute gatherers, 115-139.
9. The death scene, 141-157.
10. The *Drustansaga*, 159-167.
Bibliography, 169-179.
Index, 181-189.

288. Fichte, Joerg O. "Die englischsprachige Artusromanze
im 15. Jahrhundert: Kritik—Groteske—Burleske." Wolfzettel [362]. 47-59.

Claims that the 15th-century treatment of Arthur
took three distinct routes: a critical/political
use, a transformation into the grotesque, and an
embodiment of parody. The new focus on Gawain in a
bizarre adventure world with a mixture of folklore

and fairy tale motifs (e.g., impossible tasks and magic potions) allowed a distancing from reality, with works like *Weddynge of Sir Gawen* taking on aspects of parody and other works like *Turke and Gowin* moving toward the grotesque.

289.   ------. "The Middle English Arthurian Romance: The Popular Tradition in the Fourteenth Century." *Literature in Fourteenth-Century England*. The J.A.W. Bennett Memorial Lectures, Perugia, 1981-1982. Ed. Piero Boitani and Anna Torti. Tübinger Beiträge zur Anglistik 5. Tübingen: Gunter Narr; Cambridge: Brewer, 1983. 137-153.

Analyzes *Libeaus Desconus* and *Sir Perceval* in terms of their internal and external form, authorship and presentation, content and meaning, and authorial intent and reception in order to test whether they conform to the structural pattern of classical Arthurian romance or are influenced by popular English tales.

290.   ------. "The Middle English Arthurian Verse Romance: Suggestions for the Development of a Literary Typology." *DVLG* 55 (1981): 567-590.

Proposes a heuristic model for this type of literature that comprises internal and external form, authorship and presentation, context and meaning, and authorial intent and reception. Argues that the intrinsic structure is controlled by adventure and quest, a pattern that seems to justify the distinction of Arthurian romance from other types of ME romance. Analyzes *Ywain and Gawain* and illustrates transformations of the structural pattern in *Sir Perceval*, *Sir Gawain and the Green Knight*, and *Weddynge of Sir Gawen*.

291.   Figgins, Robert Harrison. "The Character of Sir Gawain in Middle English Romance." *DAI* 34 (1973): 2556A. U of Washington.

Explores different perspectives on Gawain's shortcomings as a function of conflict, structure, and theme in individual works.

292. Fries, Maureen. "The Rationalization of the Arthurian 'Matter' in T.H. White and Mary Stewart." *PQ* 56 (1977): 258-265.

    Investigates the use of narrator, of temporal set-ting, and of characterization by both authors, who explore the interplay between Arthur and Merlin and the perennial problem of human frailty and just rule.

293. Gibson, J.W. "The Characterisation of King Arthur in Medieval English Literature." *TGB* 5 (1954-55): 137. M.A., Sheffield U.

294. Gillies, William. "Arthur in Gaellic Tradition. Part 2. Romances and Learned Lore." *CMCS* 3 (1982): 41-75.

    Explains how, when, and why Arthurian literature came into Gaelic tradition; discovers only one direct translation of *Queste of the Holy Grail* into Welsh from English in the 15th century and discusses the embroidery upon the Arthurian legend. Argues that local traditions were already flourishing around the figure of Arthur even in the 9th century during the composition of the *Historia Brittanium*.

295. Girouard, Mark. *The Return to Camelot: Chivalry and the English Gentleman*. New Haven: Yale UP, 1981.

    Studies the medieval revival in the 19th century, mainly through an examination of Victorian thought, literature, art, and politics.

296. Glasser, Marc. *"He Nedes Moste Hire Wedde*: The Forced Marriage in the 'Wife of Bath's Tale' and its Middle English Analogues." *NM* 85 (1984): 239-241.

    Differentiates Chaucer's tale from the other ME analogues, since in *Marriage of Sir Gawaine*, *Weddynge of Sir Gawen*, and Gower's *Tale of Florent*, the knight knows that marriage is the hag's demand in exchange for the answer to the question. Only in Chaucer's tale does the knight complain bitterly, an appropri-ate response to the Wife, who struggles for domination over her spouse.

297. Göller, Karl Heinz. "The Figure of King Arthur as a
Mirror of Political and Religious Views." *Functions
of Literature: Essays Presented to Erwin Wolff on
his Sixtieth Birthday.* Ed. Ulrich Broich, Theo
Stemmler, and Gerd Stratmann. Tübingen: Max Niemeyer, 1984. 55-79.

Examines the various traditions and treatments of
Arthur, one of the most ambivalent and controversial
figures in literature, from the ideal chivalric ruler
to saint or swine. Suggests that the Arthurian story
had political overtones from the beginning, that the
image of the monarch was trivialized in ballad-type
narratives, and that the monkish and clerical traditions were responsible for the growing piety and
Christian virtue attached to the legend.

298. ------. *König Arthur in der Englischen Literatur des
Späten Mittelalters.* Palaestra 238. Göttingen: Vandenhoeck & Ruprecht, 1963.

Einleitung: Geoffrey, Wace, Layamon, 13-22.
Chapter: 1. Arthur in den englischen Chroniken,
                23-40.
             2. Die biographischen Romanzen, 41-76.
                Treats *Arthour and Merlin* (under-
                lying legend, distribution of mate-
                rial, audience), *Arthur* (language,
                audience, treatment of sources),
                and *Morte Arthur* (sources and Ar-
                thur's sinking star and fate).
             3. Arthur in den Romanzen um die Ein-
                zelritter, 77-102.
                Discusses six ME romances:
                *Avowynge of Arthur, Sir Perceval,
                Libeaus Desconus, Ywain and Gawain,*
                Launfal versions, and Gawain ro-
                mances.
             4. Arthur in den moralisierenden Ro-
                manzen, 103-143.
                Examines in detail the allitera-
                tive *Morte Arthure, Golagrus and
                Gawain, Awntyrs off Arthure,* Lyd-
                gate's *Fall of Princes,* and *Lance-*

lot of the Laik.
5. Arthur im Werke Sir Thomas Malorys, 144-165.
6. Arthur in den balladenähnlichen Verserzählungen, 166-174.
Schluss, Exkurse, and Bibliographie, 175-201.

299. Goodrich, Peter Hampton. "Merlin: The Figure of the Wizard in English Fiction (Volumes I and II)." *DAI* 44 (1983): 1798A. U of Michigan.

Argues that Merlin maintains a psychological and dialectic tension relevant to his function as Wild Man, Poet, Prophet, Wizard, Counselor, and Lover. Further suggests that Merlin and Arthur form a *Doppelgänger* representing the human desire for *renovatio* but undercut by *eros*.

300. Gransden, Antonia. "The Growth of the Glastonbury Traditions and Legends in the Twelfth Century." *JEH* 27 (1976): 337-358.

Discusses the importance of both hagiography and romance in building the prestige of the Glastonbury abbey; suggests that hagiography was the principal influence on Glastonbury's literary production until 1184 and that romance was after that date. Argues that by the end of the 12th century, the monks of Glastonbury had acquired in King Arthur a much needed patron and further enhanced their own importance by dovetailing the legend of Joseph of Arimathea with that of King Arthur.

300a. Grout, P.B., R.A. Lodge, C.E. Pickford, and E.K.C. Varty, eds. *The Legend of Arthur in the Middle Ages: Studies Presented to A.H. Diverres by Colleagues, Pupils* and Friends. Cambridge, Eng.: D.S. Brewer, 1983.

Includes essays on the stanzaic *Morte Arthur* [962] and on *Sir Gawain and the Green Knight* [1221].

301. Harward, Vernon J., Jr. *The Dwarfs of Arthurian Romance and Celtic Tradition*. Diss. Columbia U,

1953. Leiden, Neth.: E.J. Brill, 1958.

Chapter: 1. Introduction, 1-5.
          2. The dwarfs of Celtic tradition, 6-20.
          3. The court dwarf, 21-27.
          4. The appearance of the romance dwarfs,
              28-32.
          5. Bilis, King of the Antipodes, 33-42.
          6. Pelles, 43-50.
          7. The truculent dwarf and his giant
              kinsman, 51-61.
          8. Guivret, the Chevalier Petit, and
              Auberon, 62-73.
          9. Morgain la Fée and the dwarfs, 74-81.
         10. The dwarf king in the Dutch *Lancelot*,
              82-87.
         11. Teodelain, 88-89.
         12. *The Turk and Gowin*, 90-98.
              Discusses the analogues from Ire-
              land and Gaelic Scotland and believes
              that there was direct transmission
              from Ireland to Britain; this would
              explain the extravagance of the
              Turk's exploits and the fidelity of
              the author to the attributes of dwarf
              helpers and of Curoi. Further refer-
              ences to this poem occur on 28, 105,
              121.
         13. Milocrates and the elf king, 99-101.
         14. Evadeam, 102-105.
         15. The spying dwarf, 106-110.
         16. The mount of the dwarf, 111-116.
         17. The strength of the dwarfs, 117-119.
         18. Conclusion, 120-123.
Appendix and index, 124-149.

302. ------. "'Celtic Myth and Arthurian Romance': A
      Reply." *MAE* 31 (1962): 43-44.

      Refutes Bliss' attack [278] against his hypothesis,
      especially the claim that there is evidence for the
      existence of dwarfs in Welsh tradition.

303. Herzog, Michael Bernard. "The Development of Gawain
      as a Literary Figure in Medieval German and English
      Arthurian Romance." *DAI* 32 (1972): 6377A-6378A. U

of Washington.

Argues that unlike French and German literature in which Gawain undergoes a consistent and chronological deterioration, the English romance inconsistently intermingles respect and disparagement because of the great variety of sources and the inferior English writers.

304. Höltgen, Karl Josef. "König Arthur und Fortuna." *Anglia* 75 (1957): 35-54.

Argues that the image of Arthur portrayed by Geoffrey of Monmouth, Wace, and Layamon was changed in ME works by the influence of the figure of Fortuna; notes how Fortuna affected the vision and interpretation of fate in poems such as *Golagrus and Gawain* and *Morte Arthure*.

305. Jenkins, Elizabeth. *The Mystery of King Arthur.* London: Michael Joseph, 1975.

Chapter: 1. Britain before Arthur, 9-25.
2. Fact and legend, 27-37.
3. Early Arthurian tales, 39-45.
4. Growth of the legend, 47-51.
5. The first recorders, 53-64.
6. English interpretations, 65-69.
7. Lancelot and Guinevere, 71-82.
8. 'Glastonbury Is Avalon,' 84-93.
9. Medieval influences, 95-102.
10. Arthur and chivalry, 105-116.
11. Decline of knighthood, 117-127.
12. The background to Malory's Arthur, 128-135.
13. Malory: the legend immortalized, 137-153.
14. The Tudors, 155-166.
15. Stuart interest, 167-174.
16. Decline, 175-181.
17. Revival, 182-189.
18. The Pre-Raphaelites, Tennyson, ourselves, 191-215.
Literary references, 216.
Bibliography of other sources used, 217.
Illustrations acknowledgments, 218-219.

Index, 220-224.

306. Jones, R.J. "Sir Kay in Medieval Arthurian Romance."
      TGB 11 (1960-61): 167. B.Litt., Oxford U.

307. Jost, Jean E. "An Annotated Bibliography of Ten Mid-
      dle English Arthurian Romances: Editions, Back-
      grounds and Interpretations." *DAI* 41 (1981): 4391A-
      4392A. U of Cincinnati.

308. Kelly, C.S. "The Northern Arthur: A Study of Two
      Alliterative Arthurian Romances in their Literary and
      Historical Context." *TGB* 26 (1977): 289. Ph.D.,
      Edinburgh U.

309. Kelly, Susan. "A Note on Arthur's Round Table and
      the Welsh *Life of Saint Carannog.*" *Folklore* 87
      (1976): 223-225.

      Notes that although the oldest specific reference
      to the Round Table is found in Wace's *Brut*, there is
      a reference in this Welsh *vita* to Arthur converting
      an altar to a table.

310. Kemper, Viktor Robert. "Middle English Merlin Leg-
      ends: A Scientific Definition, Classification, and
      Catalog." *DAI* 44 (1984): 3695A. Miami U.

      Defines the legend and the legendary hero through
      Propp's method of structural analysis and then pre-
      sents a systematic catalog of all sixteen ME Merlin
      legends according to their different types.

311. Kennedy, Edward D. "Malory and his English Sources."
      Aspects of Malory. Arthurian Studies 1. Ed. Toshi-
      yuki Takamiya and Derek Brewer. Cambridge, Eng.:
      D.S. Brewer, 1981. 27-55, 189-193.

      Argues that English influences—especially *Sir
      Torrent*, alliterative *Morte Arthure*, stanzaic *Morte
      Arthur*, and Hardyng's *Chronicle*—account for the role
      of narrator as historian, the character of Arthur,
      and the presentation of the Grail Quest as compatible

with Arthurian chivalry.

312. Kinney, Thomas L. "Arthurian Romances." *Super-natural Fiction Writers: Fantasy and Horror.* Ed. E.F. Bleiler. 2 vols. New York: Scribner's, 1985. 1: 11-18.

Traces Arthurian romance from Geoffrey of Monmouth through the *Gawain*-poet and Malory to Mary Stewart and views the genre as a vehicle for introducing and preserving the imaginative and irrational in Western literature. Argues that these works symbolize the ideal in human experience and the striving for nobility, beauty, and spirituality.

313. Köhler, Erich. *Ideal und Wirklichkeit in der höfischen Epik: Studien zur Form der frühen Artus- und Graldichtung.* 2nd ed. Tübingen: Max Niemeyer, 1970.

Vorwort zur ersten Auflage, 1-4.
Chapter: 1. König Artus und sein Reich—Geschichtliche Wirlichkeit und ritterliches Wunschbild, 5-36.
2. *Chevalerie*—*clergie*—Doppelbestimmung und Geschichtsbewusstsein des höfischen Rittertums, 37-65.
3. *Aventure*—Reintegration und Wesenssuche, 66-88.
4. Erwählung und Erlösung—Von der Unordnung der Welt zum Friedensreich, 89-138.
Notes the redemptive aspect of the knight's quest and argues that courtly romance functioned as an instrument for exploring the new secular ideals in courtly society.
5. Verdichtung und Wandlung, der Ideal—Wirklichkeitsspannung in der Liebe—*Erec, Cligès, Tristan, Lancelot, Yvain*, 139-180.
6. Perceval und der Gral—Die eschatologische Vollendung der ritterlichen Selbstauslegung, 181-235.
7. Die Form des Artusromans bei Chrestien—Das Verhältnis von Gehalt und Gestalt, 236-261.

Anhang zur zweiten Auflage, 263-261.
Namen- und Titelregister, 274-278.

314. Korrel, P.G. "The Characterization of Arthur, Mor-
      dred, and Guinevere in the Early Welsh and the Chron-
      icle Tradition and in the Middle English Romances
      Dealing with the Death of Arthur." *DAI* 46 (1985):
      2806C. National U of Ireland.

      Deals with three ME romances. In the alliterative
      Morte Arthure, Arthur is a truly great hero brought
      down as punishment for his pride; Modred is a repen-
      tant sinner; and Guinevere is not presented in a
      unified portrait. In the stanzaic *Morte Arthur*,
      Arthur is a weakling who listens to the wrong coun-
      selors and is a foil to Lancelot; Modred is totally
      unsympathetic; and Guinevere is a long-suffering
      queen. Malory further blackens Modred, turns
      Guinevere into an interesting character, but does not
      succeed in combining chronicle and romance traditions
      in the figure of Arthur.

315. Lagorio, Valerie M. "The Glastonbury Legends and the
      English Arthurian Grail Romances." *NM* 79 (1978):
      359-366.

      Assesses the impact of Glastonbury's Arthurian and
      Arimathean claims on the ME romances from *Arthour and
      Merlin*, *Joseph of Arimathie*, *Awntyrs off Arthure*, and
      Arthur through the stanzaic *Morte Arthur* and the al-
      literative *Morte Arthure* and Malory.

316. Leible, Arthur Bray. "The Character of Gawain in
      English Literature." *DA* 22 (1962): 3648. U of Mis-
      souri.

      Explores the legend of Gawain from its first ap-
      pearance in Celtic mythology through metrical ro-
      mances to later works of E.A. Robinson. Finds two
      traditions: the older, native tradition with Gawain
      as noble and courteous and the later French tradition
      with Gawain as treacherous and amorous.

317. Lewes, Ülle Erika. *The Life in the Forest: The*

Influence of the Saint Giles Legend on the Courtly Tristan Story. Tristania Monograph Series 1. Chattanooga: Tristania 1978.

Introduction, 1-5.
Chapter: 1. Background material on St. Giles, 6-14.
2. The court of Henry II and its connections with the Giles legend and the Tristan myth, 15-17.
3. Comparison of *St. Gilles*, *Trierer Aegidius* and Latin *Vita*, 18-22.
4. Comparison of the "Life in the Forest" in the courtly and the vulgar Tristan story, 23-27.
5. Comparison of *Trierer Aegidius*, Guillaume's *St. Gilles*, Gottfried's *Tristan*, *Tristrams Saga*, and *Sir Tristrem*, 28-52.
6. Conclusions, 53-56.
Appendices, 57-68.
Bibliography and index, 69-78.

318. Littleton, C. Scott. "The Holy Grail, the Cauldron of Annwn, and the Nartyamonga: A Further Note on the Sarmatian Connection." *JAF* 92 (1979): 326-333.

Suggests that accounts of the Sacred Cup of the Nartyamonga, which reflects a Sarmatian concern with magical cups and cauldrons, may have influenced stories about the Holy Grail.

319. ------, and Ann C. Thomas. "The Sarmatian Connection: New Light on the Origin of the Arthurian and Holy Grail Legends." *JAF* 91 (1978): 513-527.

Question the Celtic origin and heritage of the Arthurian stories and hypothesize a prototype among the Iranian-speaking people of the steppes in southern Russia. Explore evidence and outline the new theory as to when, where, and how the Sarmatian tales came to England; suggest Sarmatians at Hadrian's Wall in 175 A.D.

320. Loomis, Roger Sherman, ed. *Arthurian Literature in*

the Middle Ages: *A Collaborative History*.   Oxford:
Clarendon P, 1959.

Forty-one chapters by thirty scholars with varying
approaches and emphases.   Includes essays on alliterative romances [254], verse and prose Arthurian romances [267], and Breton lays [374].

321.   ------. "Arthurian Tradition and Folklore." *Folklore* 69 (1958): 1-25.

Reviews scholarship on the Arthurian connections to
Irish and Welsh motifs and story patterns; points to
the Breton *conteurs* as playing a large role in shaping and disseminating legends about Arthur.

322.   ------. *The Development of Arthurian Romance*.   London: Hutchinson, 1963.

Chapter: 1. Arthurian origins, 13-22.
           2. The *Mabinogion*, 23-31.
           3. The intermediaries, 32-43.
           4. Chrétien de Troyes, 44-66.
           5. Wolfram von Eschenbach's *Parzival*,
               67-73.
           6. Tristan and Isolt, 74-91.
           7. The Vulgate Cycle, 92-111.
           8. Joseph of Arimathea and Glastonbury,
               112-123.
           9. Merlin, 124-130.
          10. The rimed English romances, 131-146.
               Discusses *Libeaus Desconus*, *Sir
               Perceval*, and *Sir Tristrem* as repre-
               sentatives of Arthurian romances in
               tail rhyme and the stanzaic *Morte
               Arthur* and *Ywain and Gawain* as ex-
               amples in rhymed couplets.
          11. The alliterative English romances,
               147-165.
               Assesses *Morte Arthure* and *Sir
               Gawain and the Green Knight* as the
               two best alliterative romances.
          12. Sir Thomas Malory, 166-185.
       Epilogue, 186-190.
       Bibliography and index, 191-199.

323. ------. *The Grail: From Celtic Myth to Christian Symbol.* Cardiff: U of Wales P; New York: Columbia UP, 1963.

> Chapter: 1. The chief romances of the Grail: a preview, 1-6.
> 2. The origins and growth of Arthurian romance, 7-19.
> 3. Celtic myths: their mutations and combinations, 20-27.
> 4. The first Grail story: the *Conte del Graal* of Chrétien de Troyes, 28-45.
> 5. The Grail bearer, the question test, and the Fisher King, 46-64.
> 6. The first sequel to the *Conte del Graal*: the corpse on the bier and the broken sword, 65-73.
> 7. Irish *Echtrai*: the Waste Land and the bleeding lance, 74-81.
> 8. Manessier's sequel and *Peredur*: the mission of revenge, 82-96.
> 9. *Perlesvaus*: Welsh talismans and a Welsh elysium, 97-134.
> 10. *Sone de Nansai* and the *Mabinogi* of *Branwen*, 135-145.
> 11. The Prose *Lancelot*: combat and scandal in the castle of King Pelles, 146-164.
> 12. The *Queste del Saint Graal*: Celtic story-patterns in Cistercian allegory, 165-195.
> 13. *Parzival*, the spiritual biography of a knight, 196-222.
> 14. Joseph of Arimathea, an evangelist by error, 223-248.
> 15. Glastonbury, school of forgery and Isle of Avalon, 249-270.
> 16. The end of the quest, 271-277.
> Appendixes and index, 278-287.

324. ------. "Objections to the Celtic Origin of the 'Matière de Bretagne,'" *Romania* 79 (1958): 47-77.

Reviews and rebuts the major objections brought against the Celtic hypothesis while admitting the validity of particular arguments against it.

325.   ------.   "Scotland and the Arthurian Legend." *PSAS*
       89 (1955-56): 1-21.

       Sifts evidence and information concerning the per-
       sonages in Arthurian legend. For example, Arthur
       never crossed the Tweed; Gawain never reigned in Gal-
       loway; Father Loth had no connection with Lothian;
       Sinadon is not Stirling; and Tristan was a historic
       person, a king of the Picts, but did not live in
       Arthur's time.

326.   Machann, Clinton. "A Structural Study of the English
       Gawain Romances." *Neophil* 66 (1982): 629-637.

       Analyzes the fourteen Gawain romances using Vladi-
       mir Propp's method (in *Morphology of the Folktale*),
       by dividing them into seventeen units of action or
       functions and then turns to a consideration of ab-
       stract units of opposition, replacing the syntagmatic
       chain with a paradigmatic set.

327.   Markman, Alan Mouns. "Sir Gawain of Britain: A Study
       of the Romance Elements in the British Gawain Litera-
       ture." *DA* 15 (1955): 1613. U of Michigan.

       Studies nine of the English metrical romances that
       exhibit no courtly love and that pay attention to the
       human qualities of the characters.

328.   Matthews, William. "The Egyptians in Scotland: The
       Political History of a Myth." *Viator* 1 (1970): 289-
       306.

       Suggests that the Scottish portrait of Arthur (in
       Lancelot of the Laik and *Golagrus and Gawain*, for
       example) as a contemptible tyrant is a clear reaction
       to the political implication of the legend of Brutus
       and Arthur.

329.   ------.   "Where was Siesia-Sessoyne?" *Speculum* 49
       (1974): 680-686.

       Reviews possible sites for Siesia and suggests
       Val-Suzon, thirty-seven miles southwest of Langres,

as a likely candidate since it meets the requirements
of "topography, language, and familiarity as the true
site of that great Arthurian battle."

330. Meale, Carol.   "Manuscripts, Readers and Patrons in
      Fifteenth-Century England: Sir Thomas Malory and Ar-
      thurian Romance." *ArthurL* 4 (1985): 93-126.

      Considers evidence about the existence and extent
      of English libraries and collections of books in the
      15th century; the problems encountered in any study
      of book ownership, including the unreliability of
      wills, bequests, and contemporary records; the Eng-
      lish works to which Malory had access; the function
      of patronage in relation to the writer or distributor
      of literary texts and the benefits to the patron; the
      possible connection between Malory and Wydville; and
      the necessity for collaboration and research to shed
      light on 15th-century writers like Malory.

331. Mercer, Mary Ellen.   "A Violent Order: Moral Vision
      in Late Arthurian Romance, 1215-1500." *DAI* 36 (1976):
      6708A. Syracuse U.

      Distinguishes works according to their treatment of
      knightly values: heroic chivalry (*Morte Arthure*),
      high, chivalric *courtesie* (*Sir Gawain and the Green
      Knight* and *Lancelot of the Laik*), and burlesque (*Sir
      Degrevant*).

332. Merriman, James Douglas.   *The Flower of Kings: A
      Study of the Arthurian Legend in England between 1485
      and 1835*. Diss. Columbia U, 1962. Lawrence: U of
      Kansas P, 1973.

          Introduction, 3-6.
          Chapter: 1. The growth of a legend: Arthur in the
                        Middle Ages, 9-29.
                    2. A slow decline: Arthurian story and
                        tradition in the English Renaissance,
                        31-48.
                    3. The death of a legend: Arthurian
                        story in the seventeenth and early
                        eighteenth centuries, 49-80.
                    4. Arthur stirs in Avalon: Arthurian

story among the Pre-Romantics, 83-
112.

5. The past restored: romantic medievalism as preparation for Arthur's return, 113-136.

6. Arthur wakes in Avalon: Arthurian
literature of the Romantic period,
137-177.

Notes, 179-269.
Bibliography and index, 271-307.

Medieval romances: antagonism to, 5, 32-33, 54,
75-76; narrative method of, 19-20; Arthurian story
in, 24, 128-129; Renaissance attitudes toward, 32-34;
decline of, 52, 71; and Milton, 54-55; in 18th century, 75-76, 89-91, 96; Percy's knowledge of, 95;
return of interest in, 96-97; Hole's attitude toward,
107; and Romanticism, 115-116, 137; and Scott's romances, 118, 150, 156-157; in 19th century, 127-128,
176; and Wordsworth, 158-159.

333. Moorman, Charles. "King Arthur and the English
National Character." *NYFQ* 24 (1968): 103-112.

Traces the growth of Arthur as a national hero. As
the legend and the sense of national importance grew,
so the figure of the king took on a greater shape,
but a lesser function. Arthur became the archetype
of heroism, the center from which all heroic action
stemmed, a symbol of his nation—idealist, man of
vision, creator of a stable and beneficent government
in times of adversity.

334. Morris, Rosemary. *The Character of King Arthur in
Medieval Literature.* Arthurian Studies 4. Cambridge, Eng.: D.S. Brewer, 1982.

Introduction, 1-7.
Chapter: 1. Antecedents, 8-23.
        2. Conception and birth, 24-35.
        3. Accession, 36-49.
        4. Arthur at war, 50-69.
        5. Peacetime, 70-93.
        6. Relationships, 94-118.
        7. Personal attributes, 119-129.
        8. Death and aftermath, 130-142.

Notes, 144-160.
Bibliography and index, 161-175.

335. Morton, A.L. "The Matter of Britain: The Arthurian
Cycle and the Development of Feudal Society." *ZAA* 8
(1960): 5-28.

Argues that in England a strong popular culture, an
epic strain in the literature, and a national spirit
reacted strongly upon the character of the Arthurian
Matter, sharply differentiating it from the French.

336. Neaman, Judith Silverman. "The Distracted Knight: A
Study of Insanity in the Arthurian Romances." *DA* 29
(1968): 573A. Columbia U.

Explores insanity in Arthurian romances written
between the 12th and 15th centuries. Argues that the
hero never suffers from *amour heroicus* (love madness), but rather from excessive shame, jealousy, or
grief. Also studies the wildman.

337. Newstead, Helaine. "Arthurian Legends." Severs
[90]. 38-79.

Gives a background study, including Layamon's *Brut*,
and then divides the chapter into sections on individual romances under the general rubrics of whole
life of Arthur, Merlin, Lancelot, Gawain, Perceval,
Holy Grail, Tristram, and Arthur of Little Britain.

338. Olstead, Myra Mahlow. "The Role and Evolution of the
Arthurian Enchantress." *DA* 24 (1963): 731. U of
Florida.

Argues that major enchantresses in Arthurian legend—Morgan la Fee, Lady of the Lake, and Nyneve—
derive from Celtic tradition, representing the survival of pagan deities. Claims they emphasize the
supernatural and miraculous in the Arthurian narratives.

339. Owen, D.D.R., ed. *Arthurian Romance: Seven Essays.*

Rpt. of *FMLS* 6.1 (1970). Edinburgh: Scottish Academic P, 1970; New York: Barnes and Noble, 1971.

Includes essays on irony in romance [40] and *Turke and Gowin* [1593].

340.   ------. *The Evolution of the Grail Legend*. St. Andrews U Publications 58. Edinburgh: Oliver and Boyd, 1968.

Introduction, 1-4.
Chapter: 1. Ireland: point of departure, 5-16.
          2. The passage to Wales, 17-32.
          3. Caer Seint, 33-49.
          4. From the Welsh to the French-speaking world, 50-81.
          5. The bridge, 82-101.
          6. The French master: Chrétien de Troyes, 102-129.
          7. The first Grail romance, 130-164.
          8. Perspectives, 165-198.
Conclusion, 199-202.
Bibliography and index, 203-213.

341.   Paton, Lucy Allen. *Studies in the Fairy Mythology of Arthurian Romance*. 2nd ed. enlarged by a survey of scholarship since 1903 and a bibliography by Roger Sherman Loomis. Burt Franklin Bibliographical Series 18. New York: Burt Franklin, 1960.

Chapter: 1. The fairy queen, 1-12.
           2. Morgain's hostility to Arthur, 13-24.
           3. The sojourn of Arthur in Avalon, 25-48.
           4. Morgain's retention of Renoart, Lancelot, and Alisander l'Orphelin, 49-59.
           5. Morgain and Guiomar, 60-73.
           6. Morgain and Ogier le Danois, 74-80.
           7. The Val sanz Retor, 81-103.
           8. Morgain in the horn and mantle tests, 104-123.
           9. Morgain and Auberon, 124-135.
          10. Morgain, the sister of Arthur, 136-144.
          11. Morgain la Fée, 145-166.

        12. La Dame du Lac, 167-203.
        13. Niniane and Merlin, 204-227.
        14. La Damoisele Cacheresse, 228-247.
        15. The three important fays of Arthurian
             romance, 248-249.
Excursus, supplements, and indexes, 250-316.

342. Quinn, Esther C. "Chaucer's Arthurian Romance."
      ChauR 18 (1984): 211-220.

      Argues that the *Wife of Bath's Tale* is best under-
stood if considered in relation to Arthurian romance,
in particular *Sir Gawain and the Green Knight* and
Marie de France's *Lanval*. Suggests that Chaucer's
tale echoes *Sir Gawain and the Green Knight* and is an
ironic parallel to it, that Chaucer depended on
audience familiarity with the conventions and motifs
of the genre of Arthurian romance, and that the use
of the Wife as narrator is ironic because her voice
is female and bourgeois, not the typical aristocratic
male voice of romance.

343. Rhŷs, John. *Studies in the Arthurian Legend.* 1891.
      Rpt. New York: Russell & Russell, 1966.

    Chapter: 1. Arthur, historical and mythical, 1-
               24.
           2. Arthur and Airem, 25-48.
           3. Gwenhwyvar and her captors, 49-70.
           4. Peredur and Owein, 71-97.
           5. Peredur and the Empress, 98-126.
           6. Peredur and Lancelot, 127-144.
           7. Lancelot and Elayne, 145-165.
           8. Galahad and Gwalchaved, 166-183.
           9. Cúchulainn and Heracles, 184-210.
         10. Cúchulainn and Heracles (continued)
               211-237.
         11. Urien and his Congeners, 238-272.
         12. Pwyil and Pelles, 273-299.
         13. The origin of the Holy Grail, 300-
               327.
         14. Glastonbury and Gower, 328-347.
         15. The Isles of the Dead, 348-369.
         16. Great Britain and Little Britain,
               370-390.
Additions and corrections, 391-396.

Index, 397-411.

344. Rogers, G.E. "Themes and Variations: Studies in Some
      English Gawain Poems." *TGB* 29 (1981): 258. U of
      Wales.

345. Schmolke-Hasselmann, Beate. "Die Bedeutung der
      französischen Artusdichtung für England." Chapter 3
      in Part II of *Der arthurische Versroman von Chrestien
      bis Froissart*. Beihefte zur Zeitschrift für ro-
      manische Philologie 177. Tübingen, Max Niemeyer,
      1980. 237-248.

      Briefly discusses some of the English and Scottish
      romances as a reaction against the courtliness of the
      French romances and as the beginnings of a national
      literature. Treats *Weddynge of Sir Gawen*, *Golagrus
      and Gawain*, and *Awntyrs off Arthure*, as well as
      Libeaus Desconus and *Sir Perceval*, as examples of
      this tendency in deliberately English narratives.

346. Shichtman, Martin Barry. "The Gawains of English
      Arthurian Romance." *DAI* 42 (1982): 3154A. U of
      Iowa.

      Explores the changing characteristics of Gawain
      from early Welsh sources to Malory's *Morte Darthur*.

347. Shimizu, Aya. "Several Transformation Stories in
      English in the Middle Ages." *Kiyo* 19 (1981): 99-115
      [in Japanese].

      Investigates eight transformation stories: *Turke
      and Gowin*, *Libeaus Desconus*, *King Henry*, *Weddynge of
      Sir Gawen*, *Marriage of Sir Gawaine*, Florent in *Con-
      fessio Amantis*, and the *Wife of Bath's Tale*.

348. Stephany, William Alexander. "A Study of Four Middle
      English Arthurian Romances." *DAI* 30 (1969): 1537A.
      U of Delaware.

      A close textual study of *Avowynge of Arthur*,
      Awntyrs off Arthure, *Golagrus and Gawain*, and *Sir*

Gawain and the Green Knight that reveals a thematic
unity concerning the value of an individual's growth
to self-awareness in society ruled by Fortuna and
destined to fall.

349. Sunderland, S.M. "The Mysterious Challenger and
Other Strange Opponents in Middle English Arthurian
Romance." *TGB* 17 (1966-67): 319. M.A., Leicester U.

350. Taylor, Beverly White. "Wandering Fires: Studies in
Medieval and Nineteenth-Century Arthurian Literary
Tradition." *DAI* 38 (1978): 4853A-4854A. Duke U.

Discusses the meaning of medieval Arthurian romances, their consistency in themes and pervasive
irony and humor; then reassesses Victorian accomplishments in treating Arthurian material.

351. ------, and Elisabeth Brewer. *The Return of King
Arthur: British and American Arthurian Literature
Since 1800*. Arthurian Studies 9. Cambridge, Eng.:
D.S. Brewer; Totowa, NJ: Barnes and Noble, 1983.

Prologue: The nature of the Arthurian stories 1-13.
Chapter: 1. The return of Arthur: nineteenth-
century British medievalism and Arthurian tradition, 15-33.
2. Reawakening tradition: British literature, 1800-1830, 34-67.
3. Arthur Redux: British literature of
the mid-nineteenth century, 68-88.
4. An epic in 'the Fashion of the Day':
Idylls of the King, 89-128.
5. The Pre-Raphaelites: Morris and Swin-
burne, 129-161.
6. Arthur's 'return' in the New World:
American literature of the nineteenth
and early twentieth centuries, 162-
203.
7. Dramatic new developments: early
twentieth-century British literature,
204-234.
8. 'The Waste Land' and after, 235-289.
9. Arthurian literature since World War
II, 290-321.

Appendix I: Arthurian editions published between 1800 and 1850, 322-323.
Arthurian literature since 1800: a chronological list, 324-364.
Notes and index, 365-382.

352. Thompson, Raymond H. "Gawain Against Arthur: The Impact of a Mythological Pattern upon Arthurian Tradition in Accounts of the Birth of Gawain." *Folklore* 85 (1974): 113-121.

Suggests that accounts of Gawain's birth (in French prose *Parlesvaus*, *Les Enfances Gauvain*, and *De Ortu Waluuanii*) all conform to Rank's formula for the birth of heroes.

353. ------. "'Muse on þi mirrour...': The Challenge of the Outlandish Stranger in the English Arthurian Verse Romances." *Folklore* 87 (1976): 201-208.

Examines eleven English Arthurian romances for which no source has been found and finds an uncommon feature in nine: an outlandish figure whose activities undercut the sophistication of Arthur and his knights; in eight poems he is also a shape shifter who has symbolic value or thematic appropriateness in seeking to expose the reality behind the illusions of Arthur and his knights.

354. Treharne, R.F. *The Glastonbury Legends: Joseph of Arimathea, the Holy Grail, and King Arthur*. London: Cresset, 1967.

A work of synthesis for the general reader interested in Glastonbury legends and their meaning.

355. Utley, Francis Lee. "Arthurian Romance and International Folktale Method." *RPh* 17 (1964): 596-607.

Urges the use of folklore science for Arthurians, since it affords revelations of cultural transformation and offers clues to artistic structure.

356. Varin, Amy. "Mordred, King Arthur's Son." *Folklore* 90 (1979): 167-177.

Compares episodes in *Math vab Mathonwy*, the reconstructed Welsh source, to the Irish story of Lui Lavada and the story of Modred; then suggests a pre-Geoffrey version of the Modred story.

357. Varty, Kenneth, ed. *An Arthurian Tapestry: Essays in Memory of Lewis Thorpe*. Glasgow: French Dept. of U of Glasgow, 1981.

A collection of twenty-nine essays centered mainly on Chrétien de Troyes, though also encompassing the broader topic of Arthurian studies. Includes essays on the wild hunt [939], Yvain's lion [1626], and medieval treatments of Yvain [1635].

358. Ven-Ten Bensel, Elise Francisca Wilhelmina Maria Van der. *The Character of King Arthur in English Literature*. New York: Haskell House, 1966.

    Chapter: 1. Introductory, 1-4.
              2. Arthur, historical, legendary and mythical, 5-51.
              3. King Arthur in the chronicles, 52-75.
              4. The creation of Arthur as king of romance, 76-113.
              5. King Arthur in the English metrical romances and ballads, 114-138.
                 Claims that in their fragmentary and "homely, less exalted" treatment of the character of the king, the ME romances generally fall "far below their originals."
              6. Malory's *Morte Darthur*, 139-154.
              7. King Arthur in Tudor and Elizabethan literature, 155-168.
              8. The barren age of Arthurian literature, 169-174.
              9. King Arthur in the literature of the nineteenth century, 175-204.
    Conclusion, 205-207.
    Bibliography, 208-215.

359. Vinaver, Eugène. "King Arthur's Sword, or The Making
      of a Medieval Romance." *BJRL* 40 (1958): 513-526.

      Rejects the notion that medieval authors were
      writing folktales or psychological character studies
      and argues instead that they wrote narratives with
      rational patterns and structural themes. Uses the
      treatment of Arthur's sword from early chronicles to
      13th-century romances as an indication of the de-
      velopment of romance interests.

360. Whitaker, Muriel Anna Isabel. "The Idealized World
      of Malory's 'Morte Darthur': A Study of the Elements
      of Myth, Allegory and Symbolism in the Secular and
      Religious Milieux of Arthurian Romance." *DAI* 32
      (1971): 406A. U of British Columbia.

      Examines elements of British chronicle history,
      Celtic myth, French *courtoisie*, Catholic theology,
      and chivalric conventions, including the quest.

361. Williams, Mary. "King Arthur in History and Legend."
      Folklore 73 (1962): 73-88.

      Summarizes the state of scholarship on Arthur's
      historicity and appearance in Welsh traditions and
      discusses Geoffrey of Monmouth's contribution to the
      complex Arthurian portrait.

362. Wolfzettel, Friedrich, ed. *Artusrittertum im Späten
      Mittelalter: Ethos und Ideologie*. Vorträge des Sym-
      posiums der deutschen Sektion der Internationalen
      Artusgesellschaft vom 10. bis 13. November 1983.
      Giessen: Wilhelm Schmitz, 1984.

      Includes articles on the character of Gawain [276]
      and 15th-century treatments of Arthur [288].

SEE ALSO items 55 (144-146, 167-168), 85 (14-17, 18-23, 23-
48, 75-78), 108, and 414 (69-96).

363. Baader, Horst. *Die Lais: Zur Geschichte einer Gattung der altfranzösischen Kurzerzählungen.* Analecta Romanica 16. Frankfurt am Main: Vittorio Klostermann, 1966.

Vorbemerkung, 9
Chapter: 1. "Lai": Der Name und seine Bedeutungen, 11-36.
2. Die Quellen der erzählenden Lais nach deren eigenem Zeugnis, 37-73.
3. Die Herkunft der "aventures," 74-103.
4. Die Lais und die Volksmärchen, 104-151.
5. Die Lais als Kunstmärchen, 152-184.
6. Die Lais ausserhalb Frankreichs, 185-225.
7. Die schriftliche Überlieferung der altfranzösischen Lais, 226-243.
8. Die Chronologie der Lais, 244-264.
9. Der historische Wandel der Lais als Gattung, 265-318.
10. Die Lais und die erzählende Literatur des französischen Mittelalters, 319-348.
Verzeichnis der häufigsten Abkürzungen, 349-350.
Bibliographie, 351-373.
Register der zitieren mittelalterlichen Autoren und Werke, 375-382.

364. Beston, John Bernard. "The Breton Lai and *Lay le Freine.*" Diss. Harvard U, 1966.

365. ------. "How Much Was Known of the Breton Lai in Fourteenth-Century England?" Benson [8]. 319-336.

Distinguishes between two clear groups of English lays: those in couplets from northeast England or the south Midlands and those in tail-rhyme from East Anglia; further suggests that the lay sank in prestige during the 14th century in England.

366. Bromwich, Rachel. "A Note on the Breton Lays." *MAE* 26 (1957): 36-38.

Argues that because similarities in form and technique of story-telling between Welsh and Irish sagas and that *lai* and *laoidh* came into use in French and Irish at nearly the same date, it seems possible that there existed a parallel literary form to Breton lays in the 12th-century Irish lays of Finn.

367. Bullock-Davies, Constance. "The Form of the Breton Lay." *MAE* 42 (1973): 18-31.

Argues that the distinguishing feature of the lay is its technical form, not its subject matter or language. Suggests that it could be purely instrumental or accompanied by singing, with its metrical form made to fit its melody.

368. Colopy, Cheryl Gene. "Into the Thick of the Forest: A Study of the Breton Lays in Middle English." *DAI* 42 (1981): 238A. U of California, Berkeley.

Approaches the five lays psychoanalytically as symbolic stories of the basic predicaments of childhood and adolescence.

369. Day, Dennis Michael. "A Structural Analysis of the Syntagmatic Organization of the So-Called Breton Lais: Towards the Definition of a Literary Set." *DAI* 36 (1976): 4460A. U of Wisconsin-Madison.

Explicates a systematic theoretical framework, a transformational-generative theory, which accounts for the structure of this genre. Tries to define inherent semiotic properties that identify these works as a literary set.

370. Donovan, Mortimer J. *The Breton Lay: A Guide to Varieties*. Notre Dame: U of Notre Dame P, 1969.

    Chapter: 1. Marie de France and the Breton lay, 1-64.
            2. The later Breton lay in French, 65-120.
            3. The Middle English Breton lay in octosyllabic couplets, 121-172.
            4. Chaucer and the *Franklin's Tale*, 173-189.
            5. The Middle English Breton lay in tail-rhyme stanzas, 190-234.
    Appendix, 235-236.
    Bibliography, 237-255.
    Indexes, 257-267.

371. ------. "Breton Lays." Severs [90]. 133-143.

Treats the seven poems that exemplify the Breton lay: a short narrative poem of 100-1000 lines treating an aspect of love in a single adventure and without digression. Contains background information (including dating, rhyme scheme, provenance, and summary) of *Lai le Freine*, *Sir Orfeo*, *Emare*, *Sir Launfal*, *Sir Landeval*, *Sir Degare*, *Sir Gowther*, and *Earl of Toulous*.

372. ------. "The Form and Vogue of the Middle English Breton Lay." Diss. Harvard U, 1957.

373. Finlayson, John. "The Form of the Middle English Lay." *ChauR* 19 (1985): 352-368.

Reviews ideas about the ME lays and their connections to the *lais* of Marie de France. Concludes that there is no uniform genre, but rather two subtypes: lays with a heroine, no combat, and no fairy land; and those with a chivalric hero, combat, and a fairy world.

374. Hoepffner, Ernest. "The Breton Lais." Loomis [320]. 112-121.

Discusses the Breton lays attached to the Arthurian cycle, especially *Lai du Cor*, *Lanval*, *Graelent*, and *Tyolet*.

375. Johnston, Grahame. "The Breton Lays in Middle English." *Iceland and the Medieval World: Studies in Honour of Ian Maxwell*. Ed. Gabriel Turville-Petre and John Stanley Martin. Victoria, Australia: Wilke, 1974. 151-161.

Attempts to distinguish features shared by the eight ME poems, reviews Smithers' types, notes that the four earlier lays are in couplets whereas the later four are in tail rhyme, and calls for analytical studies rather than discussions of them *en bloc*.

376. ------. "Chaucer and the Breton Lays." *Proceedings and Papers of the 14th Congress of Australasian Universities Language and Literature Association*. Ed. K.I.D. Maslen. Dunedin, NZ: AULLA, 1972. 230-241.

Proposes a paradigm of four early lays in couplet form (*Sir Orfeo*, *Lai le Freine*, *Sir Degare*, and the shorter version of *Sir Launfal*), which are based on Marie de France's *lais*, and then argues for a hiatus until Chaucer revived the form in *The Franklin's Tale*, which began a new vogue with the pseudo-lays of *Emare*, *Earl of Toulous*, *Sir Gowther*, and Chestre's *Sir Launfal* (all in tail-rhyme), which had no genuine Breton connections at all.

377. Kahlert, Shirley Ann. "The Breton Lay and Generic Drift: A Study of Texts and Contexts." *DAI* 42 (1981): 1629A. UCLA.

Discusses definitions of the lay as an historical genre (Todorov) or as a strategic generic response to dynamic cultural situations (Burke) and suggests that the *merveilleux topos* best characterizes the form.

378. Petricone, Ancilla Marie, S.C. "The Middle English Breton Lays: A Structural Analysis of Narrative Technique." *DAI* 34 (1973): 1251A-1252A. Catholic U of America.

Emphasizes the primacy of dynamism as the structural principle central to the lay, compares *Lai le
Freine* and *Sir Launfal* to Marie de France's *lais*, and
finds that Chestre's technique, unlike Marie's pro-
gression-through-stasis, increases suspense with
progression-through-digression episodes.

379.   Stemmler, Theo. "Die mittelenglischen Bearbeitungen
zweier Lais der Marie de France." *Anglia* 80 (1962):
243-263.

Treats the ME versions of the OF *Lanval* and *Le
Fraisne* by analyzing the intentions of the English
adapters and their less aristocratic audience, which
significantly affected their versions. Claims that
the authors conformed to the common tastes of their
audience, included more realistic scenes, and changed
the indirect discourse to direct speech in order to
develop the epic tendencies of their stories.

380.   Yoder, Emily K. "Chaucer and the 'Breton' Lay."
ChauR 12 (1977): 74-77.

Argues that the "Breton Lay" was not a lay composed
by minstrels from Brittany, but rather British lays,
composed either by ancient Britons who inhabited the
island or by Welshmen or Cornishmen of a later time.
Concludes that the title "Breton" is misleading,
since the poems had nothing to do with Brittany or
Breton.

SEE ALSO items 93 (139-167), 108, 163 (40-48, 269-270),
and 340 (60-62).

CHIVALRY AND KNIGHTHOOD

381. Barnie, J.E. "The Ideal of the Knight in English
      Vernacular Romance, 1330-1400." *TGB* 17 (1966-67):
      314. M.A., Birmingham U.

382. ------. "Aristocracy, Knighthood and Chivalry."
      Chapter 3 in *War in Medieval English Society: Social
      Values in the Hundred Years War 1337-99*. Ithaca:
      Cornell UP, 1974. 56-96, 163-171.

      Discusses the difficulties in evaluating the nature
      and significance of chivalry in late medieval society
      and in assessing the influence of the clerical ideal
      in the 14th century. Examines evidence from the
      lives of great aristocrats, Edward III and John II,
      and contrasts two knights, Sir John Chandos and Sir
      Thomas Gray. Argues that chivalry, despite its im-
      precision and self-contradictions, provided a sub-
      structure of ideas and values that influenced the
      outlook and actions of aristocrats and knights close-
      ly connected to the war with France. Includes Appen-
      dix D: *"Morte Arthure* and the Hundred Years War,"
      147-150, which corrects Matthew's overstatement of
      the connection between the poem and the years of Ed-
      ward III's reign [*The Tragedy of Arthur*, Berkeley: U
      of California P, 1960, pp. 178ff.]. Argues that
      there are no exact parallels between Arthur and Ed-
      ward, but Arthur's conquests are set in the context
      of English military practice.

383. Barron, W.R.J. "Knighthood on Trial: The Acid Test
      of Irony." *FMLS* 17 (1981): 181-197.

      Deals with the paradox of romance that "expresses
      man's need to see life not as it is but as it might
      be, yet the very formulation of the ideal rests upon

his awareness of personal and social imperfections."

384.   Benson, Larry D.   "Courtly Love and Chivalry in the
        Later Middle Ages." Yeager [109]. 237-257.

        Reviews the critical controversies surrounding the
        concept of courtly love and discusses the value of
        love as a source of chivalric virtue in the litera-
        ture as well as in the handbooks of conduct for the
        aristocracy in the 14th and 15th centuries.

385.   ------, and John Leyerle, eds. *Chivalric Literature:*
        Essays on Relations between Literature & Life in the
        Later Middle Ages. Studies in Medieval Culture 14.
        Kalamazoo, MI: Medieval Institute, 1980.

        Includes essays on chivalry in the 15th century
        [396], *Morte Arthure* [1021], *Sir Gawain and the Green*
        Knight [1369], and *Paris and Vienne* [1701] as well as
        other articles intended to counter the attitude that
        late medieval culture was in decline.

386.   Brewer, Derek. "The Arming of the Warrior." *Chau-*
        cerian Problems and Perspectives: Essays Presented
        to Paul E. Beichner. Ed. Edward Vasta and Zacharias
        P. Thundy. Notre Dame: U of Notre Dame P, 1979.
        221-243.

        Reviews the literary uses of this *topos*, including
        it as a mark of the hero or the beginning of an
        adventure; *Sir Gawain and the Green Knight* natural-
        izes the literary *topos*; *Bevis of Hampton* has a
        formal arming appropriately placed after the dubbing
        and before the battle; *Guy of Warwick* combines real-
        istic and formalistic elements; and *Octavian* contains
        a poetic use with Clement arming his foster son with
        the rusty armor.

387.   Colman, Rebecca V. "Mud Huts and Courtly Love." *RUO*
        53 (1983): 147-153.

        Focuses on two scholarly myths that have structured
        much writing: the myth of chivalry, of which courtly

love is a significant aspect, and the "mud hut syndrome," a set of assumptions that produced a negative image of early medieval life as primitive. Suggests that, as with all myths, there was some foundation in fact: the shift in patronage from church to court and the mixture of the ascetic and hedonistic in the literature itself. Further suggests that the age of chivalry is better viewed, not in contrast with the age of heroism, but as an age at the end of a long historical process that owed much to feudal ideas of faith, honor, and personal loyalty.

388. Ferguson, Arthur B. *The Indian Summer of English Chivalry: Studies in the Decline and Transformation of Chivalric Idealism.* Durham: Duke UP, 1960.

Introduction: ix-xviii.
Chapter: 1. A chivalric "revival"? 3-32.
2. Chivalry teaching by example, 33-74.
3. A new example and a new context, 75-103.
4. Chivalry and the commonwealth, 104-141.
5. Chivalry and chauvinism, 142-181.
6. Chivalry and the education of the citizen, 182-221.
7. Conclusion, 222-226.
Works cited and index, 227-242.

Chivalric romances are specifically mentioned on 8-11, 13, 15, 23, 27, 36, 111, 126, and 183-184.

389. Green, Dennis. "The King and the Knight in the Medieval Romance." *Festschrift for Ralph Farrell.* Australian and New Zealand Studies in German Language and Literature 7. Ed. Anthony Stephens, H.L. Rogers, and Brian Coghlan. Bern, Switz.: Peter Lang, 1977. 175-183.

Suggests that the medieval romance represents the first sustained literary attempt to find expression for a secular ideal, that of the knightly hero, which derives its validity in part from the extension to the knight of social and ethical demands that had earlier pertained only to the king.

390.   Hanning, Robert W. "The Audience as Co-Creator of the First Chivalric Romances." *YES* 11 (1981): 1-28.

      Speculates about the nature of the audience of the first chivalric romances, which intertwined most medieval genres, and claims that they had great versatility and breadth of interest that helped develop a new relationship between the poet and his audience. Further claims that the audience responded by a series of judgments that amounted to a process of self-definition in relation to the story told.

391.   Jackson, W.T.H., ed. *Knighthood in Medieval Literature.* Woodbridge, Eng.: D.S. Brewer, 1981.

      Includes six articles dealing with knighthood in literature.

392.   Keen, M.H. "Chivalry and Courtly Love." *Peritia* 2 (1983): 149-169.

      Examines the role of love as a spur to virtue and self-achievement in the chivalric context and argues that the harnessing of self-esteem (in chivalry) with sexuality (in courtly love) had the strong psychological effect of suffusing martial adventure with ennobling and erotic undercurrents. Further suggests that the most marked influence of courtly love on chivalry was the new focus on combative and competitive individualism.

392a. Kennedy, Beverly. *Knighthood in The Morte Darthur.* Arthurian Studies 11. Cambridge, Eng.: D.S. Brewer, 1985.

        Introduction, 1-12.
        Chapter: 1. The high order of knighthood, 13-55.
                      Discusses late medieval views of knighthood, the office of kingship, King Arthur's knights, and the office of the king's knights.
                2. A typology of knighthood, 56-97.
                      Examines the triple quest pattern of Gawain, Tor, and Pellinor, which is repeated by Gawain, Harhalt, and

Ywain; further discusses the literary
ancestry of Malory's type of knights.
3. True knighthood, 98-147.
4. Worshipful knighthood, 148-213.
5. Happy and unhappy knights, 214-275.
6. Standing with 'true justyce,' 276-
327.
Conclusions, 328-346.
Notes, bibliography, and index, 347-394.

393. Marchalonis, Shirley Louise. "The Chivalric Ethos
and the Structure of the Middle English Metrical Romances." *DAI* 33 (1973): 6876A. Pennsylvania State U.

Examines the initiation structure and test-reward
pattern in nine romances.

394. Markland, Murray Faulds. "The Vogue of the Medieval
Chivalric Romance in Fifteenth Century England."
Diss. UCLA, 1957.

395. Palmer, David Andrew. "Chaucer and the Nature of
Chivalric Ideas." *DAI* 37 (1977): 6507A-6508A.
McMaster U.

Re-examines the scope of chivalric theory and
practice; suggests that the chivalric knight became
the focus for an accumulation of ideas and myths
about temporal power and secular life in general.
Examines medieval romances, including *Sir Gawain and
the Green Knight*, Malory, and many OF examples.

396. Ruff, Joseph R. "Malory's Gareth & Fifteenth-Century
Chivalry." Benson and Leyerle [385]. 101-116,
169-171.

Suggests interrelationships among didactic manuals,
chivalric biographies, and romances, which all have
the same purpose of offering instruction in the order
of chivalry and the same mixed combination of idealism and realism.

397. Wimsatt, James. *Allegory and Mirror: Tradition and*

Structure in Middle English Literature.   New York:
Pegasus, 1970.   202-204, 212.

   Suggests that *Syre Gawene and the Carle of Carelyle*
and *Weddynge of Sir Gawen* reflect the common use of
chivalric narratives to display presumed ideals of
conduct.

CONVENTIONALITY AND THE POPULAR NATURE
OF MIDDLE ENGLISH ROMANCE

398. Baugh, Albert C. "Convention and Individuality in
the Middle English Romance." Mandel and Rosenberg
[63]. 123-146.

Tries to redress the critical imbalance that focuses on the conventionality of ME romance and instead stresses the creative originality of many of
the "humbler" English poets whose distinguishing
characteristic is a concern for plausibility. Using
Bevis of Hampton and *Octavian* as study examples, the
author appraises the individual contribution of the
English authors to the final result of their literary
works.

399. ------. "Improvisation in the Middle English Romance." *PAPS* 103 (1959): 418-454.

Outlines the theory of oral composition as it has
been developed for Homeric poems and OF *chansons de
geste* with their formulas and themes. Then shows
that formulas and themes are present in ME romance to
as great a degree as in Greek epics or French *chansons*, and demonstrates that these features cannot be
accounted for by oral composition, since so many of
the ME works are translations or adaptations. Finally, emphasizes the role of improvisation in final
versions of the romances.

400. ------. "The Middle English Romance: Some Questions
of Creation, Presentation, and Preservation." *Speculum* 42 (1967): 1-31.

Questions the assumptions about the minstrel composition of ME romance and assesses the evidence for

semi-learned, clerical origins with works altered by
minstrel presentation, whether by singing, recitation
with a musical accompaniment, or reading.

401.   Bordman, Gerald Martin.   "The Folklore Motifs in the
        Matter of England Romances." *DA* 19 (1958): 764.   U
        of Pennsylvania.

        Concludes that the Matter of England is a legiti-
        mate grouping, since most of the works revolve around
        political or romantic exile and contain other con-
        sistent, recurring folklore motifs.

402.   ------.   *Motif-Index of the English Metrical Ro-
        mances*. FF Communications 190. Helsinki: STA, 1963.

        Designed to fill the gap in Stith Thompson's *Motif
        Index of Folk Literature*, but does not include prose
        romances.   Corrects some motifs that were wrongly
        identified earlier.

403.   Burrow, J.A.   *Ricardian Poetry: Chaucer, Gower,
        Langland and the Gawain Poet*. New Haven: Yale UP;
        1971.

        Deals with the minstrel style of ME romances (13-
        14, 15, 17, 71, 82, 95) and the alliterative revival
        (3-4, 23, 26, 27, 33-34, 144).

404.   Curschmann, Michael.   "Oral Poetry in Mediaeval Eng-
        lish, French, and German Literature: Some Notes on
        Recent Research." *Speculum* 42 (1967): 36-52.

        Reviews the characteristics associated with oral
        poetry: formulaic diction, a limited selection of
        standard motifs, and a certain set pattern of ac-
        tions.   Suggests that individuality arises from ar-
        rangements of motifs or deviations from set patterns
        and warns against claims of direct influence, since
        many medieval works shared a vast storehouse of
        loosely connected topics, motifs, patterns, and forms
        of narration.

405. Evarts, Peter G. "Themes, Motifs, and Formulae in the Tail-Rhyme Romances." *DAI* 32 (1972): 6372A-6373A. Wayne State U.

    Establishes evidence for oral improvisation in twenty-seven tail-rhyme romances of the east Midlands during 1300-1450.

406. Fowler, David C. *A Literary History of the Popular Ballad*. Durham: Duke UP, 1968.

    Chapter: 1. The evolution of balladry, 3-19.
              2. The folksong tradition, 20-64.
              3. Rymes of Robyn Hood, 65-93.
              4. The new minstrelsy, 94-131.
              5. The Percy Folio manuscript, 132-182.
              6. Revenant ballads, 183-206.
              7. The eighteenth century, 207-234.
              8. Bishop Percy, 235-270.
              9. David Herd, 271-293.
              10. Mrs. Brown of Falkland, 294-331.
    Conclusion, 332.
    Bibliography and index, 334-352.

407. Friedman, Albert B. "Folklore and Medieval Literature: A Look at Mythological Considerations." *SFQ* 43 (1979): 135-148.

    Suggests that folklore motifs functioned in diverse ways, sometimes acting as an obstacle to meaning, sometimes reinforcing it. Uses *Sir Gawain and the Green Knight* as an example of a work in which the poet overcame popular associations of a symbol, namely the pentangle (11. 623-665). Argues that the extensive passage was necessary to overwhelm its folklore connotations as a diabolic, witch-prevention sign or as a necromancer's tool in conjuring spirits.

408. Heffernan, Thomas J., ed. *The Popular Literature of Medieval England*. Tennessee Studies in Literature 28. Knoxville: U of Tennessee P, 1985.

    Includes thirteen articles, including one on romance [177] and one on folkloric sources of popular literature [414].

409. Hilligoss, Susan Jane. "Conventional Style in Middle
      English Tail-Rhyme Romance." *DAI* 38 (1978): 4844A-
      4845A. U of Pennsylvania.

      Argues that in the fourteen romances of pathos and
      piety, the stanza is developed to express and refine
      emotion.

410. Hornstein, Lilian Herlands. "Eustace-Constance-Flor-
      ence-Griselda Legends." Severs [90]. 120-132.

      Discusses the romances that emphasize the virtue of
      a meek Job-like faith and patience: *Sir Isumbras*, *Sir
      Eglamour*, *Sir Torrent*, *Octavian*, *Sir Triamour*, *King
      of Tars*, and *Bone Florence of Rome*.

411. Quinn, William Anthony. "The Oral Performance of
      Medieval Poetry and Regular End-Rhyme." *DAI* 40
      (1979): 2051A. Ohio State U.

      Reviews current theories regarding the nature of
      end-rhyme and analyzes Welsh end-rhymes. Gives a
      detailed analysis of rhyme-words in *King Horn*, which
      seem to demonstrate an improvisational system that
      helps maintain the flow of the recitation. Suggests
      that the *Havelok*-poet merely imitates this tradition
      of orally improvised performance.

412. ------, and Audley S. Hall. *Jongleur: A Modified
      Theory of Oral Improvisation and its Effects on the
      Performance and Transmission of Middle English Ro-
      mance*. Washington, D.C.: UP of America, 1982.

                  Chapter: 1. Introduction, 1-10.
                            2. The oral theory and medieval litera-
                                ture, 11-24.
                            3. Specific backgrounds: *King Horn* and
                                Havelok the Dane, 25-31.
                            4. A modified oral theory: the theory in
                                theory, 33-47.
                            5. Jongleur performance: intratextual
                                analyses, 49-76.
                            6. Oral transmission: intertextual anal-
                                yses, 77-110.
                            7. Some further stylistic contrasts be-

tween the rhyme-crafts of *Havelok the Dane* and *King Horn*, Manuscript C, 111-117.

8. Implications textual and critical, 119-130.

Methodology, 131-141.

Appendix A: The end-rhymes of *King Horn*, MS. C, 142-234.

Appendix B: The end-rhymes of *King Horn*, MS. L, 235-316.

Appendix C: The end-rhymes of *King Horn*, MS. O, 317-403.

Appendix D: *Havelok the Dane*, 404-423.

413. Ramsey, Lee C. *Chivalric Romances: Popular Literature in Medieval England*. Bloomington: Indiana UP, 1983.

Chapter: 1. The French book, 1-25.
Discusses the nature and history of romance, its audience, authors, and manuscripts.

2. The child exile, 26-44.
Focuses on *King Horn* and *Havelok* and includes treatment of the fall of the old king, the evil force of invaders and traitors, the beauty and power of the hero and heroine, and trials and adventures.

3. The best knight in the world, 45-68.
Discusses *Bevis of Hampton*, *Guy of Warwick*, and *Ipomadon*: the superman with the enemy, usually noblemen; the disguises and false identities of the hero; love, friends, and family; and service to man and society.

4. History and politics, 69-96.
Treats all the romances with historical figures: the Troy, Arthurian, and Alexander stories; *Richard Coer de Lyon*; and *Titus and Vespasian*. Focuses on the warriors of God, marvels and magic, violence, and *Gamelyn* and *Athelston* as romances of rebellion, with a different view of history and politics.

5. Love stories, 97-131.

Discusses the love potion in the
Tristan stories, the child love in
Floris and Blauncheflur, the frater-
nal love in *Amis and Amiloun*, love
and courtesy in *William of Palerne*,
and love and religion in the stanzaic
Morte Arthur.

6. The fairy princess, 132-156.

Discusses the hero's failing, the
rewards of fairy land, the juxtaposition of wilderness and civilization;
fairies and Christian belief; revelations and resolutions in *Sir Launfal*,
Partonope of Blois, *Libeaus Desconus*,
Romauns of Partenay, and *Eger and
Grime*. Discusses the abducted queen
in *Sir Orfeo*.

7. Family affairs, 157-188.

Treats the fatherless child in *Sir
Degare*; giants and monsters in *Sir
Eglamour*, *Sir Triamour*, *Sir Torrent*,
and *Sir Degare*; animal children in
Chevalere Assigne; feuds in *Earl of
Toulous* and *Sir Degrevant*; perils of
Florence in *Bone Florence of Rome*;
and world travelers, especially in
Octavian and *Generides*.

8. *Gentils* and *Vilains*, 189-208.

Focuses on the uncouth knight in
Sir Perceval, the upstart in *Taill of
Rauf Coilyear* and *Squyr of Lowe
Degre*, and the monstrous churl in all
the Gawain stories.

9. Satire, sermons, and sentiment, 209-
231.

Treats the parody of romance in *Sir
Thopas*; faith, humility and charity
in *Lancelot of the Laik*, *King of
Tars*, *Sir Gowther*, *Sir Cleges*, *Sir
Amadace*, *Sir Isumbras*, and *Roberd of
Cisyle*; and sentimentality and sensa-
tionalism in *Knight of Curtesy*,
Amoryus and Cleopes, *Roswall and Lil-
lian*, and *Clariodus*.

Chronological list of romances, notes, and index,
232-245.

414. Rosenberg, Bruce A. "Medieval Popular Literature: Folkloric Sources." Heffernan [408]. 61-84.

    Analyzes some ME romances according to folklore types and then classifies them into three structural groups: stories of crime and punishment (such as *Gamelyn* and *Athelston*), of lovers united after separation (such as *King Horn*, *Sir Launfal*, *Bevis of Hampton*, *Guy of Warwick*, and *Sir Eglamour*), and of tests passed (such as *Sir Gawain and the Green Knight*, *William of Palerne*, *Sir Isumbras*, and *Sir Degare*).

415. Spearing, A.C. "Problems for the Critic." *Criticism and Medieval Poetry*. London: Edwin Arnold, 1964. 1-27.

    Discusses problems for a modern reader in dealing with the formulaic and conventional nature of much medieval poetry, especially alliterative works.

416. Wittig, Susan. "Formulaic Style and the Problem of Redundancy." *Centrum* 1 (1973): 123-136.

    Views formulaic style from the perspective of information theory, which provides a framework for the psychological, social, and artistic functions of redundancy in literature.

INFLUENCE STUDIES

417. Adams, Robert P. "Bold Bawdry and Open Manslaughter: The English New Humanist Attack on Medieval Romance." *HLQ* 23 (1959-60): 33-48.

 Outlines the main features of the humanist attack on romance, which he argues is related to problems of early Tudor society. Humanists saw romances upholding a pagan social order that glorified injustice, violence and war, antisocial concepts of the superman-hero, and false ideas of honor and glory.

418. Barber, Vivian Ann Greene. "Medieval Drama and Romance: The Native Roots of Shakespearean Tragicomedy." *DAI* 42 (1981): 1156A. U of Texas at Austin.

 Explores the tragicomic pattern from medieval romance of the man-tried-by-fate traditions and analogues of the St. Eustache legend.

419. Blessing, James Hartman. "A Comparison of Some Middle English Romances with the Old French Antecedents." *DA* 20 (1960): 3281-3282. Stanford U.

 Argues that the ME romances retain the elements, structure, and generic qualities of French romances, with a fundamental difference only in style.

420. Boots, John Philip. "The French Connection: A Comparative Study of Selected Middle English Romances and Their Old French Antecedents." Diss. U of Chicago, 1980.

421. Braswell, Laurel. "The Influence of Romantic Anti-
      quarianism upon Medieval English Studies." *RUO* 52
      (1982): 273-285.

      Considers the consequences of the interest of such
      people as Douce, Dibdin, Sir Walter Scott, and Madden
      in medieval literature. The practical effects of
      their labors included the physical assemblage of li-
      braries, the systematic cataloguing and publication
      of medieval manuscripts through private clubs and
      societies (EETS, Roxburghe, Camden Society), the be-
      ginnings of textual criticism, and notions of his-
      toricity and views of the Middle Ages, which rein-
      forced the philosophical ideas of primitivism and
      transcendentalism.

422. Burnley, J.D. "An Investigation of the Differences
      in Ideas and Emphases in Five Middle English Romances
      and the Old French Versions of the Same Subjects."
      TGB 18 (1967-68): 301. M.A., Durham U.

423. Dannenbaum, Susan. "Anglo-Norman Romances of English
      Heroes: 'Ancestral Romance'?" *RPh* 35 (1982): 601-
      608.

      Argues that the AN romances are centrally concerned
      with the working of the English feudal and legal sys-
      tems and that the heroes exemplify in idealized form
      the qualities important to AN baronry, but rejects
      the ancestral theory.

424. ------. "Insular Tradition: Anglo-Norman Romances
      and Their Middle English Descendants." *DAI* 37
      (1976): 328A. U of California, Berkeley.

      Considers AN and ME romances as integrally related
      parts of an insular tradition and emphasizes the
      lines of continuity from AN to ME in contrast to Con-
      tinental traditions. Discusses *King Horn*, *Havelok*,
      Bevis of Hampton, *Guy of Warwick*, *Sir Tristrem*,
      Ipomadon, and their AN analogues.

425. Edwards, James Arthur. "Some Influences of Medieval
      Romances in the English Language on 'The Faerie

Queene.'" *DAI* 34 (1973): 1276A. U of Missouri-Columbia.

Demonstrates that many of Spenser's poetic details can be traced to English romances and that he developed the romance tradition by tying the supernatural more plainly to allegory, by clarifying the moral, and by developing sophisticated irony.

426. Handelman, Anita Fern. "The Influence of the Old English Heroic Tradition on the Middle English Romance." *DAI* 41 (1980): 2100A-2101A. U of Michigan.

Argues that some of the ME works are closer to English heroic poetry than to French romance in their taste for formality, their dramatic voice, the rhetorical patterns associated with boasts, and their inclination toward a kind of discourse that operates in terms of the story.

427. Hays, Michael Louis. "Shakespeare's Use of Medieval Romance Elements in his Major Tragedies." *DAI* 34 (1974): 5102A-5103A. U of Michigan.

Suggests that Shakespeare used the following elements from romance: knights and courtiers, courtly love, ideas of justice and honor, false stewards, exile motif, and restoration of order, especially to the kingdom, in *Hamlet*, *King Lear*, *Macbeth*, and *Othello*.

428. Howard, Douglas Turner, Jr. "The Literary Uses of Religious Images and References in the Middle English Metrical Romances of the Fourteenth Century." *DAI* 39 (1978): 3567A. U of Arkansas.

Determines how religious expressions contribute to plot, character, and theme in four groups of thirty-one metrical romances: those involving the testing of individual knights, the Christian-Saracen opposition, tests of a protagonist's patience and suffering, and secular subjects with religous overtones.

429. Hume, Kathryn. "Medieval Romance and Science Fic-

tion: The Anatomy of a Resemblance." *JPC* 16 (1982): 15-26.

Finds five basic relationships between the two genres and discusses the last three: explicit borrowing, non-specific borrowing, inheritance of a type of hero, parallels from shared narrative structure, and similarities from the social function of both literary forms.

430. Lambert, Roy Eugene. "French Vocabulary Influences in Some Thirteenth-Century English Works." *DA* 18 (1958): 585. U of Illinois.

From data showing that *King Horn* has proportionately more French loan words than *Floris and Blauncheflur*, a translation, the author concludes that the French influence is stronger than supposed and that Norman is largely responsible for this.

431. Lewis, Janet E., and Barry N. Olshen. "John Fowles and the Medieval Romance Tradition." *MFS* 31 (1985): 15-30.

Provide evidence for a continued presence of courtly love conventions and curious and deliberate parallels between the actions and adventures of Fowles' protagonists and those of the heroes and heroines of medieval romance. Argue that medieval romance is at the root, both consciously and unconsciously, of Fowles' fiction and thought through his use of the exotic and mysterious, his Edenic settings, adventure and fantasy, and his major theme of love and the proper relationship between the sexes.

432. Richmond, Velma E. Bourgeois. "The Humanist Rejection of Romance." *SAQ* 77 (1978): 296-306.

Argues that the humanists' moral antipathies to medieval romance were related to the new sophistication of Renaissance thinking and Reformation zeal; literary objections developed from the standards of classicism and rationalism. Further defends the romance against such attacks and tries to rescue them from the obscurity to which "prejudiced tastes" have banished them.

433. Rubey, Daniel Robert. "Literary Texts and Social Change: Relationships between English and French Medieval Romances and Their Audiences." *DAI* 42 (1982): 3153A-3154A. Indiana U.

   Analyzes relationships between romances and the social nexus and argues that works in the French tradition echo Chrétien's concerns, but that AN works reflect expulsion-return plot structures and unification-of-the-kingdom motifs.

434. Wadsworth, Rosalind. "Historical Romance in England: Studies in Anglo-Norman and Middle English Romance." *TGB* 22 (1971-72): 385. D.Phil., York U.

MANUSCRIPTS AND EDITORS

Editions and Facsimiles:

435. Brewer, D.S., and A.E.B. Owen. Introduction. *The Thornton Manuscript* (*Lincoln Cathedral MS. 91*). London: Scolar P, 1975.

436. Kölbing, E. "Vier Romanzen-Handschriften." *EStn* 7 (1884): 177-201.

Lists the works in each manuscript, its folio designation, idiosyncrasies, and publication information: 1) Auchinleck MS (178-191), 2) Manuscript of the Duke of Sutherland (191-193), 3) Lincoln's Inn Library (194-195), and 4) Chetham 8009 (195-201).

437. McSparran, Frances, and P.R. Robinson. Introduction. *Cambridge University Library MS Ff.2.38.* London: Scolar P, 1979.

438. Pearsall, Derek, and I.C. Cunningham. Introduction. *The Auchinleck Manuscript: National Library of Scotland Advocates' MS. 19.2.1.* London: Scolar P, 1977.

Introduction includes the literary and historical significance of the manuscript (vii-xi), a physical description (xi-xiv), script and ornament (xv-xvi), binding (xvi), notes and bibliography (xvi-xviii), and contents of the manuscript (xix-xxiv).

Criticism:

439. Ackerman, Robert W. "Sir Frederic Madden and Medieval Scholarship." *NM* 73 (1972): 1-14.

Discusses the importance of the man who edited *Sir Gawain and the Green Knight*, *William of Palerne*, and *Havelok*; who had a career-long dedication to restoring the supposedly ruined or lost Cotton MSS, which form the nucleus of the manuscript collection of the British Museum Library; and who insisted on the necessity of strict literary editorial methods.

440. Burrows, Jean Harpham. "The Auchinleck Manuscript: Contexts, Texts and Audience." *DAI* 45 (1985): 3633A. Washington U.

Examines six didactic works and romances: *Amis and Amiloun*, *Speculum Gy de Warewyke*, AN *Gui de Warewic* (three texts), and the *Short Metrical Chronicle*. Shows how they reinforce and illuminate each other and offer insights into the tastes and interests of the times. Suggests that the audience wanted models for spiritual and secular conduct and were interested in local history and topography.

441. Cunningham, I.C. "Notes on the Auchinleck Manuscript." *Speculum* 47 (1972): 96-98.

Includes corrections and additions to the notes published by Bliss [*Speculum* 26 (1951): 52-58] and also new notes on the gathering of leaves and binding from a detailed examination of the manuscript when it was being rebound.

442. ------, and J.E.C. Mordkoff. "New Light on the Signatures in the Auchinleck Manuscript (Edinburgh National Library of Scotland Adv. MS. 19.2.1)." *Scriptorium* 36 (1982): 280-292.

Note the existence of additional signatures and other marks relating to the make-up of the manuscript (after publication of the facsimile). Supplement previously published lists and include a list, description, and analysis of all findings of signatures seen on the manuscript and on E fragments.

443. Daly, Owen James. "This World and the Next: Social and Religious Ideologies in the Romances of the

Thornton Manuscript." *DAI* 38 (1977): 3473A-3474A. U of Oregon.

Discusses a group of six works aimed at the country gentry and unified by their celebration of family, their portrayal of women, and their efforts to resolve the tensions between otherworld piety and secular chivalry by means of a hero who synthesizes these values.

444. Doyle, A.I. "The Shaping of the Vernon and Simeon Manuscripts." Rowland [81]. 328-341.

Describes each manuscript in terms of size, binding, ordering, division, and contents.

445. Dwyer, Richard A. "The Appreciation of Handmade Literature." *ChauR* 8 (1974): 221-240.

Discusses a collection of manuscript curiosities, including the Lincoln's Inn 150 (which contains *Libeaus Desconus*, *Arthour and Merlin*, *King Alexander*, *Seege of Troye*, and *Piers Plowman*). Views the maker as a conservative enthusiast for old forms and stories, namely alliteration and romances, and sees in the scribes a reflection of aesthetic tastes.

446. Guddat-Figge, Gisela. *Catalogue of Manuscripts Containing Middle English Romances*. Text und Untersuchungen zur englischen Philologie 4. Munich: Wilhelm Fink, 1976.

General introduction, 17-62, which includes types of manuscripts, methods of production, contents, format, audience, origin, and evaluation. Lists and describes in detail all known manuscripts containing ME romances.

447. Hanna, Ralph, III. "The London Thornton Manuscript: A Corrected Collation." *SB* 37 (1984): 122-130.

Sheds light on some mistaken assumptions shared by Horrall [450] and others concerning the composition of English literary manuscripts. Suggests that ff.

104-108 of watermarked leaves and ff. 111-115 of
unwatermarked leaves compose a single quire, rather
than Horrall's two quires, and interprets other
codicological information to reduce the number of
quires from Horrall's thirteen to eleven. Further
argues that Thornton began copying with a stock of
paper folded in folio, but increased his working
space and quire size by inserting separately folded
bifolia into the center of his quire.

448. Hardman, Phillipa. "A Medieval 'Library *in Parvo.*'"
     MAE 47 (1978): 262-273.

     Examines the contents of MS Advocates 19.3.1 and
     sees three groups of booklets representing three
     different kinds of works that could be put together
     to form a small library. Studies the four volumes of
     religious narratives and three volumes of entertain-
     ing romances.

449. Hirsh, John C. "Additional Note on MSS. Ashmole 61,
     Douce 228 and Lincoln's Inn 150." *NM* 78 (1977):
     347-349.

     Argues that there is no evidence to support the
     minstrel-ownership theory for any of the three manu-
     scripts, but there are convincing indications that
     they are professional productions.

450. Horrall, Sarah M. "The London Thornton Manuscript: A
     New Collation." *Manuscripta* 23 (1979): 99-103.

     Suggests the following arrangement of the sections
     of the manuscript: e, ff. 74-81, with one or more
     leaves lost after ff. 77 and 79; f, ff. 82-97 with a
     leaf lost after f. 96; g, ff. 98-101; h, ff. 102-110;
     j, ff. 111-119 with at least two leaves missing at
     the beginning; k, ff. 120-124.

451. ------. "The Watermarks of the Thornton Manu-
     scripts." *N&Q* ns 27 (1980): 385-386.

     Reviews watermarks in both London Thornton and
     Lincoln Cathedral MS 91 and discovers that of the

nine in the London MS, five also appear in the Lincoln. This finding supports Brewer's claim [435] that Thornton prepared papers, copied texts, and accumulated unbound quires, which only later became separated and bound as different manuscripts.

452. Hudson, Harriet. "Middle English Popular Romances: The Manuscript Evidence." *Manuscripta* 28 (1984): 67-78.

Argues that the manuscripts are a rich source of information about the roles of the audience, bookmaking practices, cultural contexts of the stories, characteristics of late medieval popular culture in England, and the nature and extent of the popularity of romances. Sees the extreme popularity of some of these romances tied to their association with the gentry.

453. Keiser, George R. "Lincoln Cathedral Library MS. 91: Life and Milieu of the Scribe." *SB* 32 (1979): 158-179.

Considers information concerning Thornton's life and affairs, ownership of books in the area, and evidence in the manuscript itself; further examines the possible effects of these factors on the availability and importance of books for the middle classes in late medieval society in Yorkshire.

454. ------. "More Light on the Life and Milieu of Robert Thornton." *SB* 36 (1983): 111-119.

Discusses the ways Thronton may have acquired texts for his two manuscripts; explores circumstantial evidence for his relationship with his neighbors, the Pikeryngs of Oswaldkirk, who owned a text to which a scribe of the Rawlinson MS had access; and looks to the priory of Nun Monkton, which had a collection of books and an association with Joan Pikeryng, for a link to Thornton.

455. ------. "The Nineteenth-Century Discovery of the Thornton Manuscript (Lincoln Cathedral Library MS.

91)." *PBSA* 77 (1983): 167-190.

Suggests that the Thornton MS came to Lincoln through the agency of the clergyman Thomas Comber, who married Alice Thornton of East Newton and either gave or sold it to Daniel Brevint, the successor to Honywood as Dean of Lincoln. Further traces the history of the manuscript and its connections with early editors such as Ritson, Laing, Madden, and Halliwell. Calls for study of the whole manuscript as devotional literature, rather than study of individual works in the collection.

456.   ------.   "A Note on the Descent of the Thornton Manuscript." *TCBS* 6 (1976): 346-348.

Slightly emends Owen's conjecture [462] by suggesting that the manuscript probably reached Lincoln Cathedral Library through Comber, not to Michael Honywood, but to his successor Daniel Brevint, Dean of Lincoln from 1682 to 1695.

457.   Macrae-Gibson, O.D.   "The Auchinleck MS.: Participles in *-and(e).*" *ES* 52 (1971): 13-20.

Evaluates the different theories about the northern participle endings in the London MS and suggests three causes: professional scribes may have immigrated to London, the authors' use depended on a rhyming value, or a familiarity with French influenced the scribes to prefer this form.

458.   ------.   "Walter Scott, the Auchinleck MS., and MS. Douce 124." *Neophil* 50 (1966): 449-454.

Suggests that the Douce MS is a transcript supplied by Walter Scott to George Ellis, who was preparing his *Specimens of Early English Metrical Romances* [584a].

459.   Moe, Phyllis.   "Cleveland Manuscript Wq 091.92-C468 and the Veronica Legend." *BNYPL* 70 (1966): 459-470.

Shows that Cleveland MS Wq 091.92-C468 contains a

different version of the Veronica Legend from that of
Vindicta Salvatoris, *Destruction of Jerusalem*, and
Titus and Vespasian.

460. Mordkoff, Judith Crounse. "The Making of the Auchinleck Manuscript: The Scribes at Work." *DAI* 42 (1981):
207A. U of Connecticut.

Focuses primarily on the physical make-up of the
manuscript, reviews Loomis's bookshop theory, and
concludes that the manuscript was not a commercial
product, but the product of a traditional scriptorium
of a religious house in which inmates worked together
with lay craftsmen.

461. Morgan, Hubert Eric. "Middle-English Romances in
Manuscript." *DAI* 33 (1972): 2336A. U of Washington.

A thorough examination of the manuscripts, including historical and topical categories that reflect
different phases of the development of romance and
the different literary traditions.

462. Owen, A.E.B. "The Collation and Descent of the
Thornton Manuscript." *TCBS* 6 (1975): 218-225.

Corrects a mistake in the facsimile edition, discusses the ordering of the quires and *lacunae*, and
suggests that Thomas Comber (1645-1699) may have
passed the manuscript to Honywood.

463. Pearsall, Derek, ed. *Manuscripts and Readers in
Fifteenth-Century England: The Literary Implications
of Manuscript Study*. Essays from the 1981 Conference
at the of York. Cambridge, Eng.: Brewer, 1983.

Includes essays on Thornton MS [472], manuscripts
of the Midlands [475], Lydgate [483], and *Troy-Book*
[1587].

464. ------. "Texts, Textual Criticism, and Fifteenth-
Century Manuscript Production." Yeager [109]. 121-
136.

Examines the problems of manuscripts as well as the valuable information to be gained from manuscript study: a better understanding of texts, of the assumptions about the nature and function of literature on the part of the scribal editors, of techniques for book production, of the historical context of the works, and of editorial recomposition.

465. Rambo, Sharon M. "Technique in Five Verse Narratives of the Auchinleck MS." *DAI* 40 (1980): 6268A. Michigan State U.

Investigates *Sir Degare*, *Lai le Freine*, *Sir Orfeo*, *Sir Tristrem*, and *Amis and Amiloun* for Cawelti's four categories of formula: adventure, romance, mystery, and alien being; of these five works, only *Sir Tristrem* does not fit the formulaic patterns studied.

466. Sajavaara, Kari. "The Relationship of the Vernon and Simeon Manuscripts." *NM* 68 (1967): 428-439.

Discusses the conflicting evidence of the relationship between the two manuscripts, but concludes that both were certainly produced in the same scriptorium, perhaps a Cistercian house of northern Worcestershire or Warwickshire.

467. Shonk, Timothy A. "A Study of the Auchinleck Manuscript: Bookmen and Bookmaking in the Early Fourteenth Century." *Speculum* 60 (1985): 71-91.

Adapts the findings of Doyle and Parkes [*Medieval Scribes, Manuscripts and Libraries*, 1978, 163-210] by proposing that the major scribe served as editor, copying much of the material himself, farming out other pieces to independent scribes, and then completing the work of putting the book into its final form. Rejects the theory of a single workshop with a team of versifiers and scribes.

468. ------. "A Study of the Auchinleck Manuscript: Investigations into the Processes of Book Making in the Fourteenth Century." *DAI* 42 (1982): 4012A. U of Tennessee.

Focuses on a detailed physical description of the manuscript and offers evidence that it was produced by independent scribes working to fulfill a contract for this codex.

469. Sklar, Elizabeth S. "MS Douce 124, Sir Walter Scott and George Ellis." *Bibliotheck* 7 (1975): 89-97.

Gives a complete account of the manuscript, including letters between Ellis and Scott. Finds that MS Douce 124 is a transcription of the Auchinleck *Arthour and Merlin*, produced under the auspices of Sir Walter Scott for Ellis' preparation of his *Specimens of Early English Metrical Romances* [584a].

470. Smith, Kathleen L. "A Fifteenth-Century Vernacular Manuscript Reconstructed." *BLR* 7 (1966): 234-241.

Reconstructs the single 15th-century volume of vernacular literature, which has been divided into seven parts, now separately bound and catalogued as six Rawlinson MSS (which include the *Prose Siege of Thebes* and *Prose Sege of Troy*) as well as Douce 324 (which includes *Awntyrs off Arthure*).

471. Stern, Karen. "The London 'Thornton' Miscellany: A New Description of British Museum Additional Manuscript 31042." *Scriptorium* 30 (1976): 26-37, 201-218.

A detailed description of the scribal hand, the organization of the manuscript, and its watermarks.

472. Thompson, John J. "The Compiler in Action: Robert Thornton and the 'Thornton Romances' in Lincoln Cathedral MS 91." *Manuscripts and Readers* [463]. 113-124.

Discovers the unorthodox compiling method of Thornton, whose ordering of the manuscript was probably determined by the piecemeal way in which he received his exemplars and the necessity of filling blank space. Reconstructs the chronology in which Thornton

probably copied items into gathering I: first *Awntyrs
off Arthure* into ff. 154r-161r, originally the first
nine folios; then needing extra paper, he refolded
his paper so that ff. 153-154 became the center bifo-
lium; then he copied *Sir Eglamour* into I and at later
stages *De Miraculo beate Marie*, *Lyarde*, and finally
Thomas of Erceldoune.

473.   ------. "Robert Thornton and his Book Producing
        Activities: Aspects of the Transmission of Certain
        Late Medieval Texts in the Light of Their Present
        Context in Thornton's Manuscripts." *DAI* 45 (1984):
        9/3866C. York U.

        Examines the range of physical and textual evidence
        indicating the practical conditions under which
        Thornton copied items into the Lincoln and London
        MSS.

474.   Turley, Raymond V. "Edward Vernon Utterson: Artist,
        Book Collector and Literary Antiquary." *BC* 25
        (1976): 21-44.

        Views the man through the eyes of his contemporar-
        ies and his own writing; lists all his editions and
        their chronology and genesis: *Arthur of Little
        Britain*, *Chevalere Assigne*, and *Roberd of Cisyle*.

475.   Turville-Petre, Thorlac. "Some Medieval English
        Manuscripts in the North-East Midlands." *Manuscripts
        and Readers* [463]. 125-141.

        Emphasizes the need for local contexts for ME lit-
        erature and pieces together some of the puzzle of
        Midlands literature by examining in detail Middleton
        MS 01 and Advocates MS 19.3.1 and the literary
        tastes—including romance reading—of four families:
        the Berkeleys, Chaworths, Sherbrookes, and Finderns.

476.   Van Buuren-Veenenbos, C.C. "John Asloan, an Edin-
        burgh Scribe." *ES* 47 (1966): 365-372.

        Investigates the two different handwritings in MS
        Douce 148, which contains *Troy-Book* and *Scottish Troy*

Book fragments and establishes that Scribe A, who wrote ff. 1-44, 139, and 257, is John Asloan.

477. Weiss, Judith. "The Auchinleck MS. and the Edwardes MSS." *N&Q* ns 16 (1969): 444-446.

Questions the assumption that the compilers of the Auchinleck MS made use of the Edwardes MS and doubts that the volume existed at the time of the Auchinleck bookshop.

478. Zettersten, Arne. "Further Notes on the Robartes Manuscripts." *NM* 67 (1966): 382-384.

Discusses parts of what was once the Robartes MS, expecially nos. 157-158 of the guard-book, which contains ten leaves of the 15th-century manuscript of *Partonope of Blois*.

479. Benson, C. David. *The History of Troy in Middle English Literature: Guido delle Colonne's Historia Destructionis Troiae in Medieval England.* Woodbridge,
Eng.: D.S. Brewer, 1980.

      Chapter: 1. The medieval history of Troy: Guido
                delle Colonne, 3-31.
                Explores Troy in historical ac-
                counts and the clerical and aristo-
                cratic chronicles; discusses the pes-
                simism, style, and focus on battles
                and heroes in *Historia Destructionis
                Troiae.*

            2. History into verse: the prologues to
                the Middle English history of Troy,
                35-41.
                Suggests that the prologues reveal
                that the ME translators were dedi-
                cated to both history and poetry with
                the expressed goals of preserving a
                true historical record while present-
                ing it in a form that would appeal to
                contemporary audiences.

            3. *The Destruction of Troy:* history as
                poetry, 42-66.
                Argues that this work is the most
                faithful to Guido's and that the poet
                was a diligent historian who brought
                to life in his alliterative verse the
                dull facts of his original.

            4. *The Laud Troy Book:* history as ro-
                mance, 67-96.
                Characterizes the author as an exu-
                berant story teller who tried to
                write a Hector romance for his lis-
                tening.

            5. John Lydgate's *Troy Book:* history as

learned rhetoric, 97-129.
Claims that Lydgate tried to coun-
ter Guido's pessimism by pointing to
the moral lessons and the virtue of
prudence, especially in his account
of the death of Hector.
6. The history of Troy in Middle English
poetry, 133-150.
Focuses mainly on Chaucer's *Troilus
and Criseyde* and Henryson's *Testament
of Cresseid*.
Notes, 151-168.
Index, 169-174.

480.   ------. "The Medieval English History of Troy." *DAI*
31 (1971): 6539A. U of California, Berkeley.

Compares the efforts of *Laud Troy-Book*, Lydgate's
Troy-Book, and *Destruction of Troy* to provide an accurate secular history of the Trojan War without allegorical interpretation.

481.   Blake, N.F. "John Lydgate and William Caxton."
LeedsSE ns 16 (1985): 272-289.

Argues that Caxton was familiar with both *Siege of
Thebes* (referred to in his epilogue to *Jason*) and
Troy-Book (possibly used as a source of the divisions
in the Malory text). Further suggests that both authors shed light on the use and nature of patronage.

481a.   Ebin, Lois A. *John Lydgate*. Twayne's English Authors Series. Boston: Twayne, 1985.

Chapter: 1. John Lydgate: monk of Bury, 1-19.
2. The courtly poems, 20-38.
3. Poetry and politics: Troy and Thebes,
39-59.
Argues that in *Siege of Thebes* and
Troy-Book, Lydgate first directs his
skills as a poet-craftsman explicitly
to concerns of the state by under-
scoring the political relevance of
the past for the future. Lydgate
also links a poet's eloquence with

wisdom, virtue, and order and sees a
poet's function as civilizer of men.
4. The *Fall of Princes*: fortune and the
lives of men, 60-75.
5. Laureate Lydgate: public and political poems, 76-91.
6. The poet of "Hie sentence": moral
and didactic poems, 92-112.
7. Religious poems: saints' lives, lyrics, *The Life of Our Lady*, 113-138.
8. Lydgate's achievement and impact,
139-142.
Notes and references, 143-154.
Selected bibliography and index, 155-163.

482. Edwards, A.S.G. "Additions and Corrections to the
Bibliography of John Lydgate." *N&Q* ns 32 (1985):
450-452.

Corrects entries in Severs [90] and gives updated
information on *Siege of Thebes* and *Troy-Book* manuscripts.

483. ------. Lydgate Manuscripts: Some Directions for
Future Research." *Manuscripts and Readers* [463].
15-26.

Reviews current scholarship and points to specific
areas for further necessary work, including a systematic study of the decorations in Lydgate's manuscripts for the information it would yield about
15th-century book production and contemporary responses to his work; a study of scribes, patrons, and
the audience of Lydgate's work; a list of early
owners of Lydgate's manuscripts; and a fresh study of
evidence from the manuscripts for the canon.

484. ------. "Lydgate Scholarship: Progress and Pros-
pects." Yeager [109]. 29-47.

Reviews trends in the past twenty-five years and
critiques recent work on Lydgate.

485. Fuller, Donald Ames. "The Style and Example of Lyd-

gate's Literary Art." *DAI* 44 (1983): 1092A. Northern Illinois U.

   Studies the confused and repetitive characteristics
of Lydgate's style and finds the approach of synonymy
the best, because it develops the distinction between
the syntactic and semantic dimensions of his work.

486. Hinton, Norman Dexter. "A Study of the Medieval
      English Poems Relating the Destruction of Troy." *DA*
      17 (1957): 2010-2011. U of Wisconsin.

         Investigates each poem individually for its rela-
      tion to the Troy tradition and for its own intrinsic
      artistic worth.   Works studied include the three
      versions of *Seege of Troye*, *Laud Troy-Book*, *Destruc-
      tion of Troy*, and Lydgate's *Troy-Book*.

487. Kaufmann, Bruce Frank. "Middle English Accounts of
      the History of Troy." *DAI* 39 (1978): 2249A. U of
      Toronto.

         Distinguishes English treatment into two separate
      traditions: the clerical in which Troy is the Earthly
      City divinely punished (*Troy-Book* and *Destruction of
      Troy*) and the secular in which Troy is the place of
      chivalric accomplishments (*Seege of Troye* and *Laud
      Troy-Book*).

488. Lumiansky, R.M. "Legends of Thebes." Severs [90].
      119. "Legends of Troy." Severs [90]. 114-118.

         A brief treatment of the four verse and two prose
      ME romances having Thebes or Troy material for their
      subjects.

489. McGunnigle, Michael Gerard. "Romanticized History
      and Historicized Romance: Narrative Styles and Strat-
      egies in Four Middle English Troy Poems." *DAI* 41
      (1980): 2616A. Northwestern U.

         Tries to develop a procedure for classifying and
      evaluating *Destruction of Troy*, *Laud Troy-Book*, *Seege
      of Troye*, and *Troilus and Criseyde* with their tenden-

cies to historicize and romanticize.

490. Mieszkowski, Gretchen. "The Reputation of Criseyde 1150-1500." *Transactions of the Connecticut Academy of Arts and Sciences* 43 (1971): 71-153.

Discusses three ME versions of the Troilus-Criseyde story (113-126). Argues that in *Laud Troy-Book*, the shortest version, the treatment of Criseyde is sarcastic; in *Destruction of Troy*, the character of Troilus is reworked to reflect the poet's value of Troilus' love, whereas Criseyde's reputation as a type personifying womanly fickleness is increased; in Lydgate's *Troy-Book*, Criseyde is treated ironically and is like the 16th-century Criseyde—promiscuous and opportunistic. Suggests that Lydgate acts as the earnest defender of women whose intractable traits defeat him.

491. Pearsall, Derek. "The English Chaucerians." Brewer [15]. 201-239.

Examines the nature of Lydgate's indebtedness to Chaucer for *Siege of Thebes* and *Troy-Book*. In the former, Lydgate plunders the *Knight's Tale* and models his prologue on a Canterbury link while building on Chaucer's moral and political concerns; in the latter, Lydgate follows Chaucer in his use of aureate vocabulary and rhetorical *topoi*.

492. ------. *Gower and Lydgate*. Ed. Geoffrey Bullough. Writers and Their Work 211. Harlow, Eng.: Longmans, Green, 1969.

Includes the chapter "John Lydgate," 23-42, which reviews Lydgate's extensive accomplishments; criticizes some of his long works for mechanical use of rhetorical devices and his lack of poetic understanding, but praises his intensity and success in his Marian hymns and gnomic moralizing poems.

493. ------. *John Lydgate*. London: Routledge & Kegan Paul; Charlottesville: UP of Virginia, 1970.

Chapter: 1. John Lydgate: the critical approach, 1-21.
         2. The monastic background, 22-48.
         3. Chaucer and the literary background, 49-82.
         4. The courtly poems, 83-121.
         5. *Troy* and *Thebes*, 122-159.
                Argues that Lydgate tried to define and consolidate the new status of English in his works; he drew upon every resource of medieval rhetoric to amplify his treatment of the story, broaden its scope, and drive home the moral lessons in his *Troy-Book*. In *Siege of Thebes*, however, Lydgate is at his best, exhibiting deep moral concern, good sense, and sober style.
         6. Laureate Lydgate, 160-191.
         7. Fables and didactic poems, 192-222.
         8. *The Fall of Princes*, 223-254.
         9. Lydgate's religious poetry, 255-292.
        10. Conclusion, 293-300.
  Bibliography and index, 301-312

494. Renoir, Alain. "The Binding Knot: Three Uses of One Image in Lydgate's Poetry." *Neophil* 41 (1957): 202-204.

     Discusses Lydgate's use of the binding knot, which traditionally functions as a metaphor for marriage as in two passages in *Troy-Book* and three passages in *Siege of Thebes*, in fresh contexts in three other places.

495. ------. "John Lydgate: Poet of Transition." *EM* 11 (1960): 9-19.

     Points to a shift in Lydgate's attitude toward classical antiquity from that of the Middle Ages to that of the Renaissance as he grew older. Argues that his *Troy-Book* (1412) reveals medieval suspicions toward the ancient poets and deities, but that his *Siege of Thebes* (1421) reflects a more Renaissance attitude of respect and admiration for the pagans.

496.   ------.   "A Note on Saintsbury's Criticism of Lyd-
       gate."   *NM* 58 (1957): 69-71.

       Counters the charge that Lydgate's poetry reflects
       an "intolerable prolixity" and suggests it is time to
       reconsider the negative verdict passed on the poet's
       work.

497.   ------.   *The Poetry of John Lydgate.*   Cambridge:
       Harvard UP, 1967.

          Chapter: 1. Opinions about Lydgate, 1-12.
                     2. The opinions reconsidered, 13-31.
                     3. The period of transition, 32-45.
                     4. The mediaeval tradition, 46-60.
                     5. Classical antiquity, 61-73.
                     6. The paragon of animals, 74-94.
                     7. The nation and the prince, 95-109.
                     8. The story of Thebes, 110-135.
                         Argues that this work is represen-
                         tative of the author's own thinking,
                         since it was not written under the
                         patronage system and is the only
                         attempt at narrating the entire
                         Theban legend in English. Further
                         suggests that it is a kind of "Eng-
                         lish Renaissance epic" illustrating
                         the evils of war.
                     9. Another point of view, 136-143.
          Notes, 145-165.
          Index, 167-172.

498.   Scherer, Margaret R. *The Legends of Troy in Art and
       Literature.* New York: Phaidon P, 1963.

       Reproduces   illuminations   from   manuscripts   of
       Lydgate's *Troy-Book* (xiii, xiv, 16, 55, 57, 122, 123,
       226.

499.   Schirmer, Walter F.   *John Lydgate: A Study in the
       Culture of the XVth Century.*   Trans. Ann E. Keep.
       London: Methuen; Berkeley: U of California P, 1961
       [originally published in German in 1952].

          Chapter: 5. Lydgate's *Troy Book*, 42-51.

Briefly discusses Henry V as Lydgate's patron, the significance of
this work, his treatment of sources,
and his conception of poetry and attitude to political questions.
7.   Lydgate and the Chaucer family; the
     Siege of Thebes, 59-65.
     Briefly describes this work as a
     Canterbury Tale, its content, and
     Lydgate's attitude to contemporary
     problems.

Of the twenty-three chapters in this book only
these two deal specifically with Lydgate's treatments
of Thebes and Troy.

500.   Stainer, P.A. "The Interpretation of the Troy Legend
       in English Literature, 1300-1637." *TGB* 19 (1968-69):
       359. M.Phil., Southampton U.

501.   Strohm, Paul. *"Storie, Spelle, Geste, Romaunce,
       Tragedie*: Generic Distinctions in the Middle English
       Troy Narratives." *Speculum* 46 (1971): 348-359.

       Considers the terms that ME poets used to describe
       their own work and argues that these reflect certain
       criteria: relationship to actual events (*storie* and
       fable), mode of narration (*spelle* and *tale*), language
       (*romaunce*), literary tradition (*romaunce*, *legende*,
       and *lyf*), proportion of represented action to argu-
       ment (*geste* and *treatise*), and movement of the for-
       tunes of the protagonist (*tragedie* and *comedie*).

THEMATIC STUDIES

502. Aljubouri, D.A.H. "The Medieval Idea of the Saracen, as Illustrated in English Literature, Spectacle and Sport." *TGB* 22 (1971-72): 372. Ph.D., Leicester U.

503. Benecke, Ingrid. *Der gute Outlaw: Studien zu einem literarischen Typus im 13. und 14. Jahrhundert.* Tübingen: Max Niemeyer, 1973.

   Einleitung, 1-28.
   > Attempts to find an explanation for the idealization of the outlaw by investigating four works: Latin *Gesta Herwardi*, AN *Fouke Fitz Warin*, and ME *Gamelyn* and *Gest of Robin Hood*.

   Chapter: 1. Die ritterlich-kämpferische Vorbildlichkeit des Outlaw, 29-55.
   2. Die Outlaw-Motivik als Mittel z. dichterischen Idealisierung der Helden, 56-86.
   3. Der Outlaw als rechtmässiger Sieger im feudalen Konflikt, 87-118.
   4. Die feudalethische Vorbildlichkeit des Outlaw im Wandel, 119-149.
   Schlussbemerkungen, 150-154.
   Summary, 155-161.
   Literaturverzeichnis, 163-170.
   Namenregister, 171.

504. Breuer, Rolf. *Die Funktion der Naturschilderungen in den mittelenglischen Versromanzen.* Diss. Georg-August U, Göttingen, 1966.

   Einleitung, 1-17.
   Chapter: 1. Landschaftsbeschreibungen als dekorative Kulissenschilderungen, 18-30.

2. Landschaftsbeschreibung zur Darstellung wunderbarer Handlungsschauplätze, 31-60.
3. Naturbilder als Einleitungen von Handlungsabschnitten, 61-76.
4. Die Handlung vordeutende und deutende Naturschilderungen, 77-95.
5. Naturszenen als Kontrast zur Handlung oder als deren Untermalung, 96-110.
6. Die Natur als Ausdruck der Psyche des Helden 111-137.
7. Naturschilderung zur Darstellung von Raum und Zeit, 138-150.
Zusammenfassung, 151-155.
Exkurs I: Die Funktion der Jagdszenen in den mittelenglischen Romanzen, 156-167.
       II: Die Landschaftsbeschreibung in *The Pearl*, 168-175.
Bibliographie, register, 176-198.

Many of the ME romances are mentioned in the various chapters.

505. Brockman, Bennett A. "Children and Literature in Late Medieval England." *ChildL* 4 (1975): 58-63.

First suggests that all literature of 14th- and 15th-century England was children's literature and then explores the treatment of children in that literature. Claims that the Middle Ages conceived of childish innocence in broader, more theological terms than did the 19th century.

506. Doob, Penelope B.R. *Nebuchadnezzar's Children: Conventions of Madness in Middle English Literature.* New Haven: Yale UP, 1974.

Chapter: 1. Backgrounds: medieval attitudes toward madness, 1-53.
2. Nebuchadnezzar and the conventions of madness, 54-94.
3. The mad sinner: Herod and the pagan kings, 95-133.
4. The unholy and holy wild man, 134-207.

   Discusses *Sir Orfeo* (164-207) and

Ywain and Gawain (139-153). Views the former in terms of the conventions of the Holy Wild Man (seen as Christ and his suffering in the desert) with the loss of Herodis analogous to the loss of one's soul through sin. In the latter, uses Ywain as one of the best examples of the Unholy Wild Man, whose failure to keep his word to his wife leads to his loss of her, to madness, and finally to atonement and restoration.
    5. Conclusion: Thomas Hoccleve, 208-231.
Index, 233-247.

507. Ellis, Patricia Carol. "The Journey Motif in Fourteen Non-Cyclical Middle English Verse Romances." *DAI* 44 (1983): 1447A. U of Georgia.

    Suggests that although travel is conventional in most narratives, in six romances it becomes a thematic motif, an image of man's movement from inexperience to experience, from sin to salvation.

508. Flemming-Blake, Anthony. "The Hunt in Middle English Romance: A Study in Tradition and Influence." Diss. U of Alberta, 1981.

509. Graeffe, Lotte Burchardt. "The Child in Medieval English Literature from 1200 to 1400." *DA* 29 (1968): 869A. U of Florida.

    Contends that children are not treated as real children, but unrealistically as accomplished miniature adults, if not perfect heroes.

510. Gwilliams, F.L. "The Disguise Theme in the Middle English Metrical Romances: Its Use, Origins and Influence." *TGB* 31 (1982): 4403. M.Phil, London U.

511. Keen, Maurice. *The Outlaws of Medieval Legend*. Toronto: U of Toronto P, 1977. Rpt. from 1961 ed., with new introduction, xiii-xxi.

Chapter: 1. The matter of the Greenwood 1-8.
           2. The story of Hereward, 9-22.
           3. The historical background of the
               Hereward legend, 23-38.
           4. The romance of Fulk Fitzwarin, 39-52.
           5. The romance of Eustace the Monk, 53-
               63.
           6. William Wallace and the Scottish out-
               laws, 64-77.
           7. The Tale of Gamelyn, 78-94.
           8. The Robin Hood ballads (I), 95-115.
           9. The Robin Hood ballads (II), 116-127.
          10. The historical background of the
               Robin Hood ballads, 128-144.
          11. The outlaw ballad as an expression of
               peasant discontent, 145-173.
          12. The historicity of Robin Hood, 174-
               190.
          13. The outlaw in history, 191-207.
          14. Conclusions, 208-218.
Appendix: I.   The supposed mythological origin of
               the Robin Hood legend, 219-222.
          II. Sources and bibliography, 223-225.
          III. Robin Hood's good yeomanry, 226-227.
Index, 228-235.

512. Kordecki, Lesley Catherine. "Traditions and Develop-
      ments of the Medieval English Dragon." *DAI* 41
      (1981): 4708A. U of Toronto.

      Argues that in the ME romances, the dragon degener-
      ates from the polyvalent symbolic level into a more
      rigidly defined level of sign.

513. Lane, Daryl F., Jr. "An Historical Study of the
      Giant in the Middle English Metrical Romances." *DAI*
      33 (1973): 5683A. U of New Mexico.

      Tries to formulate a definition of the function and
      characteristics of the giant, who is always evil and
      inimical to mankind, often an obstacle to national or
      religious interests.

514. Lovecy, Ian Charles. "A Study of the Supernatural in
      Some Selected Mediaeval Romances." *TGB* 25 (1976):

248. Ph.D., Cambridge U.

515. McAlindon, T. "The Emergence of a Comic Type in Middle-English Narrative: The Devil and Giant as Buffoon." *Anglia* 81 (1963): 365-371.

Traces the development of the devil from fearful to ludicrous in 14th-century crusade romances and the parallel development of the giant, who had a similar function, behavior, and appearance and was commonly confused with the devil in popular belief. Notes this process of degradation in *Bevis of Hampton* and *Sowdon of Babylon*, which reaches its comic nadir in *Sir Eglamour*.

516. ------. "The Treatment of the Supernatural in Middle English Legend and Romance, 1200-1400." *TGB* 11 (1960-61): 159. Ph.D., Cambridge U.

517. Taitt, Peter Stewart. "The Quest Theme in Representative English Works of the Thirteenth and Fourteenth Centuries." *DAI* 35 (1974): 3703A. U of British Columbia.

Suggests a twofold evolution in the artistic adaptation of the quest theme in romance literature before the 14th century: a shift from works in which the quest plays an exterior public role to interiorization of the quest to probe the ambiguity and fallibility of the hero as well as a shift from presenting the ideals unambiguously to questioning them.

518. Tonguç, Sencer. "The Saracens in the Middle English Charlemagne Romances." *Litera* 5 (1958): 17-24.

Explores romance's two approaches to the Saracens: one, the old Orthodox Church view, derived from ecclesiastical literature and stories about martyrs; the other derived from the chivalric point of view.

519. Collins, Marie. "Feminine Response to Masculine Attractiveness in Middle English Literature." *E&S* ns 38 (1985): 12-28.

Argues that medieval heroines usually respond to personality, the sum of abstract and concrete qualities, rather than to handsomeness. Argues that many romances stress the importance of cautious deliberation and consideration of the whole person, not just words or appearances. Examples include *Bevis of Hampton*, *King Horn*, *Sir Launfal*, *Romauns of Partenay*, and *Partonope of Blois*.

520. Eckhardt, Caroline D. "Woman as Mediator in the Middle English Romances." *JPC* 14 (1980): 94-107.

Contends that the woman as intercessor, rather than being based on medieval English social realities, is really a complex character type encompassing Lady Philosophy and *Maria mediatrix*.

521. Ferrante, Joan M. "Male Fantasy and Female Reality in Courtly Literature." *WS* 11 (1984): 67-97.

Treats in detail the woman who attacks a man's fantasies with words in *pastorelas* and debates and with deeds in the romances. Suggests that the two kinds of women in courtly literature are both projections of a man's self-image: the ideal woman, the part with which he must be united in order to be whole; and the realist, the debunker of male fantasy, who projects his own doubts. Argues that the courtly French romances question not only the male fantasy but also the very stereotyping of the sexes: the strength of men and the weakness of women, whether moral, intellectual, or physical.

522. Fries, Maureen. "*Feminae Populi*: Popular Images of Women in Medieval Literature." *JPC* 14 (1980): 79-86.

Argues that popular conceptions, like courtly images, tend to be dualistic, deriving from two archetypes: Eve (representing disobedience, vanity, *cupiditas*) and the Virgin Mary (representing chastity, virginity, sainthood). Examines the negative views of women, especially in fabliaux and ME romances (where virtues are chastity and obedience).

523. ------. "The Characterization of Women." Levy and Szarmach [242]. 25-45.

Applies the three modes of characterization developed by Sister Ritamary Bradley (archetype, stereotype, and depiction of reality) to three alliterative works, which present an unusual treatment of women in a "refreshing range" from limited but realistic representation in *Morte Arthure* to archetype in *Awntyrs off Arthure* and to a mixture of archetype, stereotype, and realism in *Sir Gawain and the Green Knight*.

524. ------. "Images of Women in Middle English Literature." Notes from Kalamazoo, Workshop 12. *CE* 35 (1974): 851-852.

Suggests that both Mary and Eve are dangerous archetypes, one pushing women towards supernatural virtue, the other towards unnatural vice. Further suggests that virtues are as oversimplified as vices, especially chastity and obedience, which are portrayed as the ideal in romances such as *Amis and Amiloun*.

525. Hanson-Smith, Elizabeth. "A Woman's View of Courtly Love: The Findern Anthology Cambridge University Library MS. Ff.1.6." *JWSL* 1 (1979): 179-194.

After considering the themes in the Findern lyrics, the author sees reflected specific details "of social realities in the fifteenth century as experienced by women," whose role remains obedience to male author-

ity. Contrary to the convention of the haughty mistress, these women do take the initiative and declare
their love openly although they seldom rail at fate,
but rather resign themselves to their lot and express
a sense of helplessness as the stay-at-home and
abandoned.

526. Harrison, Ruth Howard. "The Spirited Lady Through
Nicolete to Rosalind." *DAI* 35 (1975): 5346A. U of
Oregon.

Examines the development of the spirited lady in
romance, especially its particular motifs and themes
as well as story patterns, to help establish her as a
genuine conventional literary character type.

527. Lasry, Anita Benaim. "The Ideal Heroine in Medieval
Romances: A Quest for a Paradigm." *KRQ* 32 (1985):
227-244.

Identifies and analyzes two types of heroine in
medieval romance: the manly heroine and the feminine
heroine, both of whom act with autonomy and are able
to survive independently.

528. MacCurdy, Marian Mesrobian. "The Polarization of the
Feminine in Arthurian and Troubadour Literature."
DAI 41 (1980): 2596A. Syracuse U.

Views the image of woman as the focal point of the
Christian-Gnostic controversy regarding the good or
evil nature of the physical universe. Demonstrates
the polarization of woman as either spiritual guardian or demonic temptress and sees the literature as
trying to come to terms with the problem of how to
join flesh and spirit.

529. Magaw, Barbara Louise. "The Female Characters in
Prose Chivalric Romance in England, 1475-1603: Their
Patterns and Their Influences." *DAI* 34 (1973):
3412A. U of Maryland.

Characterizes three types of female characters who
derive from or echo the basic character in medieval

chivalric romances: the simplest (an exemplary daughter or wife) representing patient obedience, the most
complex (a reflective, constant heroine) who disobeys
her guardian, and the most popular (the active female) who proves superior in her chastity.

530.   Marchalonis, Shirley.   "Above Rubies: Popular Views
       of Medieval Women." *JPC* 14 (1980): 87-93.

       Suggests that women in romances are vehicles of
       passive virtue, depending on men and complementing
       them. Romances depict a masculine world in which
       women's roles are mainly to inspire, assist, adorn,
       or reward men.

531.   Morley, K.E.   "The Role of Women in Middle English
       Versions of the Downfall of the Fellowship of the
       Round Table." *TGB* 27 (1980): 4589. M.A., Manchester
       U.

532.   Murphy, Michael.   "Vows, Boasts and Taunts, and the
       Role of Women in Some Medieval Literature." *ES* 66
       (1985): 105-112.

       Argues that boasts often establish credentials and
       remind the hero of his past reputation (as in *Morte
       Arthure*, 1688, 2595), and that *flyting* has an impor-
       tant role in *Morte Arthure*, 1058ff, 1650ff, 2530ff;
       however, vows and boasts were not always taken seri-
       ously as in *Avowynge of Arthur*, *Sir Thopas*, and *Sir
       Gawain and the Green Knight*, which mocks the conven-
       tions in subtle ways. Concludes that the real possi-
       bility of female influence in a male world of epic is
       mocked in the "feminized" world of romance.

533.   Roberts, Nanette McNiff.   "Making the Mold: The
       Roles of Women in the Middle English Metrical Ro-
       mance, 1225-1500." *DAI* 37 (1977): 5812A. NYU.

       Suggests that romance, unlike the folktale, concen-
       trates on the male protagonists and their adventures
       and successes; only fourteen of the eighty-one ro-
       mances considered have women as protagonists or
       co-protagonists, half of whom are victims. Examines

women in their supernatural aspects, as fairy mis-
tresses, accused queens, persecuted wives, wooing
princesses, and in the realm of eros. Challenges the
assertion that romance is a "feminine" genre.

534. Thompson, Raymond H. "'For quenys I might have
now...': The Knight Errant's Treatment of Women in
English Arthurian Verse Romances." *Atlantis* 4.2
(1979): 34-47.

Concludes that of the twenty-seven English poems
dealing with Arthur and his knights, only seventeen
are devoted to the activities of knights errant, and
in these the role of women has been diminished, the
love theme suppressed in favor of a political one,
and women discredited or generally looked upon with
suspicion.

535. Ziegler, Georgianna. "The Characterization of Guinevere in English and French Medieval Romance." *DAI*
35 (1975): 5371A. U of Pennsylvania.

Examines Guinevere's mythical and pseudo-historical
background and the linguistic forms of her name,
tracing the theme of sovereignty manifested in her
role as queen and wife.

OTHER STUDIES

536. Allen, Mark Edward. "Personal Names in Old and Middle English Poetry." *DAI* 43 (1982): 784A. U of Illinois at Urbana-Champaign.

Traces patterns in onomastic function, language philosophy, and the literary form of names from *Beowulf* to Henryson. Defines four types of names: denotative or etymological, personifying, allusive, and connotative. Major texts considered include *Havelok*, *Sir Gawain and the Green Knight*, and Lydgate's *Troy-Book*.

537. Barnickel, Klaus Dieter. *Farbe, Helligkeit und Glanz im Mittelalters*. Düsseldorfer Hochschulreihe 1. Diss. Düsseldorf, 1974. Düsseldorf: Stern-Verlag Janssen, 1975.

Approaches a structural analysis of color vocabulary in ME texts, including many romances. Emphasizes the research in the theory of semantic fields and suggests that formal criteria (frequency, morphological structure, stylistic restrictions) indicate a hierarchy of primary words (red, green, blue, brown, white) and two classes of secondary words for color, which are not hue-oriented, but tied to brightness. Looks at the use of color and brightness words in traditional descriptions such as spring, feminine beauty, armor and arming, and *locus amoenis*.

538. Benskin, Michael, and M.L. Samuels, eds. *So Meny People Longages and Tonges: Philological Essays in Scots and Mediaeval English Presented to Angus McIntosh*. Edinburgh: Middle English Dialect Project, 1981.

Includes essays on alliteration [247] and *Havelok* [867].

539.   Blaicher, Günther.   "Das Weinen in mittelenglischer Zeit: Studien zur Gebärde des Weinens in historische Quellen und literarische Texten." Diss. U of Saarbrücken, 1966.

Examines historical and literary instances of weeping under various headings, one of which is "in romances." Claims that tears were used as a method of indirect characterization in order to excite emotion and as signs of a maiden in distress, which could open a new episode in the plot.

540.   Boone, Lalia Phipps.   "Criminal Law and the Matter of England." *BUSE* 2 (1956): 2-16.

Reviews the legal conditions in medieval England and examines legal practices in the Matter of England romances, finding that crimes are realistically portrayed and reflect with fair accuracy the workaday criminal law of England. Points to trial by compurgation and judicial combat in *Guy of Warwick*, trial by ordeal in *Athelston*, two separate trials before the king's council in *Havelok*, two appearances before King Edgar and his parliament in *Bevis of Hampton*, and trial by a jury of twelve in *Gamelyn*.

541.   Brook, E.J.   "The Position, Attitudes and Methods of the Noble Warrior in English Medieval Poetry." *TGB* 5 (1954-55): 138. M.A., Wales U.

542.   Cassidy, Marsha J. Francis.   "Narrative Formula and Structure in Middle English Romance." Diss. U of Chicago, 1979.

543.   Culbert, Taylor.   "The Single Combat in Medieval Heroic Narrative." *DA* 18 (1958): 1416-1417. U of Michigan.

Divides the single combat into four components: motives, boasts or challenges, conditions of fighting, and physical struggle and then examines its dramatic and structural functions, concluding that its narrative purpose changes from an interest in the hero to illustrations of pious or patriotic behavior.

544. Davis, Robert Evan, Jr. "Justice in the Middle English Metrical Romances." *DAI* 40 (1979): 3312A. Pennsylvania State U.

Argues that romances advocate support of and obedience to the legal structure as the best means of preserving order and justice.

545. Dowell, Paul Wilson. "Vestiges of Rule Ritual in the Matter of England Romances." *DAI* 32 (1972): 4559A. U of Tennessee.

Contends that rule ritual existed and survived in the Matter of England romances and that it exerted a strong influence on literature by providing archetypal conflicts and motifs.

546. Dürmüller, Urs. *Narrative Possibilities of the Tail-Rime Romance.* Swiss Studies in English 83. Bern, Switz.: Francke, 1975.

Introduction, 1-11.
    Discusses the tail-rhyme stanza, criticism of this kind of romance, and an approach to his study, which includes six chapters specifically on *Earl of Toulous* and single chapters on several other tail-rhyme romances.

Part 1: *The Erl of Tollous*: an analysis, 12-174.
Chapter: 1. Narrative structure, 13-26.
        2. The stanza, 27-70.
            Discusses parallelism, links between structures, the stanza as a narrative unit.
        3. The tail-lines, 71-118.
            Includes tag phrases, formulas and alliteration, and conclusions.
        4. Direct speech, 119-142.
            Treats the formal opening of

passages in direct speech, the use
of the tail-rhyme stanza for speech,
and the narrative function of direct
speech.

5. Themes, 143-164.

Focuses on *ryght* and *trowthe* and
their socio-historical background.

6. Appreciation and evaluation, 165-
174.

Discusses this poem as a successful one with careful structure and
symmetry and a skillful use of the
stanza.

Part 2:   *The Erl of Tollous* among the shorter
tail-rime romances, 175-229.

7. *Emaré*, 177-183.

Concludes that the poem lacks the
control and artistry of *Earl of
Toulous*.

8. *Athelstone*, 184-189.

Points to its lack of success,
awkward handling of stanza, and
unnecessary repetition.

9. *Sir Cleges*, 190-194.

Concludes that although a mixture
of fabliau, exemplum, and Christmas
tale, it takes advantage of the
stanza as a narrative device.

10. *King Edward and the Shepherd*, 195-
199.

Believes this is close to balladry, but a successful tail-rhyme
work.

11. *Sir Gowther*, 200-206.

Points to its elaborate stanza
linking with direct speech in twenty-one of its twenty-three stanzas.

12. *Sir Launfal*, 207-215.

Points to its skillful use of the
stanza in its narration.

13. *Sir Thopas*, 216-222.

Uses the advantages of the tail-
rhyme stanza.

14. Final conclusions, 223-228.

Discusses the narrative possibilities of the tail-rhyme stanza, the
relationship between an effective
use of the stanza and general artis-

tic standard of the romance itself,
mances.
Appendices, 230-237.
Abbreviations and bibliography, 238-245.

547. Duncan, Patricia Jean. "From Folklore to Archetype:
Analyses of Four Middle English Romances." *DAI* 37
(1976): 3606A. SUNY, Albany.

Examines the use of literary myth in *Sir Gawain and
the Green Knight*, *King Horn*, *Sir Orfeo*, and *Morte
Arthure* in terms of Frye's archetypal pattern of
death and rebirth.

548. Dunn, Charles W. "Romances Derived from English Legends." Severs [90]. 17-37.

Includes background, rhyme scheme, dating, sources,
dialect, and often a plot sketch, followed by some
brief literary comments, of *King Horn*, *Horn Child*,
King Ponthus, *Havelok*, *Bevis of Hampton*, *Guy of
Warwick*, *Gamelyn*, *Athelston*, and *William of Palerne*.

549. Dykstra, Timothy Eugene. "Humor in the Middle English
Metrical Romances." *DAI* 36 (1976): 5313A. Ohio
State U.

Explores four broad categories of humor: character
humor, contemporary sociological matters, erotic humor, and dark or grotesque humor.

550. Ewald, Robert James. "The Jungian Archetype of the
Fairy Mistress in Medieval Romance." *DAI* 38 (1978):
5451A. Bowling Green State U.

Traces the fairy mistress, not to folklore origins
in Celtic myth, but to the Jungian archetype of the
anima, which explains her multiple aspects, inconsis-
tencies, and role as motivator of trials or quests.
Discusses her three aspects (as fairy queen, helpful
fay, and harmful fay) in all the works in which she
appears.

551. Feinstein, Sandra. "Identity in Romance." *DAI* 45
      (1985): 2532A-2533A. Indiana U.

      Finds the identity of the hero is predetermined by
      his name and heritage and that the hero recognizes
      his identity and recovers it rather than discovers
      it. Traces the development of this idea from early
      ME romances such as *Sir Orfeo*, *Havelok*, and *King Horn*
      to later works such as *Sir Gawain and the Green
      Knight* and Spenser's poem.

552. Hadsel, Martha Elizabeth. "Prudence in the Middle
      English Metrical Romances of the Thirteenth and Four-
      teenth Centuries." *DAI* 38 (1978): 6114A. Pennsyl-
      vania State U.

      Traces prudence and imprudence in kings, knights,
      and commoners as a moral and political concept.

553. Hamilton, Gayle Kathleen. "Chaos and Conclusion in
      Late Middle English Romance." *DAI* 39 (1978): 1538A.
      U of Rochester.

      Treats romances as reflections of issues concerning
      proper authority, healthy community, and the restora-
      tion of order.

554. Hermann, Ulrike. "Stofflich Verwandte Englisch-
      Schottische Volkballaden und Mittelalterliche Epische
      Erzahlungen (Romanzen)." Diss. Innsbruck, 1960.

555. Hoffman, Bonnie. "The *Turnament of Totenham* and the
      Feest: A Critical Edition." *DAI* 45 (1985): 2520A.
      SUNY at Stony Brook.

      Discusses the use of conventional romance phrases
      and scenes in *Turnament of Totenham*.

556. Hornstein, Lillian Herlands. "Miscellaneous Roman-
      ces." Severs [90]. 144-172.

      Deals with romances of Greek or Byzantine origin,
      composites of courtly romance, romances on historical

themes that are not covered under a different heading, romances of family tradition, and legendary romances of didactic intent.

557. Kirkpatrick, Hugh. "The Bob-Wheel and Allied Stanza Forms in Middle English and Middle Scots Poetry." *DAI* 37 (1976): 3608A. North Texas State U.

Formulates a definition of the bob-wheel stanza, inventories and describes forty-seven poems, identifies their periods and dialects, and traces the origin and development of this stanza from the 13th to 16th centuries.

558. Klausner, D.N. "The Nature and Origin of Didacticism in Some Middle English Romances." *TGB* 18 (1967-68): 299. Ph.D., Cambridge U.

559. Knopp, Sherron Elizabeth. "The Figure of the Narrator in Medieval Romance and Dream Vision." *DAI* 36 (1976): 4471A. UCLA.

Shows the increasingly important role of the narrator as mediator between the material and the audience, from the impersonal voice to the master of ceremonies and shaper of the narrative.

560. Kratins, Ojars. "Treason in Middle English Metrical Romances." *PQ* 45 (1966): 668-687.

Surveys the degree of coincidence in the treatment of treason in the legal practice and in fiction and points out that the practice of *judicium Dei* was nearly obsolete and antiquated but still believed in.

561. Leo, Diana Thomas. "The Concept of the Hero in the Middle English Verse Romances." *DAI* 31 (1971): 6558A. U of Pittsburgh.

Describes the nature and idealization of the hero and his role in seventy romances, which stress the humanity of the hero, usually a vigorous transmitter of heroic ideals.

562. Leonardi, Phyllis. "An Analysis of the Feast Scene in the Middle English Metric Romances." Diss. U of Ottawa, 1980.

563. Lumiansky, R.M. "Legends of Godfrey of Bouillon." Severs [90]. 101-103.

Deals with the Swan Knight legend in two ME romances: *Chevalere Assigne* and *Helyas, the Knight of the Swan*.

564. Martin, J.E. "Studies in Some Early Middle English Romances." *TGB* 18 (1967-68): 300. Ph.D., Cambridge U.

565. Mitchell, L.E. "Aspects of the English Romance Tradition: Studies in Certain English Romances and Their Literary and Social Background." *TGB* 25 (1977): 5364. M.Litt, Cambridge U.

566. Mittermann, Harald. *Untersuchungen zum historischen Präsens und Perfekt in frühen mittelenglischen Romanzen*. Diss. Vienna, 1973. Vienna: Verband der Wissenschaftlichen Gesellschaft Österreichs, 1975.

Discusses the historic present and perfect tenses in twenty of the romances.

567. O'Brien, Timothy David. "Authority and Character in Middle English Literature." *DAI* 42 (1982): 3993A. U of California, Santa Barbara.

Argues that authority is the central issue involved in concepts of character and the relationships between characters in *Havelok*, *King Horn*, and *Sir Orfeo*, in which the unifying theme is each character's development to true authority and avoidance of tyranny.

568. Otlewski, Eleanor. "The Story of the Parents in Medieval Romance: A Study of Medieval Narrative Unity." *DAI* 32 (1972): 4574A. Indiana U.

Examines external structure and inner form as they tend toward bipartition. Applies general principles of structure to Wolfram von Eschenbach's *Parzival*, Chrétien de Troyes' *Cligès*, and Gottfried von Strassburg's *Tristan and Isolde*.

569. Pratt, John Harvey. "The Middle English Historical Battle Poem." *DAI* 37 (1977): 5811A-5812A. U of Missouri-Columbia.

Defines the generic nature of forty topical battle poems and considers features common to other medieval forms such as balladry and the combat *topoi* of medieval romance.

570. Purdon, Liam Oliver. "Thirteenth- and Early Fourteenth-Century English Short Verse Romance as Mirror of Morality." *DAI* 42 (1981): 696A. Rice U.

Studies *King Horn*, *Havelok*, *Amis and Amiloun*, and *Floris and Blauncheflur* as another literary means for disseminating moral theological instruction to ecclesiastical communities and laity.

571. Robertson, M.J. "Literariness and the Structure of Medieval Otherworld Tales." *DAI* 42 (1982): 1555C. York U.

Explores connections between *Sir Gawain and the Green Knight* and OF and ME lays and romances.

572. Rouillard, Zelda Jeanne. "An Analysis of Some Patterns of Comparison in the Matter of England Romances." *DA* 20 (1960): 4099-4100. U of Colorado.

Examines fourteen adjective, verb, and noun patterns of comparison, which can all be reduced to formula, with the exception of hyperbole and metaphor.

573. Slater, David T. "The Hero-Traitor Relationship in the English Metrical Romances." *DAI* 37 (1976): 2205A-2206A. U of New Mexico.

Treats this important relationship in *Athelston*, *Gamelyn*, *King Horn*, *Havelok*, and *Generides*.

574.   Smyser, H.M.   "Charlemagne Legends."   Severs [90].
       80-100.

Treats the twelve romances having Charlemagne material as their subject under the three broad headings of Firumbras Group, Otuel Group, and detached romances.

575.   Swanzey, Thomas Brian.   "Studies in English Histori-
       cal Poetry of the Middle Ages: Morality and English
       Historical Poetry; Romance and English Historical
       Poetry." *DAI* 34 (1973): 289A-290A. Rutgers U.

Examines the confusions between romance and reality, the romanticization of history in several famous works, and the hyperbolic portraits of historical figures as a reflection of romantic ideals in medieval romance.

576.   Walsh, Edward Michael.   "The Meaning of Rhythmic
       Changes in Fourteenth-Century English Poetry." *DAI*
       35 (1975): 7883A.   Southern Illinois U.

Discusses the major structural principle of medieval works, described as "panel-structure," and a theory of prosody accounting for alliterative poetry, including *Parlement of Thre Ages*, *Siege of Jerusalem*, and *Sir Gawain and the Green Knight*. Argues that changes in rhythm reflect cultural values and world views.

577.   Whitebook, Budd Bergovoy.   "Individuals: Eccentric-
       ity and Inwardness in English and French Romance,
       1170-1400." *DAI* 32 (1971): 3275A-3276A.   Yale U.

Claims that there are two kinds of society in romance: one in which the individual is expected to conform to the community's ideas of order (*Lanval* and *Amis and Amiloun*) and the other in which the individual is allowed to express personal choice (*Yvain* and *Sir Gawain and the Green Knight*).

578. Wittig, Susan. *Stylistic and Narrative Structures in the Middle English Romances.* Diss. U of California, Berkeley, 1972. Austin: U of Texas P, 1978.

Introduction, 3-9.
Chapter: 1. Problems of stylistic analysis in the Middle English romance, 11-46.
2. Larger structural units: the motifeme, 47-101.
3. Larger structural units: the typescene, 103-134.
4. Larger structural units: the typeepisode, 135-178.
5. Speculations and conclusions 179-190.
Notes, bibliography, and index, 191-223.

COLLECTIONS OF ROMANCES

579. Amours, F.J. *Scottish Alliterative Poems in Riming Stanzas*. STS 27, 38. Edinburgh: Blackwood, 1892, 1897.

   Includes *Awntyrs off Arthure, Golagrus and Gawain,* and *Taill of Rauf Coilyear*.

580. Beattie, William. *The Chepman and Myllar Prints; Nine Tracts from the First Scottish Press, Edinburgh 1508, Followed by the Two Other Tracts in the Same Volume in the National Library of Scotland: A Facsimile*. Edinburgh: Edinburgh Bibliographical Society, 1950.

   Contains *Gest of Robin Hood, Golagrus and Gawain,* and *Sir Eglamour*.

581. Bennett, J.A.W., and G.V. Smithers. *Early Middle English Verse and Prose*. 1968. 2nd ed. Oxford: Oxford UP, 1982.

   Includes complete texts of *King Alexander, Floris and Blauncheflur,* and *Havelok*.

582. Benson, Larry D. *King Arthur's Death: The Middle English Stanzaic Morte Arthur and Alliterative Morte Arthure*. Indianapolis: Bobbs-Merrill, 1974.

583. Brookhouse, Christopher. *Sir Amadace and the Avowing of Arthur: Two Romances from the Ireland MS*. Anglistica 15. Copenhagen: Rosenkilde and Bagger, 1968.

583a. Child, Francis James. *English and Scottish Ballads.*
       8 vols. Boston: Little, Brown, 1857-1859.

       Includes *Carle off Carlile*, *Gest of Robin Hood*,
       Grene Knight, *Knight of Curtesy*, and *Sir Gowther*.

 584. Dunn, Charles W., and Edward T. Byrnes. *Middle Eng-
       lish Literature.* New York: Harcourt Brace Jovano-
       vich, 1973.

       Includes *King Horn*, *Sir Orfeo*, *Sir Gawain and the
       Green Knight*, as well as lines 4154-4346 of *Morte Ar-
       thure* and lines 66-193 of *Siege of Thebes*.

584a. Ellis, George. *Specimens of Early English Metrical
       Romances.* 3 vols. London, 1805. 2nd ed. London,
       1811. Rev. J.O. Halliwell [-Phillipps]. London:
       Henry G. Bohn, 1848.

       Includes only selections, sometimes substantial, of
       many ME romances.

 585. Ford, Boris, ed. *The Age of Chaucer*. Vol. 1 of *The
       Pelican Guide to English Literature*. 7 vols. Balti-
       more: Penguin, 1954.

       Contains *Roberd of Cisyle*, *Sir Gawain and the Green
       Knight*, and *Sir Orfeo*.

 586. French, Walter Hoyt, and Charles Brockway Hale. *Mid-
       dle English Metrical Romances*. New York: Prentice-
       Hall, 1930. Rpt. New York: Russell & Russell, 1964.

       Includes complete texts of seventeen ME romances,
       as well as selections from five others.

586a. Garbáty, Thomas J. *Medieval English Literature.*
       Lexington, MA: Heath, 1984.

       Contains texts from many different ME genres, in-
       cluding the romances *Havelok*, *King Horn*, *Sir Gawain
       and the Green Knight*, *Sir Launfal*, and *Sir Orfeo*.

587. Grant, A.D. "An Edition of the Middle English Roman-
      ces, *Roland and Vernagu*, *The Sege off Melayne*, and
      Duke Rowlande and Sir Ottuell of Spayne. *TGB* 18
      (1967-68): 307. Ph.D., London U.

588. Gray, Douglas. *The Oxford Book of Late Medieval
      Verse and Prose*. With a Note on Grammar and Spelling
      in the Fifteenth Century by Norman Davis. Oxford:
      Clarendon P, 1985.

      Includes texts of *Gest of Robin Hood* and *Knight of
      Curtesy*, with excerpts from many other medieval
      works.

589. Hales, John W., and Frederick J. Furnivall. *Bishop
      Percy's Folio Manuscript: Ballads and Romances*. 3
      vols. London: Trübner, 1868. Rpt. Detroit: Singing
      Tree P, 1968.

      Includes *Arthour and Merlin*, *Carle off Carlile*,
      Eger and Grime, *Grene Knight*, *Libeaus Desconus*,
      Marriage of Sir Gawain, *Prose Merlin*, *Sir Degare*, *Sir
      Eglamour*, *Sir Triamour*, an abridged and mutilated
      version of *Squyr of Lowe Degre*, and *Turke and Gowin*.

590. ------. *The Percy Folio of Old English Ballads and
      Romances*. 4 vols. The King's Library. London: De
      La Mere P, 1905-1910.

      Reprints the texts from their earlier edition
      [589], but contains no critical apparatus.

591. Hall, Joseph. *King Horn: A Middle English Romance*.
      Oxford: Clarendon P, 1901.

      Includes *Horn Child* and *King Horn*.

592. Halliwell [-Phillipps], James Orchard. *Illustrations
      of the Fairy Mythology of A Midsummer Night's Dream*.
      London: Shakespeare Society, 1845. Rpt. New York:
      AMS P, 1970.

      Includes texts of *Sir Launfal* and *Sir Orfeo*.

593.   ------. *The Thornton Romances: The Early English
        Metrical Romances of Perceval, Isumbras, Eglamour,
        and Degrevant.* Camden Society 30. London, 1843.

        Includes texts of *Sir Degrevant*, *Sir Eglamour*, *Sir
        Isumbras*, and *Sir Perceval*.

594.   Hartshorne, Charles Henry. *Ancient Metrical Tales:
        Printed Chiefly from Original Sources.* London, 1829.

        Includes *Athelston* and *Floris and Blauncheflur*.

594a.   Haskell, Ann S. *A Middle English Anthology.* Garden
        City, NY: Anchor, 1966.

        Contains *Sir Gawain and the Green Knight*, *Sir Laun-
        fal*, and *Sir Orfeo*, as well as complete texts and
        selections of many other ME works.

595.   Hazlitt, W. Carew. *Early Popular Poetry of Scotland
        and the Northern Border, Edited by David Laing LL.D.
        in 1822 and 1826.* 2 vols. London: Reeves and Tur-
        ner, 1895.

        A revised and rearranged version of Laing [601,
        602], with additions and a glossary, including
        Awntyrs off Arthure, the Aberdeen version of *Eger and
        Grime*, *Roswall and Lillian*, *Sir Orfeo*, and *Taill of
        Rauf Coilyear*.

596.   ------. *Fairy Tales: Legends and Romances Illustrat-
        ing Shakespeare and Other Early English Writers.*
        London: Frank & William Kerslake, 1875.

        Text is reprinted from Halliwell [-Phillipps]
        [592].

597.   ------. *Remains of the Early Popular Poetry of Eng-
        land.* 4 vols. London: John Russell Smith, 1864-
        1866.

        Includes *Knight of Curtesy*, *Roberd of Cisyle*, and
        Squyr of Lowe Degre.

598. Herrtage, Sidney J. *"The Sege off Melayne"* and *"The Romance of Duke Rowland and Sir Otuell of Spayne."* EETSES 35. London: Trübner, 1880.

Printed from the unique Thornton MS in the British Museum, MS Additional 31.042, together with a fragment of "The Song of Roland" from the unique MS Lansdowne 388.

599. ------. *The Taill of Rauf Coilyear, With the Fragments of Roland and Vernagu and Otuel.* EETSES 39. London: Trübner, 1882. Rpt. London: Oxford UP, 1931, 1969.

600. Kurvinen, Auvo. *Sir Gawain and the Carl of Carlisle in Two Versions.* Series B, Vol. 71, pt. 2. Helsinki: Suomalaisen Tiedeakatemian Toimituksia Annales Academiae Scientiarum Fennicae, 1951.

A parallel text of the extant versions of *Syre Gawene and the Carle of Carelyle* and *Carle off Carlile*.

601. Laing, David. *Early Metrical Tales; Including the History of Sir Egeir, Sir Gryme and Sir Gray-Steill.* Edinburgh, 1826. Rpt. in *Early Scottish Metrical Tales.* London: Hamilton, Adams; Glascow: Thomas D. Morison, 1889.

A supplement to Laing [602] with the Aberdeen version of *Eger and Grime* and *Roswall and Lillian*.

602. ------. *Select Remains of Ancient Popular Poetry of Scotland.* Edinburgh, 1822. Re-edited with a memorial introduction and additions by John Small, Edinburgh: Blackwood, 1885.

Includes *Awntyrs off Arthure*, *Sir Orfeo*, and *Taill of Rauf Coilyear*.

603. Lumby, J. Rawson. *King Horn, With Fragments of Floriz and Blauncheflur, and of the Assumption of Our Lady.* EETSOS 14. London: Trübner, 1866.

Includes *Floris and Blauncheflur* and *King Horn*.

604.   McKnight, George H.   *King Horn, Floriz and Blaunche-*
       flur, The Assumption of Our Lady.   EETSOS 14.   Lon-
       don: Kegan Paul, Trench, Trübner, 1901.   Rpt. London:
       Oxford UP, 1962.

       Supplants Lumby [603] with re-edited texts.

605.   Madden, Sir Frederic.   *Syr Gawayne; A Collection of*
       Ancient Romance-Poems, by Scotish and English Au-
       thors, Relating to that Celebrated Knight of the
       Round Table.   Bannatyne Club 61.   Edinburgh: Taylor,
       1839.   Rpt. New York: AMS P, 1971.

       Includes *Awntyrs off Arthure, Carle off Carlile,*
       Golagrus and Gawain, Grene Knight, Jeaste of Syr
       Gawayne, Syre Gawene and the Carle of Carelyle, Sir
       Gawain and the Green Knight, Turke and Gowin, Wed-
       dynge of Sir Gawen, and fragments of *Marriage of Sir*
       Gawaine and *King Arthur and King Cornwall.*

606.   Michel, Francisque.   *Horn et Rimenhild, Recueil de ce*
       qui reste des poems relatif à leurs aventures.   Banna-
       tyne Club 80.   Paris: Maulde et Renou, 1845.

       Includes *Horn Child* and *King Horn* as well as four
       versions of the Hynd Horn ballad.

607.   Mills, Maldwyn.   *Six Middle English Romances.*   London:
       Dent; Totowa, NJ: Rowman and Littlefield, 1973.

       In addition to a 25-page introduction and critical
       notes, contains *Emare, Octavian, Sege of Melayne, Sir*
       Amadace, Sir Gowther, and *Sir Isumbras.*

608.   Morris, Richard.   *Specimens of Early English: A New*
       and Revised Edition with Introduction, Notes and
       Glossarial Index.   2 vols.   Oxford: Clarendon P,
       1882.

       Includes *Havelok, King Horn,* and *William of*
       Palerne.

609. O'Sullivan, Mary Isabelle. *Firumbras and Otuel and Roland*. EETSOS 198. London: Oxford UP, 1935. Rpt. Millwood, NY: Kraus, 1971.

    Edited from MS. British Museum Additional 37492 [Fillingham].

610. Pinkerton, John. *Scottish Poems, Reprinted from Scarce Editions*. 3 vols. London: Nichols, 1792.

    Includes *Awntyrs off Arthure* and *Golagrus and Gawain*.

611. Ritson, Joseph. *Ancient Engleish Metrical Romanceës*. 3 vols. London: Nicol, 1802. Rpt. Edinburgh: Goldsmid, 1884.

    Includes *Bone Florence of Rome*, *Chronicle of England*, *Earl of Toulous*, *Emare*, *Horn Child*, *King Horn*, *King of Tars*, *Knight of Curtesy*, *Libeaus Desconus*, *Sir Launfal*, *Sir Orfeo*, *Squyr of Lowe Degre*, and *Ywain and Gawain*.

612. Robson, John. *Three Early English Metrical Romances*. Camden Society 18. London, 1842.

    Contains *Avowynge of Arthur*, *Awntyrs off Arthure*, and *Sir Amadace*.

613. Rumble, Thomas C. *The Breton Lays in Middle English*. Detroit: Wayne State UP, 1965.

    Includes texts of *Emare*, *Earl of Toulous*, *Lai le Freine*, *Sir Degare*, *Sir Gowther*, *Sir Launfal*, *Sir Orfeo*, and the *Franklin's Tale*, with bibliographies.

614. Sands, Donald B. *Middle English Verse Romances*. New York: Holt, 1966.

    Includes *Athelston*, *Floris and Blauncheflur*, *Gamelyn*, *Havelok*, *King Horn*, *Lai le Freine*, *Sir Launfal*, *Sir Orfeo*, *Squyr of Lowe Degre*, *Syre Gawene and the Carle of Carelyle*, and *Weddynge of Sir Gawen*.

615. Schlobin, Roger Clark. *"The Turke & Gowin, The Marriage of Sir Gawaine,* and *The Grene Knight:* Three Editions with Introductions." *DAI* 32 (1972): 6391A. Ohio State U.

      Edited from the Percy Folio with all variant readings.

616. Schmidt, A.V.C., and Nicolas Jacobs. *Medieval English Romances.* 2 vols. London Medieval and Renaissance Series. London: Hodder and Stoughton; New York: Homes & Meier, 1980.

      Includes complete texts of *Athelston, Havelok, Sir Degare,* and *Sir Orfeo,* as well as excerpts from *Ipomadon, Morte Arthur, Morte Arthure,* and *Ywain and Gawain.*

617. Skeat, Walter W. *Joseph of Arimathie: Otherwise Called the Romance of the Seint Graal, or Holy Grail.* EETSOS 44. London: Trübner, 1871. Rpt. New York: Greenwood P, 1969; Millwood, NY: Kraus, 1973.

      Includes *Here Begynneth the Lyfe of Joseph of Arimathia* with *A Praysing to Joseph, Joseph of Arimathie,* prose *Lyfe of Joseph,* and prose *De Sancto Joseph.*

618. ------. *The Romance of William of Palerne: (Otherwise Known as the Romance of "William and the Werwolf"); to Which is Added a Fragment of the Alliterative Romance of Alisaunder.* EETSES 1. London: Trübner, 1867. Rpt. Millwood, NY: Kraus, 1973.

      Includes *Alexander A* and *William of Palerne.*

619. Stevenson, George. *Pieces From the Makculloch and the Gray MSS. Together With the Chepman and Myllar Prints.* STS 65. Edinburgh: Blackwood, 1918.

      Includes *Gest of Robin Hood, Golagrus and Gawain,* and *Sir Eglamour.*

620. Turnbull, W.B.D.D. *The Romances of Rouland and Vernagu, and Otuel: From the Auchinleck Manuscript.* Abbotsford Club 4. Edinburgh, 1836.

 Includes *Otuel A Knight* and *Roland and Vernagu*.

621. U[tterson], E.V. *Select Pieces of Early Popular Poetry: Re-published Principally from Early Printed Copies, in the Black Letter.* 2 vols. London: Longman, 1817.

 Includes *Sir Degare*, *Sir Gowther*, *Sir Isumbras*, and *Sir Triamour*.

622. Weber, Henry. *Metrical Romances of the Thirteenth, Fourteenth, and Fifteenth Centuries: Published from Ancient Manuscripts.* 3 vols. Edinburgh: Constable, 1810.

 Includes *Amis and Amiloun*, *King Alexander*, *Lai le Freine*, *Lyfe of Ipomydon*, *Octavian*, *Richard Coer de Lyon*, *Sir Amadace*, and *Sir Cleges*.

THE ALLITERATIVE ALEXANDER FRAGMENTS [65]

Alexander A or *Alisaunder*
Alexander B or *Alexander and Dindimus*
Alexander C or *Wars of Alexander*

Editions:

623. Duggan, Hoyt N. "A Critical Edition of *The Wars of Alexander*: Passus I-XIV." *DAI* 31 (1970): 728A. Princeton U.

Critical edition of first fourteen passus based on MS Ashmole 44, with all significant variants recorded from Trinity College D.4.12. Introduction, notes, and critical apparatus.

624. Magoun, Francis Peabody, Jr. *The Gests of King Alexander of Macedon: Two Middle-English Alliterative Fragments Alexander A and Alexander B.* Cambridge: Harvard UP, 1929.

Chapter: 1. The English manuscripts, 3-14.
2. Previous editions, 14-15.
3. The sources, 15-77.
4. Dialect and scribal transmission, 77-95.
5. Metre, 96-100.
6. Date of composition, 100-101.
7. The diction and style of *Alexander A* and *Alexander B*, 101-112.
8. Authorship, 112-113.
9. Texts, 113-116.
10. Abbreviations, 117-118.
Texts, 121-216.
Notes, 217-240.
Appendices, 243-254.
Index, 257-261.

Edited with parallel Latin sources (Orosius and the *Historia de Preliis*, J²-Recension). *Alexander A*: 121-170, 217-233; *Alexander B*: 171-216, 234-240.

625. Skeat, Walter W. *Alexander and Dindimus: Or, The Letters of Alexander to Dindimus, King of the Brahmans, With the Replies of Dindimus.* EETSES 31. London: Trübner, 1878. Rpt. Millwood, NY: Kraus, 1973.

Includes introduction (vii-xxxv), text of *Alexander B* (1-43), notes (45-58), and indexes (59-93).

618. ------. xxix-xliv, 177-218, 236-249, 327-328.

First edition of *Alexander A* from the unique manuscript in the Bodleian Library, Greaves 60. Here called "þe Gestes of þe Worthie King and Emperour, Alisaunder of Macedonie." Introduction, text, notes, and index of names.

626. ------. *The Wars of Alexander: An Alliterative Romance Translated Chiefly from the Historia Alexandri Magni de Preliis.* EETSES 47. London: Trübner, 1886. Rpt. Millwood, NY: Kraus, 1973.

Text of *Alexander C*, re-edited from MS Ashmole 44 in the Bodleian Library, Oxford, and MS D.4.12 in the Library of Trinity College, Dublin. Also includes introduction and notes.

627. Stevenson, Joseph. *The Alliterative Romance of Alexander.* Roxburghe Club 67. London, 1849.

Texts of *Alexander B* and *Alexander C*.

Criticism:

628. Duggan, Hoyt N. "The Source of the Middle English *The Wars of Alexander.*" *Speculum* 51 (1976): 624-636.

Argues that the major source is the I³ recension of *Historia de Preliis* and that the *Wars of Alexander* and the *Prose Alexander* are independently translated from related but different manuscripts of I³. Further adds that there is no evidence to support an I³ᵃ recension and that Hamilton [*Speculum* 2 (1927): 113-146] began the misinformation appearing in standard histories and bibliographies that *Wars of Alexander* is generally closer to the Cambridge and Glasgow MSS, but differs from any surviving manuscript.

629. Hahn, Thomas George. "God's Friends: Virtuous Heathen in Later Medieval Thought and English Literature." *DAI* 35 (1975): 4428A-4429A. UCLA.

Examines both *Alexander B* and *Awntyrs off Arthure*, among other texts, and shows the intellectual development and 14th-century backgrounds that affected attitudes towards heathens.

630. Lawrence, R.F. "A Critical Study of Verse Techniques in *The Wars of Alexander*." *TGB* 17 (1966-67): 324. M.Phil., London U.

631. ------. "Formula and Rhythm in *The Wars of Alexander*." *ES* 51 (1970): 97-112.

By means of detailed illustration from the poem, the author argues that contrary to orthodox definitions, a formula can exhibit more than one rhythmic form and that variations in formulas often perform rhythmic functions in preserving desired stress patterns.

632. Lawton, D.A. "The Middle English Alliterative *Alexander A* and *C*: Form and Style in Translation from Latin Prose." *SN* 53 (1981): 259-268.

Examines in detail two sections of the source in the hands of the two translators and argues that such a study illuminates the line-by-line mechanism of alliterative verse composition.

633. Ronberg, Gert. "The Two Manuscripts of *The Wars of Alexander*: A Linguistic Comparison." *Neophil* 69

(1985): 604-610.

Compares MSS Ashmole 44 (A) and Trinity College
Dublin 213 (D), perhaps both copies of the same exemplar, with notable differences in orthography and
morphology: D uses *o* more frequently than A for OE
ā; unlike A, D uses *qu/qw* for OE *hw*; and there is a
different distribution of *s(c)h* for OE *sc*. Concludes
that A is unmistakably northern and D less so, that
there is no evidence that the original was of western
composition, and that the differences between D and A
are attributable less to different ME dialects than
to the incipient effect of Modern English on the
language.

634.   Suzuki, Eiichi. "A Note on the Use of Middle English
       Airen in *The Wars of Alexander*." *ESELL* 66 (1977).

635.   Turner, Jerry David.   "'The Harm of Hem That Stoode
       in Heigh Degree': A Critical Study of the Middle
       English Alliterative Romance *The Wars of Alexander*."
       DAI 34 (1974): 5126A-5127A. U of Texas at Austin.

       Analyzes theme and structure to determine the
       extent and nature of the poet's adaptations; argues
       that the poet presents the theme more emphatically,
       has a stronger sense of scene, and speaks in a more
       subjective narrative voice than the authors of his
       sources.

636.   Turville-Petre, Thorlac.   "Emendation on Grounds of
       Alliteration in *The Wars of Alexander*."   *ES* 61
       (1980): 302-317.

       Contends that a comparison of the two manuscripts
       points unquestionably to one basic pattern: aa/ax,
       often with ornamental alliteration in the first
       half-line. Also suggests that within a rigid frame-
       work, great flexibility is possible, arising mostly
       from variations in the stress patterns.

637.   ------. "Nicholas Grimald and *Alexander A*." *ELR* 6
       (1976): 180-186.

Suggests that the poem, which appears in Greaves MS 60, circa 1551, is written in the hand of Nicholas Grimald.

SEE ALSO items 79 (35-36), 110 (179-189), 181 (141-180), 197 (242-243), 201, 203, 204, 212, 221, 222, 225, 230, 234, 238, 263 (36-37, 73-77, 88-90, 94-104), 266, 1002.

Editions:

638. Kölbing, Eugen. *Amis and Amiloun, zugleich mit der altfranzösischen Quelle.* Altenglische Bibliothek 2. Heilbronn: Henninger, 1884.

All manuscripts with French, Latin, and Norse texts.

639. Leach, MacEdward. *Amis and Amiloun.* EETSOS 203. London: Oxford UP, 1937. Rpt. 1960.

Text (1-100) from the Auchinleck MS, with the first 97 and last 112 lines from Egerton MS 2862 and variants from other manuscripts. Also includes introduction (ix-cii) and notes (113-130).

622. Weber. 1: lii-lv; 2: 369-473, 478-479; 3: 364-366.

Text is from the Auchinleck MS.

Criticism:

640. Baldwin, Dean R. "*Amis and Amiloun*: The Testing of *Treuþe.*" *PLL* 16 (1980): 353-365.

Argues that the poem can best be understood as an example of "test literature"; the poem is meant to be a moral laboratory showing the value of loyalty to a sworn oath, but also its limitation as an imperfect substitute for faith and grace.

641. Brody, Saul Nathaniel. "The Disease of the Soul: A

Study in the Moral Associations of Leprosy in Medieval Literature." *DAI* 32 (1971): 379A-380A. Columbia U.

Attempts to define and explain the association of leprosy with moral defilement in medieval European literature; its portrayal often has a popular moral association, as in *Amis and Amiloun*, in which leprosy is a consequence of falsehood.

642.   Dannenbaum, Susan. "Insular Tradition in the Story of Amis and Amiloun." *Neophil* 67 (1983): 611-622.

Explores the relationship between the ME and AN versions of the tale and shows that an insular tradition, including a stylistic heritage and a similar treatment of theme, strongly unites the two.

643.   Fewster, C.S. "Narrative Transformations of Past and Present in Middle English Romance: *Guy of Warwick*, *Amis and Amiloun* and the *Squyr of Lowe Degre*." *DAI* 47 (1986): 77C. Liverpool U, 1984.

Describes the audience, distinctive style, and structure of ME romances and tests these three texts against generic theories.

644.   Homan, Delmar Charles. "Old Gods in New Garb: The Making of *Amis and Amiloun*." *DA* 24 (1964): 5386. Columbia U.

Argues that the story is best accounted for by a combination of Celtic sources, with *Mabinogion* supplying the friendship plot and contaminations from the Curoi-Blathnat abduction.

645.   Hume, Kathryn. "*Amis and Amiloun* and the Aesthetics of Middle English Romance." *SP* 70 (1973): 19-41.

Judges the poem against three standards for romance: the care with which relevant details are presented; narrative economy; and the suitability of the chosen story to the form, determined by its structure, theme, and moral scheme.

646. ------. "Structure and Perspective: Romance and Hagiographic Features in the Amicus and Amelius Story." *JEGP* 69 (1970): 89-107.

Argues that while sharing many motifs and patterns, romance and hagiography differ in aesthetic structure and perspective; hagiography traces a saint from birth to death and sometimes beyond, whereas romance focuses on one period of a hero's life. The nature of the testing is also different; the saint is often tempted, whereas the hero is tested or initiated through a quest or series of adventures.

647. Kramer, Dale. "Structural Artistry in Amis and Amiloun." *AnM* 9 (1968): 103-122.

Points to the poet's use of three primary structural devices for organizing the poem: his method of presentation (scene-like dramatic quality marked by much dialogue and little description), recurrence of various events or motifs, and moral background. Divides the poem into five major sections.

648. Kratins, Ojars. "The Middle English *Amis and Amiloun*: Chivalric Romance or Secular Hagiography?" *PMLA* 81 (1966): 347-354.

Raises generic questions and treats the poem as a secular hagiographic legend rather than an unsatisfactory romance.

649. Mathew, Gervase. "Ideals of Friendship." *Patterns of Love and Courtesy: Essays in Memory of C.S. Lewis.* Ed. John Lawlor. Evanston: Northwestern UP, 1966. 45-53.

Investigates the origins of medieval concepts of friendship in both the classical (Aristotelian and Ciceronian) tradition and heroic (bonds of *comitatus*) tradition. Suggests that the emphasis on the friendship between males and the successful testing of their mutual love and friendship (as in *Amis and Amiloun*) affected the relationship between men and women from the 12th century on, thus providing a framework for the new analysis of love and marriage.

SEE ALSO items 57 (119-121), 80, 144, 163, (105-111), 166, 413, 440, 465, 504 (38-39), 524, 556, 570, 577, 578, 911, 1539.

AMORYUS AND CLEOPES [71]

Editions:

650. Craig, Hardin. *The Works of John Metham; Including the Romance of Amoryus and Cleopes.* EETSOS 132. London: Kegan Paul, Trench, Trübner, 1916. Rpt. Millwood, NY: Kraus, 1973.

651. Furnivall, Frederick J. *Political, Religious, and Love Poems.* EETSOS 15. 1866, re-ed. 1903. Rpt. London: Oxford UP, 1965. 301-308.

Includes "a sketch, with the prolog and epilog, of the Romance of *The Knight Amoryus and the Lady Cleopes* by John Metham, scholar of Cambridge, A.D. 1448-9."

SEE ALSO items 204, 413.

APOLLONIUS OF TYRE [95]

Editions:

652. Halliwell [-Phillipps], J.O. *A New Boke about Shake-
      spear and Stratford-on-Avon.* London, 1850.

      The text is from Douce MS 216.

653. Raith, Josef. *Die alt- und mittelenglischen Apollo-
      nius-Bruchstücke.* Munich: Max Hueber, 1956.

      Includes a short introduction (67-68) and the text
      from MS Douce 216 (78-84).

654. Smyth, Albert H. "Shakespeare's Pericles and Apollo-
      nius of Tyre." *PAPS* 37 (1898): 206-312.

      Reprints the fragment from Halliwell [-Phillipps]
      [652], with some normalization of the orthography
      (249-255).

Criticism:

655. Archibald, Elizabeth Frances. "*Apollonius of Tyre* in
      the Middle Ages and the Renaissance." *DAI* 46 (1985):
      697A. Yale U.

      Offers a literary history to 1609 and ends with a
      discussion of the story as perceived by medieval
      readers and modern scholars. Although it has charac-
      teristics of romance, history, and hagiography, *Apol-
      lonius of Tyre* presents an exemplary story of Man
      Tried by Fate.

656. Lawrence, Harold Whitney. "'To Sing a Song that Old
      Was Sung': *Pericles* and *Apollonius of Tyre*, the Play
      and the Tradition." *DAI* 31 (1971): 6062A-6063A.

Texas Christian U.

Studies the tradition told from Anglo-Saxon times
as an example of chaste self-discipline and magister-
ial virtue as it was understood by the 17th-century
audience.

657.   Pickford, T.E. "*Apollonius of Tyre* as Greek Myth and
       Christian Mystery." *Neophil* 59 (1975): 599-609.

Suggests reasons for the popularity throughout the
Middle Ages of this romance, one of the most frequently copied and translated of all Greek romances.
Claims the main reason is that the work is capable of
full Christian meaning with Apollonius as a Christ
figure; the theme of resurrection; the Jonas parallel; and the story of exile, slavery, and return as a
symbolic representation of the human loss of heaven
through sin, earthly exile, and the purification and
reward in an afterlife.

SEE ALSO item 556.

Editions:

658. Cylkowski, David Gerard. "An Edition of the Middle English Romance *A Lytel Treatyse of Ye Byrth & Pphecye of Marlyn*." *DAI* 42 (1982): 4005A. U of Michigan.

Provides an introduction, text, notes, glossary, and bibliography of *Arthour and Merlin*—the second, shorter version printed by Wynken de Worde in 1510.

589. Hales and Furnivall. 1: 417-496.

590. ------. 2: 1-68.

659. Holland, William Edward. "Merlin, MS. Lincoln's Inn 150: A Critical Edition." *DAI* 32 (1972): 5764A. Stanford U.

Re-edits the poem as a single text from Lincoln's Inn with variants from Auchinleck and Douce MSS. Includes glossary, annotation, and introduction.

660. Kölbing, Eugen. *Arthour and Merlin, Nach der Auchinleck-Hs*. Altenglische Bibliothek 4. Leipzig: Reisland, 1890. Rpt. Amsterdam: RODOPI, 1968.

Text from Auchinleck MS (3-272), followed by text in parallel columns of Lincoln's Inn and Douce MSS (273-370). Linear notes and glossary are also included, as well as a partial text of Lovelich's *Merlin* (lines 1-1638) and a study of the Merlin story in England (ix-clxxxix).

661.   Macrae-Gibson, O.D.   *Of Arthour and of Merlin*.
       EETSOS 268, 279.   Diss.   Oxford U, 1965.   London:
       Oxford UP, 1973, 1979.

       Full text from Auchinleck and Lincoln's Inn MSS,
       with partial text from Additional MS 27879 and vari-
       ants from Douce MSS 124 and 236 and Harley MS 6223.
       An introduction, commentary, and glossary in the
       second volume.

662.   Turnbull, W.B.D.D.   *Arthour and Merlin, a Metrical
       Romance*.   Abbottsford Club.   Edinburgh, 1838.

       Texts from the Auchinleck MS and Harley 6223 frag-
       ment.

       Criticism:

663.   Holland, William E.   "Formulaic Diction and the
       Descent of a Middle English Romance."   *Speculum* 48
       (1973): 89-109.

       From studies of the five existing manuscripts of
       Arthour and Merlin, the author suggests transmission
       was primarily oral, not written, except for two
       manuscripts, with changes occurring mainly by substi-
       tution of formulaic half-lines.

664.   McCoy, Dorothy Schuchmann.   "Devious Devil and
       Ubiquitous Arab: The Importance of the Auchinleck
       Arthour and Merlin for Chaucer's Use of Arthurian
       Legend."   Abstracts of papers delivered at the
       Twelfth International Arthurian Congress, Regensburg,
       1979.   *BBSIA* 31 (1979): 288-289.

       Proposes that the poem's muddy morality, its mud-
       dled history, and the English poet's lack of narra-
       tive skills and techniques can begin to elucidate
       Chaucer's satiric reaction to ME romance.

665.   Macrae-Gibson, O.D.   *"Of Arthour and of Merlin* in
       Sussex?"   *ELN* 17 (1979): 7-10.

       Replies to Sklar's suggestion [668] that Sussex is

the poem's most likely provenance and argues that
London is preferable since the *i*-mutated vowel and
the *e*- and *a*-alternatives for unshortened OE *ae* are
typical of the London dialect about 1300.

666. Matheson, Lister M. "The Arthurian Stories of Lambeth Palace Library MS 84." *ArthurL* 5 (1985): 70-
91.

Reproduces the four interpolated passages and
examines their possible sources and connections to
other medieval works. Finds that the second passage,
"The Birth and Childhood of Merlin," shares marked
similarities to both *Arthour and Merlin* and Lovelich's *Merlin*; delineates these shared features.
Speculates that the interpolation could be a unique
translation of an otherwise unknown French source
underlying *Arthour and Merlin*, a copy of a now lost
English work, or a compilation that derives its
conception of the birth of Merlin from *Merlin* and its
account of the journey to Vortiger's court from
Arthour and Merlin.

667. Sklar, Elizabeth S. "*Arthour and Merlin*: The Eng-
lishing of Arthur." *MichA* 8 (1975): 49-57.

Points to the poet's intensive focus on England,
his determined insularity in omitting Continental
digressions, treatment of British geography, replacing French nomenclature by English names, reducing
thematic materials to political concerns by ignoring
religious and romantic material, and diminution of
the role of Merlin.

668. ------. "The Dialect of *Arthour and Merlin*." *ELN* 15
(1977): 88-94.

Questions London as the provenance of the poem and
offers Sussex as a more likely source of origin; the
development of OE *e* from *i*-mutated *a* before a nasal
resembles the Sussex, not London dialect, which uses
the *a*-form.

669. ------. "England's Arthur: A Study of the Middle

English Poem *Arthour and Merlin*." *DAI* 30 (1970): 5004A. U of Pennsylvania.

Examines the poem's style, theme, narrative techniques, provenance in Sussex, and dating during the period of Edward I.

670. Wallner, Björn. "The Distribution and Frequency of Scandinavian and Native Synonyms in *Kyng Alisaunder* and *Arthour and Merlin*." *ES* 40 (1959): 337-352.

Discusses fifty-seven native and Scandinavian synonyms and concludes that there is no striking northern influence on the vocabulary of the two texts; rather the two texts follow usage prevalent in the east Midlands.

SEE ALSO items 89, 163 (239-242), 174, 272 (73-75), 274, 277, 285, 298, 305 (117-119), 307, 315, 334 (42-44), 337, 445, 469, 504 (68ff), 955, 995.

ARTHUR [15]

Editions:

671. Bryan, Mildred Willingham. "A Critical Edition and
      Verse Translation of *Arthur*." *DAI* 39 (1978): 2246A-
      2247A. U of Alabama.

672. Furnivall, Frederick J. *Arthur; A Short Sketch of*
      His Life and History in English Verse. EETSOS 2.
      London: Trübner, 1864. 2nd ed. 1869. Rpt. London:
      Oxford UP, 1965.

      Edited from the Marquis of Bath's MS, Liber Rubeus
      Bathoniae, 1428 A.D. Text only.

Criticism:

673. Finlayson, J. "The Source of 'Arthur,' an Early Fif-
      teenth-Century Verse Chronicle." *N&Q* ns 7 (1960):
      46-47.

      Suggests that Wace, rather than Geoffrey of Mon-
      mouth, is the source of this poem.

SEE ALSO items 298, 315, 337.

Editions:

586. French and Hale. 179-209.

594. Hartshorne. 1-34.

674. Hervey, [Lord] Francis. *Corolla Sancti Eadmundi: The Garland of Saint Edmund King and Martyr.* London: John Murray, 1907. 525-555, 669-672.

614. Sands. 130-153.

Reprint of French and Hale [586] with regularized orthography.

616. Schmidt and Jacobs. 1: 15-21, 123-150, 187-196.

Introduction, text, and commentary.

675. Taylor, George. "An Edition of the Middle English Romance of 'Athelston.'" M.A., Leeds U, 1934. Cited in "Theses Added to Leeds University Library," *LeedsSE* 3 (1934): 64.

676. Trounce, A. McI. *Athelston: A Middle English Romance.* Philological Society Publication 11. London: Oxford UP, 1933.

This book was revised and reissued as EETSOS 224, London: Oxford UP, 1951. Rpt. 1957. Includes introduction (1-61), bibliography (62-66), text (67-92), notes (93-136), appendix and glossary (137-156), and index of names (157).

677. Wright, Thomas, and James Orchard Halliwell [-Phillipps]. *Reliquiae Antiquae: Scraps from Ancient Manuscripts, Illustrating Chiefly Early English Literature and the English Language.* 2 vols. London: Pickering, 1841, 1843. Rpt. New York: AMS P, 1966. 2: 85-103.

A complete text of *Athelson*, with brief fragments of *Bevis of Hampton* (2: 58-64), *Libeaus Desconus* (2: 65-67), and *Sir Isumbras* (2: 67).

678. Zupitza, Julius. "Die Romanze von Athelston." *EStn* 13 (1889): 331-414; 14 (1890): 321-344.

Uses texts of Hartshorne [594] and Wright and Halliwell [-Phillipps] [677], with extensive notes and discussion of variants and dialect in the manuscripts.

Criticism:

679. Dickerson, A. Inskip. "The Subplot of the Messenger in *Athelston*." *PLL* 12 (1976): 115-124.

Argues that the three episodes in which the messenger is involved are a distinct and coherent subplot that parallels and reinforces the main action. Further points to the messenger as a link between the audience and the main narrative and as a figure deriving from a stock character in ME romance who embodies bourgeois views.

680. Johnson, Donald Dodge, Jr. "The Structure of *Athelston*." *DAI* 31 (1971): 3505A. U of North Carolina at Chapel Hill.

Explores the interrelationships among grammatical, prosodic, rhetorical, and narrative structures and concludes that the second plot seems grafted on to the original tale of falseness.

681. Kiernan, Kevin S. *"Athelston* and the Rhyme of the English Romances." *MLQ* 36 (1975): 339-353.

    Refutes Trounce's idea [676] of the integrity of tail-rhyme and demonstrates that what has previously been called spurious or feeble is intentional variation of the rhyme and rhythm. Also proposes that the poem's four-line lacuna may be filled according to the conscious paralleling techniques of the author, who creates a structural and thematic diptych.

SEE ALSO items 31, 80 (88-92), 110, 163 (146-152, 276-277), 166, 179, 413, 414, 540, 546 (184-189), 548, 573, 814.

THE AVOWYNGE OF KING ARTHUR, SIR GAWAN, SIR KAYE, AND SIR BAWDEWYN OF BRETAN [32]

Editions:

583. Brookhouse. 9-16, 24-30, 60-96, 106-108.

682. Dahood, Roger. *The Avowing of King Arthur*. Diss. Stanford U, 1970. Garland Medieval Texts 10. New York: Garland, 1984.

   An edition of the Ireland-Blackburne MS with critical notes, introduction, and glossary.

586. French and Hale. 607-646.

612. Robson. 57-93, 105-110.

683. Smith, James A. "The Avowynge of King Arthur, Sir Gawan, Sir Kaye and Sir Bawdewyn of Bretan: A Middle English Romance from the Ireland MS." M.A., Leeds U, 1938.

Criticism:

684. Dahood, Roger. "Dubious Readings in the French and Hale Text of 'The Avowing of King Arthur' (MS. Ireland-Blackburne)." *N&Q* ns 18 (1971): 323-326.

   Notes the most serious errors in the text, particularly *hapnes*, line 442; *luffe/stuffe/buffe*, lines 61-63; *mere*, line 1090; *store*, line 110; *strete*, line 664; *sum*, line 156; *thurst*, line 898; *wayt*, line 24; and *worlyke*, line 852.

SEE ALSO items 231, 272 (76-77), 285, 298, 307, 337, 348, 353, 504 (159-160), 532.

Editions:

579. Amours. xl-xlvi, 116-171, 329-364, 480-481.

Contains Douce MS on even-numbered pages (116-170) and Thornton MS on odd-numbered (117-171).

685. Christianson, Clayton Paul. "*The Awntyrs off Arthure*: An Edition." *DA* 26 (1965): 352. Washington U.

Presents all four known texts in parallel form.

686. Gates, Robert J. *The Awntyrs of Arthure at the Terne Wathelyne: A Critical Edition*. Diss. U of Iowa, 1967. Haney Foundation Series 5. Philadelphia: U of Pennsylvania P, 1969.

The first published edition to collate all four known manuscripts, including the Lambeth MS. Also contains introduction, notes, glossary, and index of names.

687. Hanna, Ralph, III. *The Awntyrs off Arthure at the Terne Wathelyn: An Edition Based on the Bodleian Library MS. Douce 324*. Diss. Yale U, 1967. Manchester: Manchester UP, 1974; New York: Barnes & Noble, 1974.

Includes introduction (1-55), text of *Awntyrs* A, lines 1-338, *Awntyrs* B, lines 339-702 (80-96), concluding stanza (97), notes (98-142), linguistic appendix (143-154), and glossary and index (155-190).

595. Hazlitt. 1: 1-42.

602. Laing. 81-113.

   Includes an account of the Cathedral Library Lincoln MS in an appendix (389-391).

605. Madden. 95-128, 326-336.

   Text is from the Thornton and Douce MSS.

688. Paton, Florence Ann. "A Critical Edition of the
   Aunturs of Arthur." *DA* 26 (1966): 1634. U of Colorado.

   Reproduces Lambeth text with critical apparatus.

610. Pinkerton. 3: 197-226.

   Text is from the Douce MS. Title here appears as
   "Sir Gawan, and Sir Galaron of Galloway."

612. Robson. 1-26, 94-100.

   Text is from the Ireland MS.

Criticism:

689. Allen, R.S. "A Textual Study of *The Awntyrs of Arthur*." *TGB* 18 (1967-68): 305. M.A., London U.

690. Boswinkel, J. "The Structure of the Aunters of
   Arthur." *Handelingen van het achtentwitigste Neder-
   lands Filologencongres*. Groningen, Neth.: Wolters,
   1964. 141-143.

   Rejects critical opinion that the poem has no unity
   and argues instead that its unity is in keeping with
   the didactic nature of the romance with its themes of
   the sin of pride and the inevitability of death. Its
   unity is reinforced by parallels between the individ-

ual prospect of death and the disintegration of the Arthurian world, as well as between the two unwanted intruders, the ghost and Galeron.

691. Clark, John Frank. "The Hunt as Metaphor: A Study of the Theme of Death in Four Middle English Poems." *DAI* 43 (1983): 3590A. U of Wisconsin-Madison.

A close study of *Parlement of Thre Ages*, *Sir Gawain and the Green Knight*, *Awntyrs off Arthure*, and *Book of Duchess* to establish the role of the hunt in the structure and metaphysical composition of each work.

692. Cox, R.C. "Tarn Wadling and Gervase of Tilbury's 'Laikibrait.'" *Folklore* 85 (1974): 128-131.

Suggests that Tilbury's valley, which is surrounded by a forest from Carlisle to Penrith and known by local inhabitants as "Laikibrait," is actually the Tarn Wadling of this poem; confirmation comes from the claim of Adam de Felton, Prior of St. Mary's in Carlisle, and his canons to tithe for fish caught "in lacu de Terwathelan qui dicitur Laykebrayt."

693. Dean, Christopher. "The 'Mirror for Princes' Genre and Two Late Arthurian Romances." Abstracts of papers delivered at the Twelfth International Arthurian Congress, Regensburg, 1979. *BBSIA* 31 (1979): 267-268.

Finds that *Awntyrs off Arthure* and *Lancelot of the Laik* differ from other Arthurian romances in their lengthy passages of direct admonition and counsel to rulers and suggests the genre of "mirror for princes" as a possible source.

694. Eadie, John. "Two Notes on the *Awntyrs of Arthure*." *ELN* 21.2 (1983): 3-7.

Clarifies two problems: 1) *Rayked to Rondolesette Hall* (1. 337), which may refer to Randulph Seat, a piece of raised ground considered a landmark in the Middle Ages, four miles west of the village of Cald-

beck; 2) *Hay hertly pay heued in haches on hight* (l.
448), which presents difficulties concerning the word
haches. The word *hekke* meant "manger" or "hay-rack"
only in those areas of strong Scandinavian influence;
it was never transferred in everyday usage to the
form *hache*.

695.   Hanna, Ralph, III.   "The *Awntyrs off Arthure*: An
       Interpretation." *MLQ* 31 (1970): 275-297.

       Argues that the poem is composed of two separate
       pieces: *Awntyrs* A reveals the perceptual and moral
       failure of the Arthurian court through a skillful
       blend of romance and religious *topoi*, whereas B,
       which is less skillful, draws on stock chivalric
       situations in demonstrating the futility of settling
       complicated social problems by martial prowess alone.

696.   Kelly, Susan. "Place-Names in the *Awntyrs off Ar-
       thure*." *LOS* 6 (1979): 162-199.

       A complete survey of the place names of sixteen lo-
       calities in southwestern Scotland with a detailed
       discussion of the evidence for positive identifica-
       tion.

697.   Klausner, David N. "Exempla and *The Awntyrs of Ar-
       thure*." *MS* 34 (1972): 307-325.

       Viewing the poem as a moral tale that illustrates
       both *luxuria* and *avaritia*, the author first places
       the poem's treatment of *luxuria* in the tradition of
       sermon exempla, with special attention to the English
       versions of Gregory's *Trental* and other minatory
       poems in the manuscripts of the 13th and 14th centu-
       ries. The second part of the article argues that the
       poem's major structural problems arise from the non-
       religious origins of the *avaritia* theme.

698.   Leach, H.G. "*The Auntyrs of Arthur at the Tarn
       Wadling*." Abstracts of papers delivered at the
       Seventh International Arthurian Congress, 1963.
       BBSIA 15 (1963): 145.

Argues that the poem was probably composed in the Cumbrian dialect by a minstrel in the 12th century to glorify the Scottish border by setting an Arthurian tournament there.

699.   Lowe, Virginia A.P. "Folklore as a Unifying Factor in *The Awntyrs off Arthure*." *FForum* 13 (1980): 199-223.

Views the poem as a unified whole given its cultural components: the activities of the hunt and a belief in spiritual manifestation. The poem is a conglomeration of elements from folk Christianity, and these folkloric beliefs constitute the framework that imparts symbolic meaning to both episodes in the poem.

700.   Spearing, A.C. "The *Awntyrs off Arthure*." Levy and Szarmach [242]. 183-202.

Refutes Hanna's claim [695] of separate narratives and argues that the poem should be viewed as a single narrative, not necessarily with modern unity, but with the coherence and connectedness of a medieval diptych or a modern montage; in both halves, Arthurian civilization is faced with the challenge of an apparently hostile outsider.

701.   ------. "Central and Displaced Sovereignty in Three Medieval Poems." *RES* ns 33 (1982): 247-261.

Applies the analytical methods of Alastair Fowler (in *Triumphal Forms*) to *Awntyrs off Arthure*, Henryson's *Morall Fabillis*, and *Sir Gawain and the Green Knight*. In *Awntyrs off Arthure* there is almost perfect symmetry between the two parts with the king enthroned at the exact center of the poem; *Sir Gawain and the Green Knight*, on the other hand, involves displacement of sovereignty with Gawain replacing Arthur; at the midpoint of the poem, Gawain is midway between two opposing ladies who represent ascetic Christian values and secular, courtly ones.

702.   Turville-Petre, Thorlac. "'Summer Sunday,' 'De Tri-

bus Regibus Mortuis,' and 'The Awntyrs off Arthure':
Three Poems in the Thirteen-Line Stanza." *RES* ns 25
(1974): 1-14.

Examines these three poems in order to show the existence of a school of poets using the 13-line stanza
to express similar themes. All three poets use the
hunt to introduce a somberly didactic vision of
death.

703. White, Beatrice. "Of Ghosts and Spirits Walking by
Day and by Night." Schlauch Essays [14]. 473-483.

Argues that English works are not so fertile as the
Icelandic sagas in numbers of ghosts, but that the ME
romances are full of other supernatural figures such
as wizards, witches, dwarfs, and fairies. Points to
only two instances of ghosts: the brief appearance
of the White Knight in *Sir Amadace* and the terrifying
ghost in *Awntyrs off Arthure*, a ghost straight from
monkish purgatory, but which may have a tenuous link
with the robust ghosts of Scandinavia.

SEE ALSO items 93 (252-262), 179, 212, 220, 224, 225, 227,
230, 231, 241, 243, 263 (65-66), 266, 272, 282, 298, 307,
315, 337, 345, 348, 353, 406 (201-202), 469, 470, 472, 504
(43ff), 523, 629, 1276.

Editions:

584a. Ellis. 239-281.

Text is from the Caius College MS with omissions supplied from Pynson's printed copy.

705. Fellows, J.L. "*Sir Beves of Hampton*: Study and Edition." *TGB* 31 (1982): 285. Ph.D., Cambridge U.

706. Kölbing, Eugen. *The Romance of Sir Beues of Hamtoun.* EETSES 46, 48, 65. London: Kegan Paul, Trench, Trübner, 1885-1894. Rpt. as one vol. Millwood, NY: Kraus, 1973.

Contains all manuscripts except Trinity. Extensive introduction and notes.

707. Turnbull, William B.D.D. *Sir Beves of Hamtoun: A Metrical Romance.* Maitland Club Publication 44. Edinburgh, 1838. Rpt. New York: AMS P, 1973.

Text is from the Auchinleck MS, with no critical apparatus.

Criticism:

708. Baugh, Albert C. "The Making of *Beves of Hampton*." *Bibliographical Studies in Honor of Rudolf Hirsch.* Ed. William E. Miller and Thomas G. Waldman with Natalie D. Terrell. Philadelphia: U of Pennsylvania Library, 1975. 15-37.

Argues that all the extant versions are derived
from the same adaptation of the AN text; that the
Auchinleck version is the best; that the other four
manuscripts contain three separate redactions, each
representing a version as recited from memory by a
minstrel or *disour*, who sometimes resorted to improvisation when memory failed; that the versions in
couplets are new tellings; and that it is better to
see not a single ME romance, but at least five versions of it.

709.   Jacobs, Nicolas. *"Sir Degarré, Lay le Freine, Beves
        of Hamtoun* and the 'Auchinleck Bookshop.'" *N&Q* ns 29
        (1982): 294-301.

        Offers possible hypotheses concerning the relation-
        ships among the three poems and concludes that both
        stages of the interpolation in *Sir Degare* involve the
        use of a redaction of *Beves of Hampton*, which sur-
        vives only in the Auchinleck MS; that more than one
        copy of *Sir Degare* was made in the Auchinleck scrip-
        torium; and that the 'Auchinleck bookshop' theory
        should not be ruled out.

710.   Lister, W. *"Sir Bevis of Hampton*: A Study of the
        Vogue and Successive Transformations of this Popular
        English Romance from the Middle Ages to the Present
        Day." *TGB* 21 (1970-71): 340. M.Phil., Southampton
        U.

711.   Schendl, Herbert. "Me. *randon* in *Sir Bevis of Hamp-
        ton.*" *Anglia* 102 (1984): 101-107.

        Provides a syntactic and semantic reading of line
        4277 and all its variants; considers a possible
        French influence on the syntax, but dismisses this
        hypothesis. Concludes that *randown* is a modal adverb
        with the meaning "fast" or "impetuous" and that "They
        saylyd ouyr the randown" is the best reading of this
        line.

712.   Spector, Sheila Abbye. "Studies in *The Bovo Buch* and
        Bevis of Hampton." *DAI* 38 (1977): 3523A. U of Mary-
        land.

Compares the ME poem and the 16th-century Yiddish version written in Italy, which is an epic romance. Examines differences in narrative techniques, oral and written composition, and the effects of interlacing and irony.

713. Weiss, Judith. "The Major Interpolations in *Sir Beues of Hamtoun*." *MAE* 48 (1979): 71-76.

Analyzes the adapter's two substantial interpolations in the AN source—the dragon fight at Cologne and the hero's battle in the streets of London—as reflections of the growth of patriotic sentiment and a pride in England and in the achievements of English heroes as also seen in other 13th-century adaptations such as *Guy of Warwick* and *Havelok*.

SEE ALSO items 67 (126-133), 79 (43-44), 89, 110, 122, 161, 163 (211-220), 166, 174, 386, 398, 413 (45-68), 414, 424, 504 (163-164), 515, 519, 540, 548, 578, 1539.

LE BONE FLORENCE OF ROME [84]

Editions:

714. Heffernan, Carol Falvo. *Le Bone Florence of Rome*. Diss. NYU, 1973. Manchester: Manchester UP; New York: Barnes & Noble, 1976.

    Includes introduction (1-41), bibliography (42-50), text (53-123), textual notes (124-150), glossary (151-203), and an index of proper names (204-205).

715. Knobbe, Albert. *Über die mittelenglische Dichtung Le Bone Florence of Rome*. Marburg, 1889.

    Contains the introduction to the text in Viëtor [717].

716. Lee, Anne Thompson. *"Le Bone Florence of Rome*: A Critical Edition." Diss. Harvard U, 1974.

611. Ritson. 3: 1-92, 340-342, 440-441.

717. Viëtor, Wilhelm. *Le Bone Florence of Rome*. Diss. U of Marburg, 1893. Marburg, 1899.

    Text only; accompanying introduction in Knobbe [715].

Criticism:

718. Heffernan, Carol Falvo. *"Raptus*: A Note on Crime and Punishment in *Le Bone Florence of Rome."* Bessinger and Raymo [9]. 173-179.

Argues that the poet's handling of crime and punishment for *raptus* in the poem suggests that much before the Council of Trent (1545-63) there was a growing respect for the sanctity of marriage and a woman's right to consent freely to the selection of her mate.

719.   Lee, Anne Thompson.   *"Le Bone Florence of Rome*: A Middle English Adaptation of a French Romance." Benson [8].   343-354.

Illustrates the radical alterations in descriptive technique, narrative order, and dramatic focus to the OF original by the ME author, whose deliberate changes produced a tight structure and dramatic realism lacking in the OF source.

SEE ALSO items 79 (106-107), 163 (140-146), 164, 181 (114-132), 410, 413.

BUIK OF KING ALEXANDER [69]

Editions:

720. Cartwright, John Francis. "Sir Gilbert Hay's *Buik of King Alexander the Conquerour*: A Critical Edition of Lines 1-4263." *DAI* 38 (1977): 3455A. U of Toronto.

Includes introduction, text, and commentary.

721. Macdonald, A. Text in preparation for STS.

SEE ALSO items 79 (54-55, 66-67), 204.

Edition:

722. Rosskopf, Karl. *Editio princeps des mittelenglischen Cassamus [Alexanderfragmentes] der Universitats-bibliothek Cambridge*. Diss. U of Munich, 1911. Erlangen: Junge, 1911.

    F. Holthausen emends lines 57, 74, 117, 329, and 461 of Rosskopf's text in "Zum mittelenglischen Cassamusbruchstück." *EStn* 51 (1917): 23-24.

SEE ALSO item 204.

CARLE OFF CARLILE [29]

Editions:

583a. Child. 1: 58-79.

589. Hales and Furnivall. 3: 275-294.

590. ------. 3: 277-294.

600. Kurvinen. 115-159 on odd-numbered pages.

Parallel text with *Syre Gawene and the Carle of Carelyle*.

605. Madden. 256-274, 356.

Criticism:

723. Sevier, Marcus W. "Adventures of the Ego in the Un-conscious: A Jungian Analysis of the Unspelling Group of Sir Gawain Poems in Middle English." *DAI* 40 (1979): 1456A. U of Texas at Austin.

Treats the five Gawain poems connected by the fol-lowing four traits: an otherworld character is a major figure; Gawain is tested unawares; Gawain develops a relationship with a woman he disenchants; and a beheading occurs. Views all five works from a Jungian perspective of the ego trying to recognize and assimilate the shadow and anima.

SEE ALSO items 93 (206-211), 105 (90-93), 326, 337, 723, 1276

CHEVALERE ASSIGNE [62]

Editions:

586. French and Hale. 859-873.

724. Gibbs, Henry H. *The Romance of the Cheuelere As-
     signe*. EETSES 6. London: Trübner, 1868. Rpt. 1898,
     1932. Rpt. Millwood, NY: Kraus, 1973.

     Re-edited from the unique manuscript, with preface,
     notes, and index.

725. Hoffman, Donald Lee. "The *Cheuelere Assygne*: An Edi-
     tion With Introduction, Notes and Glossary Together
     With the Legend of the Swan-Knight from Bodleian MS.
     Rawlinson Misc. 358 and the Previously Inedited 'The
     Ferst Yntroyte of Sapyens' from Cotton Caligula
     A.ii." *DA* 28 (1968): 4600A. NYU.

726. Stratton, Russell Edgar. "A Critical Edition of
     Cheuelere Assigne." *DAI* 40 (1979): 1457A. U of
     Southern Mississippi.

     Contends in introduction that the work is a book of
     conduct for young children; also includes explanatory
     notes, glossary, and selected bibliography.

727. U[tterson], E.V. *Cheuelere Assigne*. Roxburghe Club.
     London, 1820.

728. Williams, E.G. "A Critical Edition of the *Cheuelere
     Assigne*, from the Fifteenth Century MS. Cotton Cali-
     gula A II., with Introduction, Notes, Glossary and

Bibliography." *TGB* 14 (1963-64): 183. M.A., London
U.

Criticism:

729.   Barron, W.R.J. "*Chevalere Assigne* and the *Naissance
       du Chevalier au Cygne.*" *MAE* 36 (1967): 25-37.

       Finds that the English poet knew more of the French
       tradition than he could have found in the short
       redaction of the Beatrix texts, and that the English
       alliterative poem has connections with the long verse
       redaction and prose versions, although none is its
       immediate source.

730.   Stratton, Russell Edgar. "*Cheuelere Assigne*: Sim-
       plicity With a Purpose?" *AN&Q* 18 (1980): 118-121.

       Suggests that the poem's simplicity is a direct re-
       sult of its intended use in the Church as a book for
       the guidance of young children.

SEE ALSO items 82 (70-71), 163 (156-158), 212, 224, 239,
266, 361, 413, 474, 563.

CLARIODUS [105]

Editions:

731. Chapman, Robert Lundquist. "An Edition of the Middle Scots Romance *Clariodus*." *DA* 13 (1953): 382-383. U of Michigan.

   Edited from the unique Advocates MS 19.2.5. Includes introduction, textual and explanatory notes, and glossary.

732. Irving, D. *Clariodus: A Metrical Romance*. Maitland Club 9. Edinburgh, 1830. Rpt. New York: AMS P, 1973.

   Includes a brief preface and text printed from a 16th-century manuscript, with no notes or background information.

SEE ALSO items 413, 556.

Edition:

733. Panton, George A., and David Donaldson. *The "Gest Hystoriale" of the Destruction of Troy: An Alliterative Romance Translated from Guido de Colonna's "Hystoria Troiana."* EETSOS 39, 56. London: Trübner, 1869, 1874. Rpt. London: Oxford UP, 1968.

Includes preface, text, notes, and index.

Criticism:

734. Baskerville, Mary Pennino. "Two Studies in the Redaction of the Mediaeval Troy Story: Guido delle Colonne's *Historia Destructionis Troiae* and the Alliterative *Destruction of Troy*." *DAI* 39 (1978): 2244A-2245A. Columbia U.

Demonstrates how the English author refashioned the didactic history into a colorful tale by using conventions from the alliterative tradition and by minimizing the tendency to sermonize.

735. Benson, C. David. "A Chaucerian Allusion and the Date of the Alliterative 'Destruction of Troy.'" *N&Q* ns 21 (1974): 206-207.

Argues that lines 8051-8054, which refer to Troilus' woe, must refer to Chaucer's poem, thus dating the Troy poem no earlier than 1385.

736. Lawton, D.A. "*The Destruction of Troy* as Translation from Latin Prose: Aspects of Form and Style." *SN* 52 (1980): 259-270.

Analyzes the poet's compromise between the demands of source and meter and his use of a type of amplification distinctive to alliteration—collocational substitution. Further suggests that the poet translated not just with two correspondences (English and Latin), but also with a third, alliterative English.

737.   Luttrell, C.A. "Three North-west Midland Manuscripts." *Neophil* 42 (1958): 38-50.

Claims that the extant manuscript of *Destruction of Troy* was made in the northwest (South Lancashire) as late as 1538-1546, casting doubt on the long-accepted composition date of 1350-1400.

738.   Mustanoja, Tauno F. "The Middle English Syntactical Type *His Own Hand(s)* 'With His Own Hands, Himself': With Reference to Other Similar Expressions." *NM* 60 (1959): 267-286.

Concludes that the phrases are used primarily to intensify the subject-noun or pronoun, roughly in the sense of "himself" with only a slight implication of instrumentality.

739.   Ronberg, Gert. "The Language of *The Destruction of Troy* in Relation to Other Middle English Alliterative Texts." *TGB* 30 (1982): 224. D.Phil., Oxford U.

740.   ------. "Two North-West Midland Manuscripts Revisited." *Neophil* 67 (1983): 463-467.

Gives linguistic evidence that the two hands belong to two different scribes, and that the cursive hand in the manuscript of *Destruction of Troy* and in MS Chetham 6696 of Gower's *Confessio Amantis* is the same.

741.   Sundwall, McKay. "The *Destruction of Troy*, Chaucer's *Troilus and Criseyde*, and Lydgate's *Troy Book*." *RES* ns 26 (1975): 313-317.

Suggests that the author of *Destruction of Troy* borrowed Diomede's gesture of grasping Criseyde's rein (1. 8078) either from Chaucer's *Troilus and Criseyde* (11. 85-91) or from Lydgate's allusions to Chaucer in his *Troy-Book*. Either inference affects the dating of *Destruction of Troy*.

SEE ALSO items 34 (57-58), 80 (29-34), 82 (87-90), 222, 224, 225, 230, 236, 255, 259 (58-59, 65-71, 110-114), 263 (58-59, 85-86), 266, 479 (42-66), 480, 486, 487, 488, 489, 490, 504 (56ff, 107ff, 153f), 934, 1002.

DUKE ROLAND AND SIR OTUEL OF SPAIN [57]

Editions:

587.   Grant.

598.   Herrtage.   55-104, 147-159.

Text and notes.

SEE ALSO item 574.

EARL OF TOULOUS [94]

Editions:

742. Clark, J.H. "A Critical Edition of *The Earl of Toulouse*." *TGB* 20 (1969-70): 312. M.Phil., London U.

586. French and Hale. 383-419.

Text is from Cambridge University MS Ff.2.38.

743. Hülsmann, F. "Erle of Toulous: Eine neu Edition mit Einleitung und Glossar." Diss. Münster. [In *NM* 86 (1985): 122.]

744. Lüdtke, Gustav. *The Erl of Tolous and the Emperes of Almayn: Eine englische Romanze aus dem Anfange des 15. Jahrhunderts.* Sammlung englischer Denkmäler 3. Berlin: Weidmannsche, 1881.

A critical edition containing texts from all manuscripts, with extensive introductory material, but no textual notes.

611. Ritson. 3: 93-144, 342-344, 441.

Text is from Cambridge University MS Ff.2.38.

613. Rumble. 134-177.

Criticism:

745. Cabaniss, Allen.   "Judith Augusta and Her Time."
      UMSE 10 (1969): 67-109.

      Surveys the actual historical record in the chron-
      icles concerning Empress Judith, second wife of Louis
      the Pious, and concludes that she deserves better
      treatment than history has accorded her.

746. Hülsmann, Friedrich.   "The Watermarks of Four Late
      Medieval Manuscripts Containing *The Erle of Toulous*."
      N&Q ns 32 (1985): 11-12.

      Corrects Robinson's description of the number and
      dating of the watermarks in the Cambridge University
      manuscript and argues that all four watermarks date
      from 1470-1490, not the 16th century.   Checks the
      watermarks in the Ashmole MS 45, which originated in
      the mid-16th century.

747. Reilly, Robert.   "*The Earl of Toulouse*: A Structure
      of Honor." *MS* 37 (1975): 515-523.

      Argues that the poem's four-part structure with its
      system of comparisons and contrasts presents an
      idealistic picture of honor, which includes justice,
      fidelity, trust, and truth.

SEE ALSO items 55 (146-147), 163 (85-93), 363 (223-224),
370 (204-216), 371, 375, 376, 413, 443, 546, 578.

EGER AND GRIME [100]

Editions:

748. Caldwell, James Ralston. *Eger and Grime: A Paral-
      lel-Text Edition of the Percy and the Huntington-
      Laing Versions of the Romance, with an Introductory
      Study.* Harvard Studies in Comparative Literature 9.
      Cambridge: Harvard UP, 1933.

      Includes extensive introduction (3-176) and texts
      (177-353).

586. French and Hale. 671-717.

      Text of the Percy Folio.

589. Hales and Furnivall. 1: 341-400.

      Percy Folio, British Library Additional MS 27879.

590. ------. 1: 205-246.

749. Hales, John W., and Frederick J. Furnivall. *Eger and
      Grime: An Early English Romance Edited from Bishop
      Percy's Folio MS., About 1650 A.D.* London: Trübner,
      1867.

595. Hazlitt. 2: 119-210.

601. Laing. 53-134.

Criticism:

750.   Faris, David E. "The Art of Adventure in the Middle
       English Romance: *Ywain and Gawain*, *Eger and Grime*."
       SN 53 (1981): 91-100.

       Drawing on Frye's concept of romance as "an imagi-
       native model of desire," the author compares the
       aesthetic conventions of two romances of adventure
       and concludes that *Ywain and Gawain* is an imagina-
       tively forceful romance, whereas *Eger and Grime* fails
       to become a model of desire.

751.   Van Duzee, Mabel. *A Medieval Romance of Friendship:*
       Eger and Grime. New York: Burt Franklin, 1963.

           Chapter: 1. Introduction, 1-17.
                     2. *Pwyll*: the tradition, 18-32.
                     3. The friendship romances, 33-40.
                     4. The combat at the ford, 41-52.
                     5. Loosepine, the Lady of the Thorn, 53-
                         72.
                     6. Winliane, 73-88.
                     7. Eger and Grime, 89-96.
                            Points to similarities between the
                         friendship of Eger and Grime and that
                         of Yder and Gawain. Focuses on other
                         parallels and suggests this story has
                         connections to Arthurian traditions
                         concerning Gawain.
                     8. Graysteel, 97-121.
                     9. The land of Beame, 122-131.
                    10. Conclusion, 132-143.
           Notes, bibliography, and index, 144-198.

SEE ALSO items 18 (62-64), 406 (142-146), 413, 556.

Editions:

586. French and Hale. 423-455.

Text from MS Cotton Caligula A.2, but with some of Rickert's emendations [753].

752. Gough, A.B. *Emaré*. Old and Middle English Texts 2. London: Sampson Low Marston, 1901.

Includes preface and text only

607. Mills. 46-74, 197-200.

753. Rickert, Edith. *The Romance of Emaré*. Diss. U of Chicago, 1907. EETSES 99. London: Kegan Paul, Trench, Trübner, 1908. Rpt. London: Oxford UP, 1958.

Includes introduction, re-edited text, notes, and indexes.

611. Ritson. 2: 204-247; 3: 323-333, 440.

613. Rumble. 96-133.

Criticism:

754. Donovan, Mortimer J. "Middle English *Emare* and the Cloth Worthily Wrought." Benson [8]. 337-342.

Explores the possible significance or justification

for the long descriptive passage of the cloth, lines 82-180.

755. Hanks, D.T. "*Emaré*: An Influence on the *Man of Law's Tale*." *ChauR* 18 (1983): 182-186.

   Argues that both manuscript evidence and six close verbal parallels not found in Trivet or Gower support the claim that *Emare* influenced Chaucer's tale.

756. Isaacs, Neil D. "Constance in Fourteenth-Century England." *NM* 59 (1958): 260-277.

   Discusses the major points of divergence in the three ME versions dealing with false accusation of monstrous offspring: Chaucer's Man of Law, *Emare*, and Gower's version.

SEE ALSO items 34 (21-22), 80 (61-65), 93 (157-161), 161, 163 (135-140), 164, 181 (97-113), 363 (216-220), 368, 370 (216-225), 371, 375, 376, 410, 548 (177-183), 578.

FLORIS AND BLAUNCHEFLUR [96]

Editions:

581. Bennett and Smithers. 40-51 (text), 282-288 (notes).

757. DeVries, F.C. *Floris and Blauncheflur.* Diss. U. of Utrecht, 1966.

Presents four fragments in parallel columns, with introduction, notes, and glossary.

586. French and Hale. 823-885.

Text is from MS Egerton 2862.

594. Hartshorne. 81-116.

Text is from Auchinleck MS.

758. Hausknecht, Emil. *Floris and Blauncheflur: Mittel- englisches Gedicht aus dem 13. Jahrhundert.* Sammlung englischer Denkmäler 5. Berlin: Weidmannsche, 1885.

Text is a composite of all MSS.

759. Laing, David. *A Penni Worth of Witte: Florice and Blauncheflour, and Other Pieces of Ancient English Poetry Selected from the Auchinleck Manuscript.* Abbotsford Club 29. Edinburgh, 1857.

603. Lumby. 51-74 (text), 122-124 (notes).

   Text is from MSS Cambridge University Gg.4.27.2 and
   Cotton Vitellius D.3.

604.   McKnight.   xxx-xliv, 71-110, 146-147.

   Supplants Lumby [603] in the EETS series; text is
   reedited from MSS Cambridge University Gg.4.27.2,
   Cotton Vitellius D.3, and Egerton 2862.   Introduction, text, and notes.

614.   Sands.   279-309.

   Reprint of McKnight [604] with regularized orthography.

760.   Taylor, A.B.   *Floris and Blancheflour: A Middle-
   English Romance.*   Oxford: Clarendon P, 1927.

   Text is edited from MSS Auchinleck and Egerton
   2862.

   Criticism:

761.   Barnes, Geraldine.   "Cunning and Ingenuity in the
   Middle English *Floris and Blauncheflur.*"   *MAE* 53
   (1984): 10-25.

   Argues that the ME version subordinates love to
   engin or *gin*, so the result is an "entertaining account of an extended exercise in wit and ingenuity,"
   consisting largely of dupings, double-crossings, and
   duplicity more in the spirit of New Comedy than in
   that of the *roman idyllique.*

762.   Britton, G.C.   "Three Notes on 'Floris and Blancheflour.'"   *N&Q* ns 17 (1970): 366-367.

   Suggests readings for line 64 of Egerton MS as
   *Lady, you decide on behalf of both of us what is to
   be done,* and for lines 140-141 as accusing Blauncheflur of treason for bewitching his son.   Also rejects
   Smither's reading [581] for lines 741-742 and rein-
   states *heui* as the correct reading.

763. Geddes, Sharon S. "The Middle English Poem of *Floriz and Blauncheflur* and the *Arabian Nights* Tale of "Ni'amah and Naomi": A Study in Parallels." *ESRS* 19.1 (1970): 14-24.

Suggests that the English poem has its roots in Oriental tales and notes the following parallels between the two tales: the couples are young when they marry, are reared as siblings, are educated together, are separated; the girl is sold into bondage; the young men receive help from wiser individuals, enter the harem in disguise, are conveyed to the wrong chamber, are befriended by a woman within the harem; the rulers forgive the lovers and sanction their reunion; and the faithful are rewarded.

764. Giacone, Roberto. "*Floris and Blauncheflur*: Critical Issues." *RSC1* 27 (1979): 395-405.

Summarizes scholarly opinion on the question of an Oriental source and the relationships of the various European versions of the poem and provides a tentative, up-to-date chronological arrangement of the versions.

765. Pelan, Margaret M. *Floire et Blancheflor: Édition du MS. 1447 du Fonds Francaise avec notes, variantes et glossaire.* Publications de la Faculté des Lettres de l'Université de Strasbourg 7. 2nd ed. Paris: Les Belles Lettres, 1956. *Floire et Blancheflor: Seconde Version: Édition du MS. 19152 du Fonds Francaise avec introduction, notes et glossaire.* Paris: Ophrys, [1975].

Discusses the relationship between the "roman idyllique" and "roman d'aventures" versions of the poem and suggests that the ME poem antedates the division of the French story into two versions.

766. Reiss, Edmund. "Symbolic Detail in Medieval Narrative: *Floris and Blancheflour*." *PLL* 7 (1971): 339-350.

Argues that symbolic details such as floral references, colors, the garden, and the chess game all function to relate the characters' love to the Christian concept of charity as well as the hero's journey

767.   Wentersdorf, Karl P. "Iconographic Elements in *Floris and Blancheflour*." *AnM* 20 (1981): 76-96.

Stresses the ambiguous nature of the imagery, including the gold cup with its scenes depicting the cause of the Trojan War and the passion of Paris and Helen, which point to destructive, passionate love; the carbuncle as an ancient symbol of love; the chess game's connection with traditions dealing with courtly love as well as general life and sin; and flowers as a symbol of erotic passion. These elements together seem to create an atmosphere of youthful and passionate, sensual love.

SEE ALSO items 11 (52-53), 16, 67 (191-192, 243-244, 249-250), 135, 174, 413, 419, 430, 504 (23-24), 556, 570, 578.

Editions:

768. Anderson, Robert. *The Works of the British Poets*. 13 vols. London: John & Arthur Arch, 1795. 1: 203-217.

769. Bell, John. *Poetical Works of Chaucer*. Vol. 6 of *The Poets of Great Britain*. 108 vols. Edinburgh: Apollo P, 1777-1782. 109 vols. London, 1777-1787.

770. Bell, Robert. *Poetical Works of Geoffrey Chaucer*. 8 vols. London: Griffin, 1854. Rev. W.W. Skeat. London, 1885. 1: 238-267.

771. Chalmers, Alexander. *The Works of the English Poets, from Chaucer to Cowper*. 21 vols. London: J. Johnson, 1810. 1: 607-623.

   Text is reprinted from Urry [777].

772. Daniel, Neil. "*The Tale of Gamelyn*: A New Edition." *DA* 28 (1967): 2241A-2242A. Indiana U.

   Based on a complete collation of all twenty-five manuscripts with critical apparatus.

586. French and Hale. 209-235.

773. Furnivall, Frederick J. *The Ellesmere MS of Chaucer's Canterbury Tales*. Chaucer Society Publications 6.1, ser. 1. London: Trübner, 1868.

"The Spurious Tale of Gamelyn" appears in Appendix to Group A (Royal MS 18.C.2.).

774. Morris, Richard. *The Poetical Works of Geoffrey Chaucer*. 6 vols. London: George Bell, 1891-1893. 2: 138-169.

614. Sands. 154-181.

Reprint of French and Hale [586] with regularized orthography.

775. Skeat, Walter W. *The Tale of Gamelyn*. 1884. 2nd ed. Oxford: Clarendon P, 1893. Rpt. New Rochelle, NY: Elston P, 1901; [Folcroft, PA]: Folcroft Library Editions, 1971.

Edition of MSS Harley 7334 and 1758, Corpus Christi Oxford 198, Lansdowne, Petworth, Royal 18, and Sloane 1685.

776. ------. *The Complete Works of Geoffrey Chaucer*. 6 vols. Oxford: Clarendon P, 1894. 3: 399-405; 4: 645-667; 5: 477-489; 6: 347-358.

Contains introduction, text, notes, and glossary.

777. Urry, J. *The Canterbury Tales of Chaucer, Modernis'd by Several Hands*. 3 vols. London, 1741. 2: 9-96.

Boyse prepared the text, called "Gamelyn or, The Cook's Tale." According to Skeat [775], this is "a worthless text, with capricious alterations."

778. Wright, Thomas. *The Canterbury Tales of Geoffrey Chaucer*. 3 vols. Percy Society 24-26. London: Richards, 1847-1851. 1: 176-201.

Criticism:

779. Coggeshall, John M. "Champion of the Poor: The Out-

law as a Formalized Expression of Peasant Alienation." *SFQ* 44 (1980): 23-58.

In the section under "England," the author discusses *Gamelyn* as the first known outlaw legend in England, one which paints an unsavory picture of the
corruption of justice. Argues that Gamelyn is no
social revolutionary, only a hero trying to reinstate
the *status quo*; Also discusses *Gest of Robin Hood* in
terms of popular support for the oppressed and
antagonism toward the oppressor. Concludes that the
powerlessness and alienation of the English peasant
in the 14th and 15th centuries were expressed in the
structure and presentation of the heroes in these
works.

780. Daniel, Neil. "A Metrical and Stylistic Study of *The
Tale of Gamelyn*." Colquitt [25]. 19-32, 191-192.

Shows that the poem does not fit the prosodic system of either Chaucer or *Piers Plowman*, but falls
somewhere in between, partaking of both, with the
distribution of stress more important than the number of syllables.

781. Kaeuper, Richard W. "An Historian's Reading of *The
Tale of Gamelyn*." *MAE* 52 (1983): 51-62.

After sifting through thousands of petitions
against injustice sent to the crown, the author
argues that this poem faithfully mirrors contemporary
practice and attitudes regarding law and order.

782. Menkin, Edward Z. "Comic Irony and the Sense of Two
Audiences in the *Tale of Gamelyn*." *Thoth* 10 (1969):
41-53.

Interprets the poem as a conscious effort to address two distinct audiences, the bourgeois and
courtly, which results in an artful irony through the
"juxtaposition and satirization of both sets of
values."

783. Pickles, J.D. "*The Tale of Gamelyn*." *TGB* 18 (1967-

68): 295. M.A., Birmingham U.

784.   Rogers, Franklin R.   "The *Tale of Gamelyn* and the
        Editing of the *Canterbury Tales*."   *JEGP* 58 (1959):
        49-59.

        Argues that a study of *Gamelyn* reveals at least in
        one instance the nature of the relationship between
        the ancestor of group C and that of group A of the
        Canterbury Tales and explains the editorial liberties
        taken by the copyist-editor of MS Harley 7334.

785.   Ruthrof, Horst G.   "The Dialectic of Agression and
        Reconciliation in *The Tale of Gamelyn*, Thomas Lodge's
        Rosalynde and Shakespeare's *As You Like It*."   *UCTSE* 4
        (1973): 1-15.

        Views *As You Like It* as a reintroduction of the
        spirit of correction and reconciliation, a spirit
        inherent in *Gamelyn*'s structure of dialectical pat-
        terns, but lost in *Rosalynde*, which does, however,
        retain elements of aggression and violence from its
        source.

786.   Swanton, M.J.   "'A Ram and a Ring,' *Gamelyn* 172 et
        seq."   *ELN* 20.3 (1983): 8-10.

        Believes that there is a point of traditional
        reference behind this phrase; the ram was the custo-
        mary prize for wrestling contests, but was set upon a
        pole.   The ring was a circular brace, possibly a
        cartwheel, over which the ram could be tied.

SEE ALSO items 110, 166, 413, 414, 503, 511 (78-94), 540,
548, 573, 805 (70-74), 814.

Editions:

787. Furnivall, Frederick J. *A Royal Historie of the Ex-
cellent Knight Generides.* Roxburghe Club 85. London, 1865. Rpt. New York: Burt Franklin, 1971.

   Text is edited from a manuscript once belonging to
   John Tollemache, MP, now known as the Helmingham MS,
   as well as from early printed fragments.

788. Wright, W. Aldis. *Generydes, A Romance in Seven-Line
Stanzas.* EETSOS 55, 70. London: Trübner, 1873,
1878. Rpt. as one volume, Millwood, NY: Kraus, 1973.

   Text is from MS Trinity Cambridge 0.5.2.

Criticism:

789. Pearsall, Derek. "*The Assembly of Ladies* and *Generydes.*" *RES* ns 12 (1961): 229-237.

   Suggests the possibility of common authorship based
   on internal evidence such as extensive line parallels; distinctive use of rhyming tags, especially
   certayn and *wise*; handling of the line and stanza;
   partiality for dialogue; and a strong gnomic and
   proverbial strain in both.

790. ------. "Notes on the Manuscript of 'Generydes.'"
Library 5th ser. 16 (1961): 205-210.

   Describes the fourteen coats of arms decorating the
   margins of the manuscript pages and discusses possible dating and the connections between the Knevets

and Thwaites.

SEE ALSO items 53 (188-189, 235-236), 413, 556, 573, 578.

A GEST OF ROBIN HOOD

Editions:

580. Beattie. 197-200.

583a. Child. 5: 42-123.

791. Child, Francis James. *The English and Scottish Popular Ballads.* 10 vols. Boston: Houghton Miflin, 1882-1894. Rpt. in 5 vols. New York: Cooper Square, 1962. 5: 39-89.

Collates the seven early printed texts.

792. Dobson, R.B., and J. Taylor. *Rymes of Robyn Hood: An Introduction to the English Outlaw.* Pittsburgh: U of Pittsburgh P, 1976.

Includes an introduction (8-24, 30-37) and text (71-112).

588. Gray. 180-185, under "Ballads and Verse Romances."

793. Gutch, John Mathew. *A Lytell Geste of Robin Hode: With Other Ancient & Modern Ballads and Songs Relating to this Celebrated Yeoman.* 2 vols. London: Longman, Brown, Green, & Longmans, 1847. 1: 145-219.

794. Ritson, Joseph. *Robin Hood: A Collection of All the Ancient Poems, Songs and Ballads, Now Extant, Relative to that Celebrated English Outlaw.* London: Ad-

lard, 1823, a re-issue of 1795 2-vol. ed. Rpt. with
a new introduction by Jim Lees. Totowa, NJ: Rowman
& Littlefield, 1972.

Text of *Gest of Robin Hood*, 1: 1-59.

795.   ------. *Robin Hood: A Collection of All the Ancient
Poems, Songs and Ballads, Now Extant, Relative to
that Celebrated English Outlaw.* 2 vols. London: John
C. Nimmo, 1887. Printed from an 1832 ed., which was
edited and printed from Ritson's own annotated 1795
copy.

Text of "A Lytel Gest," 1: 1-80.

619.   Stevenson. 267-290.

Criticism:

796.   Aston, T.H. "Robin Hood." *P&P* 20 (1962): 7-9.

Agrees with Holt [804] that the Robin Hood ballads
do not reflect peasant discontent, but appealed to a
mixed audience of the gentry.

797.   Bellamy, John. *Robin Hood: An Historical Enquiry.*
Bloomington: Indiana UP, 1985.

Chapter: 1. The search and the searchers I, 1-15.
          2. The search and the searchers II, 16-
              37.
          3. The chronology of the *Gest*, 38-42.
                 Re-examines the possibility that
              Robin Hood was a chamber porter in
              the service of Edward II.
          4. The Sheriff of Nottingham, 43-57.
          5. The *Gest*, public order and crime, 58-
              72.
                 Concludes that the poet's concern
              was not with social evil, lack of
              governance, partial or corrupt jus-
              tice, the realities of criminal law
              administration, but rather with one

or two particular crimes and the
drama of those events.
6. Sir Richard at the Lee, 73-109.
7. Other 'personae' of the *Gest*, 110-
128.
   Notes the abbot of St. Mary's,
   York, the predatory creditor of
   Richard at the Lee, as well as possible historic sources for Little John
   and Scarlet.
8. Conclusions and additional considerations, 129-138.
   Suggests a good basis of historical
   fact in *Gest of Robin Hood*, since it
   was intended as much for political
   propaganda as for entertainment.
Bibliography and index, 139-150.

798. Bessinger, J.B., Jr. "*The Gest of Robin Hood* Revisited." Benson [8]. 355-369.

Mentions how various approaches—Biblical exegesis,
comparative mythology, folklore, and genre studies—
could be applied to this work and then suggests a
deliberate episodic interlace structure.

799. ------. "Robin Hood: Folklore and Historiography,
1377-1500." *TSL* 11 (1966): 61-69.

Briefly reviews what is known of the outlaw's origin, the growth of the legend, and sympathetic and
unsympathetic treatments of him in folklore and
ballads from 1377.

800. Coss, P.R. "Aspects of Cultural Diffusion in Medieval England: The Early Romances, Local Society and
Robin Hood." *P&P* 108 (1985): 35-79.

Raises serious questions about the genesis of ME
romance; the cultural channels between social classes; and the nature of the origin, transmission, and
social meaning of literature of social protest.
Reinterprets the probable demand for romance and the
possible lines of supply, doubting the Auchinleck

bookshop theory, because there was no strong mer-
cantile interest in romance, as evidenced by data
in wills and other documents. Points to local
society—gentry and clergy, not the aristocracy—as
the audience for early ME romance.

801.   Crook, David. "Some Further Evidence Concerning the
       Dating of the Origins of the Legend of Robin Hood."
       EHR 99 (1984): 530-534.

       Indicates the existence of some form of the legend
       by the mid-1200s.

802.   Harris, P. Valentine. *The Truth about Robin Hood: A
       Refutation of the Mythologists' Theories with New
       Evidence of the Hero's Actual Existence.* Mansfield,
       Eng.: Linneys, 1951. Rpt. and enl. in 1978.

       Discussion and extracts from *Gest of Robin Hood*,
       15-25, 50-51.

803.   Hilton, R.H.   "The Origins of Robin Hood."   *P&P* 14
       (1958): 30-44.

       Using *Gest of Robin Hood* for evidence, the author
       suggests a 13th-century origin of the story, which
       seems to be a by-product of the agrarian social
       struggle.

804.   Holt, J.C. "The Origins and Audience of the Ballads
       of Robin Hood." *P&P* 18 (1960): 89-110.

       Refutes Hilton [803], finding no exclusive class
       interests or agrarian discontent; argues instead that
       this was literature of the gentry.

805.   ------.   *Robin Hood.*   London: Thames and Hudson,
       1982.

       Chapter: 1. Prologue, 7-13.
                  2. The legend, 15-39.
                  3. Who was Robin Hood? 40-61.

4. The original Robin Hood, 62-81.
5. The physical setting, 83-108.
6. The audience, 109-158.
7. The later tradition, 159-186.
8. Epilogue, 187-190.
Notes, sources and further reading, list of illustrations, and index 191-208.

Gest of Robin Hood: 122-126, 144, 146, 147, 164, 166, 170, 171, 174, 176, 179, 184.

806. ------. "Robin Hood: Some Comments." *P&P* 19 (1961): 16-18.

Argues that *Gest of Robin Hood* must not be confused with composite ballads that matured over a long peri- od of time. Suggests that its topics reflect the ec- clesiastical and legal interests of the gentry.

807. Keen, Maurice. "Robin Hood—Peasant or Gentleman?" *P&P* 19 (1961): 7-15.

Refutes Holt [804] and sees a natural connection between the literary bias of the Robin Hood stories and contemporary protests of peasants against oppres- sion.

808. Kevelson, Roberta. *Inlaws/Outlaws. A Semiotics of Systemic Interaction: "Robin Hood" and the "King's Law."* Studies in Semiotics 9. Bloomington, IN: Re- search Center for Language and Semiotic Studies; Lisse, Neth: Peter de Ridder P, 1977.

Brings together two seemingly unrelated points of view to focus on the interaction between two social subsystems—poetics and jurisprudence—with specific references to *Gest of Robin Hood*, especially pp. 71- 80.

809. Maddicott, J.R. "The Birth and Setting of the Bal- lads of Robin Hood." *EHR* 93 (1978): 276-299.

Rebuts arguments placing *Gest of Robin Hood* in the

13th century. Finds the early 14th century more
likely, since possible historical identification of
Robin is no earlier than 1330s.

810. Oates, J.C.T.   *"The Little Gest of Robin Hood*:   A
      Note on the Pynson and Lettersnijder Editions." *SB*
      16 (1963): 3-8.

      Describes in detail the printed features of both
      editions and then suggests that the Lettersnijder
      edition is a reprint of the Pynson text.

811. Parker, David. "Popular Protest in 'A Gest of Robyn
      Hode.'" *MLQ* 32 (1971): 3-20.

      Argues that the poem is not an idealistic, but a
      protest poem, and that Robin's virtues demonstrate
      those of the rising class he represents.

812. Scattergood, V.J. "English Society III: Verses of
      Protest and Revolt." Chapter 10 of *Politics and
      Poetry in the Fifteenth Century*. History and Litera-
      ture in Blandford History Series. London: Blandford
      P, 1971. 350-377.

      Treats the protest in *Gest of Robin Hood* (362-367),
      not as ideologically based nor directed at the po-
      litical system, king, or aristocracy, but rather
      against unscrupulous landowners and corruptions in
      the law. Views the poem as the latent aspiration of
      the yeoman audience, with Robin Hood as an agent for
      moral good, rectifying abuses of the contemporary
      society.

813. Steckmesser, Kent L. "Robin Hood and the American
      Outlaw: A Note on History and Folklore." *JAF* 79
      (1966): 348-355.

      Argues that like most outlaws, Robin Hood was a
      champion of the socially and economically oppressed
      classes and a symbol of resistance to corrupt nobil-
      ity, more legend and folk tradition than history.
      Points to similarities between Robin Hood and Ameri-

can outlaws like Jesse James and Billy the Kid, who follow the same pattern as "friend of the poor," a folk tradition of generosity specific to *Gest of Robin Hood*.

814. Zellefrow, William Kenneth, Sr. "The Romance of Robin Hood." *DAI* 35 (1975): 5370A. U of Colorado.

Examines this poem, not as a ballad, but as a metrical romance, especially in terms of its narrative movement, motifs, and verse form. Compares this work to *King Horn*, *Havelok*, *Athelston*, and *Gamelyn*.

SEE ALSO items 406 (72-86), 503, 511 (99-115), 779.

GOLAGRUS AND GAWAIN [31]

Editions:

579. Amours. x-xx, 1-46, 249-287, 478-479.

580. Beattie. x, 7-48.

814a. Laing, David. *The Knightly Tale of Golagrus and Gawane, and Other Ancient Poem.* Edinburgh: W. Chepman and A. Myllar, 1827.

Contains the complete text of *Golagrus* plus fragments of *Gest of Robin Hood* and an abstract by Ellis of *Sir Eglamour.*

605. Madden. 131-183, 336-344.

610. Pinkerton. 3: 65-123.

619. Stevenson. 67-110.

815. Trautmann, Moritz. "Golagrus und Gawain." *Anglia* 2 (1879): 395-440.

Includes an introduction (395-409) and text (410-440) without any textual commentary.

Criticism:

816. Barron, W.R.J. "'Golagrus and Gawain': A Creative Redaction." *BBSIA* 26 (1974): 173-185.

Argues that the English author saw in his sources the potential of a genuinely human story and then created an organic whole that was highly original and positive.

817.   ------.   "*Golagrus and Gawain*: A Scot's Conception of Love and Honour."   Abstracts of papers delivered at the Seventh International Arthurian Congress, Aberdeen, 1963.   *BBSIA* 15 (1963): 131-132.

Argues that this version is so distinctive it cannot be called merely a redaction and then suggests that it marks the emergence of a distinctive Scottish literature.   This involves not just a rejection of the erotic, but a positive reinterpretation of chivalry in terms of personalities rather than codes of conduct.

818.   Jack, R.D.S.   "Arthur's Pilgrimage: A Study of Golagros and Gawane."   *SSL* 12 (1974): 3-20.

Explores the skilled artistry of this work, which uses a narrative form based on parallels, contrasts, and variations to test the nature of chivalry and the problem of fealty and freedom, which had a pointed political focus for contemporary Scotland.   Argues that the development of Arthur is crucial to the poem's meaning as he moves from an apparent to a real pilgrimage to distinguish between false and true chivalry.

819.   Ross, F.M.   "The Treatment of Romance Subjects in *Lancelot of the Laik*, *Golagrus and Gawain*, and *Rauf Coilyear*."   *TGB* 18 (1967-68): 316.   B.Litt., Oxford U.

SEE ALSO items 212, 224, 227, 231, 243, 263 (115-116), 269, 272 (115-117), 275, 282, 285, 298, 304, 307, 326, 328, 334, 337, 345, 348, 1276.

GRENE KNIGHT [26]

Editions:

583a. Child. 1: 35-57.

Only in 1857, not in later editions of this work.

589. Hales and Furnivall. 2: 56-77.

590. ------. 2: 120-137.

605. Madden. 224-242, 352-354.

SEE ALSO items 285, 326, 337, 723, 1276, 1374.

Editions:

820. Mills, Maldwyn, and Daniel Huws. *Fragments of an Early Fourteenth-Century Guy of Warwick*. Medium Aevum Monographs ns 4. Oxford: Blackwell, 1974.

Prints and describes the manuscripts, their provenance, and the textual affiliation of the two fragments of *Guy of Warwick*: British Library Additional 14408 and National Library of Wales 572 (a total of 2872 lines in both manuscripts).

821. Phillips, Sir Thomas. *Romance of Guy of Warwick; Fragment*. Middlehill, Eng: Gilmour, 1838.

822. Schleich, Gustav. *Guy of Warwick nach Coplands Druck*. Palaestra 139. Leipzig: Mayer & Müller, 1923.

823. T[urnbull], W.B.D.D. *The Romances of Sir Guy of Warwick, and Rembrun His Son*. Abbotsford Club 18. Edinburgh, 1840.

Texts are from the Auchinleck MS.

824. Zupitza, Julius. *The Romance of Guy of Warwick: The First or 14th-Century Version*. EETSES 42, 49, 59. London: Kegan Paul, Trench, Trübner, 1883-1891. Rpt. as one volume. London: Oxford UP, 1966.

Texts are from Auchinleck and Caius 107 MSS. No critical apparatus.

825.   ------. *The Romance of Guy of Warwick: The Second or*
        15th-Century Version. EETSES 25, 26. London: Trüb-
        ner, 1875, 1876. Rpt. as one vol. London: Oxford UP,
        1966.

        Text is from Cambridge University MS Ff.2.38.   In-
        cludes textual notes.

826.   ------. "Zur Literaturgeschichte des Guy von War-
        wick." *Sitzungberichte der Philosophisch-Histor-*
        ischen Classe der Kaiserlichen Akademie der Wissen-
        schaften 74 (1873): 623-668.

        Text is from MS Sloane 1044.

Criticism:

827.   Barron W.R.J. "The Penalties for Treason in Medieval
        Life and Literature." *JMH* 7 (1981): 187-202.

        Reviews and analyzes the legal, historical, and
        literary records of flaying. Further suggests that
        for French and English romance writers, the potency
        and value of flaying alive may have lain in its
        ability to evoke, in a single shocking image, the
        primitive significance of treason for an age of
        waning feudalism.

828.   Beck, Astrid Billes. "A Comparative Analysis of *Guy*
        of Warwick and *Engelhard* in Light of Their History
        and Contemporary Mode of Thought." *DAI* 45 (1984):
        1391A. U of Michigan.

        Compares the ME and MHG poems in terms of their
        scope, intentions, emphasis, cultural values, and
        their frame of reference in relation to other works
        of the same period. Concludes that both reflect
        shifting values and that the expiation of sin results
        in the ultimate testing of the hero through an Old
        Testament biblical motif.

829.   Dannenbaum, Susan Crane. "Guy of Warwick and the
        Question of Exemplary Romance." *Genre* 17 (1984):
        351-374.

Argues that "exemplary romances" are best understood, not as a generically separate group, but as
romances that validate secular concerns. Unlike
hagiographic works, these romances focus on the
centrality of the hero's power and value earthly life
and worldly achievement.

830.   Gaunt, J.L.   "An Unremarked Fictional Version of the
Legend of Guy of Warwick."   *AN&Q* 16 (1978): 103-104.

Points to the earliest surviving fictional version
of the Guy story in *The Heroick History of Guy Earle
of Warwick* published in 1656 by Humphrey Crouch.

831.   Klausner, David N.   "Didacticism and Drama in *Guy of
Warwick*."   *M&H* ns 6 (1975): 103-119.

Examines the changes made in the tale in its transition from saint's life to romance by pointing to
the latter's different didactic orientation, which
involves the audience's emotional and moral involve-
ment with the character, as well as an emphasis on
the real political setting.

832.   Mason, Emma.   "Legends of the Beauchamps' Ancestors:
The Use of Baronial Propaganda in Medieval England."
JMH 10 (1984): 25-40.

Argues that the Warwickshire branch of the family
generated propaganda culminating in *Guy of Warwick* to
romanticize the family's activities and to reinforce
widespread acceptance of their status, which they
tried to maintain in face of the powers of the mon-
archy and economic pressures. Points to the historical facts and L'Oilly-inspired material, upon which
the narrative is loosely based.

833.   Richmond, Velma Bourgeois.   "Chaucer's *The Book of
the Duchess* and *Guy of Warwick*."   *PLL* 11 (1975):
404-407.

Suggests that the poet's use of dramatic irony may
have influenced the manner of Chaucer's dreamer, especially in the deliberate and consciously obtuse

questioning.

834.   ------. *"Guy of Warwick*: A Medieval Thriller." *SAQ*
        73 (1974): 554-563.

        Draws parallels between a modern thriller and this
        medieval poem: both present a highly conventional
        world and a hero with essentially orthodox values,
        use disguise, stress action, and show the limitations
        of pursuing worldly triumphs.

835.   Siciliano, Francis Xavier, "Narrative Technique in
        Guy of Warwick." *DAI* 37 (1976): 3651A. U of Wiscon-
        sin-Madison.

        Argues that the poet uses repetition to order the
        work about a man's progress to independent decision
        after he realizes the inadequacies of the code of
        honor.

SEE ALSO items 5, 10, 79 (39-40, 59-62, 107-108), 80 (149-
193), 88, 89, 111 (172-173), 122, 161, 163 (220-227), 174,
181 (133-148), 386, 413 (45-68), 414, 419, 424, 504 (74ff),
540, 548, 578, 643, 713, 1175, 1478, 1539.

Editions:

581. Bennett and Smithers. 52-64 (text) and 288-297 (notes).

586. French and Hale. 73-176.

586a. Garbáty. 181-253.

836. Holthausen, F. *Havelok*. Old and Middle English Texts 1. London: Sampson Low Marston & Cie, 1901.

837. Madden, Sir Frederic. *The Ancient English Romance of Havelok the Dane*. Roxburghe Club. London, 1828.

608. Morris. 1: 222-236, 352.

Taken from Madden [837]. Re-ed. by Skeat for EETS.

614. Sands. 55-129.

Reprint of French and Hale [586] with regularized orthography.

616. Schmidt and Jacobs. 1: 7-15, 30-31, 37-121, 172-187.

Introduction, text, and commentary.

838. Sisam, Kenneth. *The Lay of Havelok The Dane*. Ox-

ford: Clarendon P, 1915.

A re-edited version of Skeat [839].

839.   Skeat, Walter W.   *The Lay of Havelok the Dane: Com-
       posed in The Reign of Edward I, About A.D. 1280.*
       EETSES 4.   London: Trübner, 1868.   Corr. and rpt.
       1889. Re-ed. Oxford, 1902. Rpt. Millwood, NY: Kraus,
       1973.

       A re-edited version of Madden [837].

       Criticism:

840.   Bennett, P.E.   "Havelok and Rainoart."   *Folklore* 90
       (1979): 77-90.

       Examines parallels between the two heroes: both
       are exiled princes forced to work as scullions, are
       set adrift at sea and encounter pirates, wage war
       against their countrymen, acquire a relationship by
       marriage with the king in whose country they reside,
       serve intrinsically evil kings, and are remarkable
       for their size and physical strength.   Also suggests
       that the Rainoart stories may have influenced the
       changes in the Havelok story.

841.   Britton, G.C.   "A Note on the Word *Thing* in *Havelok
       the Dane.*" *NM* 61 (1960): 77-79.

       Challenges the reading of the word as a singular
       and defends the manuscript reading as a weak plural.

842.   ------.   "*N*-Plurals in the Nouns of *Havelok the
       Dane.*" *NM* 60 (1959): 175-179.

       Discusses the special circumstances in which n-plu-
       rals occur and offers possible explanations for the
       form (most often the need for rhyme).

843.   Delaney, Sheila, and Vahan Ishkanian.   "Theocratic
       and Contractual Kingship in *Havelok the Dane.*" *ZAA*
       22 (1974): 290-302.

The authors see the poem as a literary expression of the concern with the nature of kingship, which dominated English public life in the 13th century. Like contemporary treatments, the poem presents kingship as a compromise between the divinely ordained royal prerogative and the practical limitations imposed by social necessity.

844. Dunn, Charles W. "Havelok and Anlaf Cuaran." *Franciplegius: Medieval and Linguistic Studies in Honor of Francis Peabody Magoun, Jr.* Ed. Jess B. Bessinger, Jr., and Robert P. Creed. New York: NYU P, 1965. 244-249.

Clarifies difficulties raised by G. Storm's identification of Havelok with the Viking king Anlaf Cuaran and claims that Havelok is entirely unrelated to any form of the name Anlaf; at most, it is a temporary loan of the nickname.

845. Gadomski, Kenneth E. "Narrative Style in *King Horn* and *Havelok The Dane*." *JNT* 15 (1985): 133-145.

Examines the differences in narrative style between the two poems not accounted for by date or locale but by the role each poet intended for his audience. Concludes that *King Horn* seems impersonal and objective because there is no overt sense of narrator, but that a narrative voice is cleverly hidden within the action and dialogue; the *Havelok*-narrator, on the other hand, elicits audience participation by telling, not showing, and by other devices such as a changing point of view.

846. Ganim, John. "Community and Consciousness in Early Middle English Romance." Ganim [38]. 16-54, 158-161.

Concentrates on *Havelok* and *King Horn* in a discussion of the relationship between the poets and their audiences and the stories. Sees the poets as desperately searching for a form that would express important historical issues despite a language that was neither forceful nor subtle enough to express content. Also suggests that the poets, in collusion

with their audiences, accepted the limitations of
their stories, rather than exploring the possibilities.

847.   Green, Richard Firth. "Arcite at Court." *ELN* 18
       (1981): 251-257.

       Compares the long digression about the page's
       duties in the *Knight's Tale* to *Havelok*, in which a
       nobleman is reduced to menial service. Suggests that
       Havelok presents a more convincing picture of the
       realities of court life than the *Knight's Tale*,
       because Chaucer seems to be idealizing the Arthurian
       court in order to point out the venality and oppor-
       tunism of court life in his own day.

848.   Halverson, John. "*Havelok the Dane* and Society."
       ChauR 6 (1971): 142-151.

       Believes that the English writer displays familiar-
       ity with peasant life and advocates "middle-class"
       values toward work, marriage, and children. These
       attitudes suggest the political, moral, and histor-
       ical situation of 14th-century England that antici-
       pates the Peasants' Rebellion.

849.   Hanning, Robert W. "*Havelok the Dane*: Structure,
       Symbols, Meaning." *SP* 64 (1967): 586-605.

       Argues that the progression from loss of power to
       recovery of power is clearly marked in the structure
       of the poem by a symbolic beginning and repetition of
       a key line about homage (11. 484 & 2172), and that
       the other central theme from helpless youth to capa-
       ble adult is represented by a series of repeating
       symbols: feasts, feats of strength, and Havelok's
       birth or destiny marks.

850.   Haskin, Dayton, S.J. "Food, Clothing and Kingship in
       Havelok the Dane." *ABR* 24 (1973): 204-213.

       Discusses the poem as a portrait of an ideal earth-
       ly king that draws on traditional descriptions of
       Christ as king and judge, who rewards benefactors and

punishes malefactors, as in the Matthean portrait.

851. Hench, Atcheson L. "'Game' in *Havelok* 996." *ChauR* 7 (1973): 297-298.

Discovers two 16th-century examples of *game* meaning "rabbit warren" and uses them to clarify the line.

852. Hirsh, John C. "*Havelok* 2933: A Problem in Medieval Literary History." *NM* 78 (1979): 339-347.

Identifies the scribal error in MS Laud 108 as a result of eye-skip, not as evidence for the minstrel exemplar theory, which is based on the prevailing romantic conception of the minstrel's role in late medieval England, for which there is no external evidence.

853. Izzard, E.R. "Aspects of the Style of *Havelok the Dane*." *TGB* 21 (1970-71): 321. M.Litt., Aberdeen U.

854. Jack, George B. "The Date of *Havelok*." *Anglia* 95 (1977): 20-33.

Finds Meyer-Lindenberg's thesis [858] implausible, especially the parallels to Arthur of Brittany. Suggests that the story more likely conforms to basic story patterns from folklore motifs in other romances such as *William of Palerne* and *King Horn*, and that the most precise date can be fixed in the late 13th century, circa 1272.

855. Kretzschmar, William A., Jr. "Three Stories in Search of an Author: The Narrative Versions of Havelok." *Allegorica* 5 (1980): 21-97.

Includes a discussion of the differences between the ME and the two AN versions of the Havelok story, an analysis of arguments for the interrelationship of all texts, and a translation of *Lai d'Haveloc*.

856. McCreesh, Bernadine. "The Problem of Goldborough's

Age in 'The Lay of Havelok the Dane.'" *N&Q* ns 19 (1972): 442.

The poem's discrepancy concerning Goldborough's age as both twelve (1. 192) and twenty (1. 1259) can be explained by AN laws; a girl could legally marry at age twelve, but if still single by age twenty-one, she could alienate her lands, goods, and chattel and be her own master. Thus Godrich was obliged to marry her so she would be ineligible to rule, because she had assumed her husband's status as villein.

857. McIntosh, Angus. "The Language of the Extant Versions of *Havelok the Dane.*" *MAE* 45 (1976): 36-49.

After a detailed examination of the linguistic evidence, the author suggests that Laud MS 108 was written in ME characteristic of Norfolk, rather than Lincolnshire, and that the fragments preserved in Additional MS 4407 are dialectically, though not textually close to the Laud MS.

858. Meyer-Lindenberg, Herlint. "Zur Datierung des *Havelok.*" *Anglia* 86 (1968): 89-112.

Argues that the poem must have been composed between 1206 and 1216 and thus was a source of the French *Lai d'Haveloc*.

859. Miller, B.D.H.   "A Primitive Punishment: Further Instances." *N&Q* ns 10 (1963): 366-368.

The punishment of mounting offenders nose to tail on a horse, donkey, or camel is cited in the following ME romances: *Havelok*, 2449-2452; *King Alexander*, 4699-4710; and *Lyfe of Ipomydon*, 1493-1498.

860. Mills, M.   "Havelok and the Brutal Fisherman." *MAE* 36 (1967): 219-230.

Suggests that the author's treatment of Grim's inconsistent behavior may be due less to originality than to the established character-type of the "brutal fisherman" as depicted in Hartmann von Aue's *Gregor-*

ius and Wirnt von Gravenberc's *Wigalois*.

861. ------. "Havelok's Return." *MAE* 45 (1976): 20-35.

Considers the return of Havelok (ll. 1625-2187), despite its shortcomings in terms of narrative economy and logic, as a surprisingly consistent view of human life, a life filled with the unexpected and uncertainties in which the "instinctive and altruistic behaviour of men of good will" is the only guide to truth.

862. Mitchell, Bruce. "The Couplet System in 'Havelok the Dane.'" *N&Q* ns 10 (1963): 405-406.

Argues that the couplet system in ME is not inviolate; thus sense can be restored to the hiatus between lines 546 and 547 by inserting the line from Cambridge Additional MS 4407, resulting in a triplet on -*aste*; by inserting the line but changing *finaste* to *grede* at the end of line 548, resulting in five lines rhyming in -*ede*; or by reading *te* instead of *led* in line 552, resulting in a triplet on -*e* in lines 552-554.

863. [Osselton, N.E.] "*Havelok*, Lines 1100-1102." *N&Q* ns 3 (1956): 236.

Suggests emending *shop* to *swok* in line 1101 and adding *that* to line 1100 as a class-noun in reference to Judas.

864. Radcliffe, Clara Jane. "The Double: A Study of Narrative Technique in Two Early Middle English Metrical Romances, *King Horn* and *Havelok the Dane*." *DAI* 35 (1975): 6677A. SUNY at Buffalo.

Examines echoic, contrastive, and completive doubles of both character and plot, as well as the chain, block, and lineal constructs in the two romances.

865. Reiss, Edmund. "*Havelok the Dane* and Norse Mythol-

ogy." *MLQ* 27 (1966): 115-124.

Suggests that Grim may be related to the great
Norse god Odin, who, disguised as a poor cotter named
Grimnir, rescues two youths from the sea, as told in
the initial prose episode of the *Grimnismal* in the
Poetic Edda.

866. Signer, Deborah A. "A Note on *Havelok the Dane*."
      Lydgate Newsletter 1.1 (1972): 14-15.

Views the recurring (although slightly varying)
couplet "He was þe wihtest man at nede/þat þurte
riden on ani stede" (11. 9-10, 25-26, 87-88, 1970-
1971, and 2894-2895) as a structural device that
functions as a leitmotif reflecting moral and political change.

867. Smithers, G.V. "Four Notes on *Havelok*." Benskin and
      Samuels [538]. 191-210.

Briefly discusses four problems: lines 263-269 with
Dover and Roxburgh as terminal points on a route
lying along one of the four royal roads; line 1317
with *trone*, not meaning "throne," but "firmament" or
"heaven"; lines 2549-2574 as a literary version of a
writ of military summons; and lines 2611-2613 with
late as a corruption of *lace*, "to lace up," with
rithe an adverb meaning "correctly."

868. ------. "The Scansion of *Havelok* and the Use of ME
      -*en* and -*e* in *Havelok* and by Chaucer." *Middle Eng-*
      lish Studies Presented to Norman Davis in Honour of
      his Seventieth Birthday. Ed. Douglas Gray and E.G.
      Stanley. Oxford: Clarendon P, 1983. 195-234.

Deduces from detailed evidence from the poem that
forms without final -*e* in words to which it was historically proper first evolved in phonetic contexts
where elision occurred and then in contexts (when
followed by an initial consonant) in which apocope
operated. Once the two forms of the word had emerged, the choice of one over the other was evidently
a matter of rhythm, in verse at least, to avoid two
successive on-beats. Argues that these findings in

Havelok apply to Chaucer's poetry and clarify problems in Chaucer's verse.

869. Staines, David. *"Havelok the Dane*: a Thirteenth-Century Handbook for Princes." *Speculum* 51 (1976): 602-623.

Argues that the poet, seeing parallels between the worlds of Havelok and Edward I, adapted and expanded his sources to create a portrait of an ideal king and a mirror for princes from the perspective of the lower classes.

870. Vause, Deborah Noble. "Figurative Language in *Havelok the Dane.*" *DAI* 43 (1983): 3607A. U of North Carolina at Chapel Hill.

By examining the schemes, tropes, metaplasms, and other figures found in the poem, the author finds the text is stylistically sophisticated and a reflection of the artist's rhetorical expertise.

871. Weiss, Judith. "Structure and Characterisation in *Havelok the Dane.*" *Speculum* 44 (1969): 247-257.

Argues that the *Havelok*-poet consciously expanded the original simple story to reflect his concerns with the problems and ideals of government, the relationship between ruler and people, and a feeling for the land itself, and thus changed his conception of character to reflect this central theme of a country and its rulers.

SEE ALSO items 5, 11 (50-52), 16, 38 (16-37, 47-54), 93 (191-200), 111 (88-89), 135, 160, 161, 163 (26-27, 159-160, 161-172, 250-251), 166, 174, 181 (31-52), 412, 413 (26-44), 424, 462, 536, 540, 548, 551, 567, 570, 573, 578, 713, 814, 911.

HERE BEGYNNETH THE LYFE OF
JOSEPH OF ARMATHIA and
A PRAYSING TO JOSEPH [42]

Edition:

617. Skeat. 37-49 (11. 1-400 of *Here Begynneth)* and 50-52
      (11. 401-456 of *A Praysyng)*, 72-74 (notes), and 97-
      100 (glossarial index).

SEE ALSO item 337.

Edition:

872. Furnivall, Frederick J. *The History of the Holy Grail by Henry Lovelich.* EETSES 20 (1874), 24 (1875), 28 (1877), and 30 (1878). Vols. 20 and 24 rpt. as one vol.; vols 28, 30, and 95 [872a] rpt. as one vol. Millwood, NY: Kraus, 1973.

872a. Kempe, Dorothy. *The Legend of the Holy Grail: Its Sources, Character and Development.* EETSES 95. London: Kegan Paul, Trench, Trübner, 1905. Rpt. with vols. 28, 30 [872] as one vol. Millwood, NY: Kraus, 1973.

The introduction to Furnivall's text [872].

SEE ALSO item 337.

HORN CHILD [2]

Editions:

873. Caro, J. *Horn Childe and Maiden Rimnild, eine Unter-
suchung.* Breslau, 1886.

874. ------. "Kleine Publicationen aus der Auchinleck-Hs.
X. Horne Childe and Maiden Rimnild." *EStn* 12 (1899):
323-366.

   A revised edition of [873]; introduction (323-350)
   and text (351-366).

591. Hall. 179-192 (text), 193-238 (glossary).

606. Michel. 341-389.

611. Ritson. 3: 282-320.

SEE ALSO items 163, 548.

IPOMADON [102]
Ipomadon (tail-rhyme)
The Lyfe of Ipomydon (couplets)

Editions:

875. Andersen, David Michael. "An Edition of the Middle English *Ipomadon*." *DA* 29 (1969): 3968A-3969A. U of California, Davis.

Based on Chetham MS 8009 with critical apparatus. Dates the poem after 1350 in the northeast Midlands.

876. Ikegami, Tadahiro. *The Lyfe of Ipomydon*. Vol. 1: Text and Introduction. Seijo English Monographs 21. Tokyo: Seijo University, 1983.

Includes text from MS Harley 2252, textual apparatus, and introduction (which includes discussion of the language of the text, its provenance, and dating). Second volume containing commentary and glossary is forthcoming.

877. Kirschten, Walther. *Ueberlieferung und Sprache der mittelenglischen Romanze The Lyfe of Ipomydon*. Marburg: Friedrich, 1885.

Text from Wynkyn de Worde's *Bagford Ballads*, 54 lines.

878. Kölbing, Eugen. *Ipomedon in drei englischen Bearbeitungen*. Breslau: Köbner, 1889.

Includes the three versions: stanzaic (3-253, 361-453), couplet (257-319, 454-461), and prose (323-358, 462-464).

879.   Roberts, Valerie Stewart Crozier. "An Edition of the
       Middle English Romance: *The Lyfe of Ipomydon*." *DAI*
       35 (1975): 4453A. U of Michigan.

       Contains the text from the MS Harley 2252 with
       commentary, glossary, and notes.

622.   Weber. 1: li-lii; 2: 281-365, 478; 3: 361-364.

       Text of couplet version is from MS Harley 2252.

Fragments:

880.   Bülbring, Karl D. "Vier Neue Alexanderbruchstücke."
       EStn 13 (1889): 153-155.

       This appendix includes two fragments (two leaves)
       of *Ipomadon* in the same manuscript in the British
       Museum as the Alexander fragments. Prints the five-
       stanza text of the first leaf and four stanzas of a
       battle scene from the second leaf.

Criticism:

881.   Bjorklund, Victoria Anne Baum. "The Art of Transla-
       tion in *Ipomadon*: From Anglo-Norman to Middle Eng-
       lish." *DAI* 39 (1978): 1580A. Yale U.

       Concludes that in translating, the ME poet pattern-
       ed choices of units in accordance with a principle of
       equivalent effect, infusing his tale with the conven-
       tions and values of his own 14th-century culture.

882.   Cowen, J.M. "'In Krystes dere blessyng and myn'—
       'Pearl' 1208." *N&Q* ns 25 (1978): 203.

       Finds in *Ipomadon*, 7095-7096, another exception in
       ME in which this phrase is not used by a parent re-
       ferring to a child.

883.   Meale, Carol M. "The Middle English Romance of
       Ipomedon: A Late Medieval Mirror for Princes and
       Merchants." *Reading Medieval Studies* 10 (1984):

136-191.

Tests the validity of the assumption that there is a direct correlation between style, content, and audience of a given work by examining in detail the manuscripts of the three versions of the Ipomadon story. Concludes that all three manuscripts, roughly of the same date, were meant as reading texts, not for oral performance, and that their appeal lay in the didactic emphasis on matters of courtesy; thus the verse and prose versions became accessible as mirrors of behavior for merchants and the increasingly literate middle class.

884. ------. "Wynkyn de Worde's Setting-Copy for *Ipomy-don.*" *SB* 35 (1982): 156-171.

Gives evidence that Harley MS 2252 is the copy for de Worde's *Bagford Ballads* edition and explores the connection of the manuscript with John Colyns, who may have instigated the publication of *Ipomydon* and then loaned his copy to de Worde.

SEE ALSO items 57 (85-96), 163 (58-68, 272-273), 224, 413 (45-68), 419, 424, 504 (161-162), 556, 578, 859.

JEASTE OF SIR GAWAYNE [36]

Edition:

605. Madden. 207-223, 348-351.

SEE ALSO items 276, 326, 337, 1276.

JOSEPH OF ARIMATHIE [40]

Editions:

885. Lawton, David A. *Joseph of Arimathea: A Critical Edition*. Garland Medieval Texts 5. New York: Garland, 1983.

   Edits the single extant manuscript, Bodleian Poet A.1, with extensive introduction, annotation, and glossary.

617. Skeat. 1-23, 53-66, 75-96.

   Includes text, notes, and glossarial index.

Criticism:

886. Barron, W.R.J. "*Joseph of Arimathie* and the *Estoire del Saint Graal*." *MAE* 33 (1964): 184-194.

   Examines nine specific incidents in *Joseph of Arimathie*, with variant readings in French versions, and considers the long French redaction the most likely source of the English story.

887. Kjellmer, Göran. "Concerning Thirst in Battle and Dog-Riding: Notes on Two Middle English Passages." *SN* 41 (1969): 162-165.

   Offers emendations for better sense in two works: *Joseph of Arimathie*, 551-554, in which *afurst* could be a variant of *a-fyrht* (frightened), but more likely a variant of *afirst*, meaning "at first." In *Sir Firumbras*, 4243-4246, a change of *lede þan* to *ledeþ an* improves the passage.

888. Lagorio, Valerie M. "The Evolving Legend of St.
      Joseph of Glastonbury." *Speculum* 46 (1971): 209-231.

      Traces the slowly evolving legend from the pur-
      ported discovery of Arthur's body by Glastonbury
      monks in 1191 to the recognition of Joseph of Arima-
      thie as a Glastonbury saint in the 15th century.
      Also assesses the factors that promoted the joining
      of Joseph with Arthur in Glastonbury.

889. ------. "The *Joseph of Arimathie*: English Hagiogra-
      phy in Transition." *M&H* ns 6 (1975): 91-101.

      Contrasts the ME and OF versions and finds that the
      former de-emphasizes the Holy Grail, consistently
      omits links with the Grail's Arthurian destiny,
      praises Joseph in his legendary role of apostle and
      preserver of the Precious Blood, and establishes a
      pattern for subsequent English encomia to Joseph.

890. ------. "The Legend of Joseph of Arimathea in Middle
      English Literature." *DA* 27 (1967): 3431A. Stanford
      U.

      Explores four phases of the legend's growth: Joseph
      legends from Scripture and ecclesiastical accretions,
      Glastonbury's role in fusing the apocryphal Joseph
      with the composite Cymric saint, non-Grail litera-
      ture, and later English grail romance.

891. ------. "St. Joseph of Arimathea and Glastonbury: A
      'New' Pan-Brittonic Saint." *Trivium* 6 (1971): 59-69.

      Explores the interrelationship between ecclesias-
      tical legends concerning the pan-Brittonic saints and
      the Arthurian romances and examines four categories
      in hagiography that influence *estoire*: Royal or Noble
      Origins, Saintly Temperament, Ecclesiastical Organi-
      zation and Activities, and the Warrior Saints.

SEE ALSO items 34 (59-61), 212, 222, 225, 239, 263 (22-25),
273 (36-39, 40-41, 52-57, 246-248, 305-306, 309-310, 343-
346), 300, 315, 323 (137-142, 224-227, 229-233, 235-247,
259-269, 274-275), 337, 343 (170-171).

KING ALEXANDER [64]

See *Lyfe of Alisaunder.*

KING HORN [1]

Editions:

892. Allen, Rosamund. *King Horn: An Edition Based on Cambridge University Library MS Gg.4.27(2)*. Garland Medieval Texts 7. New York: Garland, 1984.

Follows Kane and Donaldson's method of textual analysis for this poem and attempts to identify originality among the readings of the three manuscripts; includes an introduction explaining analytical method, textual notes, and glossary. Copy text is Gg.4.27(2) with all variants listed.

893. Church, L.B. "An Edition from the Middle English Manuscripts of the Medieval Romance *King Horn*." *TGB* 31 (1982): 283. M.Litt., Lancaster U.

584. Dunn and Byrnes. 114-149.

894. French, Walter Hoyt. *Essays on King Horn*. Cornell Studies in English 30. Ithaca: Cornell UP, 1940. 45-102, 153-204.

A reconstructed text with Harley MS 2253 preferred and extensive textual notes to the Hall edition [591].

586. French and Hale. 25-70.

Reprints Hall's edition [591] with some lines added from Laud MS wherever the Cambridge is defective.

586a.   Garbáty.   142-180.

591.   Hall.   vii-lvi, 1-89, 91-177, 193-238.

       Introduction including meter and story, parallel
       texts of the three manuscripts, notes, and glossary.

895.   Horstmann, [C].   "King Horn nach Ms. Laud 108."
       Archiv 50 (1872): 39-58.

       Edits Laud MS 108 for the first time.

603.   Lumby.   1-50, 115-120.

       Text is from Cambridge University Gg. 4.27.2, with
       notes.

604.   McKnight.   vii-xxix, 1-69, 137-146.

       Text is edited from MSS Cambridge University
       Gg.4.27.2 and Laud Misc. 108 in parallel text form.
       Harley MS 2253 is printed in full in footnote format,
       with introduction and notes.

896.   Mätzner, Eduard.   *Altenglische Sprachproben: Nebst
       Einem Wörterbuch Unter Mitwirkung von Karl Goldbeck.*
       2 vols.   Berlin: Weidmannsche, 1867, 1891.   1: 207-
       231.

       Based text on Lumby's edition [603] without seeing
       the manuscript; includes extensive notes.

606.   Michel.   lxii-lxiv, 259-338.

       First edition of MS Gg.4.27.   The text appears
       under the title "The Geste of Kyng Horn"; with intro-
       duction.

608.   Morris.   1: 237-286, 352-358.

611. Ritson. 1: xcv-xcvi, xcviii-c; 2: 91-155; 3: 221, 264-281, 439-440.

614. Sands. 15-54.

   Reprint of French and Hale [586] with regularized orthography.

897. Wissmann, Theodor. *King Horn: Untersuchungen zur Mittelenglischen Sprach- und Litteraturgeschichte.* Quellen und Forschungen zur Sprach- und Culturgeschichte der germanischen Völker 16. Strassburg: Trübner, 1876.

   An introduction to his text [898].

898. ------. *Das Lied von King Horn.* Quellen und Forschungen zur Sprach- und Culturgeschichte der germanischen Völker 45. Strassburg: Trübner, 1881.

   First critical edition of the poem. Uses Gg.4.27.2 MS as text, but relies on Michel [606] and Lumby [603] for its readings. Uses Horstmann [895] for Laud MS 108 and Ritson [611] for Harley 2153.

899. ------. "Studien zu King Horn." *Anglia* 4 (1881): 342-400.

   Contains a supplementary study of the poem.

Criticism:

900. Allen, R.S. "Some Textual Cruces in *King Horn*." *MAE* 53 (1984): 73-77.

   Briefly discusses examples of the reworking of the original text by scribes or jongleurs who introduced variation and sometimes poor sense; examples in lines 369-370 and 1105-1106, 385-386 and 653-654, 454, 753-754 and 1011-1012, 1137-1138, and 1310.

901. Arens, Werner. *Die anglonormannische und die englis-*

chen Fassungen des Hornstoffer: Ein historischgenet-
ischer Vergleich. Studien zur Anglistik. Frankfurt
am Main: Akademische Verlagsgesellschaft, 1973.

> Introduction, 1-28. Text and problems, methods.
> Chapter: 1. Place and structure as structural
> schema in Horn-works, 28-96.
> Suggests an axial symmetry of five
> parts in *King Horn.*
> 2. The time of composition of Horn, 97-
> 137.
> 3. Characterization in the Horn works,
> 138-181.
> Disputes allegorical readings of
> *King Horn.*
> 4. The central themes of each Horn work,
> 182-239.
> Views King Horn as the active
> lover.
> 5. Style and related matters, 240-287.
> Sees in *King Horn* a ballad-like
> epic.
> Conclusions, 288-298.
> English summary and bibliography, 299-320.

902. Christmann, Hans Helmut. "Über das Verhältnis zwis-
chen dem anglonormannischen und dem mittelenglischen
'Horn.'" *ZFSL* 70 (1960): 166-181.

> Divides his article into sections: the history of
> the problem of the relationship between the two
> versions and the lengthy comparison of AN and ME
> texts. Argues that a close comparison of the texts
> shows many clear parallels, indicating that the AN
> text is a possible source for the English version.
> Disproves arguments for the ME as source for the AN
> and considers the likelihood of a French source for
> both.

903. Dannenbaum, Susan. "'Fairer Bi One Ribbe/þane Eni
Man þat Libbe' (*King Horn*, C315-16)." *N&Q* ns 28
(1981): 116-117.

> Suggests that the puzzling expression refers to the
> perfection of Adam's and Christ's physical bodies.

904. Gellinek, Christian. *"The Romance of Horn*: A Structural Survey." *NM* 66 (1965): 330-333.

Outlines the tripartite structure of the AN version with its balanced double climax of winning wife and kingdom, which integrates the two main themes of wooing and exile/homecoming.

905. Gross, Laila. "Time in the Towneley Cycle, *King Horn, Sir Gawain and the Green Knight*, and Chaucer's *Troilus and Criseyde*." *DA* 29 (1969): 3097A. U of Toronto.

Argues that the continuity of the action in romance is provided by the hero, not the passage of time, and that although action occurs in short, carefully delineated scenes in time, there is no time in the intervals between scenes so there is little change or growth.

906. Hill, D.M. "An Interpretation of *King Horn*." *Anglia* 75 (1957): 157-172.

Views the poem not as a straightforward narrative, but as a mixture of symbol and nonsymbol, and examines the symbolic value of the fish and net as well as the characters of Modi, Fikenhild, and Aþulf as symbolic aspects of Horn himself, who is divided between Horn the fighter and lover.

907. Hols, Edith Jones. "Grammatical Roles of Three Sets of Prepositions in *Beowulf* and *King Horn*." *DAI* 31 (1971): 4748A. U of Iowa.

Examines the meanings and uses of *fram* and *of*, *mid*, and *on aet*.

908. Hurt, James R. "The Texts of *King Horn*." *JFI* 7 (1970): 47-59.

Reconsiders the critical and historical problem of the poem in light of oral-formulaic theory and offers sample evidence of the dense formulas and the structuring by themes, concluding that at some point in its history, this was an oral-formulaic poem.

909. Hynes-Berry, Mary. "Cohesion in *King Horn* and *Sir Orfeo.*" *Speculum* 50 (1975): 652-670.

Argues that despite superficial similarities, the two poems illustrate different kinds of interest in and perception of events and thus call for different kinds of responses; their different modes of cohesion are clarified by contrasting their presentation of events, narrative point of view, plot, and organizing structure.

910. Kealy, John Kieran, Jr. "The Horn Hero in Romance and Ballad Tradition." *DAI* 32 (1972): 6932A-6933A. Stanford U.

Focuses on the gradual disintegration of the total legend to ballads, with emphasis on episodes and the emergence of a popular, middle-class hero.

911. O'Brien, Timothy D. "Word Play in the Allegory of King Horn." *Allegorica* 7.2 (1982): 110-122.

Claims that this work is most accurately read as an allegory as defined by Maureen Quilligan [*The Language of Allegory* (Ithaca: Cornell UP, 1979)]. The essentials are the growth of the narrative out of word play, the function of action as a commentary upon words, and the dependence of the work's success on the active, self-conscious activity of its readers.

912. Pope, Mildred K. "The *Romance of Horn* and *King Horn.*" *MAE* 25 (1957): 164-167.

Suggests a common source for the AN and ME versions, points to divergent details in the two texts, and proposes features in the common source of both.

913. West, Henry S. *The Versification of King Horn.* Diss. Johns Hopkins U, 1899. Baltimore: Furst, 1907. Rpt. Folcroft, PA: Folcroft Library Editions, 1971.

Chapter: 1. The double descent of Modern English verse, the crux in Early Middle English, the 'Otfrid in England' controversy, 1-5.

2. The heart of the Middle English verse crux is *King Horn*, Schipper's 'Dreihebigkeit' of *King Horn*, the plausibility of Schipper's theory of the *Horn* verse, 6-11.

3. Schipper's "Dreihebigheit' is after all nothing but three-beat, his alleged corroborative text does not support his contention, 12-16.

4. Why not find in the *Horn* short line a two-stress rhythm?, how a free two-stress reading of the poem will afford a unifying rhythm, further analysis of *Horn* lines and couplets on a two-stress basis with wholly satisfying results, *King Horn* does not require, seems even to forbid, a three-beat scansion; and readily submits to a two-stress reading, 17-20.

5. Historic presumption favors finding in the *Horn* short line a two-stress rhythm, incomplete alliteration in *King Horn* does not disprove its claim of being in stress-verse, the alliteration in the *Horn* points to a two-stress reading of its lines, comparison of the *Horn* couplet with Middle English verse clearly in the national four-stress free-rhythm extablishes their metrical likeness, 21-48.

6. The one dissimilarity between the verse of *King Horn* and the later free-rhythm, the preservation of a recurring shorter line in the later free-rhythm not due to conservatism, the earlier lyric proves the shorter line in the cauda to be due to rime couée, comparison of *King Horn* and *The Luxury of Women*, how the native free-rhythm could be cast into rime couée without systematic alliteration, *King Horn* the natural outcome of Anglo-Saxon tendencies and its author's environment, 49-63.

7. The seven types of the *King Horn*
    verse, the *Horn* hypermetric lines,
    percentages of the several types,
    management of alliteration in *King
    Horn*, conclusion, 64-88.

Vita auctoris, 89-90.
Postscript, 91.

914. Ziegler, Georgianna. "Structural Repetition in *King
      Horn*." *NM* 81 (1980): 403-408.

Divides the work into four main sections: destruction, learning, initiation, and reconstruction, all
linked by sea voyages with recurring motifs such as
fights against pagans, the association of hunting
with love, and dreams; shows how repetitions in plot
structure build themes and weave matter with form.

SEE ALSO items 6, 11 (48-50), 16, 18 (64-66), 31, 38 (37-
54), 67 (120-121), 72, 93 (178-191), 105 (59-62), 110, 111
(137-138), 135, 161, 163 (48-56, 250-251), 166, 174, 411,
412, 413 (26-44), 414, 424, 430, 519, 547, 548, 551, 567,
570, 573, 578, 814, 845, 846, 854, 864, 1479, 1486, 1487,
1539.

Editions:

916. Krause, F. "Kleine Publicationen aus der Auchinleck-hs. IX. The King of Tars." *EStn* 11 (1888): 1-62.

   Texts from the Vernon and Auchinleck MSS, with variants from the Simeon MS, with introduction.

917. Perryman, Judith. *The King of Tars: ed. from the Auchinleck MS, Advocates 19.2.1.* Middle English Texts 12. Heidelberg: Carl Winter, 1980.

   Includes introduction (7-72), text (73-106), commentary (107-114). glossary and bibliography (115-124). This edition was presented in different form to Oxford U as a B.Litt. thesis.

611. Ritson. 2: 156-203; 3: 320-322, 440.

   Text is from the Vernon MS.

918. Shores, Doris. *"The King of Tars*: A New Edition." *DAI* 30 (1970): 3437A. NYU.

   A compromise text, not a diplomatic edition, including the complete Auchinleck and Vernon versions with variant readings from the Simeon text.

Criticism:

919. Bliss, A.J. "Notes on 'The King of Tars.'" *N&Q* ns 2 (1955): 461-462.

Suggests changing *grest* to *wrest* in line 554, that
the idiom in lines 1117-1122 means "to overturn to
the earth," that there is faulty punctuation in lines
1212-1217, and that *hal* should be *bal*.

SEE ALSO items 67 (137-140), 163 (122-124, 140-141), 410,
413.

THE KNIGHT OF CURTESY AND THE FAIR LADY OF FAGUELL [111]

Editions:

583a. Child. 1:188-210.

588. Gray. 185-199, under "Ballads and Verse Romances."

597. Hazlitt. 2: 65-87 (text), 4: 363 (notes).

920. McCausland, Elizabeth. "The Knight of Curtesy and
      the Fair Lady of Faguell: A Study of the Date and
      Dialect of the Poem and its Folklore Origins." *Smith
      College Studies in Modern Language* 4.1 (1922).

      Includes an introduction (vii-xxii), text (1-19),
      an appendix, the text of the *Chronique du Chatelain
      de Coucy et de la dame de Fayel* (20-21), and glossary
      (23-32).

611. Ritson. 3: 193-218 (text); 224, 353-357 (notes).

SEE ALSO items 413, 556.

LAI LE FREINE [85]

Editions:

613. Rumble. 80-94.

614. Sands. 233-245.

Reprint of Wattie [922] with regularized orthography.

921. Varnhagen, Hermann. "Zu mittelenglischen Gedichten. VIII. Lay le Freine." *Anglia* 3 (1880): 415-425.

Prints the Auchinleck text.

922. Wattie, Margaret. "The Middle English Lai le Freine." *Smith College Studies in Modern Languages* 10.3 (1929): 1-27.

622. Weber. 1: xlii-xlv, 357-371, 381; 3: 346.

The editor added lines 115-127 and 335-402 in order "to complete the story."

Criticism:

923. Beston, John B. "The Case Against Common Authorship of *Lay le Freine* and *Sir Orfeo*." *MAE* 45 (1976): 153-163.

Points to marked differences in intention and temperament, style, and narrative technique as evidence against common authorship.

924. Hirsh, John C. "Providential Concern in the 'Lay le
      Freine.'" *N&Q* ns 16 (1969): 85-86.

      Contrasts the emphasis in the ME lay and Marie de
      France's *Freisne* and perceives a more ecclesiastical
      focus in the English version with its emphasis on
      providential concern.

SEE ALSO items 34 (16-17), 111, 164, 364, 368, 370 (126-
139), 371, 375, 376, 378, 379, 419, 465, 504 (97-98), 578,
709, 1461.

Editions:

925. Gray, Margaret Muriel. *Lancelot of the Laik*. STS ns 2. Edinburgh: Blackwood, 1912.

Includes introduction (vii-xxxvi), text from MS Cambridge U Library (1-103), and glossary (105-113).

926. Johnston, J. "An Edition of *Lancelot of the Laik*. *TGB* 29 (1982): 4453. M.Litt., Oxford U.

927. Skeat, W.W. *Lancelot of the Laik: A Scottish Metrical Romance (About 1490-1500 A.D.)*. EETSOS 6. London: Trübner, 1865. 2nd ed. 1870, rpt. 1889, 1905. Rpt. London: Oxford UP, 1965.

Includes preface (v-xxii), extracts from the French version (xxiii-lvii), text (1-102), notes (103-113), and index (114-132).

928. Stevenson, Joseph. *The Scottish Metrical Romance of Lancelot du Lak*. Maitland Club 48. Edinburgh, 1839. Rpt. New York: AMS P, 1971.

Text (1-127) with no critical apparatus.

Criticism:

929. Kratzmann, Gregory. "The Two Traditions." Chapter 8 of *Anglo-Scottish Literary Relations 1430-1550*. Cambridge: Cambridge UP, 1980. 227-262, 272-273.

Touches on *Lancelot of the Laik*, probably written

during the reign of James III, with verbal echoes
that suggest its indebtedness to James rather than to
Chaucer. Suggests that its best poetry comes in
direct speech, especially the soliloquies of Lancelot, that the heavily anglicized form of Scots suggests imitation of the language of *The Kingis Quair*,
and that the tribute to an unnamed poet in the prologue is probably directed to James I.

930. Scheps, Walter. "The Thematic Unity of *Lancelot of the Laik*." *SSL* 5 (1968): 167-175.

Argues that the poet is concerned with reconciling
Arthurian legend, at least the part dealing with
Lancelot's early career, with orthodox Christianity,
and that the theme is symbolically represented in
terms of arms and love.

931. Wurtele, Douglas. "A Reappraisal of the Scottish *Lancelot of the Laik*." *RUO* 46 (1976): 68-82.

Draws parallels between the ideas on rulership in
this poem, especially in the long insertion of
Amytans' sermon, and those in Gower's *Confessio
Amantis* and *Secreta Secretorum* in order to demonstrate the underrated poet's inventiveness and dex-
terity.

SEE ALSO items 269, 277, 285, 298, 328, 331, 337, 413, 504
(161-162), 693, 819.

THE LAUD TROY-BOOK [74]

Edition:

932. Wülfing, J. Ernst. *The Laud Troy Book, A Romance of About 1400 A.D.* EETSOS 121, 122. London: Kegan Paul, Trench, Trübner, 1902, 1903. Rpt. as one vol. Mill-wood, NY: Kraus, 1972.

Text is edited from MS Laud Misc. 595. No introduction or critical apparatus.

Criticism:

933. Lumiansky, R.M. "The Story of Troilus and Briseida in the *Laud Troy-Book.*" *MLQ* 18 (1957): 238-246.

Considers the content and position of the ten passages in Guido's *Historia* and in this poem that present the Troilus and Briseida episode and suggests that the English poet's expansion of and emphasis on Hector's role is a result of his intention of writing a "Hector Romance."

934. Stevenson, Sharon Lynn. "An Introduction to the *Laud Troy Book.*" *DAI* 32 (1972): 6945A. U of Florida.

Shows that this 15th-century work contains ideas and techniques related to Renaissance revenge trage-dies and compares it to *Destruction of Troy.*

935. Sundwall, Harry McKay. "The *Laud Troy Book*: Intro-duction and Commentary." Diss. Harvard U, 1972.

SEE ALSO items 79, 479 (67-96), 480, 487, 488, 490.

Editions:

936. Cooper, Nancy Margaret Mays. *"Libeaus Desconus*: A Multi-Text Edition." *DA* 21 (1961): 3449. Stanford U.

Uses the five extant manuscript versions for her diplomatic edition.

589. Hales and Furnivall. 2: 404-499.

590. ------. 3: 58-126.

936a. Hippeau, C. *Le Bel Inconnu ou, Giglain Fils de Messire Gauvain et de la Fee aux Blanches Mains.* Paris: Aubry, 1860. 241-330.

The text from the Cotton Caligula MS is included as an appendix to the French edition of the poem.

936b. Kaluza, Max. *Libeaus Desconus, die mittelenglische Romanze.* Altenglische Bibliothek 5. Leipzig: Reisland, 1890.

Extensive introduction; contains a complete and critical text with variant readings from all the extant manuscripts.

936c. Mills, M. *Lybeaus Desconus.* Diss. Oxford U, 1959. EETSOS 261. London: Oxford UP, 1969.

Contains parallel texts of MSS Cotton Caligula A.2

and Lambeth Palace 306, with introduction, commentary, and glossary.

611. Ritson. 2: 1-90; 3: 220-221, 253-264, 439.

Criticism:

937. Adams, D.A. "The theme of *Le Bel Inconnu* in the Literature of England, France, Germany and Italy in the Middle Ages and After." *TGB* 25 (1974-75): 5342. Ph.D., Nottingham U.

938. Luttrell, Claude. "The Fair Unknown." Chapter 6 of *The Creation of the First Arthurian Romance: A Quest.* Evanston: Northwestern UP, 1974. 80-104.

Orders the episodes in the Fair Unknown story from his *enfances* and arrival at Arthur's court to the accomplishment of his mission and wedding; further examines variations and different orderings of the thirteen episodes in *Libeaus Desconus* and the Welsh and other versions of this story.

939. ------. "Folk Legend as Source for Arthurian Romance: The Wild Hunt." Varty [357]. 83-100.

Explores the Wild Hunt in the versions of the Fair Unknown story, including *Libeaus Desconus*; this hunt occurs as an adventure of the hero accompanied by a dwarf and a lady emissary, who keeps disparaging the hero until she is convinced of his prowess.

940. Mills, M. "The Composition and Style of the 'Southern' *Octavian*, *Sir Launfal*, and *Libeaus Desconus*." *MAE* 31 (1962): 88-109.

Proposes Chestre as the common author of all three works after investigating corruptions of source details that suggest the same habits of composition; noting favorite words, phrases, and narrative patterns common to all three; and failing to establish an order of composition that could imply a theory of simultaneous composition.

941.   ------. The Huntsman and the Dwarf in *Erec* and *Libeaus Desconus.*" *Romania* 87 (1966): 33-58.

Traces five specific parallels between the two works and concludes that Chestre was probably acquainted with *Erec*, since the use of Gyfre as a servant and the description of the pack horse laden with gifts are not found in any sources of *Libeaus Desconus*, but are in *Erec*.

942.   ------. "A Mediaeval Reviser at Work." *MAE* 32 (1963): 11-23.

Examines significant revisions of the Libeaus Desconus story in the Percy Folio in order to discuss larger issues concerning textual transmission and the validity of traditional stemma. Concludes that when a text has passed through the hands of professional reciters, the original may be improved in sense or form, or it may have motifs from parallel or unrelated stories introduced by the reviser.

SEE ALSO items 105 (85-88), 163 (69-70, 71-77), 164, 277, 289, 301 (88-90), 322 (134-138), 337, 345, 347, 413, 419, 445, 578.

LYFE OF ALISAUNDER or KING ALEXANDER [64]

Editions:

581. Bennett and Smithers. 28-39 (text), 275-282 (notes).

943. Ebsworth, Joseph Woodfall. *The Bagford Ballads: Illustrating the Last Years of the Stuarts*. 2 vols. Hertford, Eng.: Austin, 1878. 1: no. 27.

944. Smithers, G.V. *Kyng Alisaunder*. EETSOS 227. London: Oxford UP, 1952. Rpt. 1961.

   Uses Laud MS as a basis for this text, but prints in full the Lincoln's Inn MS without attempting emendation or editing, the Auchinleck MS, and the printed leaves in *Bagford Ballads* [943].

945. ------. *Kyng Alisaunder*. EETSOS 237. London: Oxford UP, 1957. Rpt. with corrections 1969.

   Introduction, commentary, and glossary for his text [944].

622. Weber. 1: xx-xxxix, lxxiii-lxxxvii, 3-327, 373-381; 3: 291-345.

Fragments:

946. Bülbring, Karl D. "Vier neue Alexanderbruchstücke." *EStn* 13 (1889): 145-153.

   Comments on the six leaves in the British Museum, which he includes.

947. Smithers, G.V. "Another Fragment of the Auchinleck
      MS." Pearsall and Waldron [73a]. 192-210.

      Finds a part of the text of *King Alexander* in MS
      593 of the U of London Library, prints the legible
      part, and discusses its relationship to other manu-
      scripts.

948. ------. "Two Newly-Discovered Fragments from the
      Auchinleck MS." *MAE* 18 (1949): 1-11.

      Mentions the fragment of *King Alexander*, 150 lines
      corresponding to 6856-6880, 6890-6924, 7170-7194,
      6944-6968, 6988-7012, 7032-7056 of the MS Laud Misc.
      622. Also prints in full the lines corresponding to
      2081-2426 of Brunner's edition of *Richard Coer de
      Lyon* [1095].

      Criticism:

949. Bunt, G.H.V. "Alexander's Last Days in the Middle
      English *Kyng Alisaunder*." *Alexander the Great in the
      Middle Ages: Ten Studies on the Last Days of Alexan-
      der in Literary and Historical Writing.* Symposium
      Interfacultaire Werkgroep Mediaevistiek Groningen
      12-15 Oct. 1977. Ed. W.J. Aerts, Joseph M.M. Her-
      mans, and Elizabeth Visser. Nijmegen, Neth.: Alfa
      Nijmegen, 1978. 202-229.

      Explores the date, provenance, and historical back-
      ground of the text, its audience, genre, character-
      ization of Alexander, and the author's treatment and
      medievalisms. Suggests that this author's portrait
      contains no moral condemnation, only a secular con-
      ception of Alexander as a great conquerer and a good,
      if pagan ruler, who suffers the same limitations of
      fame and transitoriness as all other humans.

950. Camargo, Martin. "The Metamorphosis of Candace and
      the Earliest English Love Epistle." *Court and Poet*
      [20]. 101-111.

      Shows how the author of *King Alexander*, having been
      influenced by contemporary works on *dictamen*, changed
      his source to soften Candace's character. Also

claims that he created the first extant, full-fledged love letter in English.

951. Ikegami, M. "Some Studies of English Rhymes from *Kyng Alisaunder* to Skelton." *TGB* 30 (1982): 221. M.Litt., Oxford U.

952. Tautscher, Eva Maria. "Untersuchungen zur Formenlehre und Syntax des 'Kyng Alisaunder.'" Diss. Graz, 1961.

SEE ALSO items 5, 80 (35-42), 111 (155-156), 160, 163 (208-209, 227-239, 240-241, 242-246), 174, 197 (239-240), 201, 203, 204, 445, 504 (63ff, 78ff), 670, 859.

Edition:

953. Kock, Ernst A. *Merlin: A Middle-English Metrical Version of a French Romance by Henry Lovelich, Skinner and Citizen of London (Ab. 1450 A.D.)*. EETSES 93, 112. London: Kegan Paul, Trench, Trübner, 1904, 1913. Vol. 93 rpt. Millwood, NY: Kraus, 1973; vol. 112 rpt. London: Oxford UP, 1961. EETSOS 185. London: Oxford UP, 1932. Rpt. Millwood, NY: Kraus, 1974.

    Edited from Corpus Christi MS 80, with no critical apparatus.

Criticism:

954. Macrae-Gibson, O.D. "Wynkyn de Worde's *Marlyn*." *Library* 6th ser. 2 (1980): 73-76.

    Discusses the 1510 and 1529 printings as well as fragments in Corpus Christi College and in the Library of Congress (which will be recorded in *Short Title Catalogue* as item 17840.7, not 17841 as it now stands).

955. Ransom, James Fitzhugh. "A Study of Henry Lovelich's *Merlin*." *DA* 22 (1962): 4345. Stanford U.

    Analyzes the first 7884 lines in order to establish the nature of Lovelich's source and to cast light on a widely used method of composition in late medieval England. Also compares this poem line-by-line with other available versions, including the English *Prose Merlin* and *Arthour and Merlin*.

SEE ALSO items 285, 337, 666.

LE MORTE ARTHUR [23]

Editions:

582. Benson. 1-111, 253.

956. Bruce, J. Douglas. *Le Morte Arthur, A Romance in Stanzas of Eight Lines*. EETSES 88. London: Kegan Paul, Trench, Trübner, 1903. Rpt. 1930. Rpt. Millwood, NY: Kraus, 1973.

   Text is edited from MS Harley 2252, the only extant manuscript.

957. Furnivall, Frederick J. *Le Morte Arthur*. London: Macmillan, 1864.

   Edited from MS Harley 2252, with a prefatory essay on Arthur by Herbert Coleridge.

958. Hemingway, Samuel B. *Le Morte Arthur: A Middle English Medival Romance*. Boston: Houghton Mifflin, 1912.

   Complete text with an introductory sketch of the poem and the Lancelot legend, as well as notes and a glossary.

959. Hissiger, P.F. *Le Morte Arthur: A Critical Edition*. Studies in English Literature 96. Diss. U of Pennsylvania, 1969. The Hague: Mouton, 1975.

   Complete text with an introduction, brief notes, and full glossary.

960.   Paton, Lucy Allen. *Morte Arthur: Two Early English Romances*. Everyman's Library 634. London: Dent, 1912. Rpt. 1936. 95-201.

        Text of this poem is in the ME original with no critical apparatus; also contains a modern English translation of *Morte Arthure*.

961.   Ponton, Thomas. *Le Morte Arthur: The Adventures of Sir Lancelot du Lake*. Roxburghe Club 25. London, 1819.

        Criticism:

962.   Alexander, Flora M. "'The Treason of Lancelote du Lake': Irony in the Stanzaic *Morte Arthur*." Grout et al. [300a]. 15-27, 227-228.

        Explores the poem's structural and dramatic irony, irony of events, and verbal irony, all of which contribute to a sense of detachment that prepares the audience to accept the laughter of the Archbishop and to see a fitting end in the burial of Gaynor beside her husband at Glastonbury.

963.   Beston, John, and Rose Marie Beston. "The Parting of Lancelot and Guinevere in the Stanzaic 'Le Morte Arthur.'" *AUMLA* 40 (1973): 249-259.

        Suggest that the poet drew inspiration from his own work in depicting the farewell scene since there is no known source; the scene echoes two earlier ones: the first interview between Lancelot and the queen and his return to court after the tournament and the Maid of Ascalot's letter.

964.   Bluh, Frances Adele. "The Preservation and Destruction of the Kingdom: A Study of *Sir Orfeo*, *La Chanson de Roland*, *Morte Arthure*, and *Le Morte Arthur*." *DAI* 33 (1973): 6899A-6900A. Yale U.

        Traces the different ways the kingdom is presented in the three ME works and one OF poem. Sees a pro-

gression from one extreme in *Sir Orfeo*, in which the
kingdom is unequivocally preserved, to the opposite
extreme in the two Arthurian works, which show the
destruction and dissolution of the kingdom, with the
stanzaic poem offering a more negative vision than
the alliterative work.

965. Bradstock, E.M. "The Source for Book XVIII of
      Malory's 'Morte Darthur.'" *N&Q* ns 26 (1979): 105-
      107.

      Points to specific parallels between Malory's book
      and the stanzaic *Morte Arthur*, suggesting that Malory
      actually consulted the medieval poem and could not
      have been working simply from memory.

966. Guerin, Wilfred L. "'The Tale of the Death of Ar-
      thur': Catastrophe and Resolution." *Malory's Origi-
      nality: A Critical Study of Le Morte Darthur*. Ed.
      R.M. Lumiansky. Baltimore: Johns Hopkins P, 1964.
      233-274.

      Argues that Malory used this stanzaic version as
      his primary source and the OF poem only as a secon-
      dary source, as a collation of the two possible
      sources indicates.

967. Jaech, Sharon L. Jansen. "The Parting of Lancelot
      and Gaynor: The Effect of Repetition in the Stanzaic
      Morte Arthur." *Interpretations* 15.2 (1984): 59-69.

      Demonstrates how the scene of the lovers' parting
      pulls together the most significant themes of the
      narrative and gains emotional intensity through its
      stylistic use of patterns of repetition, refrain
      lines of love and death, and stanza-linking.

968. Kennedy, Edward D. "Malory's Version of Mador's
      Challenge." *N&Q* ns 23 (1976): 100-103.

      Suggests that Malory's version, so different from
      the scene in the stanzaic *Morte Arthur*, 910-911, as
      well as from that in the OF *Mort Artu*, is not origi-

nal but influenced instead by *Suite du Merlin.*

969.   Knopp, Sherron E. "Artistic Design in the *Stanzaic Morte Arthur.*" *ELH* 45 (1978): 563-582.

Defends the poem as a coherent work of art with a structure determined by the author's deliberate focus on the abiding consequences of events, which are a complex weave of good and bad intentions, inadequate choices, chance happenings, and calculated designs.

970.   Korrel, Peter. "Arthur, Modred and Guinevere in Medieval English Romances Dealing with the Death of Arthur." Chapter 3 of *An Arthurian Triangle: A Study of the Origin, Development and Characterization of Arthur, Guinevere and Modred.* Leiden, Neth.: Brill, 1984. 173-283.

Deals with both the stanzaic and alliterative poems as well as the *Vulgate Cycle* and Malory. Argues that in the romance tradition, Modred becomes increasingly more wicked except in the alliterative poem; Guinevere is more treacherous in the alliterative version than in chronicles and is presented as inactive, emotional, and suffering in the stanzic poem; Arthur is most like the chronicle hero in the alliterative poem as a great hero but weak enough to sin and fall, whereas in the stanzaic version he is a weak king whose main function is to enhance Lancelot's prestige.

971.   Lappert, Stephen F. "Malory's Treatment of the Legend of Arthur's Survival." *MLQ* 36 (1975): 354-368.

Examines Malory's manipulation of the OF *Mort Artu,* stanzaic *Morte Arthur,* and the alliterative *Morte Arthure* by a descriptive collation of these sources. Suggests that Malory's idea of the destruction of Arthurian society comes from the stanzaic poem, but the hope that the ideal may continue comes from the alliterative poem, from which he takes the line *The once and future king.*

972. Lumiansky, R.M.   "Gawain's Miraculous Strength: Malory's Use of *Le Morte Arthur* and *Mort Artu*." *EA* 10 (1957): 97-108.

Examines the stanzaic and the OF versions and finds that the ME poet reduced the lengthy OF account of Gawain's "grace" to only twelve lines; that the ME poet makes Lancelot aware of Gawain's magical powers and, unlike the OF poet, has Lancelot overcome Gawain at the height of his powers. Suggests that Malory followed the ME version with two encounters between the knights and the reason for lifting the siege, but followed the OF in giving Gawain's powers a central place in the narrative.

973. Manzalaoui, Mahmoud.   "The Hero Transformed: A Theme in Later Medieval Narrative." *EA* 30 (1977): 145-157.

Suggests that some medieval narratives, usually unconcerned with motivation and character development, portray a transformation of character analogous to the sudden *metanoia* of religious converts. Uses this poem among others as examples of this character transformation and deformation in medieval romance.

974. Margeson, Robert Ward.   "A Key to Medieval Fiction: Romance and Didacticism in *Le Morte Arthur* and *Le Bel Inconnu*." *DAI* 33 (1972): 759A. U of Toronto.

Differentiates two types of didactic narration: the ME poem with its circular structure and static, perfect hero and the French poem with its linear, open-ended structure and imperfect hero.

975. Shimizu, Aya.   "Specific traits of *The Morte Arthur*." *Kiyo* 18 (1980): 31-47 [in Japanese].

Comments on the narrative sequences and gives evidence of the oral nature as well as dramatic aspects of the stanzaic version compared to the alliterative account.

976. Twomey, Michael.   "A Note on Detachment in the Stan-

zaic 'Morte Arthur.'" *BBSIA* 26 (1974): 206-207.

Replies to Kane's discussion of the detachment of
the poet and characters [*Middle English Literature*
(London: Methuen, 1951): 65-69] and rejects his idea
of an emotionless poem; suggests instead that the
author cultivates a *fin de siècle* mood of society
crumbling.

977. Wertime, Richard A. "The Theme and Structure of the
Stanzaic *Morte Arthur*." *PMLA* 87 (1972): 1075-1082.

Argues that the poem, which is more coherent and
serious than usually thought, is organized thematically and structurally in terms of the opposition
between Lancelot and Gawain. If the poem is best
seen as a "tragedy of consequence," then the perplex-
ing discrepancies between the narrator's point of
view and the obvious moral implications of the story
can be resolved by understanding that the "narrator's
compassion transcends, not contradicts, the rigorous
justice of events."

SEE ALSO items 80, 111, 163 (159-160, 186-193), 272 (86-
89), 274 (106-107), 298, 307, 311, 314, 315, 322 (139-140,
181-185), 337, 413, 426.

Editions:

978. Banks, Mary Macleod. *Morte Arthure: An Alliterative Poem of the 14th Century from the Lincoln MS. Written by Robert of Thornton.* London: Longmans, Green, 1900. Rpt. New York: AMS P, 1974.

582. Benson. 113-238, 253-257.

979. Björkman, Erik. *Morte Arthure.* Heidelberg: Carl Winter, 1915.

980. Brock, Edmund. *Morte Arthure, or The Death of Arthur.* EETSOS 8. London: Kegan Paul, Trench, Trübner, 1871. Rpt. London: Oxford UP, 1967.

A revised edition of Perry [986]. Includes a discussion of the meter of the poem, the text, index of names, and glossary.

981. Finlayson, John. *Morte Arthure.* York Medieval Texts. London: Edward Arnold; Evanston: Northwestern UP, 1967.

Contains a 34-page introduction dealing with romance, history, and pseudo-history, as well as the heroic tone and structure of the poem, its dialect, date, and sources. Incomplete text, including lines 1-25 and ten sections: lines 693-1221, 1279-1565, 2006-2351, 2501-2716, 3218-3467, 3598-3711, 3790-3899, 3939-4008, 4060-4160, and 4224-4346.

982. Grenier, Rachel-Ann. "The Alliterative *Morte Ar-*
      thure." *DAI* 36 (1976): 7436A. U of Rhode Island.

      Transcribed from MS Lincoln Cathedral Library with
      notes, index of names, glossary, select bibliography,
      and introduction in which she compares the poem to
      The Prick of Conscience and links Arthur to Wrath.

983. Halliwell [-Phillipps], James Orchard. *The Allitera-*
      tive Romance of the Death of King Arthur. London,
      1847.

      An edition from Lincoln MS of only seventy-five
      copies for private circulation.

984. Hamel, Mary. *Morte Arthure: A Critical Edition*.
      Garland Medieval Texts 9. New York: Garland, 1984.

      Based on a transcription of Lincoln Cathedral Li-
      brary MS 91, but takes advantage of the Winchester
      version in correcting obvious errors; extended intro-
      duction (3-99), text (103-251), textual notes (253-
      397), select bibliography (399-408), glossary, index
      of names and appendix (411-546).

985. Krishna, Valerie. *The Alliterative Morte Arthure: A*
      Critical Edition. New York: Burt Franklin, 1976.

      With an introduction, notes, and glossary by the
      editor, and a preface by Rossell Hope Robbins.

986. Perry G.G. *Morte Arthure or The Death of Arthur*.
      EETSOS 8. London, 1865.

      Later re-edited by Brock [980].

987. Spangehl, Stephen Douglas. *A Critical Edition of the*
      Alliterative Morte Arthure. Diss. U of Pennsylvania,
      1972. Philadelphia: U of Pennsylvania P, 1972.

      Introduction, notes, and glossary concordance.

Criticism:

988. Benson, Larry D. "The Alliterative *Morte Arthure* and Medieval Tragedy." *TSL* 11 (1966): 75-87.

Views the moral complexity of the poem, its ability to maintain contradictory attitudes, as its main strength. Argues further that the tension in the work is not between good and evil, but between two goods: the Christian ideal of detachment versus a complete engagement with an earthly ideal necessary for heroism; Arthur's fall is not the result of an inner flaw, but a flaw in the worldly ideal that leads even its finest adherents to the inevitable turn of Fortune's wheel.

989. ------. "The Date of the *Alliterative Morte Arthure*." Bessinger and Raymo [9]. 19-40.

Argues that both Italian and English allusions in the poem support a date around 1400, rather than 1360-1375.

990. Boren, James L. "Narrative Design in the Alliterative *Morte Arthure*." *PQ* 56 (1977): 310-319.

Explores the poet's use of Ricardian structural features as a way of demarcating distinct episodes in the narrative. These delineating devices, which begin each of the six major sections of the poem, are variations on the arrival of figures bearing messages.

991. ------. "A Reading of the Alliterative *Morte Arthure*." *DAI* 31 (1971): 4706A. U of Iowa.

Argues that the meaning of the poem is inherent in its structural design, which no literary classification has adequately defined, and proposes "ethical discourse" to describe the poet's juxtaposition of events to make his ethical vision dependent on two exemplary episodes.

992. Burrow, J. "'A maner Latyn corrupt.'" *MAE* 30 (1961):

33-37.

Points to line 3478 in *Morte Arthure*, which parallels line 519 in *Man of Law's Tale*, and suggests that
both authors knew of a passage about the development
of language in Isidore of Seville's *Etymologiae* or in
Fouke Fitz Warin (line 60 or 79).

993. Clark, George.   "Gawain's   Fall: The   Alliterative
      Morte Arthure and Hastings." *TSL* 11 (1966): 89-95.

Suggests that the account of the Battle of Hastings
by either Guy of Amiens or William of Poitier is the
likely   source   for   the   poet's   account   of   Gawain's
death.

994. Clark, Roy Peter. "*Alfin*: Invective in the Allitera-
      tive *Morte Arthure*." *ELN* 13 (1976): 165-168.

Discusses the earliest known use of this word in
line 1373, which seems to be drawing on the game of
chess as an emblem for the political situation.

995. Craft, Carolyn Martin.   "Free Will in Malory's *Le
      Morte Darthur* and in Some Earlier Arthurian Writ-
      ings." *DAI* 34 (1973): 1853A. U of Pennsylvania.

Considers the contexts of human freedom; the role
of fate, of marvels and miracles, and of God; and the
deeds of men in five works including *Morte Arthure*,
which   emphasizes   man's   dependence   on   God   and   de-
emphasizes man's own abilities.

996. Eadie, J. "The Alliterative Morte Arthure: Structure
      & Meaning." *ES* 63 (1982): 1-12.

Questions Lumiansky's emphasis   on the theme of
fortitude [1040] and instead divides the poem into
five structural divisions, which imply a working-out
of Arthur's destiny and a celebration of great prowess,   colored   by   the   recognition   that   all   human
achievements have time limits and that all men must
die.

997. Fichte, Jörg O. "The Figure of Sir Gawain." Göller [1009]. 106-116, 174-176.

Concentrates on three aspects: comparison of the figure in the poem and the image of Gawain, the relationship of Gawain and Arthur, and the consequences of an interpretative reading drawn from such an analysis. Concludes that Gawain exemplifies irrational *fortitudo*, which precipitates his and Arthur's fall, and that such a portrayal implies criticism of the imperious ruler. This criticism may also have had specific historical relevance to the 14th-century audience.

998. Field, P.J.C. "Malory's 'Morte Arthure' and the King of Wales." *N&Q* ns 19 (1972): 285-286.

Refutes McCarthy's claim that the King of Wales is a title for Arthur [1043] and argues that this is a title for a vassal whose name Sir Valiant or Vyleris appears in the poem three times.

999. Finlayson, John. "The Alliterative *Morte Arthure* and *Sir Ferumbras*." *Anglia* 92 (1974): 380-386.

Suggests that the English, not the French version of *Sir Firumbras* is the most likely source for the Gawain-Priamus episode in *Morte Arthure* (ll. 2500-3012).

1000. ------. "Arthur and the Giant of St. Michael's Mount." *MAE* 33 (1964): 112-120.

Rather than a common romantic interlude, the giant episode is more in keeping with the serious religious tone of the *chanson de geste*, with emphasis on the giant as an enemy of Christendom and a symbol of evil and the powers of disorder.

1001. ------. "The Concept of the Hero in 'Morte Arthure.'" *Chaucer und seine Zeit: Symposion für Walter F. Schirmer*. Ed. Arno Esch. Buchreihe der Anglia, Zeitschrift für englische Philologie 14. Tübingen: Max Niemeyer, 1968. 249-274.

Contrasts in detail this poet's treatment of Arthur
and Wace's handling of the king and concludes that
the ME poet created a complex and realistic character. Arthur combines traits of a romantic hero, epic
warrior, chivalric knight, champion of Christendom,
and Christian king whose downfall is not an inexplic-
able twist of Fortune's wheel, but an inevitable
consequences of his sins.

1002.   ------. "Formulaic Technique in *Morte Arthure*."
Anglia 81 (1963): 372-393.

Discusses the extent to which alliterative poetry
of a heroic nature relied on and made use of well-
established verbal-formulaic tradition and then
distinguishes this poem from both *Destruction of Troy*
and *Wars of Alexander* in terms of style and quality.
The author of *Morte Arthure* particularized general
motifs, included onomatopoeic effects, and used
formulas expected by the audience.

1003.   ------. *Morte Arthure*: The Date and a Source for the
Contemporary References." *Speculum* 42 (1967): 624-
638.

Rejects 1365 as the date of the poem and suggests
instead a date no earlier than the last quarter of
the 14th century. Also notes parallels to Chandos
Herald's *Life of the Black Prince*, dated about 1385.

1004.   ------. "Rhetorical 'Descriptio' of Place in the
Alliterative *Morte Arthure*." *MP* 61 (1963): 1-11.

Examines the four passages of *descriptio loci*
(11. 920-932, 2501-2512, 2670-2677, and 3230-3249)
and describes the poet's skillful use of this tradition for dramatic contrast of local action with the
poem's general theme and values.

1005.   ------. "The Sources, Use of Sources, and Poetic
Techniques of the Fourteenth-Century Alliterative
Morte Arthure." Diss. Cambridge U, 1962.

Chapter: 1. *Morte Arthure*: a study of its main

source.
2. *Morte Arthure* and the Hundred Years' War.
3. *Morte Arthure* and *Sir Firumbras*.
4. Concept of the hero in *Morte Arthure*.
5. Form of *Morte Arthure*.
6. Formulaic techniques in *Morte Arthure*.
7. Rhetorical "descriptio" in *Morte Arthure*.

Conclusion.

1006. ------. "Two Minor Sources for the Alliterative 'Morte Arthure.'" *N&Q* ns 9 (1962): 132-133.

Suggests "Prophecies of John of Bridlington," a political tract, as a possible influence on Arthur's prophetic dream and "Vows of the Heron" as an influence on Arthur's reception of the Roman senator's speech and the series of vows.

1007. Foley, Michael. "The Alliterative *Morte Arthure*: An Annotated Bibliography, 1950-1975." *ChauR* 14 (1979): 166-187.

A chronologically arranged bibliography of 116 items with full annotations of editions and translations, as well as books, articles, and doctoral dissertations for the 25-year period.

1008. Fries, Maureen. "The Poem in the Tradition of Arthurian Literature." Göller [1009]. 30-43, 159-161.

Reviews the varied traditions the author drew upon and suggests that he adopted the combination of prophecy and fulfillment from chronicle tradition, that much of the narrative content is Galfridian, that he pruned all traces of romance added by Wace and Layamon, and that he changed the basic chronicle structure by motifs from *chansons de geste* and by individual innovation in characterization. Concludes that the poem is a special kind of tragedy in which the poet melded Arthurian tradition and individual talent.

1009. Göller, Karl Heinz, ed. *The Alliterative Morte Ar-
       thure: A Reassessment of the Poem.* Arthurian Studies
       2. Cambridge, Eng.: D.S. Brewer, 1981.

       A collection of eleven essays, summary of research,
       and a translation by Kevin Crossley-Holland of the
       dream of the wheel of Fortune, lines 3218-3455. This
       work grew out of the XII International Arthurian Con-
       ference in Regensburg in August 1979. Includes en-
       tries 997, 1008, 1010, 1011, 1013, 1015, 1024, 1039,
       1045, 1063, 1064, and 1078.

1010. ------. "The Dream of the Dragon and Bear." Göller
       [1009]. 130-139, 177-179.

       Explores the meaning of the prophetic dream, lines
       760-805, by studying the symbolic significance of the
       dragon and bear in Christian and mythological tradi-
       tions. Discusses three levels of realization of the
       dream: 1) Just as the bear initially seemed stronger
       than the dragon, the giant nearly kills Arthur, who,
       like the dragon, finally emerges victorious; 2)
       Arthur confronts the Roman Emperor Lucius; 3) Like
       the dragon, which is an ambivalent symbol, Arthur de-
       stroys his own people and in his dark side is repre-
       sented by the image of the bear (*arth*). Arthur, who
       was once the just king becomes a tyrannical and
       barbaric conqueror embodying both symbols.

1011. ------. "Stab und Formel im Alliterierenden Morte
       Arthure." *Neophil* 49 (1965): 57-67.

       Analyzes the formulaic patterns in the poem and
       discusses verbal associations and variation in non-
       alliterative forms whose significance is lost by
       textual emendation.

1012. ------. "A Summary of Research." Göller [1009].
       7-14.

       Reviews scholarship on *Morte Arthure.*

1013. ------, with R. Gleissner and M. Mennicken. "Real-
       ity versus Romance: A Reassessment of the *Allitera-*

tive Morte Arthure. Göller [1009]. 15-29, 157-159.

Argue that the poem should be called an anti-
romance in which the poet uses structural irony to
debunk the clichés of romance. By bringing romantic
fiction into a strongly realistic context, the poet
confronts the audience with the idea that chivalric
jousting was "nothing more than a ridiculous game."
Conclude that the poem is a kind of *Fürstenspiegel*, a
death knell, or lament for the knightly ethos.

1014. Gross, Laila. "The Meaning and Oral-Formulaic Use of
       Riot in the Alliterative *Morte Arthure*." *AnM* 9
       (1968): 98-102.

Riot appears twenty-one times in the poem: eleven
times as a verb, six as an adjective, and four as a
noun.   In the formulaic phrase "reverence and
ryotte," *ryotte* can be confused with *realtee*, from OF
reiaute, with the subsequent meaning of royal dignity
rather than the usual sense of making a disturbance
or enjoying oneself.

1015. Haas, Renate. "The Laments for the Dead." Göller
       [1009]. 117-129, 176-177.

Studies the poet's use of the traditional lament in
the ten laments within the poem. Concludes that the
poet uses it to point out the frailty of the world,
providing an undercurrent of *vanitas mundi*; further
suggests that the lament exposes the discrepancy between the knightly ideal and reality as well as the
irreconcilability of the worldly and Christian components of the ideal.

1016. Hamel, Mary. "The Alliterative *Morte Arthure*, Line
       3061: The Crux *Idene*." *ELN* 17 (1980): 170-172.

Proposes the reading *indeue*, "to endow, provide
with livelihood," which requires only one emendation
to the Thornton text, the addition of an omitted
nasal. This reading would then correspond to the
Winchester Malory text.

1017.   ------. "The 'Christening' of Sir Priamus in the
         Alliterative *Morte Arthure.*" *Viator* 13 (1982):
         295-307.

         Argues against the prevailing view of Priamus as a
         pagan Saracen and claims that his lineage is explic-
         itly Greek; thus rather than asking for baptism, he
         asks for the last rites of the Greek Orthodox church.

1018.   ------. "The Dream of a King: The Alliterative *Morte
         Arthure* and Dante." *ChauR* 14 (1980): 298-312.

         Suggests the poet's familiarity with Dante's *Infer-
         no*, which would clarify the imagery of Arthur's
         dream of Fortune (ll. 3323ff) and the dreamer's dan-
         gerous spiritual condition as well as the epithet of
         "Malebranche" applied to Modred.

1019.   ------. "Scribal Self-Corrections in the Thornton
         Morte Arthure." *SB* 36 (1983): 119-137.

         A detailed analysis of the 339 cases of self cor-
         rection by Robert Thornton in order to derive conclu-
         sions about his characteristic errors, his tendencies
         to err, and his habits and system of transcription.
         Broad generalization from this study is that the
         weakest part of the alliterative long line is the
         latter part of the first half-line, b-stave, and the
         unstressed words that precede it.

1020.   ------. "The Text of the Alliterative *Morte Arthure*:
         Editorial Problems and Principles." *DAI* 32 (1971):
         388A-389A. Pennsylvania State U.

         Analyzes the textual information provided by the
         Thornton MS and Winchester MS of Malory in order to
         clarify their relationship and concludes that the
         Thornton MS is the only authoritative text.

1021.   Harder, Henry L. "Feasting in the *Alliterative Morte
         Arthure.*" Benson and Leyerle [385]. 49-62, 156-157.

         Views the feasts as a part of the "worship" or
         public honor of the king, a display of his magnifi-

cence. The feasts thus indicate the political and
social significance of honor and are a manifestation
of decorum and *fortitudo*.

1022. Howard, Douglas. "Kingship and Conquest: Tragic
Conflict in *Morte Arthure*." *ISSQ* 31.1 (1978): 29-38.

Argues that the poet, in retelling this story, did
not choose a romance hero, but a king "whose every
act must be weighed according to its potential effect" on his own troops and people as well as his
victims. Further suggests that the poet dealt with
the conflict between duties of kingship and desire
for conquest and ultimately revealed the limited
value of heroic conquest and triumph, especially when
the hero is also a king.

1023. Jacobs, Nicolas. "The Ottoman 'Porte' in Middle
English." *N&Q* ns 24 (1977): 306-307.

Refers to line 2609 of *Morte Arthure* and argues
that *porte* ought to be taken in the sense of "Ottoman
government," a meaning with no recorded instance
before 1600; further suggests that the line is an
interpolation contemporary with the manuscript or
that the poem was composed well into the 15th century.

1024. Janssen, Anke. "The Dream of the Wheel of Fortune."
Göller [1009]. 140-152, 179-181.

Suggests that the author altered the symbol of the
wheel in three ways: by uniting the wheel with the
topos of the Nine Worthies, by fusing the Boethian
concept of Fortune with the contemporary humanistic
background, and by portraying the goddess in a restricted sphere of fortune-in-war. Claims that the
dream contains "the message of the poem *in nuce*, that
the author was probably thinking of the war with
France and wanted to admonish the princes of his time
by pointing out that once a ruler entrusts his fate
to *Fortuna belli*, he has consented to his own downfall."

1025. Johnson, James D. "Formulaic Diction and Thematic
       Composition in the Alliterative *Morte Arthure*." *DAI*
       30 (1970): 3462A. U of Illinois.

       Intensive statistical and critical examination of
       formulas, formulaic systems, end-position words,
       motifs, and themes.

1026. ------. "Formulaic Thrift in the Alliterative *Morte
       Arthure*." *MAE* 47 (1978): 255-261.

       Tabulates and discusses the "FUNCTION-WORD ADJEC-
       TIVE knight" formulaic system in the poem in terms of
       thrift, a concept introduced by Milman Parry.

1027. ------. "'The Hero on the Beach' in the Alliterative
       Morte Arthure." *NM* 76 (1975): 271-281.

       Points to the occurrence of this theme in the poem
       at lines 3724-3731, a passage not in the sources, as
       a development of the formula from OE to ME.

1028. Keiser, George R. "Edward III and the Alliterative
       Morte Arthure." *Speculum* 48 (1973): 37-51.

       Finds that evidence in the poem does not support
       any extensive identification of Edward III with
       Arthur as many critics theorize; at best, it implies
       only a general attitude toward Edward that could
       reinforce the tragic vision of the poem.

1029. ------. "Narrative Structure in the Alliterative
       Morte Arthure, 26-720." *ChauR* 9 (1974): 130-144.

       Comparing this section of the poem with Wace's *Brut*
       demonstrates that the poet reshaped the chronicle
       tradition to reflect the distinctly 14th-century
       chivalric ideals; his concern with concrete and ra-
       tional detail and his drawing upon the same stock of
       conventions as romances show that this poem is very
       much a product of its age.

1030. ------. "A Note on the *Alliterative Morte Arthure*,

208-9." *NM* 76 (1975): 446-447.

Suggests that the unorthodox role of Kay as cup-
bearer may be due to the poet's misreading of line
10480 in Wace's *Brut* or to a faulty text of the
passage.

1031. ------. "The Portrait of Arthur in the Alliterative
Morte Arthure." *DAI* 32 (1971): 2645A. Lehigh U.

Closely examines the poet's adaptation of the
chronicle in forming a more complex and sympathetic
Arthur in order to show the difficulty in identifying
the hero with Edward III.

1032. ------. "The Theme of Justice in the Alliterative
Morte Arthure." *AnM* 16 (1975): 94-109.

Stresses the importance of the theme of justice and
the just king as decisive influences in the artist's
shaping of the narrative, which shows Arthur as a
just king in the first half, but his decline and restoration through the grace of God in the second half.
Thus, the poet's faith in the dominion of a just and
loving God shapes his conception of the narrative and
establishes limits to the tragic vision.

1033. Kennedy, Christopher B. "Dante Meets the Son of
Uther." *RomN* 21 (1981): 364-365.

Suggests that the author of the ME poem knew at
least the beginning of the *Inferno*, since Arthur's
dream of the wheel of Fortune is reminiscent of the
first canto of Dante's poem.

1034. ------. "'Per Ovra Delle Rote Magne': Mutability and
Providence in *Beowulf*, Layamon's *Brut* and *Morte
Arthure.*" *DAI* 40 (1980): 6266A-6267A. Duke U.

Summarizes the patristic and medieval traditions of
providential history and then demonstrates how the
three poems are illuminated by this approach.

1035. Kennedy, Edward D. "Malory's Use of Hardyng's Chron-
       icle." *N&Q* ns 16 (1969): 167-170.

           Refutes those who argue that Malory used *Morte
       Arthure*. Finds that the *Chronicle* is an equally
       likely source for the geographical place names as
       well as the overall shaping of the work.

1036. Krishna, Valerie. "The Alliterative *Morte Arthure*: A
       Verse Translation, with Introduction and Critical
       Notes." *DAI* 33 (1972): 1143A. NYU.

           Views the poem not as complex tragedy of character,
       but as simple tragedy of fortune, which exploits the
       heroic, not the romantic.

1037. ------. "Archaic Nouns in the *Alliterative Morte
       Arthure*." *NM* 76 (1975): 439-445.

           Argues that the distinctive alliterating synonyms
       for *man* do not have elevated connotations, but more
       general denotations, and that any rhetorical power
       derives from the specific context in the poem.

1038. ------. "Parataxis, Formulaic Density, and Thrift in
       the *Alliterative Morte Arthure*." *Speculum* 57 (1982):
       63-83.

           Discovers through a detailed and careful study of
       formulas that this ME poem comes closer than *Beowulf*
       to possessing the qualities singled out by Milman
       Parry as the marks of "traditional" poetry. The
       study raises questions about oral or lettered compo-
       sition and the nature of oral-formulaic study.

1039. Lippe, Karl. "Armorial Bearing and their Meaning."
       Göller [1009]. 96-105, 171-174.

           Studies coats of arms, which appear in ten pas-
       sages: lines 1374-1375, 1817-1818, 2050-2057, 2521-
       2524, 2889-2891, 3332-3337, 3645-3651, 3759, 3868-
       3869, and 4181-4186. Suggests that the author was
       familiar with the technical vocabulary of heraldry,
       but altered his descriptions in blazonry for his own

artistic ends.

1040. Lumiansky, Robert M. "The Alliterative *Morte Ar-thure*, the Concept of Medieval Tragedy, and the Cardinal Virtue Fortitude." *Medieval and Renaissance Studies: Proceedings of the Southeastern Institute of Medieval and Renaissance Studies Summer 1967.* Ed. John M. Headley. Chapel Hill: U of North Carolina P, 1968. 95-118.

Rejects the views of both Benson [988] and Matthews [1046] and instead reads the poem as an exemplum on the virtue of fortitude as it applies in both prosperity and adversity.

1041. ------. "Two Notes on Malory's *Morte Darthur*: Sir Urry in England—Lancelot's Burial Vow." *NM* 58 (1957): 148-153.

Argues that Malory found the idea of Lancelot's burial at Joyous Garden in both the OF *Mort Artu* and the ME *Morte Arthure*, but Lancelot's regret is based on the alliterative poem alone.

1042. McAlindon, T. "Comedy and Terror in Middle English Literature: The Diabolical Game." *MLR* 60 (1965): 323-332.

Suggests that both *Morte Arthure* and *Sir Gawain and the Green Knight* reflect a sardonic intermingling of grimness and jest in their supernatural figures; the horror is ritualized in sportive form, and the diabolical parodies religious themes.

1043. McCarthy, Terence. "Malory's King of Wales—Some Notes on the Text of Book II." *N&Q* ns 18 (1971): 327-329.

Argues that the King of Wales is one of Arthur's titles in *Morte Arthure*, using this as a basis for emending Vinaver's text of Malory.

1044. McIntosh, Angus. "The Textual Transmission of the

Alliterative *Morte Arthure.*" *English and Medieval Studies Presented to J.R.R. Tolkien on the Occasion of His Seventieth Birthday.* Ed. Norman Davis and C.L. Wrenn. London: Allen, 1962. 231-240.

Postulates two northeast Midlands stages in the transmission of this poem rather than a west Midlands origin.

1045.   Markus, Manfred. "The Language and Style: The Paradox of Heroic Poetry." Göller [1009]. 57-69, 164-167.

Explores the poet's use of synonyms, periphrastic constructions, and formulas; his fondness for the cumulative method of constructing passages; his larger units of style as exemplified specifically in *descriptio loci*; and his point of view with respect to characters. Concludes that the poet was fond of tension and that the poem is a "typical example of the many paradoxes of its time and in particular of the paradox which heroic poetry had become by 1400."

1046.   Matthews, William. *The Tragedy of Arthur: A Study of the Alliterative "Morte Arthure."* Berkeley: U of California P, 1960.

Chapter: 1.   Theme with variations, 3-31.
           2.   Macedon into Caerleon, 32-67.
           3.   Arms and the man, 68-93.
           4.   Structure and genre, 94-114.
           5.   Sin and punishment, 115-150.
           6.   The hub and the wheel, 151-177.
Epilogue, 178-192.
Notes and bibliography, 195-226.
Index, 227-230.

1047.   Morgan, H.E. "An Analysis of the Methods and Presumed Functions of Characterization in the Three Middle English Romances of *Ywain and Gawain, Morte Arthure,* and *Gawain and the Green Knight.*" *TGB* 20 (1969-70): 319. B.Litt., Oxford U.

1048.   Murphy, Gratia H. "Arthur as King: A Reading of the

Alliterative Morte Arthure in the Light of the *Für-stenspiegel* Tradition." *DAI* 37 (1976): 2839A-2840A. Kent State U.

Demonstrates that the tradition of educational treatises is central to the coherence and the theme of this poem, which dramatically explores the glories and dangers of kingship.

1049. Nelson, Marie. "Submorphemic Values: Their Contribution to Pattern and Meaning in the *Morte Arthure*." *Lang&S* 6 (1973): 289-296.

Argues that the poet used alliteration that is independent of lexical meaning and thus grouped details, with sound reinforcing sense. Conversely, he consistently changed alliterations to separate sections of narrative and repeated sounds to communicate meaning.

1050. Obst, Wolfgang. "The Gawain-Priamus Episode in the Alliterative *Morte Arthure*." *SN* 57 (1985): 9-18.

Interprets the Priamus episode symbolically and analogously to the preceding fight with the giant. Further explores the function of the scene and its thematic and structural connections to the rest of the poem. Treats this episode not as a turning point from Arthur's legitimate campaign to an unlawful war, but as a new stage in his continuously ascending career and as a demonstration of the consistency of Arthur's character.

1051. O'Loughlin, J.L.N. "The English Alliterative Romances." *Arthurian Literature in the Middle Ages: A Collaborative History*. Ed. Roger Sherman Loomis. Oxford: Clarendon P, 1959. 520-527.

Views Arthur as a noble king whose downfall is brought about by *hamartia*, primarily evidenced by his begetting of Modred.

1052. Onions, C.T. "The Type 'A Talbot.'" *MAE* 26 (1957): 114.

Further adds to the list of battle cries of this
type by citing its occurrence in line 1791 of *Morte
Arthure*, its earliest usage.

1053.   O'Sharkey, Eithne M. "King Arthur's Prophetic Dreams
        and the Role of Modred in Layamon's *Brut* and the
        Alliterative *Morte Arthure*." *Romania* 99 (1978): 347-
        362. Abstract in *BBSIA* 27 (1975): 216-217.

        Contrasts the two English poems with earlier ac-
        counts and then discusses the differences between the
        two; the author of *Morte Arthure* emphasizes the need
        for repentance and the ultimate subordination of Fate
        to Divine Providence, while demonstrating that Ar-
        thur's salvation is far more important than his role
        as hero.

1054.   Ovitt, George Odell, Jr. "Time as a Structural
        Element in Medieval Literature." *DAI* 40 (1980):
        4587A-4588A. U of Massachusetts.

        Argues that the Aristotelian concept of time as
        linear, continuous, and causally connected finds
        expression in this poem through the tragic rise and
        fall of Arthur.

1055.   Patterson, Lee W. "The Historiography of Romance and
        the Alliterative *Morte Arthure*." *JMRS* 13 (1983):
        1-32.

        Considers the work as a romance that tries to tell
        a truth about history, stressing both the legitimacy
        of Arthur's claim on Rome and the eschatological
        meanings implied by his imperial ambitions. Suggests
        that the poem views the past as a legitimizing au-
        thority of such value that it must be retained even
        if it costs the present its own historical identity.

1056.   Pearcy, Roy J. "The Alliterative *Morte Arthure* vv.
        2420-2447 and the Death of Richard I." *ELN* 22.4
        (1985): 16-27.

        Suggests that Arthur's behavior before Metz was
        meant to recall the circumstances of Richard's death

at the siege of Chalus and that there are even verbal echoes to reinforce audience recognition: *gadeling* (1. 2443) and *allblawsters* (1. 2426), both used for Richard's assassins in chronicle accounts.

1057. Peck, Russell A. "Willfulness and Wonders: Boethian Tragedy in the Alliterative *Morte Arthure*." Levy and Szarmach [242]. 153-182.

Views the poem, like many late 14th-century works, as a study in willful behavior based on Boethian ideas that a man's fate is his own choice and that tragedy is the condition of the will isolating the soul from its proper good through wrong choices.

1058. Porter, Elizabeth. "Chaucer's Knight, the Alliterative *Morte Arthure*, and the Medieval Laws of War: A Reconsideration." *NMS* 27 (1983): 56-78.

Argues that Chaucer's account of the knight and the portrait of Arthur in the alliterative poem are celebratory, not condemnatory as is usually claimed. Further suggests that both works can be related to the political situation in France and England in the closing decades of the 14th century.

1059. ------. "The Conduct of War as Reflected in Certain Middle English Romances, with Special Reference to the Alliterative *Morte Arthure*." *DAI* 46 (1985): 185C. Queen's U of Belfast.

Attempts a fresh analysis of this poem in relation to late medieval attitudes towards war and concludes that Arthur was a good king undertaking a just war. Relates *Siege of Jerusalem* to comtemporary legal theory and legal conventions of crusades.

1060. Regan, Charles Lionel. "The Paternity of Mordred in the Alliterative *Morte Arthure*." *BBSIA* 25 (1973): 153- 154.

Argues against O'Loughlin [1051], who claims that Arthur's fall is related to his begetting of Modred; points out that all references to Modred in the poem are to *sybb*, *cosyne*, or *neuewe*, with no hint that the traitor is Arthur's son.

1061.   ------. "The Paternity of Mordred in the Alliterative *Morte Arthure* Once More." *An&Q* 23 (1984): 35-36.

Maintains his earlier position [1060] and presents lines 1943-1944 as further evidence, since Arthur himself declares that he has no children.

1062.   Rice, Nancy Hall. "Beauty and the Beast and the Little Boy: Clues about the Origins of Sexism and Racism from Folklore and Literature: Chaucer's 'The Prioress's Tale,' *Sir Gawain and the Green Knight*, the Alliterative *Morte Arthure*, Webster's *The Duchess of Malfi*, Shakespeare's *Othello*, Hawthorne's 'Rappaccini's Daughter,' Melville's 'Benito Cereno.'" *DAI* 36 (1975): 875A. U of Massachusetts.

Examines the virulent hatred and unjust attacks against women, blacks, and other outsiders as illuminated by examples from folklore and literature.

1063.   Ritzke-Rutherford, Jean. "Formulaic Macrostructure: The Theme of Battle." Göller [1009]. 83-95, 169-171.

Points to the weakness of oral-formulaic research in not investigating the function of these patterns within the artistic framework of the poem and offers an alternative approach to the problem. Suggests that the theme of battle provides the structure of the poem with careful counterbalancing of scenes of single combat with mass warfare, but in a context differing greatly from the traditional one. This alteration is "a kind of mock-heroic parody of the original formulaic type-scene." Further suggests that the resulting form shows marked resemblances to the form of classical tragedy and that the poet transforms a war poem into one with an anti-war bias.

1064.   ------. "Formulaic Microstructure: The Cluster." Göller [1009]. 70-82, 167-169.

Introduces the concept of clusters and suggests that formulaic analysis of the poem and its treatment of the theme of battle can provide a key to the nature of the poem. Revises formulaic theory by adding the idea of cluster, a method for determining whether the poet drew on the technique and language of OE poetry. Gives examples of specific battle clusters: *dede/demen/Dryhten/dye*, *faege/fight/folk*, *shield/shoot/sharp/schalk*, *bright/byrnie/beorn*, and *hew/heathens/helm*, *head/hard*.

1065. Schelp, Hanspeter. "Gestaltung und Funktion des Auftakts in der mittelenglischen alliterierenden *Morte Arthure*." *Archiv* 207 (1971): 420-438.

Interprets lines 26-242 by examining both the chronicle sources and the parallel scene in *Sir Gawain and the Green Knight* and then demonstrates that its descriptive and dramatic elements are organized to arouse interest, provide information, and introduce Arthur.

1066. Shoaf, R.A. "The Alliterative *Morte Arthure*: The Story of Britain's David." *JEGP* 81 (1982): 204-226.

Suggests that the *exemplum* of David is crucial to the narrative of Arthur and that like David, Arthur oscillates between magnificence and wretchedness.

1067. Šimko, Ján. *Word-Order in the Winchester Manuscript and in William Caxton's Edition of Thomas Malory's Morte Darthur (1485)—A Comparison*. Halle, BRD: Max Niemeyer, 1957.

Analyzes in detail the three texts: Caxton, Winchester, and *Morte Arthure*. Finds that although in every word-order type there is a considerable proportion of instances of Winchester directly following *Morte Arthure*, there is always Winchester material with no direct parallel in *Morte Arthure*; furthermore, there is significant agreement in structure and vocabulary between Caxton and *Morte Arthure*, but not with Winchester.

1068. Stottlemyer, Ronald Steven. "The *Alliterative Morte Arthure*: The Form of Epic Tragedy." *DAI* 44 (1983): 748A-749A. U of Arizona.

       Challenges previous generic classifications and extensively analyzes the total artistic structure, narrative techniques, patterns of imagery and symbolism, and thematic development, concluding that the poem is best described as "epic tragedy."

1069. Stroud, Michael James. "Malory and the *Morte Arthure*." *DAI* 31 (1971): 4735A-4736A. U of Wisconsin.

       St. Anselm's distinction between truths of reference and truths of language is used to explain the digressive nature of the poem, the structure of which is antithetical to Aristotelean aesthetics.

1070. Suzuki, Eiichi. "Archaic Nouns in *Morte Arthure*: A Reconsideration." *PoetT* 12 (1979): 134-141.

       Rejects Krishna's theory [1037] and supports the Brink-Borroff hypothesis of alliterative rank. Stresses the importance of circumstantial evidence, formal and tangible criteria, a word's distribution, and the identification of replacements among manuscripts of a particular poem.

1071. ------. "The Substantival Adjective in *Morte Arthure*." *ESELL* 48 (1965): 1-17 [in Japanese].

1072. ------. "Tags in 'Morte Arthure.'" *ESELL* 45-46 (1964): 219-242 [in Japanese].

1073. ------. "The Uninflected Genitive in *Morte Arthure*." *ESELL* 57 (1970): 1-22 [in Japanese].

1074. Tonsfeldt, Hugh Ward. "Medieval Narrative and the Alliterative *Morte Arthure*." *DAI* 36 (1975): 1489A. U of California, San Diego.

       Analyzes the poem according to oral-formulaic

theories and the medieval rhetorical idea of *ordo artificialis*.

1075. Vale, Juliet. "Law and Diplomacy in the Alliterative *Morte Arthure*." *NMS* 23 (1979): 31-46.

Suggests that the poem offers remarkable insight into the attitudes and preoccupations of a diplomat and administrator in the second half of the reign of Edward III.

1076. Vaughan, M.F. "Consecutive Alliteration, Strophic Patterns, and the Composition of the Alliterative *Morte Arthure*." *MP* 77 (1979): 1-9.

Argues that consecutive alliteration, far from being merely ornamental, is structural in nature and that more than seventy-six of the 4346 lines of the poem are linked in this way. Further suggests that the poet composed in quatrains or larger strophic groupings.

1077. Wilson, Robert H. "Some Minor Characters in the *Morte Arthure*." *MLN* 71 (1956): 475-480.

Considers four character identification problems: Clemente (1. 1828), Ferrer and Ferawnte (1. 2421), Lowell and Lionell (1. 1826), and Valyant of Walis (1. 1982).

1078. Wurster, Jutta. "The Audience." Göller [1009]. 44-56, 161-164.

Suggests two methods of determining the nature of the medieval poem's audience: the extrinsic method that investigates political and regional background and social contexts, and the intrinsic method that analyzes the text to determine the poet's interests, intentions, and message. Concludes the study of both methods by suggesting an audience of landed gentry who may have held offices in the provinces, possibly also country clergy and substantial landowners who were intellectually active, educated, and interested in a wide range of issues. Also considers courts of nobility in the east Midlands as a possible.

1079.   Yoder, Emily. "The Wandering Jew in the *Alliterative Morte Arthure*." *FForum* 13 (1980): 254-258.

Discovers an overlooked reference to the Wandering Jew in line 2895, now the earliest known citation. Suggests that some version originated much earlier than the 17th-century German one.

1080.   Zamora, Marcela C. "'The Passing of Arthur' in Three Versions." *Verge* 2 (1968): 125-136.

Compares this poem's account of Arthur's death scene (ll. 3151-4346) with versions in Malory and Tennyson.

SEE ALSO items 11 (43-46), 16 (142-154), 17 (61-62), 34, 79 (41-42, 48-49, 52-53, 62-63, 68-69, 98-100, 102-103), 80 (47-57), 110, 160, 174, 212, 218, 224, 241, 249, 259 (52-58, 75-76, 91-96), 263 (84-85, 102-104), 264, 265, 266, 272 (48-51), 274 (53-56), 275, 277, 282, 285, 298, 304, 307, 311, 314, 315, 322 (147-152), 331, 334 (66-67), 337, 341 (36-37), 382, 426, 504 (80ff, 102ff, 117ff), 523, 532, 547, 964, 970, 971, 975.

Editions:

1081. Halliwell [-Phillipps], James Orchard. *The Romance of The Emperor Octavian.* Percy Society 14.3. London, 1844.

   Text is from MS Cambridge University Ff.2.38, with variants from Thornton MS.

1082. McSparran, Frances. *Octovian Imperator.* Middle English Texts 11. Heidelberg: Carl Winter, 1979.

   Text is from MS Cotton Caligula A.2.

607. Mills. 75-124, 201-207.

1083. Reiss, Edmund Allan. "The Northern Middle English *Octavian*: An Edition and Commentary." Diss. Harvard U, 1960.

1084. Sarrazin, Gregor. *Octavian, zwei mittelenglische Bearbeitungen der Sage.* Altenenglische Bibliothek 3. Heilbronn: Henninger, 1885.

622. Weber. 1: lviii-lix; 3: 157-239, 374-375, 461.

   Text is from MS Cotton Caligula A.2, with introduction and notes.

Criticism:

1085.   Krieg, Martha Fessler. "The Contrast of Class Cus-
        toms as Humor in a Middle English Romance: Clement
        and Florent in *Octavian*." *FCS* 9 (1984): 115-124.

        Examines three humorous passages in *Octavian*: sell-
        ing the oxen, the arming scene, and paying for the
        banquet. Points to the source of the humor in the
        contrast between the elegant knightly manners of
        Florent and the shrewd practicality of the butcher,
        with the audience identifying with the upper-class
        values regardless of their status.

1086.   Mead, Herman R. "A New Title from de Worde's Press."
        Library 5th ser. 9 (1954): 45-49.

        Suggests that the early printed copy of the romance
        in the Huntington Library is from the press of Wynkyn
        de Worde rather than from Copland.

SEE ALSO items 134, 163 (69-70, 111-119), 164, 386, 398,
410, 413, 443, 578, 940.

Editions:

599. Herrtage. 65-116, 122-124.

1087. Long, Richard A. "The Middle English versions of 'Otinel' and 'Fierabras': Aspects of Style." *Catalogue des Theses de Doctorat* 82 (1965): 4868. Poitiers U.

620. Turnbull.

SEE ALSO items 79 (92-94), 110, 163 (57-58), 419, 574.

OTUEL AND ROLAND [54]

Edition:

609. O'Sullivan. xi-xv, xlii-lxxxiii, 59-146, 147-153.

Contains introduction, text, and notes.

SEE ALSO items 67 (180-182), 79 (58-59), 110, 574.

Editions:

1088. Bödtker, A. Trampe. *The Middle-English Versions of Partonope of Blois*. EETSES 109. London: Kegan Paul, Trench, Trübner, 1912. Rpt. Millwood, NY: Kraus, 1973.

Contains all manuscripts, though MS British Library Additional 35288 is the basic text. It also reprints MS Penrose from Nichols [1090]. No introduction or notes.

1089. Buckley, W.E. *The Old English Version of Partenope of Blois*. Roxburghe Club 82. London, 1862.

Contains MS University College Oxford 188 and MS Rawl. Eng. Poetry C.3, as well as selections from MS Rawl. Eng. Poetry F.14.

1090. N[ichols], R.C. *A Fragment of Partenope of Blois, From a Manuscript at Vale Royale, in Possession of Lord Delamere*. Roxburghe Club 98. London, 1873.

The edition of this manuscript, now known as Penrose, was reprinted in Bödtker [1088], 481-488.

1091. Wülker, R. "Zu Partanope of Blois." *Anglia* 12 (1890): 607-620.

Contains MS Clifden [Robartes] with corresponding portions from MS University College Oxford 188, as well as a preceding section from MS Rawl. Eng. Poetry F.14.

Criticism:

1092. McCobb, Lilian M.   "The English *Partonope of Blois*,
its French Source, and Chaucer's *Knight's Tale*."
ChauR 11 (1977): 369-372.

Comparing the three works strongly suggests that
the English translator used the *Knight's Tale* as a
source for the tournament and that the English poem
presents stylistic differences from the French
source, probably as a result of the influence of
Chaucer.

1093. ------.   "'The Traditional Background of *Partonopeu
de Blois*': An Additional Note." *Neophil* 60 (1976):
608- 610.

Points to two further instances of Celtic tradition
affecting both the OF and ME versions of this story:
the hollow tree associated with the hero's forest
adventures (11. 664-667, 7094-7098) depends on accounts of the Wild Man, especially of Merlin Sil-
vestris in *Vita Merlini*, and the charming of the wild
beasts (11. 7202-7204, 7212-7221), which derives from
Merlin's activities in *Livre d'Artus*.

1094. Spensley, Ronald M.   "The Courtly Lady in *Partonope
of Blois*." *NM* 74 (1973): 288-291.

Examines the poet's modifications of his OF source
in his presentation of the three courtly ladies:
Melior, Uragane, and Persowis; the English poet is
more concerned with reputation, tones down the female
passions, and recommends love's virtues with some
qualification instead of bluntly condemning ladies
who reject love.

SEE ALSO items 413, 478, 504 (46-47, 57-58), 519, 556, 578.

RICHARD COER DE LYON [106]

Editions:

1095. Brunner, Karl. *Der mittelenglische Versroman über Richard Löwenherz; kritische Ausgabe nach allen Handschriften mit Einleitung, Anmerkungen und deutscher Uebersetzung.* Weiner Beiträge zur englische Philologie 42. Vienna: Wilhelm Braumüller, 1913.

Contains MS Caius Cambridge 175 with variants from all manuscripts and de Worde's editions.

622. Weber. 1: xlv-li; 2: 3-278, 475-478; 3: 347-360.

Fragments:

1096. Kölbing, E. "Kleine Publicationen aus der Auchinleck-hs. III. Zwei fragmente von King Richard." *EStn* 8 (1885): 115-119.

Prints lines 1745-1918 and 2579-2762 from Auchinleck MS.

1097. Laing, David, and W.B.D.D. Turnbull. *Owain Miles, and Other Inedited Fragments of Ancient English Poetry.* Edinburgh: Ballantine, 1837.

Contains lines 674-1774 and 2763-2936 from the Auchinleck MS (only 32 copies printed).

Criticism:

1098. Broughton, Bradford B. *The Legends of King Richard I, Coeur de Lion: A Study of Sources and Variations*

373

to the Year 1600. Diss. U of Pennsylvania, 1960. The Hague: Mouton, 1966.

Chapter: 1. Richard as prince, 11-22.
            2. Richard as king and crusader, 23-40.
            3. The Richard of legend: before the Crusade, 41-50.
            4. The Richard of legend (continued): on the Crusade, 51-65.
            5. The Richard of legend (concluded): the last years, 66-77.
            6. Sources of the legends: before the Crusade, 78-92.
            7. Sources of the legends (continued): on the Crusade, 93-110.
            8. Sources of the legends (concluded): the last years, 111-137.
            9. Conclusion, 138-142.
Bibliography, 143-153.
Index, 154-161.

The romance is mentioned on 42-45, 78-80, 82-83, 108-109, 117-119, and other single pages.

1099.   Chapman, Robert L. "A Note on the Demon Queen Eleanor." *MLN* 70 (1955): 393-396.

Suggests that Walter Map may have been responsible for attaching the folklore type "Swan-Maiden" to Eleanor or that the legend of the demon countess of Anjou may have been transferred to her successor.

1100.   Davis, Norman. "Another Fragment of 'Richard Coer de Lyon.'" *N&Q* ns 16 (1969): 447-452.

Describes the unknown fragment, which is now numbered 704.1.16 and was found in a room of the Duke of Beaufort at Badminton, and compares some lines with Brunner's text [1095].

1101.   Hauer, Stanley R. "Richard Coeur de Lion: Cavalier or Cannibal?" *MissFR* 14 (1980): 88-95.

Charts the evolution of a popular hero from history and discusses how the same character can assume different guises in different times, tempered by the spirit of each age. Examines two views of Richard: the historical/medieval view as noble and kingly, but also demonic, blood-thirsty, and cruel; and the popular, romantic view as a gentlemanly warrior-hero, civilized and urbane.

SEE ALSO items 79 (103-104), 89, 110, 122, 163 (208-209, 242-246, 258-259, 283-284), 174, 413, 556, 948.

ROBERD OF CISYLE [115]

Editions:

1102. Brotanek, Rudolf. *Mittelenglische Dichtungen aus der Handschrift 432 des Trinity College in Dublin.* Halle: Max Niemeyer, 1940.

585. Ford. 287-299.

Contains a "normalized" text with the opening stanza modernized and lines 318 and 361-364 omitted.

586. French and Hale. 933-946.

Text is from the Vernon MS.

1103. Halliwell [-Phillipps], James Orchard. *Nugae Poeticae: Select Pieces of Old English Popular Poetry, Illustrating the Manners and Arts of the Fifteenth Century.* London: Smith, 1844. 49-63, 71.

Contains MS Cambridge University Ff.2.38.

597. Hazlitt. 1: 264-288 (text), 4: 362 (notes).

Contains MS Cambridge University Ff.2.38 after Halliwell [-Phillipps] [1103] and Utterson [1107].

1104. [Horstmann, C.] "Nachträge zu den Legenden. V. Roberd of Sicily." *Archiv* 62 (1879): 416-431.

Contains MSS Cambridge University Ii.4.9, Caius College 174, and Cambridge University Ff.2.38.

1105.   ------. *Sammlung altenenglischen Legenden*. Heil-
        bronn: Henninger, 1878. 209-219.

        Contains Vernon MS as well as other manuscript
        variants in footnotes.

1106.   Nuck, Richard. *Roberd of Cisyle*. Berlin: Bernstein,
        1887.

        A critical edition, based on Vernon MS and Horst-
        mann's edition [1105].

1107.   Utterson, E.V. *Kyng Roberd of Cysylle*. London:
        [Whittingham], 1839.

        "Transcribed from a volume in the Harleian collec-
        tion, numbered 'Plutarch 1701'"; only thirty copies
        printed.

        Criticism:

1108.   Antalocy, Stephanie Clare. "Shakespeare and the
        Ruler's Disguise: The Backgrounds of *Henry V* and
        Measure for Measure." *DAI* 37 (1976): 323A-324A. U
        of California, Berkeley.

        Analyzes *Roberd of Cisyle* and *Sir Orfeo* in the
        first chapter, establishing a three-part pattern in
        this convention: the king's crisis in office, his
        withdrawal and disguise, and his return and unmask-
        ing.

1109.   Hamilton, Donna B.   "Some Romance Sources for *King
        Lear*: Robert of Sicily and Robert the Devil." *SP* 71
        (1974): 173-191.

        Traces the parallels between the two ME stories and
        King Lear.   Suggests that the theme of humbling a
        proud man, the relation of the fool and madness to
        the theme of identity, and the idea that an old
        identity is replaced by a new one only through loss
        all derive from *Roberd of Cisyle*, which was included
        in ten manuscripts between 1375 and 1500.   Further
        suggests that Robert the Devil also influenced Shake-

speare's conception in terms of the suffering of par-
ent and children and the movement towards redemption.

1110. Hornstein, Lillian Herlands. *"King Robert of Sicily*:
Analogues and Origins." *PMLA* 79 (1964): 13-21.

Studies the analogues, which reveal the superiority
of the English version and its skillful synthesis of
themes from folklore, biblical commentary, and history.

1111. ------. *"King Robert of Sicily*: A New Manuscript."
PMLA 78 (1963): 453-458.

Calls attention to another folio of MS British
Library Additional 34801, dated early 15th century.
Prints the twenty-three lines, compares them with
other manuscript readings, and determines that they
are closest to MS Harley 525.

1112. McCoy, Dorothy S. "From Celibacy to Sexuality: An
Examination of Some Medieval and Early Renaissance
Versions of the Story of Robert the Devil." *Human
Sexuality in the Middle Ages and Renaissance*. Ed.
Douglas Radcliffe-Umstead. U of Pittsburgh Publica-
tions on the Middle Ages and Renaissance 4. Pitts-
burgh: Center for Medieval and Renaissance Studies,
1978. 29-39.

Compares six versions of the story and shows
changes in views on sex, religion, and marriage. In
all the OF versions, guilt is central and is determined by the degree of violent passion; in English
versions, the audience differentiates between the
evil associated with the sex act and the specific
evil of unintentionally copulating with the Devil.

1113. Olsen, Alexandra Hennessey. "The Return of the King:
A Reconsideration of *Robert of Sicily*." *Folklore* 93
(1982): 216-219.

Suggests that the poem's deep appeal lies in its
use of mythic elements to express its religious
message about the fall of a prideful man; the life

story of Robert re-enacts the myth of the archetypal hero with double use of the mythic pattern of eternal return.

1114.   Sajavaara, Kari.   "The Sixteenth-Century Versions of *Robert the Devil.*"   *NM* 80 (1979): 335-347.

Describes the three versions: the prose text printed at least twice by Wynkyn de Worde and a later metrical re-edition.

SEE ALSO items 163 (124-125), 181 (69-83), 413, 474, 556, 1443.

ROLAND AND VERNAGU [53]

Editions:

587. Grant.

598. Herrtage. vii, xii-xvi, 35-61, 118-122.

Introduction, text, and notes.

620. Turnbull.

SEE ALSO items 67 (192-194), 163, 574.

ROMAUNS OF PARTENAY (LUSIGNAN) [110]

Edition:

1115. Skeat, Walter W. *The Romans of Partenay, or of Lusignen: Otherwise Known as the Tale of Melusine, Translated from the French of La Coudrette (about 1500-1520 A.D.).* EETSOS 22. London: Trübner 1899. Rpt. New York: Greenwood, 1969.

Edited from a unique manuscript in the library of Trinity College, Cambridge. Introduction, notes, and glossary index.

Criticism:

1116. Shull, Donald Marshall. "The Effect of the Theory of Translation Expressed in the Anonymous *Romans of Partenay* (T.C.C. MS R.3.17) Upon the Language of the Poem." *DAI* 45 (1985): 2522A. U of North Carolina at Chapel Hill.

Shows how the English translator's idiosyncratic goals account for some gallicisms in the poem, neologisms in rhyme position, but also how many anomalies are not explained. Offers the possibility that he was consciously imitating Lollard translation practices or attempting a stylistic level beyond his competence.

SEE ALSO items 79 (53-54, 55-57, 95-96), 80 (75-85), 413, 519, 556.

ROSWALL AND LILLIAN [101]

Editions:

595. Hazlitt. 2: 239-267.

601. Laing. 43-46, 283-308.

Preface and text.

1117. Laing, David. *Roswall and Lillian*. Edinburgh, 1822.

Reproduction of the 1663 text.

1118. Lengert, O. "Die Schottische Romanze 'Roswall and Lillian.'" *EStn* 16 (1892): 321-356; 17 (1892): 341-377.

Parallel texts of the black-letter print, Advocates print, and Newcastle Bodleian fragment, with variants from the 1775 Edinburgh print and Douce print.

SEE ALSO items 413, 578.

Editions:

1119. Arbuthnet, Alexander (printer). *History of Alexander the Great.* ca. 1580.

   According to Severs [90], the only copy belongs to Earl of Dalhousie.

1120. Laing, David. *The Buik of the Most Noble and Vailyeand Conquerour Alexander the Great.* Edinburgh: Bannatyne Club, 1831. Rpt. New York: AMS P, 1971.

   Reprints Arbuthnet's text [1119]. No notes or introduction.

1121. Ritchie, R.L. Graeme. *The Buik of Alexander, or the Buik of the Most Noble and Valiant Conquerour Alexander the Grit.* STS ns 12 (vol. II), ns 17 (vol. I), ns 21 (vol. III), ns 25 (vol. IV). Edinburgh: Blackwell, 1921-1929.

   Edited in four volumes from the unique printed copy in the possession of the Earl of Dalhousie, with introductions, notes, and glossary, together with the French originals (*Li Fuerre de Gadres* and *Les Voeux du Paon*) collated with numerous manuscripts.

SEE ALSO item 204.

Edition:

1122. Horstmann, C. *Barbour's des schottischen National-dichters, Legendensammlung nebst den Fragmenten seines Trojanerkrieges.* 2 vols. Heilbronn: Henninger, 1881, 1882. 2: 215.

Criticism:

1123. Farish, John. "Some Spellings and Rhymes in the Scots *Sege of Troy.*" *ES* 38 (1957): 200-206.

Suggests that the dialect of the Midlands affected Scots orthography as evidenced by the appearance in the Scots texts of Southern forms and spellings, especially the *o* for the normal Scots *a*. Examines the phenomenon in various manuscripts of the poem, finding thirty-five examples in MS Douce 148.

1124. McIntosh, Angus. "Some Notes on the Language and Textual Transmission of the *Scottish Troy Book.*" *ArL* ns 10 (1979): 1-19.

Argues that the poem is unquestionably Scottish with a veneer of English forms to lend it a fashionable neo-Chaucerian flavor.

SEE ALSO items 476, 488.

Editions:

1125. Barnicle, Mary Elizabeth. *The Seege or Batayle of Troye*. EETSOS 172. London: Oxford UP, 1927.

Edited from MSS Lincoln's Inn 150, Egerton 2862, and Arundel 22, with Harley 525 in the appendix. No notes.

1126. Bickford, Gail Holmgren. "Materials for a New Edition of the Middle English *Seege of Troye*." *DAI* 33 (1972): 1673A-1674A. U of Pennsylvania.

Transcribes the four manuscripts, normalizing punctuation and spelling; includes notes and introduction.

1127. Hibler-Lebmannsport, L. *Das mittelenglischen Versgedicht The Seege of Troye*. 2 vols. Graz, Aus.: Moser, 1928.

Uses MSS Harley 525, Egerton 2862, and Lincoln's Inn 150.

1128. Wager, C.H.A. *The Seege of Troye*. New York: Macmillan, 1899.

Edits MS Harley 525, with introduction, notes, and glossaries.

1129. Zietsch, A. "Zwei mittelenglische Bearbeitungen der Historia de Excidio Trojae des Phrygiers Dares." *Archiv* 72 (1884): 11-58.

Parallel texts of MSS Harley 525 and Lincoln's Inn 150.

SEE ALSO items 163 (228-229), 445, 486, 487, 488, 489, 504 (42-43), 1142.

SEGE OF MELAYNE [56]

Editions:

587. Grant.

598. Herrtage. 1-52, 137-146.

   Text and notes. Textual emendations by Karl D. Bülbring, *EStn* 13 (1889): 156; and by E. Kölbing, *EStn* 5 (1882): 467.

607. Mills. 1-45, 193-197.

SEE ALSO items 163 (152-156), 574.

THE SIEGE OF JERUSALEM [107]

Editions:

1130. Kölbing, E., and Mabel Day. *The Siege of Jerusalem.*
EETSOS 188. London: Oxford UP, 1932. Rpt. Millwood,
NY: Kraus, 1971.

The text is edited from Bodleian MS Laud Misc. 656,
with variants from all other extant MSS.

1131. Steffler, Gustav. *Sege of Jerusalem.* Marburg:
Elwert'sche, 1891.

Text is from the Bodleian MS Laud Misc. 656.

Criticism:

1132. Benson, L.D. "The 'Rede Wynde' in 'The Siege of
Jerusalem.'" *N&Q* ns 7 (1960): 363-364.

Discusses the traditional description of the storm,
lines 53-57, with its unusual phrase *rede wynde.*
Suggests it may be a variant of ME *rade*, meaning
"quick or speedy."

1133. McGee, Alan Van Keuren. "The Geographical Distribution of Scandinavian Loan-Words in Middle English,
with Special Reference to the Alliterative Poetry."
DAI 31 (1970): 1785A. Yale U.

Examines the number and proportion of Scandinavian
loan-words and vocabulary in *Cursor Mundi* and in
seven manuscripts (with four different dialects) of
Siege of Jerusalem.

1134. McIntosh, Angus. "Middle English 'upon schore' and
       Some Related Matters." Schlauch Essays [14]. 255-
       260.

       Clarifies the meaning of lines 61-65 in *Siege of
       Jerusalem*, in which *scher* must mean "changed direc-
       tion," the same phrase as in *Sir Gawain and the Green
       Knight*, 2331-2333.

1135. Moe, Phyllis. "The French Source of the Alliterative
       Siege of Jerusalem." *MAE* 39 (1970): 147-154.

       Suggests a French text of the 13th century, Roger
       d'Argenteuil's *Bible en francois*, as a previously
       unnoticed source for more than a third of the English
       poem.

SEE ALSO items 34 (58-59), 212, 230, 238, 263 (61-62), 504
(88-89), 556, 576, 1059, 1144.

SIEGE OF THEBES

Editions:

1136. Erdmann, Axel. *Lydgate's Siege of Thebes*. EETSES
       108. London: Kegan Paul, Trench, Trübner; Oxford UP,
       1911.

       Contains the text, edited from all known manu-
       scripts and the two oldest editions.

1137. ------, and Eilert Ekwall. *Lydgate's Siege of
       Thebes*. EETSES 125. London: Oxford UP, 1930. Rpt.
       Millwood, NY: Kraus, 1973.

       Contains an introduction, notes, rhyme-lists,
       glossary, and an appendix.

1138. Lovell, Robert Earl. "John Lydgate's *Siege of Thebes*
       and *Churl and Bird*, Edited from the Cardigan-Brude-
       nell Manuscript." *DAI* 30 (1970): 2974A. U of Texas
       at Austin.

       Intends this work as a supplement to the EETS
       edition [1136] and suggests that the Cardigan MS ver-
       sion belongs to the subgroup Ad^1, Ad^2, and I.

Fragment:

1139. Edwards, A.S.G. "Lydgate's *Siege of Thebes*: A New
       Fragment." *NM* 71 (1970): 133-136.

       Prints lines 14-16, 18-21, 54-58, 92-98, and 134-
       140 from Cambridge University Additional MS 2707 (2)
       BB, a fragment of the first leaf of this work.

Criticism:

1140.   Anderson, David. "The Legendary History of Thebes in
        Boccaccio's *Teseida* and Chaucer's *Knight's Tale*." *DAI*
        40 (1980): 4585A. Princeton U.

        Shows that the place of Thebes in the design of
        Troilus and Criseyde and Lydgate's *Siege of Thebes*
        offers further evidence that late medieval authors
        used Theban history in ways that reflect the basic
        tenets of medieval historical thought.

1141.   Ayers, Robert W.   "Medieval History, Moral Purpose,
        and the Structure of Lydgate's *Siege of Thebes*."
        PMLA 73 (1958): 463-474.

        Argues that the structure of the poem is integral
        and appropriate to Lydgate's moral purpose of writing
        a history for the edification of later generations;
        the moral and philosophical framework is basically
        Boethian, and Lydgate includes episodes to point to
        his central moral message.

1142.   Blake, N.F.   "Caxton and Chaucer."   *LeedsSE* ns 1
        (1967): 19-36.

        Argues that in praising Chaucer's style in his
        prologue to the second edition of the *Canterbury
        Tales*, Caxton borrowed from Lydgate's *Siege of Thebes*
        and *Seege of Troye*.

1143.   Bowers, John M.   "*The Tale of Beryn* and *The Siege of
        Thebes*: Alternate Ideas of *The Canterbury Tales*."
        SAC 7 (1985): 23-50.

        Argues that Lydgate intended his work to be a
        continuation of Chaucer's *Canterbury Tales*, and that
        by using "narrative congruence and verbal echoes,"
        Lydgate knit together the end of his *Siege of Thebes*
        with the beginning of the *Knight's Tale*. Further
        suggests that in its circularity, *Siege of Thebes* re-
        flects Lydgate's vision of history in which civiliza-
        tions re-enact the rise and fall of Fortune's wheel.

1144. Doyle, A.I., and George B. Pace. "A New Chaucer Manuscript." *PMLA* 83 (1968): 22-34.

Describe the contents of the Coventry MS, which includes texts of *Siege of Jerusalem* (ff. 98-129^V) and *Siege of Thebes* (ff. 137^r-167^V).

1145. Ebin, Lois. "Chaucer, Lydgate, and the 'Myrie Tale.'" *ChauR* 13 (1979): 316-336.

Argues that Lydgate's work is not an inept imitation of Chaucer's, but an extension of the *Canterbury Tales* in which Lydgate tries to deal with the artistic issue raised by the Host's and Chaucer's conflicting definitions of a "myrie" tale. Further suggests that Lydgate is successful in creating a "myrie" or fruitful tale, one that is a mirror of political morality and a testament to the power of writing in leading men to truth.

1146. ------. "Lydgate's Views on Poetry." *AnM* 18 (1977): 76-105.

Argues that Lydgate developed a new critical vocabulary to define poetry and to articulate his ideas about the poet as craftsman and his belief in the importance of amplification and high style (*enlumyn, adourn, aureate, rethorik,* and *elloquence*). Suggests that Lydgate makes the critical relationship between the poet and the well-being of the state in *Siege of Thebes*.

1147. Edwards, A.S.G. "Lydgate Bibliography 1928-1968." *BB* 27 (1970): 95-98.

An unannotated bibliography separately listing editions, general and biographical, special aspects, textual variants, manuscript and textual studies, attribution, studies of individual poems, and influence.

1148. Ganim, John. "Mannerism and Moralism in Lydgate's *Siege of Thebes*." Ganim [38]. 103-122, 167.

Argues that Lydgates's leveling tendency springs
not from a new humanistic tendency, but rather from
distinct literary styles and his conception of history. Points to his "overwhelming literalism" in accounting for his failure to acknowledge the interplay
of different levels of meaning or reality.

1149. Kimura, Takeo. "Lydgate's *Siege of Thebes*: Mo
Hitotsu no *Canterbury* Monogatari." *Omura Kiyoshi
Kyoju Taikan Kinen Ronbunsh.* Tokyo: Azuma Shobo,
1982 [in Japanese].

Discusses the relationship of Lydgate's work to the
Canterbury Tales.

1150. Kohl, Stephan. "Chaucer's Pilgrim in Fifteenth-Century Literature." *FCS* 7 (1983): 221-236.

Views *Siege of Thebes* and the *Tale of Beryn* not
only as fiction but metafictions that no longer
comply with the norms of medieval culture accepted by
Chaucer's narrator. Discusses Lydgate's pessimism
and melancholic tone caused by the invalidation of
moral norms in the everyday life of his times.

1150a. ------. "*The Kingis Quair* and Lydgate's *Siege of
Thebes* as Imitations of Chaucer's 'Knight's Tale.'"
FCS 2 (1979): 119-134.

Re-assesses 15th-century literature in terms of its
relative modernity and originality, while taking into
account the persistence of traditional features; suggests that in *Siege of Thebes* a conventional character disguises a lesson that subverts Boethian philosophy and reflects the tensions between traditional
concepts of man and society and the realities of
contemporary life.

1151. Marotta, Joseph Gerald. "John Lydgate and the Tradition of Medieval Rhetoric." *DAI* 33 (1972): 729A.
CUNY.

Reviews Lydgate's knowledge of rhetoric and gives a

detailed reading of *Siege of Thebes*, which reveals Lydgate's ability to give meaning and shape to his source material.

1152. Parr, Johnstone. "The Horoscope of Edippus in Lydgate's *Siege of Thebes*." *Essays in Honor of Walter Clyde Curry*. Nashville: Vanderbilt UP, 1954. 117-122.

Argues that Lydgate discarded the mythological oracular machinery of his sources and recast his material by using the horoscope to divine the tragedy from the child's natal configuration. However, he put Saturn rather than Sol in the house of Mars, showing that he had little insight into astrology and concocted rather than determined a malignant configuration.

1153. Renoir, Alain. "Attitudes Toward Women in Lydgate's Poetry." *ES* 42 (1961): 1-14.

Examines references to women in Lydgate's work and finds a versatility from the satirical to the deeply moving. Characterizes three distinct attitudes: of the courtly audience (women are wonderful), of the clergy (women are abominable), of Lydgate himself (women are like men and must be judged individually).

1154. ------. "Chaucerian Character Names in Lydgate's *Siege of Thebes*." *MLN* 71 (1956): 249-256.

Tries to settle the question of whether the immediate source of this work is *Ystoire de Thebes* or *Le Roman de Edipus* by comparing twenty-five character names in all three works, as well as the corresponding names in Chaucer. Concludes that Lydgate departed from Chaucerian forms only to follow *Roman de Edipus*, his source at least for characters.

1155. ------. "The Immediate Source of Lydgate's *Siege of Thebes*." *SN* 33 (1961): 86-95.

Argues that Lydgate need not have consulted the

Ystoire de Thebes, but used instead a complete text of *Roman de Edipus*.

1156.   ------.   "Lydgate's *Siege of Thebes*:   A Study in the Art of Adaptation." Diss. Harvard U, 1955.

1157.   Schlauch, Margaret.   "Polynices and Gunnlaug Serpent-Tongue: A Parallel." *E&S* ns 25 (1972): 15-22.

Compares the combat of Eteocles and Polynices in *Siege of Thebes* with the comparable situation in the Icelandic saga, claiming that a source relationship is unlikely though not impossible chronologically.

1158.   Spearing, A.C.   "Lydgate's Canterbury Tale: *The Siege of Thebes* and Fifteenth-Century Chaucerianism." Yeager [109]. 333-364.

Argues that not only did Lydgate add to the *Canterbury Tales* by writing the first tale on the homeward journey, but that he also completed Chaucer's *Knight's Tale* by recounting earlier stages of the Theban legend, bringing the end of his tale to the beginning of Chaucer's.   Further investigates the ways Lydgate interpreted and misinterpreted Chaucer's story and his stylistic, rhetorical, and literary devices of *digressio*, *sententia*, and *descriptio*.

1159.   Steinberg, Theodore.   "Poetry and the Perpendicular Style." *JAAC* 40 (1981): 71-79.

Argues that Lydgate's work—as a reflection of 15th-century literature—shares many traits with the architecture of the times, especially its linear structure.   Just as *Siege of Thebes* has a linear rather than organic unity, there are vertical layerings and facades in architecture that are not organic; just as fan vaulting uses a complex overlay for structural strength and unification, Lydgate's diction is a complex overlay to his structure.

SEE ALSO items 79 (76-77), 181 (222-236), 481, 481a, 482,

491, 493, 494, 495, 497 (110-135), 499 (59-65), 504 (70ff, 100f), 1592.

Editions:

583. Brookhouse. 9-24, 31-59, 97-106, 109-133.
Introduction, text, commentary, appendix.

1160. Brookhouse, John Christopher. *"Sir Amadas,* Edited with an Introduction, Notes, and Glossary." Diss. Harvard U, 1964.

1161. Hardman, P.M. "An Edition of a Middle English Romance: *Sir Amadace." TGB* 23 (1972-73): 304. B.Litt., Oxford U.

612. Robson. 27-56, 101-104.

1162. Smith, Marjorie N. "An Edition of the Ireland and Edinburgh Texts of 'Sir Amadace.'" M.A., Leeds U, 1934. Cited in "Theses Added to Leeds University Library," *LeedsSE* 3 (1934): 64.

1163. Stephens, George. *Ghost Thanks, or, The Grateful Unburied, A Mythic Tale in its Oldest European Form, Sir Amadace, a Middle-North-English Metrical Romance of the Thirteenth Century.* Cheapinghaven [Copenhagen]: Michaelsen and Tillge, 1860.

Texts from Robson [612] and Weber [622].

622. Weber. 1: lx-lxii; 3: 243-275, 376, 461.

SEE ALSO items 413, 504 (38-39), 556, 703.

SIR CLEGES [114]

Editions:

586. French and Hale. 877-895.

1164. Ginn, R.K.G. "A Critical Edition of the Two Texts of *Sir Cleges*." *TGB* 18 (1967-68): 317. M.A., Queen's U of Belfast.

1165. McKnight, George H. *Middle English Humorous Tales in Verse*. Boston: Heath, 1913. 38-59, 71-80. Rpt. New York: Gordian P, 1971.

Text is from the Ashmole MS 61.

1166. Morley, Henry. *Shorter English Poems*. London: Cassell, Petter & Galpin, 1876. 23-40.

1167. Treichel, A. "*Sir Cleges*: Eine mittelenglische Romanze." *EStn* 22 (1896): 345-389.

Parallel texts of the two extant manuscripts (374-389); commentary, history, and introduction (345-374).

622. Weber. 1: xxxix-xli, 331-353, 381; 3:345-346.

Criticism:

1168. Carr, Sherwyn T. "The Middle English Nativity Cherry Tree: The Dissemination of a Popular Motif." *MLQ* 36 (1975): 133-147.

Attempts to demonstrate that the Nativity cherry
tree, while derived from the well-known tree in the
apocryphal Gospel of Pseudo-Matthew, was first connected with the Nativity in *Ludus Coventriae*, and
from that source grew independently in the two popular manifestations: *Sir Cleges*, in which the motif
underwent radical transformation with no iconographi-
cal significance, and the "Cherry-Tree Carol."

SEE ALSO items 181 (84-96), 413, 546, 556.

SIR DEGARE [92]

Editions:

1169. Carr, Muriel Bothwell. *"Sire Degarre*, a Middle English Metrical Romance Edited from the Manuscript and Black Letter Texts." Diss. U of Chicago, 1924.

586. French and Hale. 287-320.

589. Hales and Furnivall. 3: 16-48.

590. ------. 3: 195-220.

1170. Laing, David. *Sire Degarre, a Metrical Romance of the End of the Thirteenth Century.* Abbotsford Club 28. Edinburgh, 1849.

1171. Rollow, Jack Wilcox. "The Text of 'Sire Degarré.'" Diss. Cornell U, 1950.

613. Rumble. 44-78.

1172. Schleich, Gustav. *Sire Degarre.* Englische Textbibliothek 19. Heidelberg: Carl Winter, 1929.

Text is based on Auchinleck MS up to line 1076, and the conclusion supplied from MS Rawlinson F. 34.

616. Schmidt and Jacobs.

621.   Utterson.   1: 113-155.

Criticism:

1173.   Colopy, Cheryl.   "*Sir Degaré*:   A Fairy Tale Oedipus."
        PCP 17 (1982): 31-39.

        Suggests that the story seems to say there is an
        inevitable connection between sexuality and the
        discovery of self, between incestuous desires and the
        growing-up process. Further argues that the story's
        muddled events, from a psychological perspective,
        become connected thematically and symbolically around
        the two pairs of potentially incestuous couples.

1174.   Jacobs, Nicolas.   "The Egerton Fragment of *Sir De-
        garre*." *NM* 72 (1971): 86-96.

        Discusses the dialect (possibly Suffolk), orthogra-
        phy, and transcription of the Egerton MS 2862 before
        printing the text of the fragment.

1175.   ------. "Old French 'Degaré' and Middle English 'De-
        garre' and 'Deswarre.'"   *N&Q* ns 17 (1970): 164-165.

        Suggests that OF *esgaré*, "lost or destitute," is
        related to ME *deswarre* in line 6003 of *Guy of War-
        wick*, and that the two forms in English suggest
        dialectical distinction in OF.

1176.   ------. "The Processes of Scribal Substitution and
        Redaction: A Study of the Cambridge Fragment of *Sir
        Degarré*." *MAE* 53 (1984): 26-48.

        Lists all variant readings in this fragment and
        compares them to all other manuscript readings and
        then discusses these findings in the broader terms of
        textual transmission.

1178.   ------. "The Second Revision of *Sir Degarre*: The
        Egerton Fragment and its Congeners." *NM* 85 (1984):
        95-107.

Analyzes in the light of known scribal tendencies the arguments for unoriginal readings in the Egerton and Rawlinson MSS and the early printed editions of the poem; further considers attributing rewritten passages to a single 14th-century revision.

1179. ------. "Two Corrections to the Auchinleck 'Sir Degarre.'" *N&Q* ns 16 (1969): 205-206.

Corrects two misreadings: line 544 of the manuscript reads *bise me*, not *vise me*, "to look after or exert"; and line 1005 reads *Belami*, not *Velami*.

1180. Kozicki, Henry. "Critical Methods in the Literary Evaluation of *Sir Degaré*." *MLQ* 29 (1968): 3-14.

Summarizes the different critical approaches to the poem and then suggests that it is best understood as a "well-knit, domestic epic of psychological growth, of *rites de passage* to maturity, skillfully augmented by residual, vegetation-myth symbolism."

1181. Rosenberg, Bruce A. "The Three Tales of *Sir Degaré*." *NM* 76 (1975): 39-51.

Challenges assumptions about romance composition by arguing that instead of a patchwork of romance motifs, this tale is a skillful conflation of three folktales: A-T Type 706, 873, and 931.

1182. Stokoe, William C., Jr. "The Double Problem of *Sir Degaré*." *PMLA* 70 (1955): 518-534.

Attempts to refute the claim that the poem has a corrupt textual tradition by showing that there are two distinct versions with major differences in style, narrative skill, and treatment of the supernatural background; denies charges of the poem's mediocrity by George P. Faust [*Sir Degare* (Princeton: Princeton UP, 1935)], Clark Slover [*TexasSE* 2 (1935): 5-23], and G.V. Smithers [*MAE* 22 (1953): 61-92].

SEE ALSO items 18 (66-71), 93 (150-157), 164, 179 (70-75), 363 (212-216), 368, 370 (158-172), 371, 375, 376, 413, 414, 465, 504 (49-50), 578, 709.

SIR DEGREVANT [97]

Editions:

1183.   Casson, L.F.   *The Romance of Sir Degrevant: A Paral-
        lel-Text Edition.*   EETSOS 221.   London: Oxford UP,
        1949.

        The text is from MSS Lincoln Cathedral 91 and
        Cambridge University Ff.1.6.

1184.   Ellis, F.S.   *The Romance of Sir Degrevant.* Hammer-
        smith, Eng.: Kelmscott P, 1896.

        Edited from Halliwell [-Phillipps] [593] with addi-
        tions and variants from Lincoln MS.

 593.   Halliwell [-Phillipps].   177-256, 288-306, 311-312.

1185.   Luick, Karl.   *Sir Degrevant.* Wiener Beiträge zur eng-
        lischen Philologie 47.   Vienna: W. Braumüller, 1917.

        Texts from the Thornton and Cambridge University
        MSS on opposite pages.

Fragment:

1186.   Schleich, G.   "Collationen zu me. Dichtungen.   3. *Sir
        Degrevant.*"   *EStn* 12 (1889): 140-142.

        A collation of the first ninety-six lines of both
        Findern and Thornton MSS.

Criticism:

1187.   Harris, Kate.   "The Origins and Make-up of Cambridge
        University Library MS Ff.1.6."   *TCBS* 8 (1983): 299-
        333.

           Suggests that the informality of the whole content
        and the shifting of the personnel making entries
        imply that the Findern MS was a loose-leaf album with
        its origins in and use by a South Derbyshire family
        (Cotton, Frauncis, Shirley, or Findern) and friends
        and associates. (*Sir Degrevant* is item 27 of this
        manuscript.)

SEE ALSO items 11 (56-57), 163 (93-99, 273-274), 331, 413,
443, 556, 578.

Editions:

580. Beattie. 53-88.

1188. Cook, Albert S. *Sir Eglamour, A Middle English Romance*. New York: Holt, 1911.

    Reprinted from Schleich [1190], but with modernized punctuation.

589. Hales and Furnivall. 2: 338-389.

590. ------. 3: 9-49.

593. Halliwell [-Phillipps]. 121-176, 273-287, 311.

1189. Richardson, Frances E. *Sir Eglamour of Artois*. EETSOS 256. London: Oxford UP, 1965.

1190. Schleich, Gustav. *Sir Eglamour: Eine englische Romanze des 14. Jahrhunderts*. Palaestra 53. Berlin: Mayer & Müller, 1906.

619. Stevenson. 115-156.

Fragments:

1191. Hall, J. "Bruchstücke eines alten Druckes des Eglamour of Artois." *Archiv* 95 (1895): 308-311.

Text consists of the Bankes fragments.

1192. Matheson, Lister M. "A Fragment of *Sir Eglamour of
       Artois*." *ELN* 17 (1980): 165-168.

       Draws attention to a previously unnoticed fragment
       in the University of Michigan MS 225 written in the
       16th century and corresponding to the first thirty-
       five lines of the Richardson text [1189] of the poem.

SEE ALSO items 79 (36-37), 163 (77-83), 179, 410, 413, 414,
443, 472, 515, 578.

SIR FIRUMBRAS [47, 48]
(Ashmole and Fillingham versions)

Editions:

1193. Herrtage, Sidney J. *Sir Ferumbras*. EETSES 34.
London: Kegan Paul, Trench, Trübner, 1879. Rpt.
London: Oxford UP, 1966.

The text is edited from the unique Ashmole MS 33
now in the Bodleian Library.

609. O'Sullivan. xv-xlii, 1-58.

Text of Fillingham version.

1194. Stevens, David. *"Sir Ferumbras*: A New Edition of the
Most Popular Charlemagne Romance." *DA* 29 (1968):
241A. U of Massachusetts.

A new transcription of the Ashmole MS 33.

Criticism:

1195. Koenig, V. Frederic. "The Etymology of *Fierabras*."
MLN 71 (1956): 356-357.

Suggests that the only phonologically acceptable
explanation for the hero's name is the imperative of
ferir + à + *bras*.

SEE ALSO items 67, 79 (51-52, 109-111), 101, 574, 887, 999,
1005.

SIR GAWAIN AND THE GREEN KNIGHT [25]

Editions:

1196. Andrew, Malcolm, and Ronald Waldron. *The Poems of the Pearl Manuscript: Pearl, Cleanness, Patience, Sir Gawain and the Green Knight.* York Medieval Texts, 2nd ser. London: Arnold, 1978. 37-43, 207-300.

Complete text with textual notes and glossary.

1197. Barron, W.R.J. *Sir Gawain and the Green Knight.* Manchester Medieval Classics. Manchester: Manchester UP; New York: Barnes & Noble, 1974.

Provides a ME text with textual notes and a prose translation on facing pages, followed by explanatory notes.

1198. Burrow, J.A. *Sir Gawain and the Green Knight.* Penguin English Poets 13. Harmondsworth, Eng.: Penguin, 1972. Rpt. New Haven: Yale UP, 1982.

Includes text (17-87), notes (88-124), manuscript readings (125-127), and glossary (129-176).

1199. Cawley, A.C. *Pearl and Sir Gawain and the Green Knight.* Everyman's Library 346. London: Dent, 1962. Rev. with J.J. Anderson, 1976.

1200. Como, Frank Thomas. *"Sir Gawain and the Green Knight*: A Normalized and Glossed Text." *DA* 30 (1969): 2512A. Arizona State U.

Aims at a text for the beginning student in ME to

minimize the distractions caused by an idiosyncratic manuscript. Eliminates obsolete orthographic symbols and corrects scribal confusions.

584. Dunn and Byrnes. 376-459.

585. Ford. 349-428.

A normalized text based on Tolkien and Gordon [1208].

586a. Garbáty. 254-332.

1201. Gollancz, Sir Israel. *Sir Gawain and the Green Knight: Re-edited from Ms. Cotton Nero, A.x., in the British Museum.* EETSOS 210. London: Oxford UP, 1940. Rpt. 1957.

Began as a revision of Morris [1205] in 1897 and in 1912 and now completed, with introductory essays by Mabel Day and Mary S. Serjeantson.

1202. Guidi, A., trans. *Galvano e il Cavaliere Verde.* Edizione Fussi. Firenze: Sansoni, 1958.

Parallel ME text with a prose translation in Italian, as well as textual notes.

594a. Haskell. 1-138.

1203. Jones, R.T. *Sir Gawain and the Grene Gome: A Regularized Text.* Pietermaritzburg, S. Afr.: U of Natal P, 1962. Rev. ed. New York: Barnes & Noble, 1972.

605. Madden. 3-92, 299-326.

First edition of "Syr Gawayn and the Grene Knyȝt" with notes and glossary.

1204. Moorman, Charles. *The Works of the Gawain-Poet*. Jackson: UP of Mississippi, 1977.

Introduction (3-65), text with notes (281-444), and glossary (445-452).

1205. Morris, Richard. *Sir Gawayne and The Green Knight: An Alliterative Romance-Poem, (ab. 1320-30 A.D.)*. EETSOS 4. London: Trübner, 1864.

First separate edition of the poem, which follows Madden [605]. Full ME text, notes, and glossary, but superseded by EETSOS 210 [1201].

1206. Pons, Émile. *Sire Gauvain et le Chevalier Vert: Poème Anglais du XIVe Siècle*. Bibliothèque de Philologie Germanique 9. Paris: Aubier, 1946.

Introduction (15-95) and text of ME and French translation on facing pages (100-259); no commentary.

1207. Silverstein, Theodore. *Sir Gawain and the Green Knight: A New Critical Edition*. Chicago: U of Chicago P, 1984.

Complete ME text with textual notes at the foot of each page, followed by explanatory notes and full glossary.

1208. Tolkien, J.R.R., and E.V. Gordon. *Sir Gawain and the Green Knight*. Oxford: Clarendon P, 1925. Corr. and rpt. 1930. 2nd ed., rev. Norman Davis, 1967.

1209. Tsuchiya, Tadayuki. *Sir Gawain and the Green Knight Annotated by OED and MED*. Tokyo: privately printed, 1976.

1210. Vantuono, William. *Patience and Sir Gawain and the Green Knight*. Vol. 2 of *The Pearl Poems: An Omnibus Edition*. The Renaissance Imagination 6. 2 vols.

New York: Garland, 1984.

Parallel texts of ME and modern translation (43-194) and commentary (237-371).

1211.   Waldron, R.A. *Sir Gawain and the Green Knight*. York Medieval Texts. London: Arnold; Evanston: North-western UP, 1970.

ME text with partially modernized spelling, textual notes, explanatory notes, and select bibliography.

Bibliographies:

1212.   Andrew, Malcolm. *The Gawain-Poet: An Annotated Bibliography, 1839-1977*. New York: Garland, 1979.

1213.   Blanch, Robert J. *Sir Gawain and the Green Knight: A Reference Guide*. Troy, NY: Whitston, 1983.

Provides annotations chronologically from 1824 to 1978, with no separation of editions and criticism. Only seventeen items for 1977 and four for 1978.

1214.   Do, Merdeka Thien-Ly Huong. "*Sir Gawain and the Green Knight*: An Annotated Bibliography, 1973-1978." *Comitatus* 11 (1980): 66-100.

1215.   Hambridge, Roger A. "*Sir Gawain and the Green Knight*: An Annotated Bibliography, 1950-1972." *Comitatus* 4 (1973): 49-84.

1210.   Vantuono.   389-430.

Criticism:

1216.   Andrew, Malcolm. "The Diabolical Chapel: A Motif in *Patience* and *Sir Gawain and the Green Knight*." *Neophil* 66 (1982): 313-319.

Considers the paradoxical combination of the hellish and sacred associations of the green chapel and the whale's belly, both settings in which the protagonist undergoes penitential experience.

1217. Arthur, Ross Gilbert. "The Signs of Sir Gawain: A Study in Fourteenth-Century Modes of Meaning." *DAI* 43 (1983): 3313A. York U, Canada.

Examines the non-verbal signs in the poem, which can be interpreted by sign theory found in medieval texts, both the analytical techniques of the logicians and signs from popular heraldic, mathematical, and devotional works.

1218. Astell, Ann W. *Sir Gawain and the Green Knight*: A Study in the Rhetoric of Romance." *JEGP* 84 (1985): 188-202.

Argues that the author uses the created "I"—the mediator between himself and the audience—as a rhetorical and didactic strategy by which he leads his audience first to recognize the fictive situation as analogous to their own and then to accept its moral teaching as applicable to them.

1219. Bachman, W. Bryant, Jr. "Lineation of the Bobs in *Sir Gawain and the Green Knight*." *ELN* 18 (1980): 86-88.

Argues that no manuscript authority exists for the bob as a separate line, since it is always written to the right of an existing line. Further suggests that not numbering them may lead to a better understanding of the numerology of the poem.

1220. ------. "*Sir Gawain and the Green Knight*: The Green and the Gold Once More." *TSLL* 23 (1981): 495-516.

Views the poem as a complex and ambitious dialectic between the green and gold, symbols that increase the tensions between impulse and repression, energy and formalism, nature and civilization, pragmatism and idealism, the demands of this world and proscriptions of the next.

1221.   Barron, W.R.J. "The Ambivalence of Adventure: Verbal Ambiguity in *Sir Gawain and the Green Knight*, Fitt I." Grout et al. [300a]. 28-40, 228-230.

Examines the poem in light of romance conventions, especially *aventure*, which the poet presents as a complex of interrelated games in a variety of ambiguous contexts. Further suggests that the poet stimulated the audience's scrutiny of the conventional quest and the relationship between romance and reality, finally calling into question their very judgment about the poem's genre.

1222.   ------. *Trawthe & Treason: The Sin of Gawain Reconsidered; A Thematic Study of "Sir Gawain and the Green Knight."* Manchester: Manchester UP, 1980.

Chapter: 1.   Hunting and wooing, 1-35.
           2.   *Trawthe* and treason, 36-81.
           3.   Treason to whom? 82-112.
           4.   The purgation of treason, 113-145.
Abbreviations, 146.
Bibliography, 146-150.

1223.   Barry, Peter. "*Sir Gawain and the Green Knight.*" *Expl* 37.1 (1978): 29-30.

Discusses the two names of the Green Knight (ll. 408 and 2445) and refutes the idea that Bercilak is his "everyday" name.

1224.   Bennett, Michael J. "Courtly Literature and Northwest England in The Later Middle Ages." *Court and Poet* [20]. 69-78.

Attempts to reassemble the community of poets and patrons who built up the literary tradition around the *Gawain*-poet; reviews the theories about interpenetration between the provincial culture and the international court; suggests that the writers acquired their sophistication outside the region; and concludes the poem can be located in the last years of Richard II's reign, with Gawain's journey paralleling the actual route of the King and his Cheshire retinue from Ireland in July 1339.

1225. ------. "Late Medieval Society in North-west England: Cheshire and Lancashire, 1375-1425." *TGB* 26 (1977): 641. Ph.D., Lancaster U.

1226. ------. "Power, Patronage and Provincial Culture." Chapter 10 of *Community, Class and Careerism: Cheshire and Lancashire Society in the Age of Sir Gawain and the Green Knight.* Cambridge Studies in Medieval Life and Thought 18, 3rd ser. Cambridge: Cambridge UP, 1983. 192-235.

Suggests that the operations of royal patronage and the progress of careerism brought large sectors of regional society into the mainstream of national life, allowed local men to attain positions of wealth and power available in their provincial settings, and fed a mutual dependence whereby local families had to seek the favor of courtiers and government officials in order to maintain their positions while royal lords recruited men for their own retinues. Concludes that the character of the literature bears eloquent testimony to the prosperity of these two northern counties and the cultural influences engendered by careerism.

1227. ------. "*Sir Gawain and the Green Knight* and the Literary Achievement of the North-west Midlands: The Historical Background." *JMH* 5 (1979): 63-88.

Draws on the social history of the area; focuses on the career of Richard Newton, a Cheshire writer; and accounts for the richness and sophistication of Midlands literature in terms of social mobility, the large number of careerists, and the possible patronage of Richard II himself.

1228. Benson, C. David. "John Mirk and the Green Knight's

Christmas." *BSUF* 20.3 (1979): 13-15.

Suggests parallels between criticism of contemporary Christmas celebrations made by John Mirk in his sermon for Septuagesima Sunday in the *Festial* and events in *Sir Gawain and the Green Knight*; believes that the audience for the poem would have recognized the potential dangers in the merriment at the castle.

1229.   Besserman, Lawrence L.   "Gawain's Green Girdle."   *AnM* 22 (1982): 84-101.

Compiles the many and diverse significances and associations of the girdle from folk belief and Christian lore, including its value as an icon of martial valor, chastity, purity, truth, eroticism, austerity, inconstancy in love, magical binding or healing, and spiritual preparedness.   Concludes that Gawain singled out its significance as broken *trawthe*.

1230.   Bishop, Ian.   "Time and Tempo in *Sir Gawain and the Green Knight*."   *Neophil* 69 (1985): 611-619.

Points to the significance of time in this narrative, which begins and ends with a historical frame; the adventure is thus placed in the context of world history. Further suggests that the final wheel contrasts with the opening in reminding the audience that for Christians the end lies outside cycles of time.

1231.   Blamires, Alcuin.   "The Turning of the Year in 'Sir Gawain.'"   *Trivium* 17 (1982): 21-38.

Argues that the iconography of the medieval calendar sheds light on the poem's meaning, especially December's pig-killing and the beheading scenes. Further argues that the poet superimposed the end of the year on the beginning, so the January feast is disrupted by the December axman.

1232.   Blanch, Robert J.   "The Game of Invoking Saints in *Sir Gawain and the Green Knight*."   *ABR* 31 (1980): 237-260.

Points out that saints' oaths ironically foreshadow Gawain's trials at the castle and at the Green Chapel as well as reinforce the symmetrical design of the poem.

1233.   ------. "Imagery of Binding in Fits One and Two of *Sir Gawain and the Green Knight.*" *SN* 54 (1982): 53-60.

Examines the images of knotting and binding and then traces Gawain and Camelot's identification with trappings and tinsel values, emblems of pride and worldliness, which emphasize their concern with external forms rather than inner spiritual values.

1234.   ------. "The Legal Framework of 'A Twelmonyth and a Day' in *Sir Gawain and the Green Knight.*" *NM* 84 (1983): 347-352.

Traces the tradition in Germanic custom and judicial procedure and the role of this legal term in English common law and then examines the poem's contexts (ll. 277-300 and 377-412), which signalize the binding nature of the compact that Gawain makes with the Green Knight, who acts as judge on a legal court day.

1235.   ------, and Julian N. Wasserman. "Medieval Contracts and Covenants: The Legal Coloring of *Sir Gawain and the Green Knight.*" *Neophil* 68 (1984): 598-610.

Trace medieval contractual tradition, especially the concepts of contract, covenant, surety, and tally in common law and juridical procedure; show how this tradition shapes the narrative and delineates the specific rules that Gawain violates.

1236.   Blenkner, Louis, O.S.B. "The Three Hunts and Sir Gawain's Triple Fault." *ABR* 29 (1978): 227-246.

Suggests that parallelism between the hunt and Gawain's activities centers on the three powers of the soul: irascible *couardise*, concupiscent *couetyse*, and irrational *untrawþe*, and that Gawain's triple fault also represents the triple wound inflicted as punishment for original sin.

1237. Boitani, Piero. "L'invenzione delle coordinate mimetiche in *Sir Gawain and the Green Knight*." *StG* 16 (1978): 267-290 [in Italian].

Using ideas from Auerbach's *Mimesis*, the author examines the "mimetic coordinates" of the poem. Sees the structure as orchestrated into four parts, including the Beheading Game and Exchange of Winnings; views the poem's temporal dimensions (real, historic, cyclic, ritualistic and mythological, and Christian) and multi-spatial dimensions (the fantastic, indefinite space of romance juxtaposed with the context of a real landscape). Sees a psychological profundity with characters that transcend mere convention to become artistic, social, and real personnages; notes the artistic self-awareness of the artist, who combines oral and literary conventions as well as romantic adventures within a historical framework.

1238. Bragg, Lois. *Sir Gawain and the Green Knight* and the Elusion of Clarity: Social Codes as Presented by the Narrator." *NM* 86 (1985): 482-488.

Argues that the narrator deliberately employs techniques to elude clarity, first offering and then discrediting religion, chivalry, courtly love, pragmatism, and revenge, in turn, as the main controlling theme. Concludes that for the *Gawain*-poet no single societal code could adequately encompass Gawain's adventures.

1239. Braswell, Mary Flowers. *The Medieval Sinner: Characterization and Confession in the Literature of the English Middle Ages*. Rutherford: Fairleigh Dickinson UP; London: Associated UP, 1983. 95-100.

Discusses the penitential motifs, especially those in Gawain's confession.

1240. Broughton, Bradford B. "Sir Gawain: From Scoundrel to Hero." *English Record* 31.1 (1980): 9-10, 16.

Suggests that the author chose Gawain as protagonist, despite his mixed nature, because he was Arthur's nephew and his name alliterates with "grene."

1241. Burrow, J.A. "Honour and Shame in *Sir Gawain and the Green Knight.*" *Essays on Medieval Literature.* Oxford: Clarendon P, 1984. 117-131.

Utilizes the ideas of social anthropologists such as Campbell and Pitt-Rivers concerning shame cultures to examine the workings of honour and shame in the Arthurian world and to distinguish between guilt and shame for Gawain and the court.

1242. ------. *"Sir Gawain and the Green Knight."* Ford [36]. 208-223.

Discusses the poem's themes, plot, and treatment of adventure, the subject of medieval romances.

1243. Callaghan, Mary. "Number and Numerical Composition: Tradition and Practice in *Sir Gawain and the Green Knight.*" *DAI* 43 (1982): 796A. Fordham U.

Examines the practice of numerical composition in classical, biblical, and medieval works and then explores ways in which these traditions and practices are present in this poem.

1244. Catalini, Claire F. "A Note on Lines 1020-23 of *Sir Gawain and the Green Knight.*" *QFG* 1 (1980): 159-163.

Argues that *sayn Jonez day* in line 1023 was probably originally *childermasse day*, the name for Holy Innocent's Day, December 18. This proposal not only fits the alliteration and meter, but also sets straight the confused dating of the poem without postulating the author's confusion, an inaccuracy in the dates, or the existence of a missing line to make sense of this passage.

1245. ------. "Two Stages in Breaking up the Deer." *QFG* 2
       (1982): 255-277.

       Deals specifically with two aspects of *gralloching*
       (disemboweling): making the *erber* and opening the
       belly prior to removing the inner organs. Also es-
       tablishes the meaning of *raven's bone* as the upper
       part of the sternum, not the pelvis. Reads lines
       1333-1334 as: "þen brek þay þe bale, þe bowelez out
       token/Lystily, for lancying and lere of þe knot,"
       meaning they opened up the belly, took out the in-
       nards, carefully, so as not to pierce the stomach or
       undo the knot. Compares the treatment of disembowel-
       ing in *Sir Gawain and the Green Knight* with that in
       French texts.

1246. Clark, S.L., and Julian N. Wasserman. "The Pearl
       Poet's City Imagery." *SoQ* 16 (1978): 297-309.

       Argue that the poet's conception of God's final
       judgment is realized through a series of spatial-
       temporal metaphors, that the poet translates the pro-
       cess of apocalyptic separation of the saved from the
       damned into secular terms, and that the poet is
       interested in the progressional nature of wisdom.

1247. Clein, Wendy Anne. "'þe Lettrure of Armes': Chiv-
       alry in *Sir Gawain and the Green Knight*." *DAI* 46
       (1985): 1619A. U of Connecticut.

       Suggests that the poem provides a setting for the
       interplay of the conflicting religious, military, and
       courtly concepts of chivalry, and that its ending
       provides an understanding of the possibilities and
       inherent tensions and limitations of knighthood.

1248. Clough, Andrea. "The French Element in *Sir Gawain
       and the Green Knight*: With Special Reference to the
       Description of Bertilak's Castle in 11. 785-810."
       NM 86 (1985): 187-196.

       Discusses the profound morphological and semantic
       influence of the French language on this poem from
       naturalized AN loan words to rare dialectical forms,

including the use of calques, which refashioned
English phraseology and syntax.

1249. Cockcroft, Robert. "Castle Hautdesert: Portrait or
Patchwork?" *Neophil* 62 (1978): 459-477.

Examines the components of the castle and setting
as they appear to Gawain: the distant view, the park,
and the nearby castle. Suggests that the knight's
eye and judgment review features embodying successive
phases of civilization: the park pale, the clearing,
and the double ditch are the first signatures on a
primitive landscape made by man as hunter and warrior; the towers reflect the movement from the world
of pioneer through increasing technology of defense
to the luxuries of high civilization. Under the roof
of a castle that is "pared out of papure," the ideal
of the pentangle is broken and ostentation replaces
defense.

1250. Cole, Carolyn Barry. "The Purpose and Practice of
Troth in Medieval English Society and Literature."
DAI 46 (1985): 1274A. U of Southwestern Louisiana.

Traces the tradition of troth from *sacramentum*, a
voluntary oath pledged by Germanic comitatus to their
chief, through feudal oaths of homage and fealty,
customary law, and the penitential literature of the
Church. Examines Anglo-Saxon literature as well as
Sir Gawain and the Green Knight.

1251. Coleman, Arthur. "Francis Macomber and Sir Gawain."
AN&Q 19 (1981): 70.

Suggests that Hemingway's story is a 20th-century
rendition of a theme and situation present in the
medieval poem, the story of a Hero-Initiate and his
ceremonial conquest of fear and his process of learning the Code and its value.

1252. Colledge, Edmund, and J.C. Marler. "'Céphalologie':
A Recurring Theme in Classical and Mediaeval Lore."
Traditio 37 (1981): 411-426.

Trace this theme from its beginnings through works such as *Sir Gawain and the Green Knight*, the most celebrated example, which combines the usually separate Paul and Denis legends. Suggest two associations with Holyhead: Holywell, where Winefrid was decapitated, and "Holy," the settlement of St. Cybi.

1253. Connelly, William. *"Sir Gawain and the Green Knight*: Mirror of an Age." *AvC* 1.2 (1983): 4-6.

Briefly reviews the poem as a reflection of the nostalgic ideal of chivalry fostered by Edward III of England.

1254. Cook, James Rhodes. "Aesthetic and Religious Symbolism in *Sir Gawain and the Green Knight*." *DAI* 39 (1978): 277A. Georgia State U.

Examines five aspects of symbolism in the poem: the grouping of details, color (and their liturgical significance), fire (an indication of the presence of God in his Trinitarian form), arms and arming, and typological matters (relationship between King Arthur and Abraham, Gawain and Lot, Morgan and Sarah, Guinevere and Hagar, Bercilak and St. Peter). Suggests that the poet was much concerned with the Old Covenant and circumcision as well as the New Covenant and baptism.

1255. Coyle, Martin. *"Sir Gawain and the Green Knight*." *Expl* 42.3 (1984): 4-5.

Suggests that line 1752 contains a deliberately ironic reference to *that day*, not only pointing to Gawain's confused and fearful state of mind but also acting as a warning that his destiny will be settled on that day, not when he meets the Green Knight.

1256. Cubbin, G.P. "Dialect and Scribal Usage in Medieval Lancashire: A New Approach to Local Documents." *Transactions of the Philological Society*. Oxford: Blackwell, 1981. 67-101.

A detailed study with 102 brief sections of features of the Lancashire dialect from the earliest ME period up to 1350. Concludes that the *Gawain*-poet, if he came from Lancashire, must have been from Clitheroe or Lancaster, since they offer the only possibilities for the transitional dialect that best accounts for the poet's linguistic peculiarities.

1257. Cuda, Margaret Curtis. "Shifting Shapes: Anglo-Celtic Christian Symbolism in *Sir Gawain and the Green Knight*." *DAI* 44 (1983): 1091A. Lehigh U.

Suggests the need for reassessing the poem by examining Celtic sources and influences from OE religious materials, the Bible, and Christian liturgy.

1258. Davenport, W.A. *The Art of the Gawain-Poet*. London: Athlone P, 1978.

Bibliographical preface, xi-xiii.
Chapter: 1. Introduction, 1-6.
2. *Pearl*, 7-54.
3. *Purity*, 55-102.
4. *Patience*, 103-135.
5. *Sir Gawain and the Green Knight*, 136-194.
   Explores the literary sophistication of the poem and the poet's treatment of the hero and his adventure, including his adversaries: the challenger, the castle, huntsman, temptress, host, and judge.
6. The poet and his art, 195-228.
Notes and index, 229-233.

1259. Day, Mildred Leake. "Scarlet Surcoat and Gilded Armor: The Literary Tradition of Gawain's Costume in *Sir Gawain and the the Green Knight* and *De Ortu Waluuanii*." *Interpretations* 15.2 (1984): 53-58.

Argues that the Latin story of Gawain's youth is essential for interpreting the significance of Gawain's red surcoat and gilded armor, which represent his reputation as a brilliant fighting knight and the glory of his early exploits.

1260.   Derolez, R. "Authorship and Statistics: The Case of the *Pearl*-Poet and the *Gawain*-Poet." *Studies in English Language and Early Literature in Honour of Paul Christophersen.* Ed. P.M. Tilling. Occasional Papers in Linguistics and Language Teaching 8. [Coleraine]: New U of Ulster, 1981. 41-52.

Questions the validity of the conclusions of Kjellmer [*Gothenburg Studies in English* 20 (1975)], because his handling of the lexical dimension cannot be conclusive—his variables are in fact dependent on each other—and he neglected to account for the constraints imposed by the poetic form.

1261.   Derrickson, Ann. "The Pentangle: Guiding Star for the *Gawain*-poet." *Comitatus* 11 (1980): 10-19.

Contends that the pentangle is the dominant symbol, rather than the conventional griffin or eagle, since the poet intended to bring form into accord with intention and to use diction and narrative design to catch traces of the humanly unattainable ideal.

1262.   de Weever, Jacqueline. "*Lufly* and Its Variants in *Sir Gawain and the Green Knight.*" *JRMMRA* 4 (1983): 33-43.

Views *lufly* and its variants, which occur with the second highest frequency of all adverbs and adjectives in the poem (twenty-one times), as a locking and linking device with words such as *know* and *lace*, thus tying together the poem's complex meanings. As one of the main devices in the poet's idiom, these words take on different meanings in different contexts, but still act as a thread connecting people and action.

1263.   Eadie, John. "Sir Gawain and the Ladies of Ill Repute." *AnM* 20 (1981): 52-66.

Examines Gawain's controversial and curious anti-

feminist speech (ll. 2407-2428) as an ironic passage
in which he says that if his values were those of the
world of Fortune/Chance, as Bercilak's and Arthur's
are, then he would be able to salve his conscience.
He cannot, however, because he has fallen from high
Christian ideals.

1264.   ------. "Sir Gawain's Travels in North Wales." *RES*
ns 34 (1983): 191-195.

Theorizes that Holyhead is indeed the "Holy Hede"
of line 700 and then offers evidence that a number of
fords linked Holy Island with Anglesey and that
Holyhead was very much associated with both fords and
forelands.

1265.   Edgeworth, Robert H.   "Anatomical Geography in Sir
Gawain and the Green Knight." *Neophil* 69 (1985):
318-319.

Suggests that the chapel and its setting are iden-
tifiable with features of the feminine genitalia: a
ravine (vulva), steep banks on either side (labia),
and the mound above (mons Veneris), overgrown with
grass (pubic hair).

1266.   Elliott, Ralph W.V. *The Gawain Country: Essays on
the Topography of Middle English Alliterative Poetry.*
Leeds Texts and Monographs ns 8.   Leeds: U of Leeds
School of English, 1984.

Chapter: 1. Prologue, 1-5.
2. The rhetoric of landscape, 6-13.
3. The landscape of spiritual pilgrimage: the Langland country, 14-33.
4. Romantic quest in the west Midlands:
Staffordshire and Cheshire landscapes
in "Sir Gawain and the Green Knight,"
34-72.
5. The Scandinavian influence: some
northern landscape features in "Sir
Gawain and the Green Knight," 73-84.
6. The topographical vocabulary I: hills
and valleys in the "Gawain" country,

85-111.
7. The   topographical   vocabulary   II:
   woods   and   forests   in   the   "Gawain"
   country, 112-133.
8. The   topographical   vocabulary   III:
   streams   and   swamps   in   the   "Gawain"
   country, 134-152.
Maps, 153-157.
Select bibliography, 158-159.
Index of words, places, 160-165.

1267. ------. "Hills and Valleys in the *Gawain* Country."
       LeedsSE ns 10 (1978): 18-41.

       Discusses thirteen sets of terms denoting hills and
       valleys in alliterative poetry, mainly of the 14th
       century, to clarify meanings and connotations, to
       bring out stylistic differences among alliterative
       poets, to explore parallels between these terms and
       their occurrence in place names, and to assign some
       words and perhaps some poems to specific regions.

1268. ------. "Staffordshire and Chesire Landscapes in *Sir
       Gawain and the Green Knight." North Staffordshire
       Journal of Field Studies* 17 (1977): 20-49.

       Explores in detail features of the north Stafford-
       shire moors near the Cheshire border and relates them
       to descriptions in the poem. The green chapel resem-
       bles a natural "chapel" known as Ludchurch, part of
       the endowment of the abbey at Dieulacres; the sur-
       rounding area has the height of Roach End with com-
       manding views to Forest Bottom, 500 feet below, as
       well as hunting lodges of the earls of Chester; there
       is a "holy head" at Poulton by the Dee, and other
       features in the area that bear close resemblance to
       specifics in the poem.

1269. ------. "Streams and Swamps in the *Gawain* Country."
       LeedsSE ns 13 (1982): 56-73.

       Reviews the usages and meanings of sixteen sets of
       "water" words and strongly suggests that the poets
       drew upon their local map.

1270. ------. "Woods and Forests in the *Gawain* Country."
       NM 80 (1979): 48-64.

       Argues that the landscapes owe a debt to the north-
       west Midlands toponymy and that the poet singles out
       features that probably belong together, evoking
       impressions of actual landscapes. Further suggests
       that the *Gawain*-poet is the first of the great Eng-
       lish nature poets and more than any other alliter-
       ative poet, he was able to translate his impressions
       of his surroundings into settings for his narrative.

1271. Finlayson, John. "The Expectations of Romance in *Sir
       Gawain and the Green Knight*." *Genre* 12 (1979): 1-24.

       In this detailed discussion of the poem, the author
       argues that the poet self-consciously exploits and
       often disappoints audience expectations of the con-
       ventions and rituals of romance. By ultimately
       reversing most of the usual patterns, the poet focus-
       es on the "fiction of chivalry."

1272. Fitzpatrick, John Francis. "Courtly Love and the
       Confessional in English Literature from 1215 to John
       Gower." *DAI* 39 (1978): 895A. Indiana U.

       Examines the history of the interaction between
       penance and courtly love. Finds that the two confes-
       sional scenes in *Sir Gawain and the Green Knight*
       point to the dramatic opposition of courtly love and
       Christianity.

1273. Ganim, John. "Disorientation, Style, and Perception
       in *Sir Gawain and the Green Knight*." Ganim [38].
       55-78, 161-164.

       Insists that the form and style, however entertain-
       ing, imply a challenge and assault on the "sensibili-
       ties and shared values" of the audience. Emphasizes
       a countertendency to the elaborate structure and ob-
       vious symmetry of the poem, a device that depends
       upon disorientation and unbalancing effects on the
       consciousness of the reader. Describes the extensive
       treatment of themes of decline, decadence, and dis-

memberment juxtaposed to themes of perfection and idealism as well as specific examples of how the poem's rhetoric disorients the reader.

1274. Gee, Elizabeth. "The Lists of Knights in *Sir Gawain and the Green Knight.*" *AUMLA* 62 (1984): 171-178.

Argues that the lists of knights (11. 109-113 and 550-555) are not inserted for tradition, grandeur, or euphony, but as a skillful artistic reminder of the internal dissent marring the Round Table, fore-shadowing the collapse of the chivalric ideal.

1275. Giaccherini, Enrico. "Gawain's Dream of Emancipa-tion." *Literature in Fourteenth-Century England.* The J.A.W. Bennett Memorial Lectures, Perugia, 1981-1982. Ed. Piero Boitani and Anna Torti. Tübin-gen Beiträge zur Anglistik 5. Tübingen: Gunter Narr; Cambridge, Eng.: D.S. Brewer, 1983. 65-82.

An archetypal reading of the poem that views sym-bolic, psychological, and ritual aspects of an initiation pattern converging in this story of Gawain's opposition to the father figure of the Green Knight with his final test occurring in the womb of the Great Mother.

1275a. Glenn, I.E. "The Beheading Scene in 'Sir Gawain and the Green Knight.'" *Communique* 7.1 (1982): 15-21.

1276. Goff, Frederick J. "A Study of the Middle English Gawain Romances." *DAI* 45 (1985): 2110A. Rutgers U.

Investigates the connections of nine Gawain poems to Cumberland and the consistent moral portrait of Gawain as a humble knight.

1277. Goltra, Robert. "The Confession in the Green Chap-el: Gawain's True Absolution." *ESRS* 32.4 (1984): 5-14.

Argues that Gawain's perspective is the most accurate of all the views offered in the poem, since he recognizes the gravity of his sins and the invalidity of his confession, later corrected by his confession to the Green Knight.

1278. Green, Richard Firth. "Sir Gawain and the *Sacra Cintola.*" *ESC* 11 (1985): 1-11.

Links Gawain's girdle to the aprocryphal story of St. Thomas and the Virgin's *sacra cintola*. Views the first arming scene as Gawain as Mary's knight and the second as a secular travesty of *sacra cintola*, with green ironically implying disloyalty in love.

1279. Griffith, Richard R. "Bertilak's Lady: The French Background of *Sir Gawain and the Green Knight.*" *Machaut's World: Science and Art in the Fourteenth Century.* Annals of the New York Academy of Sciences 314. Ed. Madeleine Pelner Cosman and Bruce Chandler. New York: New York Academy of Sciences, 1978. 249- 266.

Claims that the continuation of the Vulgate *Merlin* is essential for understanding the roles of Bercilak and his wife, who both bear grudges against Arthur's court. In the French *Merlin*, Bertelak le Rous is disinherited and exiled by Arthur's court, and his wife is the false Guinevere, the child of Leodegrance and his steward's wife.

1280. Grogan, Nedra C. "Mulier est Hominis Confusio: The Green Knight's Lady." *ESRS* 32.4 (1984): 15-27.

Argues that the lady is central to the outcome of the poem, that she has full knowledge of the plot against Gawain, and that her actions are planned to make Gawain sin; she and her husband work against Gawain for positive ends, so he will learn from his experience and take his lesson to Arthur's court.

1281. Haines, Victor Yelverton. *The Fortunate Fall of Sir Gawain: The Typology of Sir Gawain and the Green Knight.* Washington: UP of America, 1982.

Chapter: 1. The felix culpa, 1-36.
          2. The poet's intention in the framing
              prologue and epilogue, 37-56.
          3. The place for allegory, 57-73.
          4. Sir Gawain and the felix culpa, 74-
              105.
          5. Camelot and the felix culpa, 106-129.
          6. Haut Desert and the felix culpa, 130-
              162.
          7. The reader and the felix culpa, 163-
              177.
Appendix: The Shape of Gawain Criticism, 178-194.

1282. ------. *"Hony soyt qui mal pence*: Can the Reader
       Sin?" *RUO* 53 (1983): 181-188.

       Investigates the postscript, which is not the exact
       motto of the Order of the Garter, and suggests that
       the missing "y" changes the focus from the object of
       thought to the thought itself. Believes that the
       postscript applies especially to the reader, who has
       a moral responsibility to think well ethically.

1283. Hale, William C. "The Enigma of Gawain." *AvC* 1.2
       (1983): 24-25.

       Explores the origins of the name and character of
       Gawain and suggests that the resolution of the ques-
       tion of Gawain's Celtic origin as Cuchulin or Gmalch-
       mai will yield no insight into this knight of the
       Round Table.

1284. Hanna, Ralph, III. "Unlocking What's Locked: Ga-
       wain's Green Girdle." *Viator* 14 (1983): 289-302.

       Examines four possible meanings attached to the
       girdle: the lady's claim that it has magical powers,
       Gawain's view that it is a sign of his failure, the
       Green Knight's view that it is merely a token of a
       chivalric adventure, and the belief of the members of
       the Round Table that it is a sign of their fellowship
       and sympathy with Gawain. The multitude of interpre-
       tations suggests the limitation of human efforts to
       comprehend the variety of experience, and the poem

itself approximates a process of recognizing the persistent intractability of experience.

1285. Hanning, Robert W. "Poetic Emblems in Medieval Narrative Texts." *Vernacular Poetics in the Middle Ages.* Ed. Lois Ebin. Studies in Medieval Culture 16. Kalamazoo, MI: Medieval Institute, 1984. 1-32.

Treats *Sir Gawain and the Green Knight* as an example of 14th-century use of emblem; argues that the penitential fish in its sly sauce in Fitt 2 is a superb emblem pointing to the problematic relationship between appearance and reality or art and interpretation. Further suggests that as an emblem, the fish represents the subduing of nature, the disguises and sophistication of nature by saucing, and the endowment of nature with social and moral ambivalence by its being served as part of a penitential meal.

1286. ------. "Sir Gawain and the Red Herring: The Perils of Interpretation." *Acts of Interpretation.* Ed. Mary J. Carruthers and Elizabeth D. Kirk. Norman, OK: Pilgrim Books, 1982. 5-23.

Discusses the artfulness of the poet, who embellishes his poem with deliberate ambiguities, false leads, and emblems; by doing so, he draws attention to civilization's penchant for decoration or embellishment in the form of rhetorical games, rituals that partly conceal the primary levels of experience or meaning beneath artfully created surfaces.

1287. Harley, Marta Powell. "Faulkner's Medievalism and *Sir Gawain and the Green Knight.*" *AN&Q* 21 (1983): 111-114.

Sees echoes of *Sir Gawain and the Green Knight* in the very name Gavin and in the three tests of chastity of Gavin Stevens in Faulkner's *Town.* Also notes parallels between the medieval poem and the bear (like boar) hunt and test of courage of Ike in "The Bear."

1288.   Harrison, Keith.   "Primary Works in Translation: *Sir Gawain and the Green Knight*."   *AvC* 1.2 (1983): 7-8.

Discusses his own translation of the poem commissioned by the Folio Society of Great Britain as well as the radio broadcasts aired on National Public Radio.

1289.   Hendrix, Howard V.   "'To Luf Hom Wel, and Leve Hem Not': The Neglected Humor of Gawain's 'Antifeminism.'"   *Comitatus* 14 (1983): 39-48.

Argues that the so-called antifeminist tirade is "outright funny" in a vein of self-deprecating male humor; half is masculine befuddlement in the face of the oldest puzzle—women—and the rest is an excuse to salve his wounded honor.

1290.   Hieatt, A. Kent.   "Numerical Structures in Verse: Second-Generation Studies Needed (Exemplified in *Sir Gawain* and the *Chanson de Roland*)."   Eckhardt [32]. 65-78.

Offers general rules for those interested in numerical structures in literary analysis: 1) not to exclaim over arithmetical felicities that follow automatically from other felicities; 2) to consider what is entailed physically and chronologically in the origin and survival of any numerical scheme; 3) to think out carefully all the internal consequences of the pattern imputed to a work; 4) to be careful about the symbolic values assigned to particular numbers; 5) to find confirmation of a suggested numerical pattern in the subject matter of the work; 6) to avoid proposing short structural systems arbitrarily located in larger works; and 7) to talk with mathematicians specializing in probability theory or statistical analysis.

1291.   Hill, Ordelle G.   "Sir Gawain's Holidays."   *KPAB* 1980: 18-26.

Points to the rich religious associations of specific holidays emphasized in the poem: Michaelmas,

which reminds Gawain of his mission, prompting a hope
of defending his foe through the intercession of
Michael or by his identification with him as a prince
of angels and deliverer of men; All Saints' Day,
which commemorates the martyrs of the Church; St.
John's Day, which would remind the audience of a
saint who lived a long life as well as one who was
beheaded as a young man; and the Day of Circumcision,
when Gawain goes to the Green Chapel and receives his
symbolic circumcision, signifiying spiritual purification and the moritification of worldly lusts according to the *Golden Legend*.

1292.   Hill, Thomas D. "Gawain's Jesting Lie: Towards an
        Interpretation of the Confessional Scene in *Gawain
        and the Green Knight*." *SN* 52 (1980): 279-286.

        Evaluates Gawain's behavior according to St. Augus-
        tine, who asserted that a joke is not to be accounted
        a lie; thus, the crucial issue concerning the cove-
        nant to exchange winnings is whether the agreement is
        serious or jocose. If the latter, then the failure
        with the girdle is merely a breach of courtesy rather
        than a substantial moral failure—at worst, a venial
        sin.

1293.   Hollis, Stephanie J. "The Pentangle Knight: *Sir
        Gawain and the Green Knight*." *ChauR* 15 (1981): 267-
        281.

        Considers the contrasting moral evaluations in the
        final fitt and suggests that through the attitude of
        the Green Knight, Gawain's behavior should be seen as
        human comedy since he tries to maintain the original
        integrity of his knightly virtues, locating the im-
        pulses and causes of his sin outside himself.

1294.   Hunter, Susan Marie. "Tales, Tellers, and Audiences:
        Narrative Structure and Aesthetic Response in *Beo-
        wulf*, *Pearl*, *Cleanness*, *Patience*, and *Sir Gawain and
        the Green Knight*." *DAI* 45 (1984): 841A. U of Cali-
        fornia, Riverside.

        Demonstrates that both poets employ the structural

principle of tellers telling tales to listeners within their poems and try to assume voices from oral tradition to sound the meaning of the past for the present, to control the movement of the poem, to show how knowledge is received and transmitted, and to imply their aesthetics by seeming to replicate their own compositional processes.

1295. Huval, Barbara Jane. "Anglo-Saxon Lexical and Literary Implications in the Works of the *Gawain*-Poet." *DAI* 46 (1985): 1621A. Rice U.

Argues that the poet's word choice and diction reflect a pervasive Anglo-Saxon influence, which should not be ignored.

1296. Ikegami, Tadahiro. "*Cortaysye* and *Trawþe* in *Sir Gawain and the Green Night.*" *Genzobunka-Rousha* [*Studies in Languages and Cultures*] 6 (1979): 1-13 [in Japanese].

Employs *cortaysye* and *trawþe* as pivotal concepts in his discussion of Gawain's humanity and the religious aspects of this romance [author's annotation].

1297. ------. "*Gawain* Poet." *An Introduction to English Literature—Society and Literature.* Ed. Bishu Saito. Tokyo: Chukyo Shuppan, 1978. 49-52 [in Japanese].

Traces the works of the *Gawain*-poet and supplies a critical analysis of *Sir Gawain and the Green Knight* and *Pearl* [author's annotation].

1298. Ingham, Muriel, and Lawrence Barkley. "Further Animal Parallels in *Sir Gawain and the Green Knight.*" *ChauR* 13 (1979): 384-386.

Suggests two further parallels between Sir Gawain and the boar. Like the boar, Gawain refuses "ignominious flight" as the servant advises (ll. 2118-2125) and instead stands fast for the attack across the stream (ll. 1568-1570). The Green Knight vaults across the stream (ll. 2221-2222, 2229-2232) just as

Bercilak did to face the boar (ll. 1573-1576).

1299.   Jacobs, Nicolas.   "The   Green   Knight: An   Unexplored
        Irish Parallel." *CMCS* 4 (1982): 1-4.

        Investigates the connections between *Sir Gawain and
        the Green Knight* and the Irish tale *The Destruction
        of Da Derga's Hostel*, especially in terms of the
        color   motif,   the   horsemen's   physical   attributes
        because of enchantment (Morgan la Fee's part in the
        English poem), a punishment, but not involving death
        (the Knight's decapitation), and the recurring motif
        of three destructions and three blows.

1300.   Jennings, Margaret, C.S.J.   "'Heavens Defend Me from
        that Welsh Fairy' (*Merry Wives of Windsor*, V,v,85):
        The Metamorphosis of Morgain la Fee in the Romances."
        Court and Poet [20].   197-205.

        Traces the degenerating status of Morgan from the
        Great Fairy Queen, counterpart to the Welsh Modron,
        to almost a Christian demon, the view depicted in *Sir
        Gawain and the Green Knight*.

1301.   Johnson, Lynn Staley.   *The Voice of the Gawain-Poet*.
        Madison: U of Wisconsin P, 1984.

                Chapter: 1. *Patience*, 3-36.
                          2. *Sir Gawain and the Green Knight*, 37-
                              96.
                              The   author   presents   a   detailed
                              account of the poet's use of time as
                              cyclical, degenerative, and regenera-
                              tive. Cyclic history stresses the
                              lessons of the past, ways in which
                              the   present   learns   from   earlier
                              successes and failures; the degenera-
                              tive   nature   of   time   suggests   the
                              debilitating effects of time from an
                              age of gold to one of iron, from the
                              grandeur of the past to the inglo-
                              rious present; regeneration is inher-
                              ent in the liturgical calendar, which
                              transcends time, suggesting redemp-

tion through truths impervious to the
mutability of human, earthly time.
3.   *Purity*, 97-143.
4.   *Pearl*, 144-210.
Conclusion: "He Cryed So Cler," 211-226.
Appendix: De Maria Magdalena, 227-235.
Notes and index, 237-276.

1302.   Kaske, R.E. "*Sir Gawain and the Green Knight*." *Proceedings of the Southeastern Institute of Medieval and Renaissance Studies, Summer 1979*. Medieval and Renaissance Studies 10. Ed. George Mallary Masters. Chapel Hill: U of North Carolina P, 1984. 24-44.

Suggests that the governing theme is *lewté* or *trawthe*, closely supported by the heroic ideal *sapientia* and *fortitudo*, with Gawain's testers taking on overtones of *Fortuna* and *Natura*, the great regents by whom God rules the material universe.

1303.   Kean, P.M.   "Christmas Games: Verbal Ironies and Ambiguities in *Sir Gawain and the Green Knight*." *Poetica* 11 (1979): 9-27.

Examines the words for game and play in the poem (*gomen, enterludez, kauelacion, play*), all of which emphasize ironies, trickery, stage-management, and play-acting, thereby suggesting the uncertainties about the border between reality and romance.

1304.   Keenan, Joan.   "Feasts and Fasts in *Sir Gawain and the Green Knight*." *AN&Q* 17 (1978): 34-35.

Claims that the poet carefully chose to mention three holy days: Lent, Michaelmas, and Hallowmas— Lent is a penitential time; Michael the Archangel weighs souls, an activity echoed in the testing and judgments in the poem; and the gospel of Hallowmas teaches Christians how to lead a good life.

1305.   Kelly, Robert L.   "Allusions to the Vulgate Cycle in *Sir Gawain and the Green Knight*." *Literary and Historical Perspectives of the Middle Ages*. Proceedings of the 1981 SEMA Meeting. Ed. Patricia W. Cummins, Patrick W. Conner, and Charles W. Connell. Morgantown: West Virginia UP, 1982. 183-199.

Finds that all the explicit references to the Vulgate cycle occur in three passages, a total of thirty lines (107-113, 551-555, and 2444-2464), and that they reflect a consistent method of allusion, all related to the mutability pattern.

1306. Kikuchi, Kiyoaki. "'Ye' and 'Thou' in *Sir Gawain and the Green Knight*." *SELit* 58 (1981): 233-246 [in Japanese]. Synopsis in English, *SELit* 59 (1982): 158.

Refutes Tolkien's view [1208] that the poet uses the second person singular pronoun inconsistently. Sees the poet's use as a stylistic effect appropriate to varying contexts of conversations between Bercilak and Gawain and between the Lady and Gawain.

1307. Kindrick, Robert L. "Gawain's Ethics: Shame and Guilt in *Sir Gawain and the Green Knight*." *AnM* 20 (1981): 5-32.

Argues that the poem demonstrates the tensions between two sets of values: shame-honor (sanctions from without) and guilt-innocence (internalized sense of ethics). Suggests that the true knight must be personally committed to a sense of integrity that includes chivalric ideals and cannot simply pay lip service to an ideal to meet public expectation.

1308. Kooper, Erik. "The Case of the Encoded Author: John Massey in 'Sir Gawain and the Green Knight.'" *NM* 83 (1982): 158-168.

Claims that the author's name—John Massey—occurs in the poem in the form of a signature, a cryptogram, and an acrostic, all found in stanza five.

1309. Kossick, S.G. "Continuity and Contrast in *Sir Gawain and the Green Knight*." *UES* 17.1 (1979): 1-13.

Examines the poet's careful balancing of incident and aesthetic effect reflected in the patterning in the verse form, the balance of scenes, and general structure; each action, object, or character tends to have its complement or to contain within itself the antinomies inherent in creation: ambiguities, ambivalences, contradiction, yet the possibility of change and continuity.

1310.   Lee, Jennifer A. "The Illuminating Critic: The Illustrator of Cotton Nero A.X." *SIcon* 3 (1977): 17-46.

Closely examines and evaluates the twelve full-page illustrations of all four poems in this manuscript, which are the mark of a draftsman's work later painted over by an amateur. Concludes that the artist saw all the poems as moral tales and highlighted the journey of each main character to spiritual knowledge.

1311.   Lehman, David. "Fantasia on Kierkegaard and *Sir Gawain and the Green Knight*." *MQR* 23 (1984): 270-280.

A whimsical reading of the poem that sees the theme as the religious potential of human frailty, not the heroic potential of the human will. Views Gawain as an exemplification of Kierkegaard's Knight of Infinite Resignation, but as more than a failed Abraham. Finds modern images, not of Gawain, but of the Green Knight.

1312.   Levine, Robert. "Aspects of Grotesque Realism in *Sir Gawain and the Green Knight*." *ChauR* 17 (1982): 65-75.

Accounts for some of the unusual qualities of the poem by using Mikhail Bakhtin's principle of debasement techniques or grotesque realism, which include verbal excess; images of slaughter, dismemberment, and bowels; connections among food, sex, and money; and images of game playing.

1313. Lock, Richard Howard. "Aspects of Time in Medieval Literature." *DAI* 38 (1978): 4806A-4807A. U of California, Berkeley.

Attempts to develop a new approach to differences between oral and written literature; linear time is characteristic of literate society, and cyclic time of a nonliterate one. Examines texts along an oral-literary spectrum from a variety of cultures, including *Sir Gawain and the Green Knight*, which is linear and hypotactic, with objective time.

1314. Luttrell, Claude. "The Folk-Tale Element in *Sir Gawain and the Green Knight*." *SP* 77 (1980): 105-127.

Contends that the structure of the poem depends on a combination of the Beheading Game with a form of an international folktale, Type 313, and that the strength of the poem derives from this pairing, which gives the setter of tasks the added moral dimension of tempter.

1315. ------. "*Sir Gawain and the Green Knight* and the Versions of *Caradoc*." *FMLS* 15 (1979): 347-360.

Refutes the claim of Benson [*MP* 59 (1961-62): 1-12] that the long version of the First Continuation of Chrétien's *Li Contes del Graal* is the source of the beheading theme. Argues instead that the short version is the true source.

1316. Mathewson, Jeanne T. "*Sir Gawain* and the Medieval School of Comedy." *Interpretations* 15.2 (1984): 42-52.

Explores the poet's familiarity with secular comic theory and practice, especially as manifested in the works of the cathedral universities in the Loire Valley in the 12th century; draws attention to structural similarities and parallels in story motifs and imagery between this English poem and the four comedies in *Vindobonensis 312*.

1317.   Metcalf, Allan.   "Gawain's Number."   Eckhardt [32].
        141-155.

        Closely analyzes the symbolic value of the numbers
        5 and 25 in the work and argues that the narrative
        eschews the symbolism of 5's and 25's for the non-
        symbolic 2's and 3's, but that the form of the story,
        the poetic framework, is fundamentally 5's and 25's.
        Suggests that the poem is composed of 2525 lines with
        an additional five-line unit, that the average stanza
        length is twenty-five lines, that the rhyme scheme
        involves five interlocking rhyme words plus a five-
        line bob and wheel, and that at the critical turning
        point of the poem, the end of stanza forty-five, the
        stanza length is exactly twenty-five.   Concludes that
        both numerical symbolism and numerical structure are
        present in the poem and that the two interact to re-
        inforce their relevance to the story.

1318.   Morgan, Gerald.   "The Significance of the Pentangle
        Symbolism in 'Sir Gawain and the Green Knight.'" *MLR*
        74 (1979): 769-790.

        Insists upon the justice of the poet's conception
        of the pentangle for the meaning of the poem as a
        whole.   In scholastic philosophy, it is a symbol for
        the rational soul, a symbol with a system of spiri-
        tual, moral, and social values used by both Dante in
        Convivio and the author of this poem to express the
        limited perfection possible for humans.

1319.   ------.   "The Validity of Gawain's Confession in *Sir
        Gawain and the Green Knight*."   *RES* ns 36 (1985):
        1-18.

        Refutes the interpretation of J.A. Burrow [*A Read-
        ing of Sir Gawain and the Green Knight* (London: Rout-
        ledge & Kegan Paul, 1965)] that the confession is in-
        valid.   Clarifies the moral relationship between
        Gawain's acceptance of the girdle and his subsequent
        confession to the priest in order to demonstrate the
        coherence and lucidity of the moral argument of the
        poem.

1320. Morgan, Hubert E. "'To be her servant soþly': Ga-
       wain's Service." *ESC* 11 (1985): 273-281.

       Relates this poem to its sister poems in the Cotton
       Nero MS, which shed light on the moral and theologi-
       cal concerns of the age as well as on the specific
       treatment and thematic importance of cleanness and
       patience or spiritual humility in this poem.

1321. Murphy, Michael. "North: The Significance of a Com-
       pass Point in Some Medieval English Literature."
       Lore&L 3.8 (1983): 65-76.

       Investigates the significance of Gawain's journey
       into the winter landscape of a northern land in terms
       of the well-established connection of the devil with
       the north as well as the general negative attitude of
       southerners towards the north. Suggests that the
       Green Knight is a southern conception of a northern
       monster.

1322. Newman, Barbara Florence. "Sin, Judgment, and Grace
       in the Works of the *Gawain*-Poet." *DAI* 46 (1986):
       3027A-3028A. Cornell U.

       Discusses *Sir Gawain and the Green Knight* as a
       moral fable illustrating man's fallibility and need
       for grace.

1323. Nicholls, Jonathan. *The Matter of Courtesy: Medie-
       val Courtesy Books and the Gawain-Poet.* Woodbridge,
       Eng: D.S. Brewer, 1985.

       Introduction, 1-6.
       Chapter: 1. Terms, definitions, and genres, 7-21.
                 2. Courtesy and the religious orders,
                     22-44.
                 3. Courtesy books in secular society and
                     popular fiction, 45-56.
                     Suggests that romances were not
                     intended merely as a model for ex-
                     emplary conduct, but for explicit
                     pedagogical advice to promote specif-
                     ic behavior.

4. The use of courtesy books in education and private study, 57-76.
5. Social isolation in *Patience*, 79-84.
6. Feasts and feasting in *Cleanness*, 85-102.
7. Expectations of courtesy unfounded: the dreamer and the maiden in *Pearl*, 103-111.
8. The testing of courtesy at Camelot and Hautdesert in *Sir Gawain and the Green Knight*, 112-138.

Argues that the poem explores the full social meanings of courtesy with the Green Knight instigating a searching analysis of courtesy at both courts: at Hautdesert the audience is made aware of the restrictions of courtesy and its ambiguous interpretations; at Camelot the audience realizes the potential disaster for society if this code of courtesy should be broken.

Conclusion, 139-142.
Appendices, 145-202.
Bibliography and index, 203-241.

1324.   Nickel, Helmut. "The Arming of Gawain." *AvC* 1.2 (1983): 16-19.

Discusses Gawain's armor and concludes that it corresponds in every detail to surviving representations of English knights datable to the second half of the 14th century; most significantly it is the exact counterpart to the famous effigy of the Black Prince in Canterbury Cathedral.

1325.   Novak, James Ballaz. "Magic as Theme in *Sir Gawain and the Green Knight*." *DAI* 40 (1980): 6267A. Syracuse U.

Investigates the relationship between various forms of magical belief and the specific 14th-century context that shaped this poem.

1326. Olmert, Michael. "'A Man May Seye Ful Sooth in Game and Pley': The Tradition of Sport in Middle English Literature." *DAI* 42 (1981): 1649A. U of Maryland.

Examines play, including ludic theory, ecclesiastical approval of games, and the exploitation of games and sports in literary works, including *Sir Gawain and the Green Knight*, which shows the value of losing.

1327. Patrick, Marietta Stafford. "A Reading of *Sir Gawain and the Green Knight*." *BSUF* 24.4 (1983): 27-33.

Interprets this as a unique romance in its interlocking historical, natural, liturgical, and cosmic dimensions. Sees Gawain's experiences as giving wholeness and balance to the work, whose final frame sets it in eternal time with the deliberate parallel between Christ and Gawain showing spiritual renewal through suffering.

1328. Perryman, Judith. "Decapitating Drama in *Sir Gawain and the Green Knight*." *DQR* 8 (1978): 283-300.

Suggests the possibility that the poem may have been intended as a kind of drama or performance. The description of the Green Knight fits an actor wearing a false head; the action and characters are described in terms of observed scenes easily performed; and ideas of game, play, and merriment permeate the poem.

1329. Phelan, Walter S. "Playboy of the Medieval World: Nationalism and Internationalism in *Sir Gawain and the Green Knight*." *LitR* 23 (1980): 542-558.

Compares this poem and Synge's *Playboy of the Western World* as works using ancient myth as a criticism of contemporary life. Suggests further that both poets were concerned with the value of nationalism as a vehicle for human value.

1330. Piehler, Paul. "Plot Structure in an Oral Poem: The Double Audience of *Sir Gawain and the Green Knight*."

RUO 52 (1982): 247-256.

Suggests that the aim of the structuring is to
guide the imaginative responses of the audience into
complete participation in the deeds of the hero
despite the natural hesitancy to do so, a literary
technique that parallels liturgical participation in
the crucifixion of Christ. Suggests a parallel
between the girdle and crown of thorns, both symbols
of humiliation and glorious victory; like Jesus,
Gawain achieves by his ordeal and victory a vindication of all people willing to participate in them.

1331. Pollard, William F., Jr. "Images of the Apocalypse
in *Gawain and the Green Knight.*" *PPMRC* 3 (1978):
85-93.

Argues that judgment and mercy, as well as bliss
and blunder, are at the core of the poem and that
Apocalypse 4:3 helps explain these symbols. Sees the
Green Knight as a parody of *Majestas domini* and green
as the color of faith and regeneration.

1332. Prior, Sandra Pierson. "Poet of the Word: Patterns
and Images of the Apocalypse in the Works of the
Pearl-Poet." *DAI* 46 (1985): 974A-975A. Columbia U.

Relates *Sir Gawain and the Green Knight*, *Pearl*,
Patience, and *Cleanness* to writings in the apocalyptic tradition; each opens with a version of an escha-
tological story, moves to the beginning of the story
of a hero or society, and closes with a reminder of
the end.

1333. Puhvel, Martin. "Art and the Supernatural in *Sir
Gawain and the Green Knight.*" *ArthurL* 5 (1985):
1-69.

Viewing the poem as a great suspenseful mystery
drama, the author deals with the issues of preternat-
uralia in the poem and the poet's deliberate mysti-
fying techniques and game-playing. Concludes that
the magical and mysterious suggestions concerning
supernatural persons, objects, and phenomena in the

poem are undermined in the course of the action of the poem, leaving the impression of a game played out even if some of the mystery lingers at the end.

1334. ------. "Circumambulation and Medieval English Literature." *Folklore Studies in the Twentieth Century.* Proceedings of the Centenary Conference of the Folklore Society, 1978. Ed. Venetia J. Newall. Woodbridge, Eng.: D.S. Brewer; Totowa, NJ: Rowman & Littlefield, 1980. 344-347.

Deals especially with ritual circling in *Sir Gawain and the Green Knight*, resembling either Welsh *desiul* to derive benefit or *tuapholl* to counteract or foil diabolic magic.

1335. ------. "Sir Gawain's Circling of the Green Chapel." *ELN* 17 (1979): 10-15.

Interprets Gawain's circling of the chapel as a possible echo of the *desiul*, the custom in Celtic tradition of circling objects sunwise as a matter of precaution, protection, or good luck; less likely is the possibility of an allusion to the *tuapholl* tradition.

1336. ------. "Snow and Mist in *Sir Gawain and the Green Knight*—Portents of the Otherworld?" *Folklore* 89 (1978): 224-228.

Suggests that the storm raging on Gawain's last night at Hautdesert (ll. 2000-2008) reflects the tradition of the elfin storm, often encountered by a hero on his way to the otherworld.

1337. Reichardt, Paul F. "Gawain and the Image of the Wound." *PMLA* 99 (1984): 154-161.

Points to the significance and centrality of the wound in the structural and symbolic symmetry of the poem. Discusses the body wound of Gawain as counterpoint to Christ's sacred wounds and as analogous to the defect in the soul associated with disordered will. Also refers to the neck wound as a symbol of the "stiff-necked" pride of the Arthurian knights and of the dangerous willfulness in the human social order. [This article has prompted three responses by Thomas J. Farrell, Patrick D. Murphy, and Richard H. Osberg in the "Forum," *PMLA* 100 (1985): 97-98.]

1338.   Reid, Wendy M.   "The Drama of *Sir Gawain and the Green Knight*." *Parergon* 20 (1978): 11-25.

Draws parallels to masquerades and other dramatic entertainment such as the Sword Dance and suggests that dramatic rituals were a shaping force in the poet's composition.

1339.   Rigby, Marjory.   "'Sir Gawain and the Green Knight' and the Vulgate 'Lancelot.'" *MLR* 78 (1983): 257-266.

Argues that the *Gawain*-poet transformed material from the long Vulgate *Lancelot* to produce his characteristic effect of mystery and ambiguity, though he adhered to his source in the description of Morgan (ll. 2446-2455).

1340.   Ringel, Faye Joyce.   "Patterns of the Hero and the Quest: Epic, Romance, Fantasy." *DAI* 40 (1980): 5854A.   Brown U.

Examines narratives from the Middle Ages through the 19th and 20th centuries and surveys critical approaches to medieval romance and modern fantasy by examining the cycle of the monomyth, fantasy and reality, quest and return. Discusses *Sir Gawain and the Green Knight*.

1341.   Robertson, Michael.   "Stanzaic Symmetry in *Sir Gawain and the Green Knight*." *Speculum* 57 (1982): 779-785.

Disputes conventional views of the poem's symmetry and argues instead that the poem breaks into eleven-stanza groupings, reflecting the poet's concern with both the number 5 (incorruptibility) and 11 (transgression).

1342. Robinson, Noel Petri. "The Works of the *Gawain*-Poet:
       Didacticism and Artistry." *DAI* 44 (1983): 1094A.
       Drew U.

       Finds a tension between the artist's dual commit-
       ment to didacticism and artistry in each of his four
       works, which resolve the problem in different ways;
       in *Sir Gawain and the Green Knight* the poet transfers
       the preaching function from the narrator to the hero,
       and thus artistry is his first priority.

1343. Roney, L.Y. *"Sir Gawain and the Green Knight."* *Expl*
       37.1 (1979): 33-34.

       Contends that the three hunting scenes not only
       parallel the bedroom scenes, but also serve to char-
       acterize Bercilak as a man in control and a lord in
       his own right.

1344. Rudnytsky, Peter L. *"Sir Gawain and the Green Knight*:
       Oedipal Temptation." *AI* 40 (1983): 371-383.

       Compares this poem to *Oedipus Rex* in its interweav-
       ing of the themes of incest and parricide.

1345. Sanderlin, George.   "Gawain and Aeneas." *LangQ* 23
       (1984): 13-14.

1346. ------.   "The Negative Exemplum in the *Gawain*-Poet: A
       Most Ingenious Paradox." *StudH* 9.1 (1981): 52-55.

       Points to the way the author often teaches a virtue
       by illustrating its absence—a negative exemplum.

1347. ------.   "Point of View in *Sir Gawain and the Green
       Knight."* *LangQ* 18 (1980): 7-8, 14.

       Argues that the poet used the omniscient point of
       view to bring out the complexity and ambiguity of
       life by skillfully shifting "his camera to highlight
       not only Gawain's fears, religious impulses, embar-
       rassment, sexual temptation, courage and shame, but

also to reveal what others think of him and of their conflict with him."

1348. ------. "Sir Gawain and Lady Bercilak." *LangQ* 22 (1983): 17-19, 56.

Suggests that the center of the poem is the realistic relationship between Gawain and Lady Bercilak, a "convincing man-woman relationship" that adds depth to the poem's testing and makes plausible Gawain's partial failure and consequent self-knowledge.

1349. ------. "Two Transfigurations: Gawain and Aeneas." *ChauR* 12 (1978): 255-258.

Suggests the likelihood that the *Gawain*-poet got the idea for the transfiguration of Gawain from that of Aeneas (*Aeneid*, I, 588-593) and that the two heroes are linked not only by blood, but by a "love-adventure, begun amid feasting, with a glow of youth that surpasses nature."

1350. ------. "Who Was Gawain's Guide?" *StudH* 8.2 (1981): 10-12.

Offers the explanation that the Green Knight may represent fear, thus accounting for the false description of him as a universal destroyer instead of what he is; when Gawain refuses the guide's offer, he conquers his fear and can go to the appointment.

1351. Scattergood, V.J. "*Sir Gawain and the Green Knight* and the Sins of the Flesh." *Traditio* 37 (1981): 347-371.

Argues that the three temptations at Hautdesert represent the sins of the flesh, gluttony, lechery, and especially sloth—the sins of the outer man.

1352. Schopf, Alfred. "Gawains Beichte." *Goerres-Gesellschaft Literaturwissenschaftliches Jahrbuch* ns 22 (1981): 31-51.

In dealing with Gawain's confession scene, the author sees the function of the Green Knight not only as tempter and tester, but also as one whose task is *correctio fraterna* for Gawain and Arthur's court. Views the poem as the work of a priestly educator who wanted to show the spiritual danger of trying to live up to religious and chivalric ideals and losing humility.

1353.   Shaw, Ian. "Sir Gawain Lurking: A Note on *Sir Gawain and the Green Knight*, l. 1180 and l. 1195." *ELN* 18 (1980): 1-8.

Intrepets *lurken*, not as "to doze," but rather as "to be in ambush, to cower," which functions as a direct and ironic criticism of the inactive hero.

1354.   Shaw, Margaret Jane.   "Modernism in Medieval Literature: A Kierkegaardian Approach to *Sir Gawain and the Green Knight*." *DAI* 44 (1984):   3379A.   U of Mississippi.

Examines Gawain's self-discovery according to Kierkegaard's psychoanalysis of the self; Gawain's spiritual progression is traced through the confessions at the end of the poem, when he has discovered his theological self.

1355.   Shoaf, R.A.   *The Poem as Green Girdle: Commercium in Sir Gawain and the Green Knight*.   U of Florida Humanities Monograph 55.   Gainesville: U of Florida, 1984.

Introduction, 1-4.
Chapter: 1.   The poem in its commercial context, 5-14.
          Suggests that the commercial vision of the poem is linked to two related phenomena: the role of commercial discourse in the Scriptures and in Christianity as well as the economic upheaval in England in the 14th century.
        2.   The commerce of circumcision and the role of mediation, 15-30.

Discusses the antiphon "O Admirabile Commercium" and Gawain's circumcision on New Year's Day as well as the sacramental nature of the rite of circumcision as an important element in the Christian theory of mediation and signification.

3. Love's relations: the seduction of Gawain, 31-65.

Argues against the importance of *surquidré* and instead emphasizes *prys* and *cost* as well as the legality of pricing and convenants.

4. The new covenant of the green girdle, 66-76.

Inteprets the green girdle as a "mortal knot of mediation."

Appendix: Vocabulary of commercial words, 77-80. Notes, bibliography, and index, 81-105.

1356. Simpson, J.A. "Notes on Some Norse Loans, Real or Supposed, in *Sir Gawain and the Green Knight*." *MAE* 50 (1981): 301-304.

Comments on *draʒt*, *droupyng*, *faltered* and *pryve*, *slentyng*, and *welcum*.

1357. Smith, Sarah Stanbury. "*Fayre Formez*: Image and Vision in the Works of the *Gawain*-Poet." *DAI* 41 (1980): 1584A. Duke U.

Investigates the poet's concern with the art of visual perception and with the process by which a perceiver interprets and judges what he sees.

1358. Soucy, A. Francis. "Gawain's Fault: 'Angardez Pryde.'" *ChauR* 13 (1978): 166-176.

Suggests that the answer to the fundamental question of the nature of Gawain's offense lies in his excessive pride in his reputation and that the *vntrawþe* (1. 2509) refers to his forsaking the chivalric code by his sin of pride in his reputation, as Gawain himself states in lines 2429-2438.

tion of the nature of Gawain's offense lies in his excessive pride in his reputation and that the *vntrawþe* (1. 2509) refers to his forsaking the chivalric code by his sin of pride in his reputation, as Gawain himself states in lines 2429-2438.

1359. Srebnick, Walter. "Art and History: A Cultural Study of *Sir Gawain and the Green Knight.*" *DAI* 41 (1981): 4029A. U of Wisconsin-Madison.

Examines the poem in terms of the problems and tensions in late 14th-century England: aristocratic and knightly identity, military and social chivalry, and the new importance of commerce and its effects on aristocracy's role in national affairs.

1360. Stokes, Myra. "*Sir Gawain and the Green Knight*: Fitt III as Debate." *NMS* 25 (1981): 35-51.

Reads the conversations with the Lady of the Castle as a debate, identifying a very serious issue: the meaning of the vocabulary of courtesy and chivalry. Identifies debate features in these talks and explores the poet's use of this form in replacing trials of strength with verbal strife.

1361. ------, and John Scattergood. "Travelling in November: Sir Gawain, Thomas Usk, Charles of Orleans and the *De Re Militari.*" *MAE* 53 (1984): 78-83.

Suggest that to a medieval audience, Gawain's November journey would have testified to the importance of his mission and indicated the magnitude of the constraints upon him; early November was a time of transition, an apt and fitting moment for difficult choices and courses of action to which the works of the *Gawain*-poet, Usk, and Charles testify.

1361a. Suzuki, E. "Another Note on 'hyghe' in 'Sir Gawain and the Green Knight.'" *Medieval English Studies Newsletter* (Tokyo) 5 (1981): 1-2.

1362.   Tajima, Matsuji.   "Additional Syntactical Evidence
         Against the Common Authorship of MS. Cotton Nero
         A.x." *ES* 59 (1978): 193-198.

         Presents further syntactical evidence against the
         theory of common authorship of the Cotton Nero poems
         by pointing out important differences between *Sir
         Gawain and the Green Knight* and the other three
         poems in the use of the neuter personal pronoun *hit/
         hyt*.

1362a.   Tambling, Jeremy.   "A More Powerful Life: 'Sir
         Gawain and the Green Knight.'" *Haltwhistle Q* 9
         (1981): 1-23.

1363.   Torrini-Roblin, Gloria. "*Gomen* and *Gab*: Two Models
         for Play in Medieval Literature." *RPh* 38 (1984):
         32- 40.

         Suggests a new critical perspective for viewing
         Sir Gawain and the Green Knight, that of *gab*, a
         generic model proposed by John Grigsby for *Voyage de
         Charlemagne*.

1364.   Trask, Richard M.   "Sir Gawain's Unhappy Fault."
         SSF 16 (1979): 1-9.

         Views Gawain's sin as a tragicomic flaw and his
         laments as an ironic contrast to the mirth at the
         end of the poem; sees Gawain's reaction as incongru-
         ous given the theme of revelry and his response as
         food for laughter.

1365.   Tripp, Raymond P., Jr.   "The Arming Topos and the
         Comparative Modernity of Chaucer, the *Gawain*-Poet,
         and Malory." *Bulletin of Hirosaki U Coll*ege 1981:
         179-187.

         Refutes Brewer's interpretation [386] and argues
         instead that the poet is "surprisingly modern" in
         his use of the arming as a symbol of the outer uni-
         verse.

1366.   Vaghaiwalla, Feroza Rustom. "The Heroic Plot in Epic and Romance: A Study of the Monster-Fight Motif from *Beowulf* to the *Faerie Queene*." *DAI* 43 (1982): 442A. U of New Hampshire.

Traces the fight motif from OE poetry, in which martial prowess is the sole determinant of heroic worth, through Chrétien's romances, in which the fight loses its centrality and becomes symbolic or parodic, to *Sir Gawain and the Green Knight*, in which combat is taken seriously as a real encounter with the external world, but with psychological dimensions that provide new understanding of the human condition.

1367.   Van Nuis, Hermine J. "Sir Gawain's Excesses: The Tension Between his Real and Apparent Self." *CP* 17 (1984): 13-25.

Argues that while Gawain may have learned a bitter lesson about his true self, he does not return a better or changed man, but continues to fail to reconcile his inner and outer selves. Concludes that the poet's ultimate point is that given man's sinful condition (of cowardice, *covetise*, and *untrawthe*), humans have inescapable weaknesses that lead them into self-contradictions; in this, however, Gawain acts better than most.

1368.   Ward, Margaret Charlotte. "French Ovidian Beasts in *Sir Gawain and the Green Knight*." *NM* 79 (1978): 152- 161.

Maintains that there is a connection between the hunt and love scenes and that the hunts of Diana and Venus in OF versions of Ovid and "bestiaries of love" afford thematic parallels to this romance.

1369.   Wasserman, Loretta. "Honor & Shame in *Sir Gawain and the Green Knight*." Benson and Leyerle [385]. 77-90, 164-166.

Views the poem's social realism not only as a reflection of contemporary concerns, but also as the poet's handling of the conflict between reputation and goodness according to the code described by social anthropologists.

1370.   Weiss, Victoria L. "The Medieval Knighting Ceremony in *Sir Gawain and the Green Knight*." *ChauR* 12 (1978): 183-189.

Notes the resemblance between the ax strokes and the accolade or neck-blow that often served as the culmination of the medieval knighting ceremony, a ceremony that marks a kind of rebirth and, for Gawain, a maturity rite after passing the recent tests.

1371.   White, Jack H. "The Feasts in *Sir Gawain and the Green Knight* as Microcosms of Meaning and Structure." *Teaching the Middle Ages*. Ed. Robert V. Graybill, Robert L. Kindrick, and Robert E. Lovell. Warrensburg, MO: Ralph, 1982. 99-107.

Discusses the iconic quality of the festival meals in the poem, especially lines 875-927, as microcosms of the hierarchical concepts of chivalric idealism and courtly love. Suggests an emblematic approach to reading and teaching the poem—a balance of fast and feast, release and self-control.

1372.   Wilkin, Gregory J. "The Dissolution of the Templar Ideal in *Sir Gawain and the Green Knight*." *ES* 63 (1982): 109-121.

Argues that the poet knew of the Templars and the charges against them in England and that Gawain is confirmed as a failed Templar in the poem; our judgment of the abandonment of the ideal depends on our understanding of the earlier ideal of knighthood represented by the Templars.

1373.   Williams, Edith Whitehurst. "Morgan la Fee as Trickster in *Sir Gawain and the Green Knight*." *Folklore* 96 (1985): 38-56.

Examines the elements of the trickster archetype as delineated by Carl Jung and recognizes in Morgan la Fee the manifestation of the shadow-trickster, which Gawain overcomes through "relatedness" and returning to his social world.

1374. Wilson, Edward. *"Sir Gawain and the Green Knight* and the Stanley Family of Stanley, Storeton, and Hooton." *RES* ns 30 (1979): 308-316.

Collects evidence for a connection between this poem and the Stanley family, including a possible reference to the Stanleys of Hooton in *Grene Knight* and the holy bough as a heraldic pun in the Stanley crest.

1375. Wirtjes, Hanneke. "Bertilak de Hautdesert and the Literary Vavasour." *ES* 65 (1984): 291-301.

Reviews relevant parts of *Sir Gawain and the Green Knight* in light of Bercilak as a vavasour, thus placing the ME poem even more firmly in the French romance tradition. Argues that by exploiting the literary traditions associated with the vavasour, the poet creates many possibilities for irony with Bercilak as a fully developed character and mature vavasour who sees that not even Gawain can attain perfection.

1376. Zaletel, Cora. "The Green Knight as Thor." *ESRS* 32.4 (1984): 28-38.

Suggests that the poet based the Green Knight on the mythological god Thor, citing similarities between the two in dress and accoutrements, physical characteristics, geographic surroundings, behavior, and possibly even values.

SEE ALSO items 5, 7, 10, 11 (60-70), 16 (155-180), 18 (72-91), 21 (72-73, 96-97, 116-117, 127-128), 24, 34, 35, 41 (78-79, 95-96, 122-123, 138-139, 339-354), 55 (170-193), 59, 62, 72, 82 (9-11, 120-123), 93, 105 (96-108), 111 (154-162, 342- 344), 117, 125, 127, 135, 158, 161, 163, 174, 211, 212,

216, 218, 220, 222, 224, 225, 245, 230, 241, 243, 245, 249, 252, 259, (51-52, 71-74, 83-91, 115-116), 263 (51-58, 66-67, 71-82, 88-89), 264, 266, 272, 275, 282, 290, 298, 305, (122-123), 322, 331, 337, 342, 348, 386, 395, 407, 414, 426, 504 (117ff, 138ff, 162ff), 523, 532, 536, 547, 551, 571, 576, 577, 691, 701, 723, 905, 1042, 1047, 1062, 1065, 1134.

SIR GOWTHER [93]

Editions:

1378. Breul, Karl. *Sir Gowther: Eine englische Romanze ans dem XV. Jahrhundert.* Oppeln: Franck, 1886.

583a. Child. 1: 160-187.

607. Mills. 148-168, 214-218.

1379. Novelli, Cornelius. "Sir Gowther." *DA* 26 (1965): 1634. U of Notre Dame.

    Presents two versions in parallel columns with textual and explanatory notes.

613. Rumble. 178-205.

621. Utterson. 1: 157-190.

Criticism:

1380. Bradstock, E.M. "The Penitential Patter in *Sir Gowther.*" *Parergon* 20 (1978): 3-10.

    Explores the relationships between the poem's dual thematic levels: the heroic, knightly exploits that structurally reinforce and give visual expression to the process of regeneration and penance.

1381. ------. "*Sir Gowther*: Secular Hagiography or Hagiographical Romance or Neither?" *AUMLA* 59 (1983): 26-47.

Reviews generic problems in classifying pietistic romances, secular legends, and saints' legends. Discovers an underlying structure with six syntagmatic sets that are remarkably similar to Propp's functions for the folktale: injustice/justice or lack/liquidation, communication of injustice/lack or contract, departure/return, exchange, disguise/recognition, and struggle or test. This structure seems to apply to both romance and ME saints' legends with the only distinction in the position and function of marriage in the two genres. Compares individual syntagmatic sets in *Sir Gowther* and *Alexius*, with reference to *Robert le Diable*. Concludes by acknowledging that there is a group of romances dealing with the fortune of regenerate sinners, and if the term "secular hagiography" may be taken to refer to content and mode and not structure, then it is a useful term for such works.

1382. Marchalonis, Shirley. "*Sir Gowther*: The Process of a Romance." *ChauR* 6 (1971): 14-29.

Traces the growth of the story from a conversion story to a literary work shaped by principles of chivalry and alchemy into an *exemplum* of chivalric ethic, which incorporates symbolism of investiture and the color symbolism of alchemy to amplify and particularize the hero's conversion.

SEE ALSO items 80 (65-68), 163 (125-127), 181 (84-96), 368, 370 (225-232), 371. 375, 376, 413, 546 (200-206).

Editions:

1383. Broh, Charles Michelson. "A Critical Edition of the Romance of Sir Isumbras." *DAI* 31 (1971): 3496A. Case Western Reserve U.

Includes the text from the Gonville and Caius MSS, footnotes, annotated bibliography, and discussion of the poet's accomplishments in de-emphasizing the didacticism of his sources by adding details of homely realism and creating a symmetrical and entertaining poem.

1384. Ellis, F.S. *Sir Isumbras*. London: Kelmscott P, 1897.

Text is from Halliwell [-Phillipps] [593].

593. Halliwell [-Phillipps]. 88-120, 267-273, 310-311.

607. Mills. 125-147, 208-214.

1385. Schleich, Gustav. *Sir Ysumbras: Eine englische Romanze des 14. Jahrhunderts*. Palaestra 15. Berlin: Mayer & Müller, 1906.

Credits Julius Zupitza for much of the preliminary work necessary for this edition.

621. Utterson. 1: 73-112.

Fragments:

1386. Brown, Carleton. "A Passage from *Sir Isumbras*."
       EStn 48 (1914-15): 329.

       Discovered the first seventeen lines of *Sir Isum-
       bras* on the flyleaf of the University College Oxford
       MS 142 of *Pricke of Conscience* and prints them.

1387. D'Evelyn, Charlotte. "The Gray's Inn Fragment of *Sir
       Ysumbras*." *EStn* 52 (1918): 73-76.

       Prints and discusses the fragment (more legible as
       a rotograph than in the original Gray's Inn MS 20).

1388. Kölbing, E. *"Das Neapler Fragment von Sir Isumbras."*
       EStn 3 (1880): 200.

       Text from Naples Royal Library MS 13.B.29.

       Criticism:

1389. Blaicher, Günther. "Zur Interpretation der mit-
       telenglischen Romanze *Sir Ysumbras*." *GRM* ns 21
       (1971): 135-144.

       Argues that this work has allegorical dimensions,
       based on textual analysis and its closeness to devo-
       tional literature, sermon *exempla*, and the Eustache
       legend in *Gesta Romanorum*. Sees the animals as the
       incarnation of sin or the devil, the two children as
       Will and Intellect, and the final reunification of
       the family as the return of the soul to eternal life
       with the flesh, will, and intellect all in harmony.

1390. Braswell, Laurel. "'Sir Isumbras' and the Legend of
       Saint Eustace." *MS* 27 (1965): 128-151.

       Shows that the poem is the only one of the tail-
       rhyme romances to reproduce the structure and se-
       quence of events found in the Eustache legend, and
       then considers the thematic correspondences between
       this version and the saint's legend, in particular

such motifs as separation, trial, lost treasure, recognition, and reunion.

SEE ALSO items 162, 163 (128-135, 275-276), 164, 181 (53-58), 410, 413, 414, 443, 578.

Editions:

1391. Kittredge, George Lyman. "Launfal (Rawlinson Version)." *AJP* 10 (1899): 1-33.

Introduction with manuscript studies (1-21) and text (21-33).

1392. Zimmermann, R. "Sir Landeval." Diss. Köningsberg, 1900.

Criticism:

1393. Lyle, E.B. *"Sir Landevale* and the Fairy-Mistress Theme in *Thomas of Erceldoune."* *MAE* 42 (1973): 244-250.

Points to *Sir Landeval* as the main source of the fairy-mistress theme as it is assumed to have existed in the hypothetical source of *Thomas the Rhymer.*

1394. Williams, Elizabeth. *"Lanval* and *Sir Landevale*: A Medieval Translator and His Methods." *LeedsSE ns* 3 (1969): 85-99.

Separates the narrative into fifteen episodes and discusses the English translator's methods of adapting Marie de France's *lai* through additions, omissions, and compressions for a less sophisticated audience.

SEE ALSO items 31, 163 (44-48), 164, 298, 371, 375, 376, 1408.

Editions:

1395. Bliss, A.J. *Thomas Chestre: Sir Launfal*. Nelson's Medieval and Renaissance Library. London: Nelson, 1960.

Introduction (1-46), bibliography (47-52), text (53-82), notes (83-102), appendix (103-129), and glossary (131-153).

1396. Erling, Ludwig. *Li lais de Lanval*. Kempten: Dannheimer, 1883.

586. French and Hale. 345-380.

586a. Garbáty. 365-395.

592. Halliwell [-Phillipps]. 1-36, 320.

Text is from MS Cotton Caligula A.2.

594a. Haskell. 451-477.

596. Hazlitt. 47-81.

1397. Kaluza, M. "Thomas Chestre, Verfasser des Launfal, Libeaus Deconus und Octovian." *EStn* 18 (1893): 168.

611. Ritson. 1: 170-215; 3: 242-252, 438-439.

1399. Ritson, Joseph. *Launfal, an Ancient Metrical Romance
       By Thomas Chestre; to which is Appended the Still
       Older Romance of Lybeaus Disconus.* Edinburgh: Gold-
       smid, 1891.

 613. Rumble. 2-43.

 614. Sands. 201-232.

       Reprint of French and Hale [586] with regularized
       orthography.

1400. Turville-Petre, Thorlac. "Thomas Chestre: *Sir Laun-
       fal.*" Ford [36]. 440-472, 601.

       Includes the complete ME text from the MS Cotton
       Caligula A.2.

       Criticism:

1401. Anderson, Earl R. "The Structure of *Sir Launfal.*"
       PLL 13 (1977): 115-124.

       Argues that the central theme is Launfal's manhood,
       a theme developed by the convergence of various con-
       trasts: pride and humiliation, truth and falsehood,
       loyalty and treason, largesse and niggardliness,
       prosperity and poverty, chivalry and unknightly con-
       duct; further argues that the structure supports this
       theme and that incidents are arranged in a symmetri-
       cal pattern, but counterpoised to changes in setting,
       which impose an asymmetrical structure.

1402. Bliss, A.J. "The Hero's Name in the Middle English
       Versions of *Lanval.*" *MAE* 27 (1958): 80-85.

       Challenges the view of the scribe as a careless
       copier and discusses the various forms of the name,
       which throw light on the textual relationships of the
       manuscripts.

1403.   ------.   "The Spelling of *Sir Launfal*."   *Anglia* 75
        (1957): 275-289.

        Examines scribal pecularities common to MSS Cotton
        Caligula A.2 and Cotton Julius D.9 and hypothesizes a
        single scriptorium in Kent or East Sussex as an
        explanation for their shared characteristics.

1404.   ------.   "Thomas Chestre: A Speculation."   *Litera* 5
        '(1958): 1-6.

        Speculates on the possibility of Chestre as a per-
        sonal friend of Chaucer and that *Sir Thopas* may have
        been a private joke between the two, since it alludes
        to *Sir Launfal*.

1405.   Bradstock, E.M.   "'Honoure' in *Sir Launfal*."   *Parer-
        gon* 24 (1979): 9-17.

        Suggests that the main issue in the poem is the
        important dichotomy of honor and shame and that the
        tale is concerned with the protagonist's loss of
        honor in the eyes of society and his retrieving it;
        thus the three narrative movements all concern honor
        in the hero's proving his largesse, prowess, and
        honesty.

1406.   Edwards, Anthony S.G.   "Unknightly Conduct in 'Sir
        Launfal.'"   *N&Q* ns 15 (1968): 328-329.

        Replies to Hirsch [1407], arguing that Launfal is
        seen as a properly proud knight at the beginning and
        end, but in-between he exhibits two faults: improvi-
        dence and betrayal of his lady.

1407.   Hirsh, John C.   "Pride as Theme in 'Sir Launfal.'"
        N&Q ns 14 (1967): 288-291.

        Argues that the ending is the "final victory of
        Launfal over the forces that would oppose his pride
        and his honour," a graceful culmination of a romance
        tradition in which virtue is ultimately successful
        and love reciprocated.

1408. Knight, S.T. "The Oral Transmission of *Sir Launfal*."
       MAE 38 (1969): 164-170.

       Argues that Chestre knew *Sir Landeval* in an oral,
       not written form, since the evidence clearly supports
       fixed rhyme but a fluid body of lines.

1409. Lane, Daryl. "Conflict in *Sir Launfal*." *NM* 74
       (1973): 283-287.

       Contends that critical disagreement about the poem
       can be resolved by regarding it as an archetypal con-
       flict between the forces of good and evil, harmony
       and discord.

1410. Lucas, Peter J. "Towards an Interpretation of *Sir
       Launfal* with Particular Reference to Line 683." *MAE*
       39 (1970): 291-300.

       Suggests that *J nell be traytour* may have two mean-
       ings intended by the author, since it is unclear to
       whom he refuses to be disloyal, the king or his mis-
       tress.

1411. McCreesh, Bernadine. "The Use of Conversation in
       Medieval Literature: The Case of Marie de France and
       Her First Redactor." *RUO* 53 (1983): 189-197.

       Argues that the ME redactors took Marie's basic
       story and its underlying structure with its parallel-
       isms, but then adapted it to their own view of the
       world with a more active male role, an excision of
       the feminine aspects, a heavy emphasis on the theme
       of poverty, and increased direct speech.

1412. Martin, B.K. "*Sir Launfal* and the Folktale." *MAE* 35
       (1966): 199-210.

       Claims that many of the criticisms leveled against
       the poem can be explained by conventions of the
       folktale, in particular the three features of style
       identified by Max Lüthi [*Once Upon a Time: On the
       Nature of Fairy Tales* (New York: Ungar, 1970)]: one-

dimensionality, a predilection for surfaces, and an isolating technique.

1413. Mills, M. "A Note on *Sir Launfal*, 733-744." *MAE* 35 (1966): 122-124.

Wonders whether lines 733-736 and 739-744 were suggested by an earlier moment in the Lanval-Graelent story or by something in another romance, such as lines 6753-6754 of Wirnt von Gravenberc's *Wigalois*, one of the most important surviving versions of the story of the Fair Unknown.

1414. Patton, Patricia Joan. *"Sir Launfal*: A Source Study." *DAI* 34 (1973): 1250A-1251A. U of Missouri-Columbia.

Compares the poem to Marie de France's version, to *Landeval*, to the OF lay *Graelent*, and to *The Art of Courtly Love* in order to give a clear picture of Thomas Chestre's artistry.

1415. Robson, C.A. "The Technique of Symmetrical Composition in Medieval Narrative Poetry." *Studies in Medieval French Presented to Alfred Ewert in Honour of his Seventieth Birthday.* London: Oxford UP, 1961. 26-75.

Proposes a formula for *Sir Launfal* whereby twenty-seven stanzas are assigned to each of three parts: his private relationship with Guinevere and Triamour, his public trial and vindication, and the digressive incidents.

1416. Stemmler, Theo. "Die mittelenglischen Bearbeitungen zweier Lais der Marie de France." *Anglia* 80 (1962): 243-263.

Analyzes the intention of the ME adaptors and their artistic effects and concludes that they developed more realistic scenes, changed indirect speech to direct, and deleted the love psychology and subtle fairy atmosphere in Marie de France's work.

1417.   Wright, Michael J.   "The Tournament Episodes in *Sir Launfal*: A Suggestion."   *Parergon* 8 (1974): 37-38.

Suggests that the two tournaments (ll. 433-504 and 505-612) are best understood if considered with the end of the poem, since all three are manifestations of a concern with the conflict between the pleasures of requited love and a knightly duty to participate in combat.

SEE ALSO items 11 (54-56), 31, 88, 93 (161-167), 163 (44-48, 69-70, 111-112, 270-271), 164, 179 (68-70), 277, 298, 322 (131-132), 368, 370 (139-146, 200-204), 371, 375, 376, 378, 379, 413, 414, 519, 546, (207-215), 578, 940.

Editions:

1418. Bliss, A.J. *Sir Orfeo*. London: Oxford UP, 1954.
2nd ed. Oxford: Clarendon P, 1966.

   Presents texts of all three MSS: Auchinleck, Harley 3810, and Ashmole 61; with introduction, notes,
   and glossaries.

1419. Burrow, John, ed. *English Verse 1300-1500*. Longman
Annotated Anthologies of English Verse 1. London:
Longman, 1977.

   Text of *Sir Orfeo* from Auchinleck MS, except for
   lines 1-38 from Harley MS 3810. Short introduction
   (4-5) with text (5-27).

1420. Cook, Albert Stanburrough. *A Literary Middle English
Reader*. Boston: Ginn, 1915. 88-107.

   Text mainly follows that of Zielcke [1425], but
   with lines 1-24 and 33-46 from Harley MS 3810 and
   freely altered punctuation.

584. Dunn and Byrnes. 216-230.

585. Ford. 271-228.

   A "normalized" text based on Sisam [1423], with
   lines 1-24 omitted.

586. French and Hale. 323-341.

586a.   Garbáty.   349-364.

        Text from Auchinleck MS, except for lines 1-24 from
        Harley MS 3810.

1421.   Gibbs, A.C. *Middle English Romances*.   York Medieval
        Texts.   London: Edward Arnold; Evanston: Northwest-
        ern UP, 1966.   33-34, 84-103.

        Brief introduction and text from the Auchinleck MS;
        also extracts from eight other ME romances.

 592.   Halliwell [-Phillipps].   36-55.

594a.   Haskell.   247-262.

 595.   Hazlitt.   1: 59-80.

        Entitled "Orfeo and Heurodis; or King Orfeo."

 596.   ------.   82-100.

 602.   Laing.   115-136..

        The first twenty-four lines from Harley MS 3810,
        remaining text from Auchinleck.   Prologue from Ash-
        mole MS 61 appears in the appendix, 392-393.

 611.   Ritson.   2: 248-269, 3: 333-336.

 613.   Rumble.   206-226.

 614.   Sands.   185-200.

        Reprint of French and Hale [586] with regularized
        orthography.

616. Schmidt and Jacobs. 1: 21-28, 32-33, 151-171, 197-205.

1422. Shackford, Martha Hale. *Legends and Satires from Mediaeval Literature*. Boston: Ginn, 1913. 141-160, 174-176.

Text is copied from Laing [602].

1423. Sisam, Celia and Kenneth. *The Oxford Book of Medieval English Verse*. London: Oxford UP, 1970. 76-98.

Sir Orfeo appears as item 37 and is taken from Auchinleck MS. No notes or introduction.

1423a. Sisam, Kenneth. *Fourteenth Century Verse & Prose*. Oxford: Clarendon P, 1921. Rpt. with corr. 1975. 13-31, 207-212.

Text from the Auchinleck MS with lines 1-24 and 33-46 from Harley MS 3810. Also contains excerpts from *Destruction of Troy* and *Sir Gawain and the Green Knight* among other ME works.

1424. Wallace, Sylvia Crowell. *"Sir Orfeo*: An Edition." Diss. Yale U, 1963.

1425. Zielcke, Oscar. *Sir Orfeo: Ein englisches Feenmärchen aus dem Mittelalter*. Breslau: Köbner, 1880.

Text is from the Auchinleck MS.

Criticism:

1426. Allen, Dorena. "Orpheus and Orfeo: The Dead and the *Taken*." *MAE* 33 (1964): 102-111.

Rejects the notion of an elusive Celtic source and argues instead that a Gaelic or Breton narrator would have restored Orpheus' quest for his lost wife to its proper condition, the rescue of the *taken* from the *sid*, a popular and superstitious belief of the British Isles.

1427. Baldwin, Dean R. "Fairy Lore and the Meaning of *Sir Orfeo*." *SFQ* 41 (1977): 129-142.

Suggests that the poem's meaning derives not from its religious, moral, or philosophical themes, but rather from its conformity to narrative patterns and traditions of fairy lore.

1428. Ball, C.J.E. "Old Kentish *Wig* and Middle English *Owy*." *RES* ns 11 (1960): 52-53.

Proposes that *owy* is a weak stress form not connected with the Old Kentish *wig*, and thus the ME form should not be cited as a reason for denying the dialect of *Sir Orfeo* as southwest Midlands.

1429. Bergner, H. "*Sir Orfeo* and the Sacred Bonds of Matrimony." *RES* ns 30 (1979): 432-434.

Believes that the source of lines 129-130 in the Auchinleck MS is both secular (formulas of consent in marital vows of fidelity) and religious (Ruth 1:16).

1430. Blais, Ellen Anne. "A Reading of the Middle English Romance *Sir Orfeo*." *DAI* 39 (1978): 2245A. SUNY, Binghamton.

Sees the poem as a transmutation of classical and Celtic materials into an essentially Christian work, an allegory of man's fall from grace and restoration to the heavenly kingdom.

1431. Briggs, K.M. "The Fairies and the Realms of the Dead." *Folklore* 81 (1970): 81-96.

Describes the Celtic influence on *Sir Orfeo*: the interweaving of fairyland and Hades, recurrent motifs such as the danger of certain hours and seasons and the connections between the dead and fairies.

1432. Bristol, Michael D. "The Structure of the Middle English *Sir Orfeo*." *PLL* 6 (1970): 339-347.

Argues that the action of the poem sets in opposition two modes of perception: one unifies and liberates, while the other divides and destroys. The poem diminishes the elements of adversity and loss by placing them in a symmetrical and continuous structure.

1433. Bullock-Davies, Constance. "'Ympe Tre and 'Nemeton.'" *N&Q* ns 9 (1962): 6-9.

Interprets the word as "sacred grove" because of confusion between *nante*, *nemeton*, and *ante*, *ente*.

1434. Carpinelli, Francis B. *"Sir Orfeo."* *Expl* 19.2 (1960): 13.

Shows how the poet displays rhetorical skill in five successive couplets (ll. 103-112) by contrasting Heurodis' past and present conditions, by presenting Orfeo's anguish in a series of concise couplets, and by ironically switching red and white colors commonly associated with the beautiful lady in medieval romance.

1435. Cochrane, Kirsty. "Orpheus Applied: Some Instances of His Importance in the Humanist View of Language." *RES* ns 19 (1968): 1-13.

Refers to the role of Orpheus as an exemplar of the humanists' educational and ethical concepts of creative and persuasive speech (without alluding to the relevance of these ideas to the medieval versions of the Orpheus story). Examines the associations of Orpheus with both music and the figure of Christ, associations that have some relevance to *Sir Orfeo*.

1436. Coolidge, Sharon Ann. "The Grafted Tree in Literature: A Study in Medieval Iconography and Theology." *DAI* 38 (1977): 2107A. Duke U.

Examines the grafted tree in diverse medieval works, including *Sir Orfeo*, where it suggests man's temptation and fall through his inherent weakness, depicts the need for salvation, and provides an iconographic re-enactment of redemption.

1437.   ------. "The Grafted Tree in *Sir Orfeo*: A Study in the Iconography of Redemption." *BSUF* 23.2 (1982): 62-68.

Explores the enigmatic image of the grafted tree in this poem from an iconological, theological, and literary perspective. Suggests that the author of the ME poem has fused the themes of the fall of man and Christ's Passion and triumph in the Harrowing of Hell through the central figures of the *ympe* tree and its counterpart, the hollow tree. The grafted tree suggests man's temptation and fall through inherent weakness, depicts the need for salvation, and provides an iconographic re-enactment of redemption.

1438.   Davies, Constance. "Classical Threads in 'Orfeo.'" *MLR* 56 (1961): 161-166.

Suggests Map's story of the *Filii Mortue* and Virgil's description of the otherworld in *Aeneid* (Book 6) as possible explanations of the details in the poem that cannot be explained by Celtic legend or fairy belief.

1439.   Deligiorgis, Stavros George. "*Sir Orfeo*: A Study of Literary Themes." *DA* 27 (1966): 1027A-1028A. U of California, Berkeley.

Focuses on the poem's position in Western literature by drawing attention to its affinities with French *reverdies*, English lyrics, German allegories, Hellenistic dream books, Anglo-Saxon poetry, Byzantine romances, Latin Apocrypha, and Homeric *nostoi*.

1440.   Dien, Stephanie. "The Fairy King's Castle in *Sir Orfeo*." *Parergon* 4 (1972): 20-24.

Finds two features of the description of the castle puzzling: *vousour* (1. 363) and *butras* (1. 361) and wonders whether the description, far from arbitrary, is intentionally "elusive, baffling, and ambiguous" in order to maintain a sense of the intangibility of the fairy world.

1441. Donovan, Mortimer J. "Herodis in the Auchinleck *Sir Orfeo*." *MAE* 27 (1958): 162-165.

Puzzled by inconsistent spellings of the queen's name, the author offers an analogue to *Sir Orfeo* in which the names Orpheus and Herodias appear together in an incident from a 10th-century Winchester chronicle.

1442. Dronke, Peter. "The Return of Eurydice." *C&M* 23 (1962): 198-215.

Traces the journey to the underworld back to the Greeks, whose earliest instance of it is Euripides' *Alkestis*; considers the earliest evidences for Orpheus as a *figura* of Christ and suggests that the theme can be tied to the redemptive power of love over death.

1443. Eadie, J. "A Suggestion as to the Origin of the Steward in the Middle English *Sir Orfeo*." *Trivium* 7 (1972): 54-60.

Disputes claims of any Irish influence and suggests instead that the poem draws upon common European folklore motifs, especially the proud man brought low; further suggests that the angel in *Roberd of Cisyle* has been replaced by the steward in this poem.

1444. Edwards, A.S.G. "Marriage, Harping and Kingship: The Unity of *Sir Orfeo*." *ABR* 32 (1981): 282-291.

Argues that the poem's major concern is with political order and the relationship between the personal desire and feelings of the king and his role and function as ruler; the poet unifies the poem by tying together the three main problems with the king's priorities and decorous behavior in terms of harping, marriage, and kingship.

1445.   ------.   "*Sir Orfeo*, 379-384." *Expl* 29.5 (1971): 43.

Suggests an ironic reading with *solas* as entertainment to obtain "solace" for his own deprivation, which reflects a tension between the function of minstrel and husband.

1446.   ------.   "*Sir Orfeo*, 458-471." *SSF* 9 (1972): 197-198.

Believes that these lines are not only dramatically ironic, but morally evaluative, and that the scene is thematically and narratively central, since Orfeo returns and acts out a renewed sense of his responsibility as king.

1447.   Foster, Edward E.   "Fantasy and Reality in *Sir Orfeo*." *BSUF* 14.4 (1973): 22-29.

Amplifies Knapp's reading [1468] and examines the interpenetration of the fairy and human worlds that shows how the basic metaphoric structure of the poem contrasts resistance with resignation and celebrates the triumph of the latter in a thoroughly Boethian way.

1448.   Frappier, Jean.   "Orphée et Proserpine ou la Lyre et la Harpe." *Mélanges de langue et de littérature médiévales offerts à Pierre le Gentil*. Paris: S.E.D.E.S., 1973. 277-294.

Concludes that Lefèvre (in *Recueil*) probably knew and used *Lai d'Orphée*, the presumed source of *Sir Orfeo*.

1449.   Friedman, John Block.   "Eurydice, Heurodis, and the Noon-Day Demon." *Speculum* 41 (1966): 22-29.

Suggests that the author's conception of the concupiscent heroine required a Satanic attack, suggesting the noon-day demon tradition.

1450. ------. "The Figure of Orpheus in Antiquity and the
Middle Ages." *DA* 26 (1966): 4627. Michigan State U.

Outlines ways in which writers and artists, including the author of *Sir Orfeo*, have regarded the legend
of Orpheus and Eurydice, modifying it to express the
religious, philosophical, and literary beliefs of
their own times.

1451. ------. "King Orpheus and His Queen in Medieval
Romance." Chapter 5 of *Orpheus in the Middle Ages.*
Cambridge: Harvard UP, 1970. 146-210, 233-240.

Discusses *Sir Orfeo* (pp. 175-194, 237-239). Claims
that both the Celtic otherworld and romance contrib-
uted to this ME poem, which uses a tradition that
produced the allegory of Oraia-phonos and Eur-dike in
hell, the ethical tradition that sees Eurydice as a
prey for Satan.

1452. Gray, Douglas. "Sir Orfeo, 1. 565." *Archiv* 198
(1961): 167-169.

Interprets *in y nome* as "took lodging" and suggests
that *her* is an objective genitive or dative "for
her," which completes the contrast *by mi-self* in the
next line.

1453. Grimaldi, Patrizia. *"Sir Orfeo* as Celtic Folk-Hero,
Christian Pilgrim, and Medieval King." *Allegory,
Myth, and Symbol.* Harvard English Studies 9. Ed.
Morton W. Bloomfield. Cambridge: Harvard UP, 1982.
147-161.

Finds the three levels of meaning in patristic
interpretation valuable for this poem, which can be
viewed as a Celtic folktale at the literal level, a
Christian allegory with Orfeo as pilgrim at the
allegorical or moral level, and a parable about power

at the anagogic or social level.

1454.   Gros Louis, Kenneth Richard Russell. "The Myth of Orpheus and Eurydice in English Literature to 1900." *DA* 25 (1964): 2488. U of Wisconsin.

Analyzes English adaptations of the story from Alfred to the Victorians, including *Sir Orfeo*, and claims that in the oral traditions, Orfeo became a magician and a moral exemplum because of associations with David and Christ.

1455.   ------. "The Significance of Sir Orfeo's Self-Exile." *RES* ns 18 (1967): 245-252.

Refutes the statement of Bliss [1418, p. xlii] concerning Orfeo's long search for Heurodis and argues that the poet consciously altered the basic story pattern with Orfeo simply going into exile, never actively searching for his lost wife; he recovers her because of his Christian humility, sacrifice, patience, acceptance, and submission to the authority of the gods and then receives the gift of grace.

1456.   Gual, Carlos Garcia. "'Sir Orfeo': en la confluencia de dos tradiciones miticas." *Prohemio* 6 (1975): 69-81.

Claims that the ME minstrel was only vaguely familiar with the classical Ovidian account of the myth and probably relied on an unknown intermediate French Breton lay. Suggests that he altered episodes and took great liberties with the material in order to curry favor with his English audience (the happy ending and locale change from Thrace to Winchester).

1457.   Habicht, Werner. "*Sir Orfeo*: Die Gebärde als autonome Form." *Die Gebarde in englischen Dichtungen des Mittelalters*. Wissenschaften Philosophisch-Historische Klasse 46. Munich: Bayerische, 1959. 141-148.

Discusses the stylistic form, thematic function, and symbolic value of gestures in *Sir Orfeo*. Sug-

gests that gestures in this poem are not only ornamental, but also functional.

1458. Hanson, Thomas B. *"Sir Orfeo*: Romance as Exemplum."
AnM 13 (1972): 135-154.

Contrasts the Auchinleck and Harley versions and
suggests that the poet deliberately manipulated his
materials and transformed the myth, Orfeo, and his
wife, so the classical myth could be changed into a
Christian exemplum of fortitude and reward.

1459. Heitmann, Klaus. "Orpheus im Mittelalter." *Archiv
für Kulturgeschichte* 45 (1963): 253-294.

Traces the different versions of the Orpheus myth
through the Middle Ages to the end of the 15th century, thus denying that the Renaissance rediscovered
the classical story.

1460. ------. "Typen der Deformierung antiker Mythen im
Mittelalter: Am Beispeil der Orpheussage." *RomJ* 14
(1963): 45-77.

Touches on *Sir Orfeo* briefly in the detailed discussion of medieval writers' transformations of the
Orpheus myth. States that Orpheus was transformed
into a medieval king, the underworld medievalized and
christianized, and the story changed to fit the national literatures and medieval audiences.

1461. Heydon, Peter N. "Chaucer and the *Sir Orfeo* Prologue
of the Auchinleck MS." *PMASAL* 51 (1966): 529-545.

Tries to determine whether Chaucer's *Franklin's
Prologue* specifically resembles the prologue to *Sir
Orfeo* more closely than the *Lai le Freine* prologue;
shows that with regard to diction and syntax the
later Harley 3810 and Ashmole 61 MSS of *Sir Orfeo* do
present similarities to Chaucer's prologue, but that
Chaucer consistently tempered the ME poem by the
sense of his own poetic intention.

1462.   Hill, D.M.   "The Structure of 'Sir Orfeo.'"   *MS* 23
        (1961): 136-153.

        Divides the poem into three parts: lines 1-56, 57-
        476, and 477-604, rather than four sections as Bliss
        [1418] does.

1463.   Jeffrey, David Lyle.   "The Exiled King: Sir Orfeo's
        Harp and the Second Death of Eurydice."   *Mosaic* 9.2
        (1976): 45-60.

        Rejects Knapp's Boethian principle [1468] as an ex-
        planation of the poet's radical change of the tradi-
        tional conclusion of the tale and instead examines
        the symbolic objects of the poem and their spiritual
        and scriptural associations; thus, the poem becomes a
        metamorphosis of natural history by supernatural
        history.

1464.   Keeble, N.H.   "The Narrative Achievement of *Sir
        Orfeo.*"   *ES* 56 (1975): 193-206.

        Argues that the poem's achievement depends not on
        structural symmetry, but on the morality of the nar-
        rative, its concern with personal integrity, honor,
        and fidelity.

1465.   Kennedy, Edward D.   "Sir Orfeo as *Rex Inutilis.*"   *AnM*
        17 (1976): 88-110.

        Rejects the interpretations of Kinghorn [1466] and
        Gros Louis [1455], who assess Orfeo as a good king,
        and argues that Orfeo is guilty of *acedia* and with-
        draws from his royal duties because of his desire for
        or loss of a woman.   Further suggests that the story
        had special power for its audience, since there were
        three medieval cases of royal uselessness in the
        Pope, the Holy Roman Emperor, and Edward II.

1466.   Kinghorn, A.M.   "Human Interest in the Middle English
        Sir Orfeo."   *Neophil* 50 (1966): 359-369.

        Examines the characters in the poem and concludes

that the poet, who imposed a consistent moral pattern
on his narrative, was constantly concerned with human
qualities and removed all hint of supernatural powers, thus inviting a more complete identification
with the hero on the part of the audience.

1467. Klammer, Thomas P. "Multihierarchical Structure in a
Middle English Breton Lay—A Tagmemic Analysis."
Lang&S 4 (1971): 3-23.

Illustrates that monohierarchical analysis of *Sir
Orfeo* fails and indicates how an analysis of its
narrative structure might be carried out with interlocking phonological, grammatical, and lexical hierarchies.

1468. Knapp, James F. "The Meaning of *Sir Orfeo*." *MLQ* 29
(1968): 263-273.

Views the poem from a Boethian perspective, which
assumes a world in which man's affairs are always at
the mercy of fickle Fortune. At the same time, however, the poem affirms values that transcend appearance, including the principle of love, which Boethius
describes as ordering the universe.

1469. Knight, S.T. "The Characteristic Mode of *Sir Orfeo*—A
Generic Reading." *Balcony* 5 (1966): 17-23.

Examines the nature of a lay and then tests this
poem's conformity to the genre. Unlike romance, the
lay exhibits a precision of writing and an interest
in aesthetic effect that dominate any moral concern
and override narrative interest, all characteristics
that describe *Sir Orfeo*.

1470. ------. "The Fairy King's Castle in *Sir Orfeo*: Some
Comments on lines 357-68." *Parergon* 4 (1972): 25.

Answers Dien [1440] by suggesting possible meanings
for some of the problematic architectural terms:
butras as a buttress, but not a flying buttress, and
vousour as a stone in an arch.

1471. Lasater, Alice E.   "Under the Ympe-Tre or: Where the Action is in *Sir Orfeo*." *SoQ* 12 (1974): 353-363.

Suggests that the apple tree of Emain in Irish lore is a counterpart to the *ympe tre* found in the other-world in this poem, not because of the tree, but because of the grafted branches, the silver or golden boughs, which were a universal token for admission to the otherworld.

1472. Lee, M. Owen.   "Orpheus and Eurydice: Myth, Legend, Folklore." *C&M* 26 (1965): 402-412.

Supplements Dronke's study [1442] by touching briefly on all references to the descent myth in classical literature, which shows a steady develop-ment and then deterioration; the author also dis-cusses the perennial vitality of the story as three interwoven strands: part myth (mystery of death), part legend (power of music), and part folklore (love put to the test).

1473. Lerer, Seth.   "Artifice and Artistry in *Sir Orfeo*." *Speculum* 60 (1985): 92-109.

Finds that the description of the fairyland in the poem is indebted to technical terms of English paint-ing in the 13th and 14th centuries and that the poet contrasts this deceptive, artificial world with Or-feo's artistry, which harmonizes man with nature.

1474. Longsworth, Robert M.   "*Sir Orfeo*, the Minstrel, and the Minstrel's Art." *SP* 79 (1982): 1-11.

Challenges the assumption that different versions of a romance imply textual corruption and suggests rather that each is an equally authentic realization of the romance and that improvisational treatments of a story were probably welcome in a minstrel's art. Uses *Sir Orfeo* as an example of the minstrel's art, which is at once subject to change and capable of compelling change.

1475. Lovecy, Ian. "*Sir Orfeo* and Faerie." *Parergon* 7 (1973): 3-8.

Considers apparent contradictions in the presentation of the otherworld; argues that there are two sides of the fairy world and that line 387, often seen as a troublesome change in tone, heightens this presentation of the otherworld as a representation of all the forces that stand in the path of true love.

1476. Lucas, Peter J. "An Interpretation of *Sir Orfeo*." *LeedsSE* ns 6 (1972): 1-9.

Argues that the poem's central meaning concerns the testing of private love and public loyalty, the bonds of society.

1477. Lyle, E.B. "Orpheus and Tristan." *MAE* 50 (1981): 305-308.

Reconstructs the Orpheus story as a type of the woman won and lost between a mortal and immortal lover, the same plot as the basic *Tristan*, but the consolation motif is not useful in *Sir Orfeo*, because the Fairy King has his own queen and does not desire the love of the woman he has stolen. Refutes Frappier's theory [1448], since Thomas' *Tristan* and the *Recueil* share a motif not found in *Sir Orfeo*, suggesting that Lefevre's source was not the *Lai d'Orphée*, but a form of the story serving as Thomas' source.

1478. ------. "*Sir Orfeo* and the Recovery of Amis from the Otherworld in *Guy of Warwick*." *NM* 80 (1979): 65-68.

Notes that lines 347-376 of *Sir Orfeo* parallel and perhaps borrow from lines 11377-11416 of *Guy of Warwick*.

1479. McLaughlin, John. "The Return Song in Medieval Romance and Ballad: King Horn and King Orfeo." *JAF* 88 (1975): 304-307.

Delineates the elements of a narrative type called "Return Song" and claims that *Sir Orfeo*, as well as other medieval romances, fits the paradigm: return after a long exile, a deceptive story told to test the wife, a delayed recognition through a token, and the restoration to the throne.

1480. Masi, Michael. "The Christian Music of *Sir Orfeo*." *CF* 28 (1974): 3-20.

Reads the poem in light of medieval musico-philosophic thought, which demonstrates how music infused a poem whose trappings were borrowed from paganism with a Christian narrative structure; through his music, the Christian Orpheus was able to bring a new harmony to the universe.

1481. Mills, Carol. "Romance Convention and Robert Henryson's *Orpheus and Eurydice*." *Bards and Makars*. Scottish Language and Literature: Medieval and Renaissance. Ed. Adam J. Aitken, Matthew P. McDiarmid, and Derick S. Thomson. Glasgow: U of Glasgow P, 1977. 52-60.

Points to the possible influence on Henryson not only from courtly romances of the Chaucerian type, but also from *Sir Orfeo* itself.

1482. Mitchell, Bruce. "The Faery World of *Sir Orfeo*." *Neophil* 48 (1964): 155-159.

Rejects Kane's interpretation of the fairy world as evil and peopled by a hostile race [*Middle English Literature* (London: Methuen, 1951): 81] by rejecting lines 391-400 of Auchinleck MS and lines 382-389 of Ashmole MS as an early interpolation not present in the original and inconsistent with the description of the fairy world elsewhere in the poem.

1483. Mori, Yoshinobu. "Notes on *Sir Orfeo*." *SLit* 2 (1959): 99-113.

Discusses seven grammatical points of interest:

the omission of the second negative in a subordinate clause ("Not one day passed that he thinks of her"); the function of an abstract noun as an object of verbs like *tell* and *know*; the use of the preposition *of* with the verbs of the five senses ("see of a thing"); the substitution of "it is" for "there is"; the use of a single *as* form in the usual *as...as* construction denoting the superlative degree; the use of a group genitive; and the *that*-clause as an adverbial complement.

1484. Murphy, Christina J. "*Sir Orfeo*: The Self and the Nature of Art." *UMSE* 13 (1972): 19-30.

Argues that the poem analyzes the limits of art within the matrix of the individual's relation to society; Orfeo triumphs because of his ability to control the a-natural forces of the human ego and of the cosmos through the controlling and taming processes of art.

1485. Nicholson, R.H. "*Sir Orfeo*: A 'Kynges Noote.'" *RES* ns 36 (1985): 161-179.

Identifies this poem as a lay with its story of loss and recovery within two linked plots. Suggests the author's artful and purposeful opposition of the two plot threads: one passionate, irrational, and extra-human; the other human, social, and rational. The harp represents Orfeo's life as king, and the tree is associated with the passion of Orfeo and Heurodis.

1486. Nimchinsky, Howard. "The Grafted Tree: A Study of the Composition of *Sir Orfeo*." *DA* 28 (1968): 4138A-4139A. Columbia U.

Explores the classical versions of Orpheus legends that may have been known in the Middle Ages: the early Irish *Wooing of Etain*, the descriptions of the Wild Hunt by Ordericus Vitalis, Walter Map, Andreas Capellanus, *Lay du Trot*, with possible connections to *Sir Orfeo*, and the subplot connections to *Guillaume d'Angleterre* and *King Horn*.

1487.   ------. *"Orfeo, Guillaume,* and *Horn."* *RPh* 22 (1968):
         1-14.

         Finds specific correspondences among the three nar-
         ratives (man beset by fate and expulsion-return) and
         concludes that *Sir Orfeo* was most likely influenced
         by the other two works, although it is possible that
         each bequeathed some details to the others at differ-
         ent stages of transmission.

1488.   Olsen, Alexandra Hennessey. "Loss and Recovery: A
         Morphological Reconsideration of *Sir Orfeo."* *Fabula*
         23 (1982): 198-206.

         Suggests that the poet deliberately changed the
         given story to a folktale with a happy ending.
         Examines *Sir Orfeo* from the morphological point of
         view established by Propp with thirty-one functions
         from transfiguration to the marriage of the hero and
         his ascension to the throne. Concludes that the poem
         is a sub-type of a story described by Propp as "a
         married hero loses his wife; the marriage is resumed
         as the result of a quest."

1489.   Orton, P.R. "Some Problems in *Sir Orfeo."* *N&Q* ns 27
         (1980): 196-199.

         Reconsiders the passages in lines 387-408 and 303
         ff. of the Auchinleck text and proposes that there
         are two distinct types of people in the courtyard:
         those seized by the fairies at the point of violent
         or accidental death or those who have gone mad (ll.
         387-400) and those who were lying in the courtyard
         (ll. 401-408); further suggests that the hawking
         party (ll. 303ff) consists of abducted mortals.

1490.   Ovitt, George. "The Rhetoric of Negation in *Sir
         Orfeo."* *AN&Q* 19 (1980): 2-4.

         Suggests that the unraveling of social and politi-
         cal order is related through the rhetorical act of
         negation until the poem ends in a world that can be
         comprehended by affirmative language.

1491. Owen, Lewis J. "The Recognition Scene in *Sir Orfeo*."
       MAE 40 (1971): 249-253.

       Rejects Bliss' reading [1418] of lines 323-330 on
       rhetorical and thematic grounds and supports Sisam's
       punctuation [1423a] of full stops after lines 324 and
       327, rather than at line 326.

1492. Riddy, Felicity. "The Uses of the Past in *Sir
       Orfeo*." *YES* 6 (1976): 5-15.

       Disputes Donovan's assumptions [371] that the con-
       trast between the real and fairy worlds is either as
       simple or central as he claims; instead the poem as a
       whole seems to encompass two ways of looking at ex-
       perience in time: first, the nostalgic view of the
       past with a sense of discontinuity between events in
       time, and the second, which consummates the first in
       its perception of a pattern in events that does not
       obliterate suffering, but transcends it.

1493. Ronquist, E.C. "The Powers of Poetry in *Sir Orfeo*."
       PQ 64 (1985): 99-117.

       Considers the nature of the otherworld (a place
       accessible to poetry), Orfeo's uses of poetry (as an
       art dependent on reasoned inferences from emotional
       involvement), and the narrator's own poetic activity
       (as an Orphic power of ethical speculation that
       subordinates magic to ethics and poetry).

1494. Rota, Felicina. "Echi di Miti e Leggende in un
       Poemetto Medievale Inglese." *LM* 8 (1958): 439-452.

       Views the poem as a composite of classical legend,
       contaminated by Celtic myth intermingled with German-
       ic and French traditions, but essentially English in
       construction and genesis.

1495. Severs, J. Burke. "The Antecedents of *Sir Orfeo*."
       Leach [56]. 187-207.

       Examines the relationship between the English

version and its antecedents, especially the classical
origins in Alfred's adaptation of Boethius and the
Celtic sources in *Wooing of Etain* and *Filii Mortue*;
argues that the final episode is an integral part of
the poem, which is unified by suspense and parallel
developments in the plot.

1496.   Spring, Ian.   "Orfeo and Orpheus: Notes on a Shet-
         land Ballad."   *Lore&L* 3.10 (1984): 41-52.

Sees the Scottish *King Orphius* as representing a
transitional style between the ME *Sir Orfeo* and the
Shetland *King Orfeo*. Rather than viewing the ballads
as a degeneration of the medieval romance version,
the author argues that all three are independently
derived from the widespread story types of the winning hero, the master musician, and the return from
the dead.

1497.   Stewart, Marion.   "'King Orphius.'"   *ScS* 17 (1973):
         1-16.

Discusses versions of the Orpheus story (1-4),
prints a Scottish version (4-8), and comments on the
discovery of this new version (8-15). In comparing
Sir Orfeo with *King Orphius*, the author sees similarities in content and development, but very different
details, perhaps best accounted for by the theory
that both are translations of an original Breton *lai*,
but are independent versions of the same story.

1498.   Vicari, Patricia.   "*Sparagmos*: Orpheus Among the
         Christians."   *Orpheus: The Metamorphosis of a Myth*.
         Ed. John Warden.   Toronto: U of Toronto P, 1982.
         63-83.

Explores the ways the myth of Orpheus developed in
medieval culture and focuses on specific medieval
treatments, including that in *Sir Orfeo*. Disagrees
with Friedman [1451] and insists that the atmosphere
is Celtic and the treatment of the story "entirely
pagan."

1499.   Wetherbee, Winthrop. *Platonism and Poetry in the Twelfth Century: The Literary Influence of the School of Chartres*. Princeton: Princeton UP, 1972. 98-104.

   Discusses the story of Orpheus and Eurydice in terms of love and loss, as well as the restorative power of poetry.

1500.   Wright, Dorena Allen. "From *Sir Orfeo* to *King Orphius*." *Parergon* 27 (1980): 9-11.

   Points to sixteen examples of verbal parallels as evidence of the descent of the 16th-century Scottish poem from the 14th-century English one.

1501.   ------. "'Sir Orfeo': A Note on 'In Ich Ways.'" *N&Q* ns 14 (1967): 47-48.

   Examines lines 119-120 in the Auchinleck text and proposes that this was the original reading and that the common ancestor of Harley and Ashmole MSS may have been "in al(le) ways."

SEE ALSO items 11 (54-56), 16, 31, 34 (13-14), 67 (217-218), 79 (30-31), 93 (139-150), 111, 163 (42-43), 164, 363 (201-202, 203-204, 210-211) 370 (146-158), 371, 375, 376, 413, 465, 504 (39-50), 506 (164-207), 547, 551, 567, 908, 909, 923, 964, 1108, 1538.

Editions:

1502. Baldwin, Dean Richard. "Sir Perceval of Galles: An Edition." *DAI* 33 (1973): 6299A-6300A. Ohio State U.

1503. Campion, J., and F. Holthausen. *Sir Perceval of Gales*. Alt- und Mittelenglische Texte 5. Heidelberg: Carl Winter, 1913.

1504. Ellis, F.S. *Syr Percyvelle of Galles*. London: Kelmscott, 1895.

586. French and Hale. 531-603.

593. Halliwell [-Phillipps]. 1-81, 257-267, 307-310.

1505. Rodriguez, Marcia. "*Sir Perceval of Gales*: A Critical Edition." *DAI* 39 (1978): 1540A. U of Toronto.

Considers the work not as a Grail romance, but as a ME tail-rhyme romance. Includes text, bibliography, commentary, glossary, and index.

1506. Williams, M.E. "An Edition of the Romance of Sir Percyvelle de Galles, with a Discussion of the Continental and Celtic Analogues." *TGB* 12 (1961-62): 150. M.A., U of Wales.

Criticism:

1507.   Baron, F. Xavier. "Mother and Son in *Sir Perceval of
        Galles.*" *PLL* 8 (1972): 3-14.

        Argues that the ME version emphasizes the love
        between the hero and his mother, which is pointed up
        in the poem's three-part structure: as a child he is
        with her, as a youth he leaves her, as a man he is
        reunited with her. Further suggests that the opposi-
        tion is the archetypal feminine versus masculine
        principles with the feminine symbol triumphant.

1508.   Blaess, Madeleine.   "Arthur's Sisters."   *BBSIA* 8
        (1956): 69-77.

        Describes the discrepancies in the number of sis-
        ters Arthur has. In *Sir Perceval* there is an extra
        sister in Acheflour, the mother of Perceval; in
        several other romances there is an unnamed sister,
        who is the mother of Cador.

1509.   Busby, Keith.   "*Sir Perceval of Galles*, *Le Conte du
        Graal*, and *La Continuation-Gauvain*: The Methods of an
        English Adaptor." *EA* 31 (1978): 198-202.

        Argues that the English poet's methods of treating
        his sources are more sophisticated than hitherto
        suspected and that the *Continuation-Gauvain* is the
        most likely major source of the English work.

1510.   Eckhardt, Caroline D.   "Arthurian Comedy: The Simple-
        ton-Hero in *Sir Perceval of Galles.*" *ChauR* 8 (1974):
        205-220.

        Suggests that the author followed the tradition of
        Dümmling romances and that he exploited the potential
        comedy of simpleton-hero in a chivalric context
        through economy of character and incident.

1511.   Fowler, David C.   "*Le Conte du Graal* and *Sir Perceval
        of Galles.*"   Abstracts of papers delivered at the
        Eleventh Triennial Congress, Exeter, 1975.   *BBSIA* 27

(1975): 217.

Views the poem as a parody of conventional romance and an effective and artistic work in harmony with the treatment of Perceval in the OF work.

1512. ------. *"Le Conte du Graal* and *Sir Perceval of Galles."* CLS 12 (1975): 5-20.

Assumes that the English poem was inspired by Chrétien's original, despite the increased emphasis on comedy and the omission of the Grail itself in the ME version. Also argues that the English poet understood and retained Chrétien's serious theme, the conflict between prowess and charity.

1513. Galloway, Patricia Kay. "Transaction Units: An Approach to the Structural Study of Narrative Through the Analysis of *Perceval of Galles, Li Contes del Graal*, and *Parzival."* DAI 34 (1973): 2558A-2559A. U of North Carolina at Chapel Hill.

Analyzes, transcribes, and compares the deep structure of these romances and argues that the transaction form predominates.

1514. Goetinck, Glenys. *Peredur: A Study of Welsh Traditions in the Grail Legends.* Cardiff: U of Wales P, 1975.

Compares the Welsh romance with the English and Continental works on Perceval; concludes that there is no direct connection between the ME and Welsh versions, although the two do share common plot details not found in Chrétien's work.

1515. Hood, Edna Sue. *"Sir Perceval of Galles:* Medieval Fiction." DA 27 (1966): 1030A-1031A. U of Wisconsin.

Evaluates the poem as narrative fiction with a coherent and unified plot, credible characters, and other elements of successful fiction.

1516. Kindrick, Robert LeRoy.   "The Unknightly Knight:
       Anti-Chivalric Satire in Fourteenth and Fifteenth
       Century English Literature." *DAI* 32 (1972):   5742A.
       U of Texas at Austin.

       Sees two distinct trends: the political poems,
       folk literature, and sermons, which are critical of
       knights who do not live up to the ideals of their
       order; and the anti-romances, which attack the con-
       ventions of romance itself.   Uses *Sir Perceval* and
       Weddynge of Sir Gawen as examples of anti-romances.

1517. Thompson, Raymond H.   *"La Femme Fatale*:   The Rela-
       tionship between Perceval's Attitude to Women and His
       Role as a Grail Quester."   Abstracts of papers deliv-
       ered at the Tenth Triennial Congress, Nantes, 1972.
       BBSIA 24 (1972): 187-188.

       Notes that the English author deals with the non-
       spiritual aspects of Perceval's adventures and ap-
       proaches his role with women differently from the
       Continental writers, revealing the changing heroic
       ideals.

1518. Veldhoen, N.H.G.E.   "I Haffe Spedde Better Pan I
       Wend: Some Notes on the Structure of the M.E. *Sir
       Perceval of Galles.*" *DQR* 11 (1981): 279-286.

       Defends the poem's artistry against attacks of
       failed potential by describing its tightly organized
       structure of seven concentric circles, exhaustively
       investigating the relationships between the charac-
       ters.

SEE ALSO items 93 (122-138), 134, 163 (69-70, 100-105), 272
(77-80), 274 (103-104), 277, 283 (52-56, 60-61), 285, 286,
289, 290, 298, 307, 322 (137-138), 337, 340 (194-196),345,
578, 1546.

SIR TORRENT OF PORTYNGALE [80]

Editions:

1519. Adam, E. *Torrent of Portyngale*. EETSES 51. London:
       Trübner, 1887.

       Re-edited from Chetham MS 8009 with seven fragments
       included. Introduction (v-xxxiv), text (1-92), frag-
       ments (93-100), notes (101-112), and glossary and
       index of names (113-120).

1520. Halliwell [-Phillipps], J.O. *Torrent of Portugal*.
       London, 1842.

       From Chetham MS 8009 with Douce fragment in appen-
       dix.

SEE ALSO items 163 (69-70, 83-85), 311, 410, 413, 578.

Editions:

1521. Allum, Jeanne. "Syr Tryamoure: A Literary and Linguistic Study and an Investigation of Textual Relations (Together with Parallel Texts, Notes and Glossary)." *TGB* 1 (1950-51): 370. M.A., London, U.

1522. Bauszus, Hugo. *Die mittelenglische Romanze Sir Triamour mit eine Einleitung kritisch.* Königsberg: Leupold, 1902.

589. Hales and Furnivall. 2:78-135.

590. ------. 2: 138-190.

1523. Halliwell [-Phillipps], James Orchard. *The Romance of Syr Tryamoure from a Manuscript Preserved in the University Library, Cambridge.* London: Richards, 1846.

1524. Schmidt, Anna Johanna Erdman. *Syr Tryamowre; a Metrical Romance with Introduction, Glossary and Notes.* Diss. U of Amsterdam, 1937. Utrecht: Drukk. Broekhoff, 1937.

Introduction (1-47), text (48-86), notes (87-95), rhyme index and glossary (96-158), and references (159-161).

621. Utterson. 1: 1-72.

SEE ALSO items 111, 410, 413, 578.

SIR TRISTREM [43]

Editions:

1525. Kelton, Robert William. "A Critical Edition of *Sir Tristrem*, Edited from the Auchinleck Manuscript." *DAI* 35 (1975): 7258A. Ohio State U.

   Includes introduction, text, notes, and glossary.

1526. Kölbing, Eugen. *Sir Tristrem, mit Einleitung, Anmerkungen und Glossar.* Vol. 2 of *Die nordische und die englische Version der Tristan-sage.* Heilbronn: Henninger, 1882.

1527. Long, Charles Edward, Jr. "*Sir Tristrem*, Edited from Photostats of the MS Collated with Previous Editions and Provided with Introduction and Notes." *DA* 24 (1963): 1172. U of Arkansas.

   An edition from the Auchinleck MS with full collation from the editions of Kölbing [1526], McNeill [1528], and Scott [1529]. Introduction re-examines critical and textual problems.

1528. McNeill, George P. *Sir Tristrem.* STS 8. Edinburgh: Blackwood, 1886.

1529. Scott, Sir Walter. *Sir Tristrem; A Metrical Romance of the Thirteenth Century; by Thomas of Erceldoune, Called the Rhymer.* 4th ed. Edinburgh: James Ballantyne, 1819.

Criticism:

1530.   Benning, Helmut A.   "'þis Wommon woneþ by West':
        Epische Allusionen in englischen Gedichten des MS
        Harley 2253." *Festschrift für Karl Schneider*.   Ed.
        Ernst S. Dick and Kurt R. Jankowsky.   Amsterdam:
        Benjamins, 1982.   431-438.

        Feels that the French and Latin influence on Eng-
        lish lyrics has overshadowed the Celtic influence,
        especially with regard to content.   Discusses epic
        allusions and the importance of the Tristan story and
        Welsh socio-cultural interaction in the love poetry
        of Harley MS 2253 and in *Sir Tristrem*.   Suggests that
        the description of the queen in *Sir Tristrem* (11.
        1200-1206) comes from the Tristan story with its
        Irish setting, the healer who was Isolde's mother,
        and the warning to women of faithless lovers.

1531.   Dannenbaum, Susan.   "*Sir Tristrem* and its Source."
        Abstracts of papers delivered at the Twelfth Interna-
        tional Arthurian Congress, Regensburg, 1979.   *BBSIA*
        31 (1979): 266.

        Argues that the poet, after rejecting Thomas'
        psychological complexity and courtly tone, never
        found a new unifying principle, so this work suffers
        from diffusion and lack of thematic unity and inten-
        tion.

1532.   Harris, Sylvia C.   "The Cave of Lovers in the 'Tris-
        tramssaga' and Related Tristan Romances." *Romania* 98
        (1977): 306-330, 460-500.

        Analyzes in detail the variants of the Tristan
        story and argues that the author of *Sir Tristrem* must
        have worked from a copy of Thomas's romance, retain-
        ing familiar features of the Earthly Paradise, such
        as the wooded setting and a well with clear water;
        also concludes from evidence in the ME version, Gott-
        fried's *Tristan*, and the Tavolé Ritonda that the cave
        was probably on a hill in the original.   Further sug-
        gests that the ME author seems to have understood the
        kind of structure Thomas had in mind, a cave in the
        earth, a setting inspired by *fogou* at Carn Eumy, a

site in Cornwall.

1533. Hoffman, Donald L. "Cult and Culture: 'Courtly Love' in the Cave and the Forest." *Tristania* 4 (1978): 16-34.

Examines the forest, especially the cave, in versions of the Tristan story and suggests that the ON and ME versions present a cave that is intermediate between the worlds of nature and culture, a kind of protection imparting some of Ogrin's otherworldly grace upon the lovers; this cave as sanctuary is contrasted to Gottfried von Strassburg's allegorical Minnegrotte.

1534. Hynes-Berry, Mary. *"Tristan* and *Sir Tristrem*: Manner as the Heart of the Matter." Abstracts of papers delivered at the Tenth Triennial Congress, Nantes, 1972. *BBSIA* 24 (1972): 200.

Claims that the failure of the poem is due to the absence of narrative coherence and lack of dramatic focus, not in its abridgement of Thomas' work.

1535. Lewes, Ülle Erika. "Comparison of *Trierer Aegidius,* Guillaume's *St. Gilles,* Gottfried's *Tristan, Tristrams Saga,* and *Sir Tristrem*." Lewes [317]. 28-52.

Examines the theme of miraculous nourishment in the texts and suggests that since the "usually brief and superficial" *Sir Tristrem* contains a rather lengthy and dramatic passage (11. 2485-2497), then much of Gottfried's supernatural nourishment must have been present in Thomas already. The ME passage conforms quite closely to Gottfried's famous passage, lines 815-820.

1536. McCroskery, Margaret S. "Tristan and the Dionysian Sea: Passion and the Iterative Sea Motif in the Legends of Tristan and Isolde." *MidwestQ* 13 (1972): 409-422.

Traces the Tristan legend from the Middle Ages

through 19th- and 20th-century adaptations and treatments. Argues that the sea serves the legend well as a structural device and as an eternal symbol of passion and a personification of the life force.

1537. Newstead, Helaine. "The Enfances of Tristan and English Tradition." Leach [56]. 169-185.

Demonstrates that Thomas' version of the *Tristan enfances* may have been influenced by Anglo-Scandinavian traditions current in the east of England in the 12th century; suggests that a Breton *conteur* may have been responsible for the unusual treatment of the tempest and the interweaving of the Havelok, Apollonius, and Tristan stories.

1538. ------. "The Harp and the Rote: An Episode in the Tristan Legend and its Literary History." *RPh* 22 (1969): 463-470.

Investigates the episode of playing the harp or rote—in *Sir Tristrem* as well as other derivatives of Thomas' romance—which does not occur in extant abduction stories in Welsh or Irish. Suggests a Breton influence on these stories (as well as on *Sir Orfeo*), since the otherworld is associated with the dead in Brittany.

1539. ------. "Isolt of the White Hands and Tristan's Marriage." *RPh* 19 (1965): 155-166.

Suggests that the legend of the Man with Two Wives influenced the Tristan stories as well as *King Horn*, *Bevis of Hampton*, and *Guy of Warwick*. Further points to a parallel between the folk tale The Two Brothers, *Amis and Amiloun*, and the Tristan Legend, all of which use the motif of the separating sword.

1540. ------. "King Mark of Cornwall." *RPh* 11 (1958): 240-253.

Studies anew the traditions attached to Mark, the

monarch of great power (according to the biography of St. Paul Aurelian), and the chief of Britain's army and navy, but also the grotesque and sinister figure in traditions of Wales and Brittany in which he is depicted as a king with a horse's ears, who murders his barber to conceal his deformity.

1541. ------. "The Tryst Beneath the Tree: An Episode in the Tristan Legend." *RPh* 9 (1956): 269-284.

Traces the literary history of the episode of the tryst under the tree and its distinctive features, including the lovers' unusual method of communication by chips in the stream, found in the *Saga, Sir Tristrem*, and the Oxford *Folie*.

1542. Pickford, Cedric E. "*Sir Tristrem*, Sir Walter Scott, and Thomas." *Studies in Medieval Literature and Languages in Memory of Frederick Whitehead*. Ed. W. Rothwell, W.R.J. Barron, David Blamires, and Lewis Thorpe. Manchester: Manchester UP, 1973. 219-228.

Demonstrates how Scott approached the poem as part of the minstrelsy of the Scottish border and then makes a plea for better understanding of this poem, which has suffered from the enthusiasm of Scots and the critical judgment of Continental scholars.

1543. ------. "*Tristan* of Thomas, *Sir Tristrem* and Sir Walter Scott." Abstracts of papers delivered at the Tenth Triennial Congress, Nantes, 1972. *BBSIA* 24 (1972): 201.

Places the poem in its proper literary perspective, neither as the source of Thomas' poem nor as a Scottish adaptation of it, but as an English version most likely written in London.

1544. Rumble, Thomas C. "The Middle English *Sir Tristrem*: Toward a Reappraisal." *CL* 11 (1959): 221-228.

Argues against general criticism of this poem as a "garbled and condensed" version of a much finer original and suggests that it is instead a story "so rationalized and so moralized that it would satisfy in terms of its own implicit *solace* and *sentence* the expectations of its relatively uncultured audience."

1545.   Shirt, David J. "A Note on the Etymology of 'Le Morholt.'" *Tristania* 1 (1975-76): 14-18.

Suggests that the name derives from Breton for porpoise, a voracious scavenger, and that the word underwent a process of metaphorical extension.

1546.   Tamplin, Ronald. "*Sir Tristrem* and *Sir Perceval of Galles*: The Meaning of Narrative." Abstracts of papers delivered at the Eleventh Triennial Congress, Exeter, 1975. *BBSIA* 27 (1975): 215.

Suggests that *Sir Tristrem* may be understood better if it is associated with the phenomenological concept of man-in-the-world and that *Sir Perceval* anticipates a post-Renaissance tendency to build language systems, which confer power and impose limits on what is held to be meaningful.

1547.   York, Ernest C. "An Anglo-Saxon Custom in the *Tristrams Saga*." *SS* 41 (1969): 259-262.

Suggests possible English influence on the Norse saga in the blowing of the horn, an Anglo-Saxon custom required of any stranger passing through common land separating property. The horn blowing occurs in both the ON prose saga and the ME poem, a fact suggesting that either the Norse translator was English or knew of the English custom.

1548.   ------. "Isolt's Ordeal: English Legal Customs in the Medieval Tristan Legend." *SP* 68 (1971): 1-9.

Argues that the ordeal reflects features of Anglo-Saxon and later medieval English law in Westminster, but that the author of *Sir Tristrem* depicts procedures that had dropped out of use in England almost a century before he composed the poem.

1549. ------. "Sir Tristrem, 2225-2233." *Expl* 25 (1967): 76.

Describes two preliminary steps to the ordeal by hot iron, which this passage depicts: pleading and the medial judgment.

SEE ALSO items 163 (159-161, 172-179, 193-194), 272 (82-85), 274 (143-144), 283 (43-45), 287, 307, 322 (134-136), 337, 424, 465, 504 (161-162).

THE SONG OF ROLAND [58]

Editions:

598. Herrtage. 107-136 (text), 160-166 (notes).

1550. Russ, Jon Robin. "The Middle English *Song of Roland*:
       A Critical Edition." *DAI* 30 (1969): 291A-292A. U of
       Wisconsin.

       Edited from MS Lansdowne 338.

Criticism:

1551. Russ, Jon R. "For the *MED* and *OED* from the 'Song of
       Roland.'" *AN&Q* 8 (1969): 37-38.

       Cites omissions of *bent*-side and *overcourse*; a new
       meaning for *sand*; antedating in *overslide* and *stag-
       ger*; and post dating of *stem*.

SEE AlSO items 59, 574.

THE SOWDON OF BABYLON [46]

Editions:

1552. Anon. *The Romaunce of the Sowdone of Babylone and of Ferumbras his Sone Who Conquerede Rome.* Roxburghe Club 71. London, 1854.

"Copied from a manuscript in the noble collection of Sir Thomas Phillips, at Middle Hill, Worcestershire.

1553. Hausknecht, Emil. *The Romaunce of the Sowdone of Babylone and of Ferumbras His Sone Who Conquerede Rome.* EETSES 38. London: Trübner, 1881. Rpt. London: Oxford UP, 1969.

Edited from the unique manuscript of Sir Thomas Phillipps, with introduction, notes, and glossary.

1554. Lappert, Stephen Frederick. *"The Romaunce of the Sowdon of Babyloyne*: A Critical Edition." *DAI* 36 (1976): 5319A-5320A. U of Pennsylvania.

Includes introduction, all readings and emendations of previous editions, text, extensive textual commentary, and glossary.

1555. Zehringer, William Clark. "Contributions toward a New Edition of *The Sowdone of Babylone.*" *DAI* 42 (1982): 5116A. Temple U.

Includes discussion of manuscript form, language, script, sources, metrical scheme, style, language patterns, structure and characterization. Explanatory and textual notes supplement the EETS text [1553].

SEE ALSO items 67, (169-175, 188-192, 196-197), 111, 515, 574.

THE SQUYR OF LOWE DEGRE [104]

Editions:

1556. Dibdin, Thomas Frognall. *Reminiscences of a Literary Life.* 2 vols. London: J. Major, 1836. 2: 912-918.

Reproduces "the whole of the fragment in his [John Repton's] possession," the same version from which Ellis [584a] printed his extract, with woodcut and notes.

586. French and Hale. 721-755.

589. Hales and Furnivall. 3: 263-268.

"A much abridged and somewhat mutilated version."

590. ------. 4: 151-155.

597. Hazlitt. 2: 21-64 (text), 4: 362 (notes).

1557. Herbert, J.E. "*The Squyr of Lowe Degre*: A Critical Edition." *TGB* 33 (1985): 2253. M.Phil., Liverpool U.

1558. McCallum, James Dow. *English Literature, The Beginnings to 1500.* New York: Scribner's, 1932. Rpt. 1960. 402-433, 475.

1559. Mead, William Edward. *The Squyr of Lowe Degre, A Middle English Metrical Romance.* Albion Series of

Anglo-Saxon and Middle English Poetry.   Boston: Ginn, 1904.

Edited in all extant forms, with introduction, notes, and glossary.

611.   Ritson.   3: 145-192, 344-353, 441.

614.   Sands.   249-278.

Reprint of Mead [1559] with regularized orthography.

Criticism:

1560.   Allen, Margaret J.   "The Harlot and the Mourning Bride." *The Practical Vision: Essays in English Literature in Honour of Flora Roy.* Ed. Jane Campbell and James Doyle.   Waterloo, ON: Wilfrid Laurier UP, 1978.   13-28.

Shows how Spenser and the author of this poem drew on allusions to the Whore of Babylon in Revelations 3:20.

1561.   Diehl, Huston.   "'For No Theves Shall Come Thereto': Symbolic Detail in *The Squyr of Lowe Degre.*" *ABR* 32 (1981): 140-155.

Argues against Kiernan [1562] by suggesting that the story's pictorial details are symbolic, recalling the life of Christ—his sojourn in the wilderness, betrayal, Crucifixion and Resurrection—and concepts of Christian theology: *caritas*, *fides*, and the marriage of *Sponsus* and *sponsa*.

1562.   Kiernan, K.S.   "*Undo Your Door* and the Order of Chivalry." *SP* 70 (1973): 345-366.

Treats the poem as a deliberately humorous spoof of conventional romance techniques.

1563.   Rivers, Bryan. "The Focus of Satire in *The Squire of Low Degree*." *ESC* 7 (1981): 379-387.

Argues that the poem's satire embraces both lovers and that the colophon "Undo Your Door" indicates that the primary target is the sexual timidity of the princess, not, as Kiernan [1562] suggests, the mercenary aspirations of the squire.

1564.   Rona, Eva. "Hungary in a Medieval Poem 'Capystranus' a Metrical Romance." Schlauch Essays [14]. 343- 352.

Argues that the author of "Capystranus" and publisher of *Squyr of Lowe Degre* were the same, because both works come from Wynkyn de Worde's press, have settings in Hungary, and share similarities of vocabulary.

SEE ALSO item 10, 11 (56-59), 34 (5-6), 79 (94-95), 413, 504 (112-113), 556, 578, 643.

SYRE GAWENE AND THE CARLE OF CARELYLE [28]

Editions:

1565. Ackerman, Robert W. *Syre Gawene and the Carle of Carelyle*. U of Michigan Contributions in Modern Philology 8. Ann Arbor: U of Michigan P, 1947.

600. Kurvinen. 114-158 on even-numbered pages.

Parallel text with *The Carle off Carlile*.

605. Madden. 187-206, 344-348.

614. Sands. 348-371.

Uses the texts of Ackerman [1565] and Kurvinen [600] with regularized orthography.

SEE ALSO items 105 (90-93), 272 (107-109), 274 (116-117), 285, 337, 397, 1276.

THE TAILL OF RAUF COILYEAR [59]

Editions:

579. Amours. xxxiv-xl, 82-114, 317-328, 479-480.

1567. Beattie, William. *The Taill of Rauf Coilyear Printed by Robert Lekpreuik at St. Andrews in 1572: A Facsimile of the Only Known Copy.* Edinburgh: National Library of Scotland, 1966.

1568. Browne, William Hand. *The Taill of Rauf Coilyear.* Baltimore: Johns Hopkins UP, 1903.

Edited with introduction (3-68), text (69-104), notes (105-138), and glossarial index (139-163).

595. Hazlitt. 1: 212-249.

599. Herrtage. v-vii, 1-33, 117-118.

Introduction, text, and notes.

602. Laing. 1-40.

1569. Tonndorf, Max. *Rauf Coilyear.* Diss. Halle-Wittenberg. Berlin, 1893.

1570. Walsh, Elizabeth. "*Rauf Coilyear*: An Edition with an Introduction and Notes." Diss. Harvard U, 1974.
Criticism:

1571.   Walsh, Elizabeth, R.S.C.J.   "The King in Disguise."
        Folklore 86 (1975): 3-24.

        Examines other examples of this popular theme of
        the king-in-disguise in chronicles, other literary
        works, popular tales, and ballads.   Claims that the
        basic motif remains the same, although there is no
        direct literary borrowing.   Suggests that in this
        poem the folklore motif is uppermost, since the hero
        is a seller of coal.

1572.   ------.   "*The Tale of Rauf Coilyear*:   Oral Motif in
        Literary Guise."   *ScLJ* 6.2 (1979): 5-19.

        Investigates the relationship between the oral
        tradition and the literary form of this Scottish
        poem, which is a literary redaction of the popular
        motif of the king-in-disguise.   Includes an extensive
        lists of formulas found in the poem and commentary
        about the use of these formulas.   Argues that the
        poet used traditional phrases, which were not a large
        percentage of the language, but cast the story into
        alliterative and literary form.

SEE ALSO items 212, 227, 243, 413, 574, 819.

Editions:

1573. Fischer, Rudolf. "Vindicta Salvatoris." *Archiv* 111 (1903): 285-298; 112 (1904): 25-45.

Text is from MS Pepys 2014, Magdalene College, Cambridge.

1574. Herbert, J.A. *Titus and Vespasian; or The Destruction of Jerusalem in Rhymed Couplets.* Roxburghe Club 146. London, 1905.

Text is from British Library MS Additional 36523 with collation of four other manuscripts.

1575. Wilson, John Holmes. "*Titus and Vespasian*: A Trial Edition of the Osborn Manuscript." *DA* 28 (1967): 207A. Yale U.

Transcription of Osborn MS as a base text and collations from seven other manuscripts. Introduction and textual notes.

Criticism:

1576. Bühler, Curt F. "The New Morgan Manuscript of *Titus and Vespasian.*" *PMLA* 76 (1961): 20-24.

Examines the new manuscript in the Pierpont Morgan Library (MS 898) and its relationship to two other very similar versions in Additional MS 10036 and Pepys MS 2014. Argues that the short version is better than the longer one published by Herbert [1574] and that the long version is due to accretion rather than the short one to abridgement.

1577.   Moe, Phyllis Gainfort.   "Titus and Vespasian: A Study
        of Two Manuscripts."   *DA* 24 (1964): 3731.   NYU.

        Examines Pierpont Morgan Library MS 898, concluding
        that it is more closely related to Pepys 2014 than to
        British Library Additional 10036 and that the longer
        text is a later redaction.   Also accurately describes
        the contents of the Cleveland Public Library manu-
        script, which contains a prose translation of Roger
        d'Argenteuil's *Bible en francois*, not *Titus and
        Vespasian*.

SEE ALSO items 79 (45-46), 413, 459, 556.

Edition:

1578. Bergen, Henry. *Lydgate's Troy Book.* EETSES 97, 103,
106, 126. 1906-1935. Rpt. Millwood, NY: Kraus,
1973.

Edited from MS Cotton Augustus A.iv, collated with
MSS Arundel 99, Digby 232, and Digby 230. Includes
introduction, notes, and glossary.

Criticism:

1579. Benson, C. David. "The Ancient World of John Lydgate's *Troy Book.*" *ABR* 24 (1973): 299-312.

Argues that Lydgate is neither hostile to antiquity
nor using allusions as a mindless example of his no-
torious prolixity, but rather he strives to present a
believable picture of the ancient world to his medieval audience.

1580. ------. "Prudence, Othea and Lydgate's Death of
Hector." *ABR* 26 (1975): 115-123.

Argues that Lydgate replaced Guido's account of the
Greek king taken prisoner by Hector with Christine de
Pisan's account from her *L'Epistre Othea* of Hector's
plundering of the dead king's armor. Also suggests
that Lydgate changed his treatment of Hector by giving him a fatal flaw of covetousness, an attribute
stressed in Christine's work, which inspired Lydgate
to give more value to prudence.

1581. Blake, N.F. "William Caxton Again in the Light of

Recent Scholarship." *DQR* 12 (1982): 162-182.

Suggests that Lydgate may have had a shaping influence on Caxton, who possibly learned the habit of writing prologues and epilogues as well as the humility *topos* from Lydgate. Further suggests that Caxton's *History of Troy* may have been intended as an introduction to Lydgate's *Troy-Book*.

1582. Cairncross, Andrew S. "Thomas Kyd and the Myrmidons." *ArlingtonQ* 1.4 (1968): 40-45.

Suggests that epithets in Lydgate's *Troy-Book* (*base*, 1. 2653, and *cowardly*, 1. 2740) and the beheading in lines 2760-2762 act as the source for Balthazar's taking advantage of his foes in Kyd's work.

1583. Daniel, Bette L. "A Note on Lydgate's *Corious Flour of Rethorik*." *ESRS* 14 (1965): 29-40.

Discusses how Lydgate handled the problem of translating and adapting an ancient myth to the vernacular in his prologue to *Troy-Book*. Argues that Lydgate respected the truth of his model, endorsed the use of rhetorical devices since they imparted an idiomatic freshness, admitted his own deficiencies, and implied that a translator's tasks are made more difficult by attempts to reproduce the rhetorical patterns of the original.

1584. Dwyer, R.A. "Some Readers of John Trevisa." *N&Q* ns 14 (1967): 291-292.

Suggests that Trevisa's translation of the *Polychronicon* is the source for mythological as well as other usages in Lydgate and Chaucer. Finds Lydgate's misreading of *cattus* for *Cacus* in *Troy-Book* (1. 591) in Trevisa's work, evidence that this was his immediate source.

1585. Hascall, Dudley L. "The Prosody of John Lydgate." *Lang&S* 3 (1970): 122-146.

Objects to the dismissal of Lydgate's verse as "sententious, incompetent, padded, and diffuse." Applies Halle-Keyser's theory [*CE* 28 (1966): 187-219] to Lydgate's verse by analyzing 1000 lines of *Troy-Book* as well as other excerpts. Then generalizes rules for all his so-called irregularities, which can be accounted for by two phonetic conventions and two conditions of substitution.

1586. Kiser, John Edgar. "John Lydgate's *Troy Book*: A Prose Translation." *DAI* 33 (1973): 4349A. U of South Carolina.

Incomplete translation with summaries of omitted passages.

1587. Lawton, Lesley. "The Illustration of Late Medieval Secular Texts, with Special Reference to Lydgate's 'Troy Book.'" *Manuscripts and Readers* [463]. 41-69.

Outlines the possible functions of miniatures in medieval texts and then analyzes the illustrated *Troy-Book* manuscripts, finding that the miniatures were used primarily as visual indices to emphasize the formal division of the text into books.

1588. ------. "Text and Image in Late Mediaeval English Vernacular Literary Manuscripts." *DAI* 45 (1984): 9/1206C. York U.

Focuses on *Troy-Book*, *Fall of Princes*, and Mandeville's *Travels* and the three possible relationships between text and image: as decoration, as a means of providing textual interpretation, and as an indicator of important passages.

1589. Manzalaoui, M.A. "'Derring-do.'" *N&Q* ns 9 (1962): 369-370.

Shows that the misunderstanding of the word occurred in Lydgate's mind and discusses the four appearances of this phrase in *Troy-Book*.

1590. Merritt, Karen Maxwell. "The Source of John Piker-
       yng's *Horestes*." *RES* ns 23 (1972): 255-266.

       Argues that Lydgate's *Troy-Book*, not Caxton's
       Recuyll, is the primary source of plot materials,
       ideas, mood, moral outlook, vocabulary, and even
       phraseology of *Horestes*.

1591. Studer, John. "History as Moral Instruction: John
       Lydgate's Record of *Troie Toun*." *ESRS* 19.1 (1970):
       5-13.

       Views the work as an example of the medieval use of
       history for moral instruction concerned with For-
       tune's mutability, a view that helps explain the
       work's verbosity and digressions.

1592. Walsh, Elizabeth, R.S.C.J. "John Lydgate and the
       Proverbial Tiger." Benson [8]. 291-303.

       Suggests that Lydgate shaped a simile and gave it
       greater meaning and wider circulation than ever be-
       fore. Gives examples of his use of the ferocity of
       the tiger as he applied it to three categories: pa-
       gan warriors, enemies of the Church, and women.
       Troy-Book: I.217, 4283-4284; II.3857-3858; III.991,
       1142, 1394, 2054-2055, 2468-2469, 5137-5142, 5246,
       5297-5298; IV.1271, 2724, 4158-4159, 6787-6788, 6860-
       6864; V.1059-1060, 1264-1265, 2577-2578. Also *Siege
       of Thebes*: 867-868, 1013, 1356, 4274.

SEE ALSO items 79 (46-47, 63-66, 70-71), 476, 479 (97-129),
480, 481, 481a, 482, 486, 487, 490, 491, 493, 494, 495, 497
(11-12, 56-59, 66-69, 71-72, 86-87, 112-114, 141-142), 499
(42-51), 536, 741.

THE TURKE AND GOWIN [27]

Editions:

589. Hales and Furnivall. 1: 88-102.

605. Madden. 243-255, 355.

615. Schlobin.

Edited from the Percy Folio with all variant readings provided.

Criticism:

1593. Lyle, E.B. *"The Turk and Gawain* as a Source of *Thomas of Erceldoune."* FMLS 6 (1970): 98-102. Rpt. in Owen [339].

Points to similarities between the two works in words, in the sequence of narrative elements, and in direct speech, which suggest specific indebtedness, not independent use of a common stock of material.

1594. Simpson, Jacqueline. "Otherworld Adventures in an Icelandic Saga." *Folklore* 77 (1966): 1-20.

Compares the Icelandic saga *þonsteins saga boejarmagns* to its analogue *Turke and Gowin,* which preserves essentially the same plot; the ball jest is part of the tradition they share with *Pèlerinage de Charlemagne.*

1595. Thompson, Raymond H. "The Perils of Good Advice:

The Effect of the Wise Counsellor upon the Conduct of Gawain." *Folklore* 90 (1979): 71-76.

Examines *Le Livre d'Artus, Hunbaut,* and *Turke and Gowin,* which resist the tradition of praising Gawain's *sens* and which seem to be affected by the popular folklore motif of the wise counselor who provides advice and thereby preserves the hero from the disaster into which his folly is leading him.

1596. Walpole, Ronald N.   "*The Pèlerinage de Charlemagne*: Poem, Legend, and Problem." *RPh* 8 (1955): 173-186.

Suggests that the *Pèlerinage* is a parody, embodying fantastic feats of prowess and folklore motifs, such as the reproving wife, which is found in *Turke and Gowin* as well.

SEE ALSO items 93 (201-203), 231, 285, 288, 301 (90-98), 307, 326, 337, 347, 723, 1276.

THE WEDDYNGE OF SIR GAWEN AND DAME RAGNELL [34]

Editions:

1597. Clarke, S.J. *"The Weddynge of Syr Gawen and Dame Ragnell."* *TGB* 26 (1977): 285. M.A., Birmingham U.

1598. Glanville, L. "A New Edition of the Middle English Romance *The Weddyng of Syr Gawen and Dame Ragnell."* *TGB* 9 (1958-59): 139. B.Litt., Oxford U.

1599. Hartwell, David Geddes. "The Wedding of Sir Gawain and Dame Ragnell: An Edition." *DAI* 34 (1973): 3343A. Columbia U.

       Presents text for the first time as a stanzaic romance (in six-line stanzas). Includes introduction, notes, and glossary.

605. Madden. 298-298y.

614. Sands. 323-347.

       Reprints Sumner's text [1600] with regularized orthography.

1600. Sumner, Laura. "The Weddynge of Sir Gawen and Dame Ragnell." *Smith College Studies in Modern Languages* 5.4 (1924).

       The text is printed from Bodleian MS Rawlinson C.86 and collated with Madden's edition [605]. Introduction (vii-xxix), text (1-24), and glossary (25-39).

1601. Whiting, Bartlett J.   "The Wife of Bath's Tale."
       Sources and Analogues of Chaucer's Canterbury Tales.
       Ed. W.F. Bryan and Germaine Dempster. Chicago: Chi-
       cago UP, 1941. 242-264.

       A reprint of the text in Sumner [1600], with a few
       misprints corrected.

Criticism:

1602. Dannenbaum, Susan.   "*The Wedding of Sir Gawain and
       Dame Ragnell*, Line 48." *Expl* 40.3 (1982): 3-4.

       Suggests that ME *grese* or *grece*, meaning "fat or
       grease," sheds light on line 48; thus, Arthur is fol-
       lowing conventional hunting practice by examining the
       fatness of his deer.

1603. Field, P.J.C.   "Malory and *The Wedding of Sir Gawain
       and Dame Ragnell.*" *Archiv* 219 (1982): 374-381.

       Argues that Malory also wrote the *Weddynge of Sir
       Gawen.* Otherwise, the authors of the two works wrote
       at the same time and in the same region, tidied up
       the Arthurian stories, enjoyed writing about hunting,
       shared the same metrical sense, gave their work the
       same ethos, and wrote in prison.

⚡1604. Glasser, Marc.   "'He Nedes Moste Hire Wedde': The
       Forced Marriage in the 'Wife of Bath's Tale' and its
       Middle English Analogues." *NM* 85 (1984): 239-241.

       Suggests that Chaucer emphasized forced marital
       consent in his poem more than writers of the other
       three ME analogues and in so doing underscored the
       appropriateness of the tale for the wife of Bath, who
       conceives of marital relationships as contests be-
       tween spouses to dominate each other.

1605. Griffiths, J.J.   "A Re-examination of Oxford, Bod-
       leian Library, MS Rawlinson C.86." *Archiv* 219
       (1982): 381-388.

Reviews the four booklets that comprise this manuscript and concludes that it was copied in the early
16th century and that the provenance was in or near
London.

1606. Matthews, William. "The Locale of *Le Morte Darthur*."
Chapter 3 of *The Ill-Framed Knight: A Skeptical
Inquiry into the Identity of Sir Thomas Malory.*
Berkeley: U of California P, 1966. 75-114.

Suggests that Malory used this northern romance as
the source for the minor figure of Gromoresom Erioure
(102-103).

1607. Shenk, Robert. "The Liberation of the 'Loathly Lady'
of Medieval Romance." *JRMMRA* 2 (1981): 69-77.

Examines the ending that is often ignored and
argues that the poem makes a serious comment on the
general Christian concern to set men free from the
fetters that bind all humans, made possible only by
the gift of a person's will; further argues that the
romance comments not only on the liberation of men,
but women as well.

SEE ALSO items 105 (88-90), 136, 276, 288, 290, 296, 326,
337, 345, 347, 397, 723, 1276, 1516.

WILLIAM OF PALERNE [11]

Editions:

1608. Bunt, G.H.V. *William of Palerne: An Alliterative Romance*. Groningen, Neth.: Bouma's, 1985.

Text (123-281), commentary (282-327), and three appendices: the prose *William*, errors in Skeat's edition, and the poem and the computer. Also contains glossary, name index, and extensive introduction that includes discussion of the manuscript, date, authorship, audience, editors of the poem, other versions, language, dialect, versification, diction, story, and appreciation (1-111).

1609. Madden, Frederic. *The Ancient English Romance of William and the Werwolf*. Roxburghe Club. London, 1832. Rpt. New York: Burt Franklin, 1970.

608. Morris. 2: 138-150, 312-315.

1610. Simms, Norman Toby. *William of Palerne: A New Edition*. Diss. Washington U, 1969. [Philadelphia]: Norwood Editions, 1973.

Includes introduction, text (1-244), textual notes (245-268), notes on translation, appendix, and bibliography (269-348).

618. Skeat. i-xxix, xxxviii-xliv, 1-175, 219-235, 324-327.

Text is re-edited from the MS 13 King's College, Cambridge; also includes introduction, notes, and index of names.

Criticism:

1611. Bunt, G.H.V.   "Patron, Author and Audience in a
       Fourteenth-Century English Alliterative Poem." *Non
       Nova, Sed Nove: Mélanges de Civilisation Médiévale
       Dédiés à Willem Noomen.* Ed. Martin Gosman and Jaap
       van Os. Groningen, Neth.: Bouma's, 1984. 25-36.

       Reviews evidence of Humphrey de Bohun's patronage,
       suggests he commissioned the translation for himself
       and his immediate associates and not for a wider
       audience, and finds no grounds for localizing the
       poem in Gloucestershire.

1612. Dunn, Charles W. *The Foundling and the Werwolf: A
       Literary-Historical Study of Guillaume de Palerne.*
       University of Toronto Department of English Studies
       and Texts 8. Toronto: U of Toronto P, 1960.

       Specific references to *William of Palerne*: 5, 7,
       9, 10, 72, 73, 76, 135.

1613. Foster, Edward E., and Gail Gilman. "The Text of
       William of Palerne." *NM* 74 (1973): 480-495.

       List eighty-one divergences by Skeat [618] from the
       manuscript and criticize forty-three emendations by
       Madden [1609], Skeat [618], and Kaluza [*EStn* 4
       (1881): 280]; also propose sixteen new emendations.

1614. Kooper, Erik. "*Grace*: The Healing Herb in *William of
       Palerne.*" *LeedsSE* ns 15 (1984): 83-93.

       Opposes the view that the poet is limited or naive
       (Skeat [618], p. xix, and Pearsall [174], p. 158).
       Analyzes his skillful and consistent use of sickness,
       healing and medicine metaphors not in the original
       poem. Focuses specifically on lines 433-434, 540,
       558, 559, 562, 576-577, 595-597, 605, 627-628, 635-
       641, 670, 741, 799, 806-807, 834-836, 841, 847-848,
       956, 962-964, 983-986, 1025, 1030-1034, and 1039-

1040.

1615. Loughman, Thomas Patrick. *William of Palerne*: A Critical Analysis of its Structure, Theme, and Composition and a Modern English Prose Translation." *DAI* 43 (1983): 3314A. Auburn U.

Re-evaluates the poem and shows that it is among the best of the alliterative tradition.

1616. Simms, Norman. "Notes Towards a Poetics of Alliterative Verse: *William of Palerne*." *Proceedings of the AULLA Conference, Melbourne* 13 (1970): 362-381.

Explores the difference between the OF original and the ME alliterative poem in terms of meaning, mode of presentation, and tone by the analysis of a single scene and a close reading of a single figure of speech; suggests critical terminology appropriate to alliterative poetry.

1617. ------. "Partenidon, the Disappointed Prince of Greece: Some Social and Literary Backgrounds to the Alliterative *William of Palerne*." *RITL* 24 (1975): 57-65.

Suggests that the ME version deliberately deletes almost all specific historical and geographical allusions and brings to the foreground moral and philosophical implications of the motifs in the French poem and the allegorical meanings of disguise and metamorphosis; further suggests that the treatment of Partenidon is related to the English barons' opposition to Henry II's involvment in Sicilian affairs.

1618. Turville-Petre, Thorlac. "Humphrey de Bohun and *William of Palerne*." *NM* 75 (1974): 250-252.

Suggests that the author may have been a member of Humphrey's household at either Haresfield or Wheatenhurst or an Austin canon at Lanthony.

SEE ALSO items 34 (53-55), 72, 79 (90-92), 122, 163 (209-210, 246-251), 212, 229, 236, 239, 263 (24-25, 40-42, 134-135), 266, 361 (121-123, 413, 414, 419, 504 (157-158), 548, 578, 854.

Editions:

1619. Friedman, Albert B., and Norman T. Harrington. *Ywain and Gawain*. EETSOS 254. London: Oxford UP, 1964. Rpt. 1981.

Includes introduction (ix-lxii), text (1-107), commentary (108-132), glossary (133-145), and index of persons and places (146).

1620. Harrington, Norman Taylor. "*Ywain and Gawain*: A Critical Edition." Diss. Harvard U, 1960.

611. Ritson. 1: 1-169; 3: 219-220, 225-242, 437-438.

1621. Schleich, Gustav. *Ywain and Gawain*. Oppeln: Franck, 1887.

1622. Taglicht, J. "An Edition of the Middle English Romances *Ywain* and *Gawain*, with Introduction, Notes, and Glossary." *TGB* 14 (1963-64): 186. D.Phil., Oxford U.

Criticism:

1623. Ackerman, Robert W. "Arthur's Wild Man Knight." *RPh* 9 (1955): 115-119.

Interprets lines 259-260 as references to the Wild Man, whose animal muzzle or lips may have been of rubbery texture.

1624.   Ashby, Warren Delaplane, Jr.   "The Lady of the Foun-
        tain: A Study of a Medieval Myth."   *DAI* 37 (1977):
        7732A.   U of Miami.

        Examines five versions of the lady, including *Ywain
        and Gawain*, and sees her as a type of water goddess
        combining features from both classical goddesses and
        the Celtic fairy mistress.

1625.   Combellack, C.R.B.   "Yvain's Fault."   *SP* 68 (1971):
        10-25.

        Mentions the ME version as proof that the Ywain
        stories are not about his great sinful pride.

1626.   De Caluwé-Dor, Juliette.   "Yvain's Lion Again: A
        Comparative Analysis of its Personality and Function
        in the Welsh, French and English Versions."   Varty
        [357].   229-238.

        Argues that the different versions demonstrate that
        the same animal fulfills different functions depend-
        ing on the fundamental themes of each work.   In the
        English version, the lion is assimilated into a dog
        and considered a full protagonist, not as a mere
        device found along the journey of the hero.

1627.   Faris, David Earl.   "Symbolic Geography in Middle
        English Literature: *Pearl*, *Piers Plowman*, *Ywain and
        Gawain*."   *DAI* 34 (1974): 7228A.   Yale U.

        Studies the interaction between the hero and land-
        scape in these poems and argues that the *Gawain*-poet
        illustrates the conventional patterns of romance
        geography with a twist.

1628.   Finlayson, John.   "*Ywain and Gawain* and the Meaning
        of Adventure."   *Anglia* 87 (1969): 312-337.

        Views the poem as one of the most sophisticated,
        complex, and original romances in ME that possesses
        the essentials of the genre; the hero's adventures
        are motivated by a desire to fulfill obligations and

preserve justice and to prove his prowess in his attempt to win his lady—all of which are tied to contemporary realities and social ideals.

1629. Finnie, W. Bruce. "A Structural Study of Six Medieval Arthurian Romances." *DA* 27 (1966): 178A-179A. Ohio State U.

Examines *Ywain and Gawain* as well as five Old Welsh and Old French Arthurian tales by pointing out themes, motivations, plot devices, and the relationship of action to the whole.

1630. Fogg, Sarah Lucille. "Structure and Meaning: A Critical Study of Four Medieval Romances." *DAI* 36 (1976): 7398A. Indiana U.

Applies the principles of structuralism and existential hermeneutics to *Erec et Enide*, *Yvain*, Hartmann von Aue's *Eric*, and *Ywain and Gawain* in order to demonstrate the ways the English poet altered the contexts of plot structure.

1631. Fry, Norman James. "A Comparative Study of Metaphor in the *Ywain* Legend." *DAI* 34 (1973): 3392A. Stanford U.

Notes a lack of metaphor and a deliberate disregard for imagery in Norse and English adaptations, which are a reflection of their world view without the symbolic, interpretative structure that informs the French and German.

1632. Hamilton, Gayle K. "The Breaking of the Troth in *Ywain and Gawain*." *Mediaevalia* 2 (1976): 111-135.

Contends that the English author reveals a new *sens* concerned with fidelity as the basis for an honorable society and thus switches the emphasis in *Ywain and Gawain* from love to *trowth* with its positive as well as negative ramifications.

1633. Harrington, Norman T. "The Problems of the Lacunae
       in *Ywain and Gawain.*" *JEGP* 69 (1970): 659-665.

       Argues against Schleich's theory of faulty copying
       [1621], which suggests at least seven lacunae are a
       result of carelessness; defends the validity of the
       extant text by arguing that it is not due to careless
       omissions, but to the practices of the English
       adapter who deliberately abridged the original by
       eliminating the gore, high emotionalism, love rhet-
       oric, and psychology.

1634. Hunt, Tony. "Beginnings, Middles, and Ends: Some
       Interpretative Problems in Chrétien's *Yvain* and its
       Medieval Adaptations." *The Craft of Fiction: Essays
       in Medieval Poetics.* Ed. Leigh A. Arrathoon. Roches-
       ter, MI: Solaris P, 1984. 83-117.

       Relates three aspects of poetics (exploitation of
       rhetorical conventions, use of intertexual refer-
       ences, and the role of didacticism) in three versions
       of the same story: OF *Yvain*, MHG *Iwein*, and ME *Ywain
       and Gawain.* Concludes that in Chrétien, love and
       chivalry are kept separate with the love theme bur-
       lesqued and chivalry presented seriously; in Hart-
       mann, love and chivalry are united in the political
       responsibilities of the hero; and in *Ywain and
       Gawain*, the love element is subordinated to chivalric
       trowthe, with none of the irony and complexity of
       Chrétien's original.

1635. ------. "The Medieval Adaptations of Chrétien's
       Yvain: A Bibliographical Essay." Varty [357]. 203-
       213.

       Covers the MHG, ME, Swedish, Welsh versions and
       several from the 15th-century. Briefly describes the
       treatment of the hero in each.

1636. Kratins, Ojars. "A Comparative Study of the Struc-
       ture and Meaning of Chrétien de Troyes' *Yvain*, Hart-
       mann von Aue's *Iwein*, and the Middle English *Ywain
       and Gawain.*" Diss. Harvard U, 1965.

1637.   ------. "Love and Marriage in Three Versions of 'The
        Knight of the Lion.'" *CL* 16 (1964): 29-39.

        Compares the relationship that Chrétien develops
        between the Lady and Gawain with those in the MHG
        Iwein and ME *Ywain and Gawain*, which excise courtly
        love and change the hero's relationship to his lady,
        thus emphasizing the knight who has broken his word,
        not the hero as lover.

1638.   Margetts, John. "Gefühlsumschwung in *Iwein*:   minne
        unde haz, luf and envy." *Grossbritannien und Deut-
        schland: Europäische Aspekte der politish- kulturel-
        len Beziehungen beider Länder in Geschichte und
        Gegenwart*. Festschrift für John W.P. Bourke. Ed.
        Ortwin Kuhn. Munich: Goldmann, 1974. 452-460.

        Contrasts Hartmann's *Iwein* with the ME version,
        which follows Chrétien's model, and discusses the
        different treatments between the MHG and ME texts
        (especially 11. 3513-3524, 3675-3687). Argues that
        Hartmann, by returning to the feelings of hatred and
        envy in his text, heightens suspense and clarifies
        the irrationality of human behavior and changes in
        human attitudes.

1639.   Mills, Maldwyn. "The Englishness of *Ywain and Ga-
        wain*." Abstracts of papers delivered at the Eleventh
        Triennial Congress, Exeter, 1975. *BBSIA* 27 (1975):
        214-215.

        Views the "Englishness" of the poem, not in narra-
        tive detail, but in points of style.

1640.   Nolan, Edward Peter. "Medieval Versification: Style
        and Meaning in Hartmann von Aue's *Iwein* and the
        Middle English *Ywain and Gawain*." *DA* 28 (1967):
        2217A-2218A. Indiana U.

        Attempts to analyze formal patterns of meter and
        rhyme and their interaction with the narrative sur-
        face. Argues that the ME poem, which reveals no bal-
        ance of tension between sense and meter and no con-

cern with *mâze* on either a formal or thematic level,
is only a minstrel's tale.

1641. Owens, Roger John. *"Ywain and Gawain:* Style in the
Middle English Romance." *DAI* 38 (1978): 5501A. U of
California, San Diego.

Studies the poem as part of an English stylistic
tradition with controlled conventional style allowing
associative meanings to enhance the internal order of
the poem.

1642. Taglicht, J. "Notes on the Language of *Ywain and
Gawain." Studies in English Language and Literature.*
Eds. Alive Shalvi and A.A. Mendilow. Scripta Hiero-
solymitana 17. Jerusalem: Hebrew U, 1966. 301-309.

Deals with three aspects of the poem's language
that have been neglected or treated unsatisfactorily.

1643. ------. "Notes on *Ywain and Gawain." NM* 71 (1970):
641-647.

Corrects errors in the EETS edition [1619] and provides an additional eighty-eight textual or linguistic notes.

SEE ALSO items 1 (130-131), 80 (121-129), 85 (20-22), 93
(114-121), 163 (159-160, 180-185, 278-279), 272 (111-114),
274 (117-118), 277, 285, 290, 307, 322 (140-141), 506, 325,
337, 419, 426, 504 (47-48, 50ff), (139-153), 578, 750, 1047,
1059.

PROSE ROMANCES

BACKGROUND AND GENERAL

1644. Blake, N.F. "Late Medieval Prose." Bolton [13]. 371-403.

Argues that prose flourishes only when culture, learning, and peace are all present in a society, and that in England, prose developed later than poetry. Traces a line of development which had its impetus in Latinate Church writings and translations and investigates indigenous prose of the 14th century, including the mystics, Caxton, Capgrave, and Malory.

1645. ------. "Middle English Prose and its Audience." *Anglia* 90 (1972): 437-455.

Questions the legitimacy of Chambers' theory [*On the Continuity of English Prose* (London, 1932)] and suggests instead two distinct audiences for ME prose: one with religious interests (with Latin models), and the other with general interests (OE models); further suggests that the influence of French became greater in late ME writings.

1646. Bornstein, Diane. "French Influence on Fifteenth-Century English Prose as Exemplified by the Translation of Christine de Pisan's *Livre du corps de policie*." *MS* 39 (1977): 369-386.

Argues that 14th- and 15th- century writers and translators tried to adapt *style clergial* to English prose and that its primary devices (introductory phrases, doublets, and subordination) are still cultivated in modern formal prose.

1647. Davis, Norman. "Styles in English Prose of the Late Middle and Early Modern Period." *Langue et Littéra-*

ture: *Actes du VIIe Congrès de la Fédération Inter-nationale des Langues et Littératures Modernes*. Bib-liothèque de la Faculté de Philosophie et Lettres de l'Université de Liège 161. Paris: Les Belles Lettres, 1961. 165-184.

Challenges Chambers' theory by pointing to the im-portance of preaching manuals, not OE tradition, in the development of ME prose. Further suggests the importance of the spoken word, the common resources of everyday speech, and French models for ME prose style.

1648. Dolan, T.P., and V.J. Scattergood. "Middle English Prose." Ford [36]. 103-120.

Discuss the range of prose in ME from colloquial to elevated prose, with the self-conscious borrowing of Latinate style and vocabulary by the end of the 15th century. View prose as a utilitarian medium that was used to record, instruct, and exhort; only with the vogue of prose romances did prose style become more flexible and colloquial.

1649. Edwards, A.S.G., ed. *Middle English Prose: A Criti-cal Guide to Major Authors and Genres*. New Bruns-wick: Rutgers UP, 1984.

Contains eighteen essays, including one on romance [1654] and one on Caxton [1668].

1650. ------. "Towards an Index of Middle English Prose." Edwards and Pearsall [1651]. 23-42.

Assesses problems and major difficulties in compil-ing the index, including problems with dating, the first-line index, and the subject matter itself. Foresees publications of handlists and bibliographies of ME prose before the definitive index, which will probably take two decades to complete.

1651. ------, and Derek Pearsall, eds. *Middle English Prose: Essays on Bibliographical Problems*. New York: Garland, 1981.

Includes work by Edwards [1650], Lewis [1655], and Robbins [1659] on the ME prose index.

1652. Field, P.J.C. *Romance and Chronicle: A Study of Malory's Prose Style.* Bloomington: Indiana UP, 1971.

          Chapter: 1. Preliminaries, 1-7.
                  2. Background, 8-35.

Discusses the status of prose in ME and the difficulties faced by the early prose stylists; points to traditions and models available to ME writers in their early efforts at prose writing.

                  3. Narration, 36-68.

Contrasts Malory's independence from his sources with other ME writers' dependence on French diction, idiom, syntax, and style. Considers such works as *Valentine and Orson*, *Prose Merlin*, and *Foure Sonnes of Aymon*.

                  4. The rhetoric of narration, 69-82.
                  5. Description, 83-102.
                  6. Dialogue, 103-119.
                  7. The rhetoric of dialogue, 120-141.
                  8. The narrator, 142-159.
      Apendices, 160-173.
      Bibliography, notes, and index, 174-202.

1653. Gordon, Ian A. *The Movement of English Prose.* English Language Series. London: Longmans, Green, 1966.

          Part: 1. The continuity of English prose, 3-32.

Handles preliminary problems and continuity in terms of vocabulary, stress, segmentation, and sentence structure.

                  2. The Middle Ages, 35-70.

Discusses varieties of OE prose, the elevated alliterative prose of ME, the plain prose of the sermon, and the different styles with their

attendant problems; examines writers
in the 15th century with prose based
on the spoken norm and prose based on
Latin or French originals and the
deliberately conscious stylists.
3. The Renaissance, 73-101.
4. The seventeenth century, 105-129.
5. The creation of modern prose, 133-
167.
Discussion section, further reading, and index,
168-182.

1654. Keiser, Geroge R. "The Romances." Edwards [1649].
271-289.

Examines the canon, state of scholarship, and
directions for future studies in ME prose romances;
reviews critical ideas about the genre, questions the
selections listed in Severs [90], and concludes with
a new list of twenty-five works arranged chronologically.

1655. Lewis, R.E. "Editorial Techniques in the Index of
Middle English Prose." Edwards and Pearsall [1651].
43-64.

Describes major editorial decisions and the content
of each entry in the index. Argues that the first-
line index is the best of the five possible indexes:
author, title, date, genre, and first-line.

1656. Mueller, Janel M. *The Native Tongue and the Word:
Developments in English Prose Style 1380-1580*.
Chicago: U of Chicago P, 1984.

Chapter: 1. Introductory, 1-39.
"Modernity" in prose is defined as
prose that is an instrument of
thought with stabilized clausal word
order.
2. Prose in the later fourteenth and
fifteenth centuries: scripturalism
and the oral basis of composition,
40-110.
Includes a discussion of Wyclif's

English sermons, Hilton's *Scale of Perfection*, *The Cloud of Unknowing*, and *Myrrour of the Blessed Lyf of Jesu Christ*. Examines Caxton's program for ME prose.

3. Prose in the later fourteenth and fifteenth centuries: the reaches of recursion, 111-161.
4. Prose in the earlier half of the sixteenth century: resurgent scripturalism and the stylings of authority, 162-243.
5. Prose in the earlier half of the sixteenth century: sententious sentences or, forms of counsel, 244-321.
6. Prose in the later half of the sixteenth century: the belletristic circuit—from scripturalism to Euphuism, and back, 322-414.

Index, 415.

1657. Richardson, Malcolm. "The *Dictamen* and its Influence on Fifteenth-Century English Prose." *Rhetorica* 2 (1984): 207-226.

Argues that the universal use of the *dictamen* helped in regularizing written English by providing a linquistic and stylistic model for writing while English prose style was developing and maturing; the *dictamen* was also the rhetorical medium through which the English language moved toward a standardized written form.

1658. Ringler, William A., Jr. "*Beware the Cat* and the Beginnings of English Fiction." *Novel* 12 (1979): 113-126.

Investigates prose fiction in English and finds a lack of original works since most work was translated or in verse from 1050 to 1400; discusses Caxton's works, which were pseudo-histories and mostly translations or adaptations; concludes that original and inventive fiction in prose did not emerge until the mid-16th century and suggests Baldwin's *Beware the Cat* as the first prose fiction in English.

1659. Robbins, Rossel Hope. "Opening Remarks." Edwards
       and Pearsall [1651]. 3-22.

       Discusses the aim of the index to catalogue every
       piece of ME prose, providing a counterpart to the
       Index of Middle English Verse. Delineates prose as
       primarily literature, not documents, and points to
       the importance of good indexes.

1660. Scanlon, Paul A. "A Checklist of Prose Romances in
       England 1474-1603." *Library* 5th ser. 33 (1978):
       143-152.

       Lists the prose romances in two categories: those
       rendered into English and those in the original.

1661. ------. "Pre-Elizabethan Prose Romances in English."
       CahiersE 12 (1977): 1-20.

       Argues that prose romances were popularized by a
       less exclusive reading audience, who enjoyed the less
       sophisticated content and manner of presentation.

1662. Sutherland, James. *On English Prose*. Toronto: U of
       Toronto P; London: Oxford UP, 1957.

       Chapter: 1. The problem of prose, 3-30.
                     Outlines the development of prose,
                     which was slower and more uncertain
                     than that of poetry, and stresses the
                     importance of Latin for vocabulary in
                     enriching ME prose style. Claims
                     that when writers were following a
                     good story, they wrote easily with
                     natural rhythms from speech.
                 2. Apes and peacocks, 31-56.
                 3. The age of prose, 57-81.
                 4. The nineteenth century and after,
                     82-110.
            Notes and index, 113-123.

1663. Wilson, R.M. "On the Continuity of English Prose."
       *Mé langes de Linguistique et de Philologie: Fernand
       Mossé in Memoriam*. Paris: Didier, 1959. 486-494.

Stressing the importance of figures such as Malory and Caxton in the development of modern prose, the author finds fault with R.W. Chamber's claim concerning the continuation of OE tradition.

SEE ALSO items 16 (262-279), 39, 43, 60, 62 (300-302), 65, 72 (353-381, 418-438), 80, 85 (47-81), 90, 98 (335-436), 113, 145, 171, 174 (223-281), 385, 388, 394, 396, 529, 578.

CAXTON STUDIES

Bibliography:

1664. Blake, N.F. *William Caxton: A Bibliographic Guide.*
Garland Reference Library of the Humanities 524.
New York: Garland, 1985.

Includes eight sections: Reference works, Caxton's
works, Selections from Caxton, Caxton and his work,
Language and style, Literary background, Printing,
Historical background; also contains three indexes:
names, titles, and manuscripts.

Criticism:

1664a. Anon. "Caxton's Quincentenary: A Retrospect." *BC*
25 (1976): 455-480.

Reviews dating of Caxton's works, patronage, facts
about his life, and his attitude toward books and
printing; notes recent work on Caxton and gives a
brief sketch of his career as a printer.

1665. Blake, N.F. "Caxton and Courtly Style." *E&S* ns 21
(1968): 29-45.

Considers Caxton's reaction to literary English
and the development of prose in the 15th century.
Suggests that Caxton, in following Lydgate, who also
favored "compendiousness," was developing an attitude toward style and rhetoric, a task made difficult because there was no model for prose like
Chaucer for poetry. Argues that Caxton was trying to
break new ground in developing a prose style for
English.

1666.   ------. "Continuity and Change in Caxton's Prologues and Epilogues: The Bruges Period." *GJ* 1979:
72-77.

Finds that Caxton's prologues and epilogues had
little to do with each other and evolved as Caxton
learned more about what kinds of information should
be included and how they should be connected; since
there was no model to follow, Caxton "invented" the
material to be included about patronage and details
concerning the genesis and purpose of the translations.

1667.   ------. "Investigations into the Prologues and
Epilogues by William Caxton." *BJRL* 49 (1966):
17-46.

Examines the relationship between Caxton and Margaret of Burgundy, the history of the first English
printing press, questions about patronage, and the
connections between establishment of the press and
political upheavals of the times.

1668.   ------. "William Caxton." Edwards [1649]. 389-
412.

Reviews attitudes toward Caxton, facts concerning
his life and literary career, the kinds of works he
printed, his translating policies, the meanings and
importance of his prologues and epilogues, his attitudes toward language and style, and directions for
future studies.

1669.   ------. "William Caxton." *Lore&L* 2.6 (1977): 7-15.

Puts into perspective the claim that Caxton is
England's first printer; reviews his career as publisher and printer and the kinds of texts he issued;
and points to the fact that he took no part in distribution or sales and that printing and publishing
were done by the same firm.

1670.   ------. "William Caxton: His Choice of Texts."
Anglia 83 (1965): 289-307.

Points to the importance of Caxton's Burgundian connections and suggests that he was also a seller of books and manuscripts, so that he translated or printed books when he had more than one manuscript at hand. Suggests that his printing for the upper-class audience affected his choice of texts, which were never controversial religious tracts.

1671. Bornstein, Diane. "William Caxton's Chivalric Romances and the Burgundian Renaissance in England." *ES* 57 (1976): 1-10.

Discusses the effects of the Burgundian fashion during the reign of Edward IV on English aristocracy and on the specific choices printed by Caxton, whose works were all in the ducal library.

1672. Chaffee, Harry Alexander. "William Caxton and Fifteenth-Century Prose Style." *DAI* 41 (1980): 1051A. Florida State U.

Suggests that Caxton's prime compositional pattern was based on rhetorical figures and that his syntax was associational, not grammatical. Further sees Caxton in his three functions of editor, translator, and writer as one who took pains to ennoble English prose and polish a deliberate style.

1673. Fisher, John H. "Caxton and Chancery English." Yeager [109]. 161-185.

Examines similarities between Caxton's usage and Chancery English in four passages from his prose; tabulates results and analyzes findings. Concludes that in orthography and morphology, Caxton's language employed and transmitted essentially Chancery forms, with no movement toward more modern or regular forms.

1674. Montgomery, Robert L. "William Caxton and the Beginnings of Tudor Critical Thought." *HLQ* 36 (1973): 91-103.

Argues that Caxton's attitudes reflect concerns

that remained important into the Renaissance: attention to style, interest in didactic intention, preference for historical fact rather than poetry or
fiction, and insistence on the moral profitability
of reading.

1675. Nixon, Howard M. "Caxton, His Contemporaries and
Successors in the Book Trade from Westminster Documents." *Library* 5th ser. 31 (1976): 305-326.

Reviews the available records concerning the loca-
tion of Caxton's shop, the date of his death (Febru-
ary or March 1491/1492), his bequests, and information concerning how his printing and publishing were
organized and why.

1676. Sands, Donald B. "Caxton as Literary Critic." *PBSA*
51 (1957): 312-318.

Attributes "sound critical ability" to Caxton in
his choice of texts whenever he was allowed to
choose his own material. Claims that Caxton himself
chose to print Cato, Cicero, Chaucer, Gower,
Lydgate, and tales of classical antiquity—evidence
of his good judgment in matters of literary taste.

1677. Yeager, R.F. "Literary Theory at the Close of the
Middle Ages: William Caxton and William Thynne."
SAC 6 (1984): 135-164.

Claims that both Caxton and Thynne had a utilitarian theory of literature that affected their choice
of material for publishing. As a result of their
ideas that literature should instruct or reform its
audience, the Chaucer who emerges from their pages
is a more "moral" Chaucer than the one in modern
texts.

SEE ALSO items 16 (263-279), 86 (302-307), 481, 1142, 1581,
1590.

COLLECTIONS

1678. Brie, Friedrich, "Zwei mittelenglische Prosaromane:
The Sege of Thebes und The Sege of Troy." *Archiv* 130
(1913): 40-52, 269-285.

Includes a short introduction and the texts of the
Prose Siege of Thebes and *Prose Siege of Troy*.

1679. Thoms, William J. *Early English Prose Romances, with
Bibliographical and Historical Introductions*. 2nd
ed. 3 vols. London: Nattali and Bond, 1858.

Includes *Robert the Deuyll* and *Helyas, the Knight
of the Swan*. Reprinted from Wynkyn de Worde's.

ARTHUR OF LITTLE BRITAIN [44]

Editions:

1680. Mitchell, George Emil. "A Textual Edition on Modern Principles of *Arthur of Little Britain*, a Romance of the Sixteenth Century Translated by John Bourchier, Lord Berners." *DA* 29 (1969): 4463A. U of Notre Dame.

Uses the 1555 edition as copy text, with introduction, discussion of methodology, textual notes, and variants.

1681. Utterson, E.V. *The History of the Valiant Knight Arthur of Little Britain, a Romance of Chivalry.* Trans. John Bourchier, Lord Berners. London: White, Cochrane, 1814.

Rpt. from an edition by R. Copland for Robert Redborne, ca. 1550.

Criticism:

1682. Blake, N.F. "Lord Berners: A Survey." *M&H* ns 2 (1971): 119-132.

A preliminary survey of what is known of Berners' literary activity and the present state of knowledge about him and his work.

1683. Michel, G.E. "The Folio and Quarto Editions of *Arthur of Little Britain.*" *RBPH* 57 (1979): 664-666.

Discusses possible dates for the two 16th-century editions: the quarto as early as 1567 or after 1582, and the folio as early as 1555 or 1566.

1684. Mitchell, G.E. "The Sixteenth Century Edition of
       'Arthur of Little Britain.'" *RBPH* 50 (1972): 793-
       795.

       Discusses the first edition, printed by Robert Red-
       borne, ca. 1555, and the second, printed by Thomas
       East, ca. 1582. Dismisses as an "error due to care-
       lessness" the entry in Ames' *Typographical Antiqui-*
       ties, which suggested an earlier edition than Red-
       borne's.

1685. Morgan, Alice B. "'Honour & Right' in *Arthur of*
       Little Britain." Benson [8]. 371-384.

       Claims that Berners was not concerned with typical
       romance elements such as divided loyalties, mistaken
       identities, and character complexities, but rather
       with honor and status and the presentation of the
       social milieu.

1686. Oberempt, Kenneth J. "Lord Berners' *Arthur of Lytell*
       Brytayne: Its Date of Composition and French Source."
       NM 77 (1976): 241-252.

       Assesses Blake's dating [1682] and argues that this
       poem is a translation of the 1496 edition of the
       Artus, and that the *terminus a quo* for the transla-
       tion must be thirty years before the most conserva-
       tive estimate (i.e., 1525) and twenty years before
       the most liberal estimate (1514).

1687. ------. "Lord Berners' Translation of *Artus de la*
       Petite Bretagne." *M&H* ns 5 (1974): 191-199.

       Studies Berners' method of translation, which
       reveals his attachment to the principles of the
       Caxtonian school, especially its abiding concern with
       literalism and with courtly style.

1688. ------. "Sir John Bourchier's *Arthur of Lytell*

Brytayne: Its Relation to the French *Artus de la Petite Bretagne.*" *DAI* 32 (1972): 6994A-6995A. U of Iowa.

Shows how Bourchier made the narrative more explicitly coherent and placed more emphasis on the contexts of action through systematic changes from the French source.

1689. Taylor, Anne Robb. *"Grant Translateur:* The Life and Translations of John Bourchier, Second Baron Berners." *DA* 30 (1969): 343A. Brown U.

Examines aspects of Berners' life and work, claiming he deserves credit for first introducing the figure of Oberon into English literature in *Huon of Bordeux* and Proserpina as *dea ex machina* in *Arthur of Little Britain.* Argues that both works are built on the medieval aesthetic standard of infinity, not unity, and show a didactic interest.

SEE ALSO items 85 (69-75), 89, 90, 274 (136-138), 337, 474, 574.

THE BOKE OF DUKE HUON OF BURDEUX [61]

Edition:

1690. Lee, S.L. *The Boke of Duke Huon of Burdeux.* EETSES
40, 41, 43, 50. London: Trübner, 1882-1887. Vols.
40, 41 rpt. as one vol. and vols. 43, 50 rpt. as one
vol. Millwood, NY: Kraus, 1973.

Translated into English by Sir John Bourchier, Lord
Berners, and printed by Wynkyn de Worde, about 1534.

Criticism:

1691. Fisher, J.A. *"Huon of Burdeaux:* A Study in Late
Medieval Prose Romance." *TGB* 23 (1972-73): 303.
B.Litt., Oxford U.

SEE ALSO items 85 (54-55), 574, 1689.

CHARLES THE GRETE [49]

Edition:

1692.   Herrtage, Sidney J.H. *The Lyf of the Noble and Crys-*
         ten Prince, Charles the Grete. EETSES 36, 37. Lon-
         don: Trübner, 1880, 1881. Rpt. as one vol. 1967.

         Translated from the French by William Caxton and
         printed by him in 1485. Includes introduction,
         (v-xii) text (1-252), notes (253-263) and glossary
         (265- 268).

SEE ALSO item 574.

THE DUBLIN ALEXANDER EPITOME [70]

Fragment:

626. Skeat. 279-283, 317.

Appears as "The Story of Alexander" and is copied from the Dublin manuscript.

SEE ALSO item 204.

THE FOURE SONNES OF AYMON [60]

Edition:

1693. Richardson, Octavia. *The Right Plesaunt and Goodly
Historie of the Foure Sonnes of Aymon*. EETSES 44,
45. London: Trübner, 1884, 1885. Rpt. Millwood, NY:
Kraus, 1973.

Translated into English by William Caxton and
printed by him in London, 1489-1491. The edition
includes a short introduction, text, and glossaries,
but no critical apparatus.

SEE ALSO items 85 (51-54), 574.

Editions:

1693a.   Hoe, Robert. *The History of Helyas, Knight of the Swan; Translated by Robert Copland from the French Version published in Paris in 1504; a Literal Reprint in the Types of Wynkin de Worde, after the Unique Copy Printed by him upon Parchment in London MCCCCXII*. New York: Grolier Club, 1901.

1694.   Lombardo, Stanley Daniel. "Wynkyn de Worde and His 1512 Edition of *Helyas, Knyght of the Swanne*." *DAI* 37 (1977): 5107A.   Indiana U.

Introduction includes a critical study of the historical background, the work's structure, and its relation to romance and chronicle traditions.

1679.   Thoms.   3: 3-149.

SEE ALSO items 85 (57-60), 563.

IPOMEDON [102]

Edition:

878. Kölbing. 323-358, 462-464.

SEE ALSO item 556.

KING PONTHUS AND THE FAIR SIDONE [4]

Editions:

1695. Mather, F.J., Jr. *"King Ponthus and the Fair Sidone*
[MS. Digby 185, Bodleian Library. Editio princeps,
with facsimile]." *PMLA* 12 (1897): 1-150.

Introduction with a discussion of the French,
German, and English versions, sources, and a literary
consideration of the work (iv-lxvii); text (1-150).

1696. Krappe, Edith Smith. *"King Ponthus and the Fair
Sidone*: A Critical Edition." *DA* 13 (1953): 797. U
of Pennsylvania.

Includes a photocopy of Wynkyn de Worde's 1511
text. A critical edition of the Digby MS with introduction and notes.

SEE ALSO items 85 (63-64), 548, 1715.

Edition:

1697. Donald, A.K. *Melusine, Compiled (1382-94 A.D.) by Jean D'Arras, Englisht about 1500.* EETSES 68. London: Kegan Paul, Trench, Trübner, 1895. Rpt. Millwood, NY: Kraus, 1975.

Includes text (1-371), brief notes (373-386), and glossary (389-408).

Criticism:

1698. Nolan, Robert J. "An Introduction to the English Version of *Mélusine*: A Medieval Prose Romance." *DAI* 31 (1971): 5370A. NYU.

Examines the French source and past scholarship and sets new directions for scholarship by exploring the tradition of Lamias and Sirens in the Middle Ages. Further suggests that Melusine's demonic nature is suggested by a 12th-century analogue *Otia Imperialia* of Gervasius of Tilbury and the history of Geoffroy de Grand Dent.

1699. Rigsby, Roberta Kay. "'In Fourme of a Serpent fro the Nauel Dounward': The Literary Function of the Anima in *Melusine*." *DAI* 40 (1980): 5434A. Indiana U.

Explores the meaning and importance of the Melusine legend from an archetypal, literary-critical approach and finds the Jungian concept of anima most appropriate, since it allows a perception of the unity of this work's form and meaning.

SEE ALSO items 79 (55-57, 96-98), 556.

PARIS AND VIENNE

Editions:

1699a.　Hazlitt, W.C. *Paris and Vienne. Thystorye of the Noble Ryght Valyaunt and Worthy Knyght Parys, and of the Fayr Vyenne, the Daulphyns Doughter of Vyennoys.* Roxburghe Club. London, 1868.

From the unique copy printed by Caxton at Westminster, MCCCLXXV. Includes preface, glossary,and notes.

1700.　Leach, MacEdward. *Paris and Vienne.* EETSOS 234. London: Oxford UP, 1957. Rpt. 1970.

Translated from the French by William Caxton and printed by him in 1485. Includes introduction that deals with the origin and date of the story and Caxton as translator (ix-xxxi), text (1-78), notes (79-106), glossary (107-114), and a bibliographical note (115-120).

Criticism:

1701.　Cotton, William T. "Fidelity, Suffering, & Humor in *Paris and Vienne.*" Benson and Leyerle [385]. 91-100, 166-169.

Explores the nature of the new passive heroism of fidelity and suffering in love, exemplified to indecorous and humorous proportions according to modern taste in this prose romance.

1702.　Finlayson, J. "The Source of Caxton's *Paris and Vienne.*" *PQ* 46 (1967): 130-135.

Lists twenty-eight correspondences between Caxton's text and Jacques Moderne's *Paris et Vienne*, a book of 44 leaves (B.M.C.47.d.1.), tentatively dated 1540; concludes that Moderne is derived from a source closer to Caxton than MS B.N. Fr. 20044 or Leeu.

SEE ALSO items 80 (142-148), 85 (67-69).

THE PROSE ALEXANDER [67]

Editions:

1703. Neeson, Marjorie, C.S.J. "*The Prose Alexander*: A Critical Edition." *DAI* 32 (1972): 4012A. UCLA.

Includes the Thornton text with critical apparatus. The author suggests that the source is the I^3 recension of *Historia de Preliis*, its provenance is East Yorkshire in 1440, and its scribe is Robert Thornton.

626. Skeat. 279-283, 317.

1704. Westlake, J.S. *The Prose Life of Alexander*. EETSOS 143. London: Kegan Paul, Trench, Trübner, 1913. Rpt. Millwood, NY: Kraus, 1971.

Includes the text only with no critical apparatus.

SEE ALSO items 79 (115-117), 80 (42-47), 200, 203, 204.

PROSE LYFE OF JOSEPH [42]
and DE SANCTO JOSEPH

Edition:

617. Skeat.   25-32, 67-72 (*Prose Lyfe*); 33-34, 72 (*De Sancto*).

Includes the 1516 Pynson print of *De Sancto* and the 1520 Pynson print of *Prose Lyfe*.

SEE ALSO item 337.

PROSE MERLIN [19]

Editions:

589. Hales and Furnivall. 1: 417-496.

Uses Wheatley's edition [1705] as text.

1705. Wheatley, Henry B. *Merlin, or the Early History of King Arthur: A Prose Romance.* EETSOS 10, 21, 36, 112. 1865-1899. Vols. 10, 112 rpt. as one vol. and vols. 21, 36 rpt. as one vol. Millwood, NY: Kraus, 1973.

Vol. 112 includes an introduction, containing outlines of the history of the legend of Merlin by William Henry Mead, as well as essays on Merlin the enchanter and Merlin the bard by D.W. Nash and Arthurian localities by J.S. Stuart Glennie. This edition includes text (1-701), index (703-749), and glossary (751-776).

SEE ALSO items 285, 337, 955.

PROSE SIEGE OF JERUSALEM

Edition:

1706. Kurvinen, Auvo. *The Siege of Jerusalem in Prose.*
Mémoires de la Société Néophilologique de Helsinki
34. Helsinki, 1969.

A previously unedited prose romance of the 15th
century, not listed in Severs [90]. A condensation
of the couplet *Titus and Vespasian.* Includes an
introduction, text from MS Porkington 10, and discussion of the relationships of different versions of
the story.

SEE ALSO items 459, 556, 1577.

PROSE SIEGE OF THEBES [77]

Edition:

1678. Brie. 47-52, 269-272.

SEE ALSO items 470, 488.

PROSE SIEGE OF TROY [76]

Editions:

1678. Brie. 272-285.

1707. Griffin, Nathaniel E. "The Sege of Troye." *PMLA* 22
       (1907): 157-200.

       Includes an introduction that treats the manuscript
       and it sources (157-173) and the text (174-200).

Criticism:

1708. Benson, C. David. "Chaucer's Influence on the Prose
       Sege of Troy." *N&Q* ns 18 (1971): 127-130.

       Argues that although this work is essentially a
       summary of Lydgate's *Troy-Book*, its author drew on
       details from *Troilus and Criseyde* for the character
       of Calchas.

SEE ALSO items 470, 488.

ROBERT THE DEUYLL

Editions:

1709. Morley, Henry. *Early Prose Romances*. London: Routledge, 1889. 167-206.

Text is from Wynkyn de Worde, with brief mention of the story in introduction, 14-18.

1679. Thoms. 1: 1-56

Criticism:

1710. Sajavaara, Kari. "The Two English Prose Texts of *Robert the Deuyll* Printed by Wynkyn de Worde." *NM* 63 (1962): 62-68.

Compares the two prints with the 1496 copy and lists the omissions in the British Library manuscript.

SEE ALSO items 80 (60-61, 68-75, 85-86, 112-113), 1109, 1112, 1114.

THREE KINGS' SONS [108]

Edition:

1711.   Furnivall, F.J. *The Three Kings' Sons (Englisht from the French)*. EETSES 67. London: Kegan Paul, Trench, Trübner, 1895. Rpt. Millwood, NY: Kraus, 1973.

   Text is edited from MS Harley 326. No introduction or notes.

Criticism:

1712.   Grinberg, Henry. "The *Three Kings' Sons*: Notes and Critical Commentary." *DAI* 30 (1969): 280A-281A. NYU.

   Discusses the work as an expression of bourgeois common sense and the values and themes that Duke Philippe cultivated: chivalry, courtliness, and anti-Islamic crusades. Further compares this prose version with the Harley manuscript and with French versions.

1713.   ------. "The *Three Kings' Sons* and *Les Trois Fils de Rois*: Manuscript and Textual Filiation in an Anglo-Burgundian Romance." *RPh* 28 (1975): 521-529.

   Argues that the Harley MS derives from a group II source, but that none of the printed editions qualifies as that source; all are descended from a lost manuscript.

VALENTINE AND ORSON [103]

Edition:

1714. Dickson, Arthur. *Valentine and Orson*. EETSOS 204.
London: Oxford UP, 1937. Rpt. Millwood, NY: Kraus,
1971.

Text is a translation from the French by Henry
Watson, which was first printed by Wynkyn de Worde
about 1503-1505. This volume includes an introduction (ix-lxiii), text (1-327), notes (329-341),
glossary (343-363), and an index of names (365-375).

SEE ALSO items 80 (105-118), 85 (56-60), 556.

WILLIAM OF PALERNE [11]

Fragment:

1715. Brie, Friedrich. "Zwei frühneuenglische Prosaromane." *Archiv* 118 (1907): 318-328.

Contains two fragments, a prose fragment of *William
of Palerne* (318-325) and "Surdyt" (325-328), later
correctly identified by Brie [in "Zu 'Surdyt,'"
Archiv 121 (1908): 129-130] as a fragment of the
prose *King Ponthus*.

SEE ALSO item 548.

INDEX

Ackerman, Robert W. 1, 2,
267, 439, 1565, 1623
Adam, E. 1519
Adams, D.A. 937
Adams, Robert 417
Adolf, Helen 268
Aerts, W.J. 949
Aitken, Adam J. 1481
Alexander, Flora M. 269, 962
Aljubouri, D.A.H. 502
Allen, Dorena 1426
Allen, Margaret J. 1560
Allen, Mark Edward 536
Allen, Rosamund S. 689, 892,
900
Allum, Jean 1521
Amours, F.J. 579
Amsler, Mark E. 112
Anderson, David 1140
Anderson, David Michael 875
Anderson, Earl R. 1401
Anderson, J.J. 1199
Anderson, Robert 768
Andrew, Malcolm 1196, 1212,
1216
Antalocy, Stephanie Clare
1108
Anttila, Raimo 211
App, August J. 270
Arbuthnet, Alexander 1119
Archibald, Elizabeth Frances
655
Arens, Werner 901
Arn, Mary-Jo 173
Arnold, F.E.A. 194

Arrathoon, Leigh A. 1634
Arthur, Ross Gilbert 1217
Ashby, Warren Delaplane 1624
Ashe, Geoffrey 271
Astell, Ann W. 1218
Aston, T.H. 796
Auden, W.H. 3
Ayers, Robert W. 1141
Baader, Horst 363
Bachman, W. Bryant, Jr.
1219, 1220
Baird, Lorrayne Yates 4
Baldwin, Dean Richard 640,
1427, 1502
Ball, C.J.E. 1428
Banks, Mary Macleod 978
Barber, Richard W. 272,
273, 274
Barber, Vivian Ann Greene
418
Barkley, Lawrence 1298
Barnes, Geraldine 761
Barnickel, Klaus Dieter 537
Barnicle, Mary Elizabeth
1125
Barnie, J.E. 381, 382
Baron, F. Xavier 1507
Barron, W.R.J. 5, 212, 275,
383, 729, 816, 817, 827,
886, 1197, 1221, 1222, 1542
Barry, Peter 1223
Baskerville, Mary Pennino
734
Baugh, Albert C. 62, 398-
400, 708

Bauszus, Hugo 1522
Beatie, Bruce A. 6
Beattie, William 580, 1567
Beck, Astrid Billes 828
Beck, Horace 116
Beer, Gillian 113
Bell, John 769
Bell, Robert 770
Bellamy, John 797
Benecke, Ingrid 503
Bennett, J.A.W 213, 581
Bennett, Michael J. 7, 1224-
  1227
Bennett, P.E. 840
Benning, Helmut A. 1530
Benskin, Michael 538
Benson, C. David 479, 480,
  735, 1228, 1579, 1580, 1708
Benson, Larry D. 8, 384,
  385, 582, 988, 989, 1132
Bergen, Henry 1578
Bergner, Heinz 276, 1429
Bernstein, Linda 277
Besserman, Lawrence L. 1229
Bessinger, Jess B., Jr. 9,
  798, 799, 844
Beston, John Bernard 364,
  365, 923, 963
Beston, Rose Marie 114, 963
Bethurum, Dorothy 99
Bickord, Gail Holmgren 1126
Bishop, Ian 1230
Björkman, Erik 979
Bjorklund, Victoria Ann Baum
  881
Blaess, Madeleine 1508
Blaicher, Günther 539, 1389
Blais, Ellen Anne 1430
Blake, N.F. 214, 215, 481,
  1142, 1581, 1644, 1645,
  1664, 1665-1670, 1682
Blamires, Alcuin 1231
Blamires, David 1542
Blanch, Robert J. 1213, 1232-
  1235
Bleiler, E.F. 312
Blenker, Louis 1236
Blessing, James Hartman 419

Bliss, A.J. 278, 919, 1395,
  1402-1404, 1418
Bloomfield, Morton W. 10,
  115, 1453
Bloomgarden, Ira 279
Bluh, Frances Adele 964
Bödtker, A. Trampe 1088
Boitani, Piero 11, 289, 1237
Bollard, J.K. 280
Bolton, W.F. 12, 13
Boone, Lalia Phipps 540
Boots, John Philip 420
Bordman, Gerald Martin 116,
  401, 402
Boren, James L. 990, 991
Bornstein, Diane 1646, 1671
Borroff, Marie 216
Boswinkel, J. 690
Bowers, John M. 1143
Boyle, John Andrew 195
Bradstock, E.M. 965, 1380,
  1381, 1405
Bragg, Lois 1238
Brahmer, Mieczyslaw 14
Braswell, Laurel 421, 1390
Braswell, Mary Flowers 1239
Breuer, Rolf 504
Breul, Karl 1377
Brewer, Derek S. 15, 16, 17,
  18, 117, 118, 119, 281,
  311, 386, 435
Brewer, Elisabeth 351
Brie, Friedrich 1678, 1715
Briggs, K.M. 1431
Bristol, Michael D. 1432
Britton, G.C. 762, 841, 842
Brock, Edmund 980
Brockman, Bennett A. 505
Brody, Saul Nathaniel 641
Broh, Charles Michelson 1383
Broich, Ulrich 297
Bromwich, Rachel 366
Brook, E.J. 541
Brookhouse, Christopher 583,
  1160
Brotanek, Rudolf 1102
Broughton, Bradford B. 1098,
  1240

Brown, Carleton 1386
Brown, W.R.J. 217
Browne, William Hand 1568
Brownlee, Kevin 120
Brownlee, Marina Scordilis 120
Bruce, J. Douglas 956
Brunner, Karl 19, 121, 1095
Bryan, Mildred Willingham 671
Bryan, W.F. 1601
Buck, David Earle 196
Buckley, W.E. 1089
Bühler, Curt F. 1576
Bukker-Neilsen, Hans 52
Bülbring, Karl D. 880, 946
Bullock-Davies, Constance 367, 1433
Bullough, Geoffrey 492
Bunt, G.H.V. 949, 1608, 1611
Burgess, Glyn S. 20, 88
Burnley, J.D. 422
Burns, Norman T. 10
Burrow, J.A. 21, 403, 992, 1198, 1241, 1242, 1419
Burrows, Jean Harpham 440
Busby, Keith 1509
Byrnes, Edward T. 584
Cabaniss, Allen 745
Cairncross, Andrew S. 1582
Caldwell, James Ralston 748
Callaghan, Mary 1243
Camargo, Martin 950
Campbell, Alphonsus M. 282
Campbell, Jane 1560
Campbell, Leslie Jean 122
Campion, J. 1503
Caro, J. 873, 874
Carpinelli, Francis B. 1434
Carr, Muriel Bothwell 1169
Carr, Sherwyn T. 1168
Carruthers, Mary J. 1286
Cartwright, John Francis 720
Cary, George 197
Cassidy, Marsha J. Francis 542
Casson, L.F. 1183

Catalini, Claire F. 1244, 1245
Cawley, A.C. 1199
Chaffee, Harry Alexander 1672
Chalmers, Alexander 771
Chandler, Bruce 1279
Chapman, Robert Lundquist 731, 1099
Child, Francis James 583a, 791
Childress, Diana T. 123
Christianson, Clayton Paul 685
Christmann, Hans Helmut 902
Church, L.B. 893
Clanchy, M.T. 22
Clark, Donald Lemen 23
Clark, George 993
Clark, J.H. 742
Clark, John Frank 691
Clark, Roy Peter 994
Clark, S.L. 1246
Clarke, Marlene Beth 124
Clarke, S.J. 1597
Cleaves, Francis Woodman 198
Clein, Wendy Ann 1247
Clough, Andrea 1248
Cochrane, Kirsty 1435
Cockcroft, Robert 1249
Coffer, Karin Boklund 125
Coffey, Jerome Edward 218
Coggeshall, John M. 779
Coghlan, Brian 389
Cole, Carolyn Barry 1250
Coleman, Arthur 1251
Coleman, Janet 24
Colledge, Edmund 1252
Collins, Marie 519
Colman, Rebecca V. 387
Colopy, Cheryl Gene 368, 1173
Colquitt, Betsy Feagan 25
Combellack, C.R.B. 1625
Como, Frank Thomas 1200
Connelly, William 1253
Cook, Albert S. 1188, 1420

Cook, James Rhodes 1254
Cooke, Thomas D. 35
Coolidge, Sharon Ann 1436, 1437
Cooper, Helen 26
Cooper, Nancy Margaret Mays 936
Cosman, Madeleine Pelner 283, 1279
Coss, P.R. 800
Cotton, William T. 1701
Couse, G.S. 46
Cowen, J.M. 882
Cox, R.C. 692
Coyle, Martin 1255
Craft, Carolyn Martin 995
Craig, Hardin 650
Creed, Robert P. 844
Crook, David 801
Cubbin, G.P. 1256
Cuda, Margaret Curtis 1257
Culbert, Taylor 543
Cunningham, I.C. 438, 441, 442
Curschmann, Michael 404
Cylkowski, David Gerard 658
Dahood, Roger 682, 684
Daiches, David 175
Dalaney, Sheila 843
Daly, Owen James 443
Daniel, Bette L. 1583
Daniel, Neil 772, 780
Dannenbaum, Susan Crane 423, 424, 642, 829, 903, 1531, 1602
Darrah, John 284
Davenport, S.K. 199
Davenport, W.A. 1258
Davidson, Clifford 27
Davies, Constance (see also Bullock-Davies) 1438
Davis, Herbert 89
Davis, Norman 1044, 1100, 1208, 1647
Davis, Robert Evan, Jr. 544
Day, Dennis Michael 369
Day, Mabel 1201

Day, Mildred Leake 1259
De Caluwé-Dor, Juliette 1626
de Weever, Jacqueline 1262
Dean, Christopher 285, 693
Dean, Kitty Chen 28
Delaney, Sheila 843
Deligiorgis, Stavros George 1439
Dempster, Germaine 1601
Derolez, R. 1260
Derrickson, Ann 1261
D'Evelyn, Charlotte 1387
DeVries, F.C. 757
Deyermond, A.H. 20
Diamond, Sara Arlyn 219
Dibdin, Thomas Frognall 1556
Dick, Ernst S. 1530
Dickerson, A. Inskip 679
Dickson, Arthur 1714
Diehl, Huston 1561
Diekstra, F.N.M. 126
Dien, Stephanie 1440
Do, Merdeka Thien-Ly Huong 1214
Dobson, R.B 792
Dolan, T.P. 1648
Donald, A.K. 1697
Donaldson, David 733
Donovan, Mortimer J. 370-372, 754, 1441
Doob, Penelope B. 506
Dowell, Paul Wilson 545
Doyle, A.I. 29, 220, 444, 1144
Doyle, James 1560
Dronke, Peter 1442
Dubois, Marguerite-Marie 30
Dürmüller, Urs 546
Duggan, Hoyt N. 221, 222, 623, 628
Duncan, Edgar Hill 31
Duncan, Patricia Jean 547
Dunn, Charles W. 548, 584, 844, 1612
Dunn, Vincent Ambrose, III 127

Dwyer, Richard 445, 1584
Dykstra, Timothy Eugene 549
Eadie, John 694, 996, 1263, 1264, 1443
Ebin, Lois 481a, 1145, 1146
Ebsworth, Joseph Woodfall 943
Eckhardt, Caroline D. 32, 286, 520, 1510
Economu, George D. 129
Edgeworth, Robert H. 1265
Edwards, Anthony S.G. 482-484, 1139, 1147, 1406, 1444-1446, 1649-1651
Edwards, James Arthur 425
Eisner, Sigmund 287
Ekwall, Eilert 1137
Elliott, Ralph W.V. 223, 1266-1270
Ellis, F.S. 1184, 1384, 1504
Ellis, George 584a
Ellis, Patricia Carol 507
Erdmann, Axel 1136, 1137
Erdoss, Patricia, Klari 128
Erling, Ludwig 1396
Erzgräber, Willi 65
Esch, Arno 1001
Evans, W.O. 33
Evarts, Peter G. 405
Everett, Dorothy 34
Ewald, Robert James 550
Faris, David Earl 750, 1627
Farish, John 1123
Feinstein, Sandra 551
Fellows, J.L. 705
Ferguson, Arthur B. 388
Ferrante, Joan M. 129, 148, 521
Fewster, C.S. 643
Fichte, Joerg O. 288-290, 997
Field, P.J.C. 998, 1603, 1652
Field, Rosalind 224
Figgins, Robert Harrison 291
Finlayson, John 130, 373, 673, 981, 999-1006, 1271, 1628, 1702
Finnie, W. Bruce 1629
Fischer, Rudolf 1573
Fisher, J.A. 1691
Fisher, John H. 2, 35, 1673
Fitzpatrick, John Francis 1272
Flemming-Blake, Anthony 508
Flynn, Elizabeth A. 200
Fogg, Sarah Lucille 1630
Foley, Michael 1007
Foote, Peter 52
Ford, Boris 36, 585
Foster, Edward E. 1447, 1613
Foster, Robert Alfred 131
Fowler, David C. 406, 1511, 1512
Fowler, Roger 233
Frakes, Jerold C. 132
Frankis, John 225
Frappier, Jean 1448
French, Walter Hoyt 586, 894
Friedman, Albert B. 407, 1619
Friedman, John Block 1449-1451
Fries, Maureen 292, 522-524, 1008
Fry, Norman James 1631
Frye, Northrop 133
Fuller, Donald Ames 485
Furnivall, Frederick J. 589, 590, 651, 672, 749, 773, 787, 872, 957, 1711
Furrow, Melissa McCleave 134
Gadomski, Kenneth E. 845
Galloway, Patricia Kay 1513
Ganim, John M. 37, 38, 135, 846, 1148, 1273
Garbaty, Thomas J. 136, 586a
Gardner, Helen 89
Gates, Robert J. 686
Gaunt, J.L. 830
Geddes, Sharon S. 763
Gee, Elizabeth 1274

Gellinek, Christian   904
Giaccherini, Enrico   1275
Giacone, Roberto   764
Gibbs, A.C.   1421
Gibbs, Henry H.   724
Gibson, J.W.   293
Gillies, William   294
Gilman, Gail   1613
Ginn, R.K.G.   1164
Girouard, Mark   295
Glanville, L.   1598
Glasser, Marc   296, 1604
Gleissner, R.   1013
Glenn, I.E.   1275a
Glennie, J.S. Stuart   1705
Göller, Karl Heinz   297,
   298, 1009-1013
Goetinck, Glenys   1514
Goff, Frederick J.   1276
Gollancz, Sir Israel   1201
Goltra, Robert   1277
Goodrich, Peter Hampton   299
Gordon, E.V.   1208
Gordon, Ian A.   1653
Gosman, Martin   1611
Gough, A.B.   752
Gradon, Pamela   39
Graeffe, Lotte Burchardt
   509
Gransden, Antonia   300
Grant, A.D.   587
Gray, Douglas   225, 588, 868,
   1452
Gray, Margaret Muriel   925
Graybill, Robert V.   1371
Green, D.H.   40, 41, 137
Green, Dennis   389
Green, Richard Firth   847,
   1278
Grenier, Rachel-Ann   982
Griffin, Nathaniel E.   1707
Griffith, Richard   1279
Griffiths, J.J.   1605
Grimaldi, Patrizia   1453
Grinberg, Henry   1712, 1713
Grogan, Nedra C.   1280
Gros Louis, Kenneth Richard

Russell   1454, 1455
Gross, Laila   905, 1014
Grout, P.B.   300a
Gual, Carlos Garcia   1456
Guddat-Figge, Gisela   446
Guerin, Wilfred L.   966
Guidi, A.   1202
Gunn, Alan M.F.   138
Gutch, John M.   793
Gwilliams, F.L.   510
Haarder, Andreas   52
Haas, Renate   1015
Habicht, Werner   1457
Hadsel, Martha Elizabeth   552
Hahn, Thomas George   629
Haidu, Peter   41a, 139, 139a
Haines, Victor Yelverton
   1281, 1282
Hale, Charles Brockway   586
Hale, William C.   1283
Hales, John W.   589, 590,
   749
Hall, Audley S.   412
Hall, J.   1191
Hall, Joan Krakover   11
Hall, Joseph   591
Halliwell, [-Phillipps],
   James Orchard   592, 593,
   652, 677, 983, 1081, 1103,
   1520, 1523
Halverson, John   848
Hambridge, Roger A.   1215
Hamel, Mary   984, 1016-1020
Hamilton, Donna B.   1109
Hamilton, Gayle Kathleen
   553, 1632
Handelman, Anita Fern   426
Hanks, D.T.   755
Hanna, Ralph, III   447, 687,
   695, 1284
Hanning, Robert W.
   148, 390, 849, 1285, 1286
Hanson-Smith, Elizabeth   525
Hanson, Thomas B.   1458
Harder, Henry L.   1021
Hardman, Phillipa M.   448,
   1161

Harley, Marta Powell 1287
Harrington, Norman Taylor
  1619, 1620, 1633
Harris, Kate 1187
Harris, P. Valentine 802
Harris, Sylvia C. 1532
Harrison, Keith 1288
Harrison, Ruth Howard 526
Hartle, P.N. 226
Hartshorne, Charles 594
Hartwell, David Geddes 1599
Harward, Vernon J., Jr.
  301, 302
Hascall, Dudley L. 1585
Haskell, Ann 594a
Haskin, Dayton, S.J. 850
Hauer, Stanley R. 1101
Hausknecht, Emil 758, 1553
Haymes, Edward R. 140
Hays, Michael Louis 427
Hazlitt, W. Carew 595, 596,
  597, 1699a
Headley, John M. 1040
Heffernan, Carol Falvo 714,
  718
Heffernan, Thomas J. 408
Heitmann, Klaus 1459, 1460
Helsztynski, Stanislaw 14
Hemingway, Samuel B. 958
Hench, Atcheson L. 851
Hendrix, Howard V. 1289
Herbert, J.A. 1574
Herbert, J.E. 1557
Hermann, Ulrike 554
Hermans, Joseph M.M. 949
Herrtage, Sidney J.H. 598,
  599, 1193, 1692
Herschel, James A. 227
Hervey, Lord Francis 674
Herzog, Michael Bernard 303
Heydon, Peter N. 1461
Hibler-Lebmannsport, L. 1127
Hieatt, A. Kent 1290
Hieatt, Constance B. 228
Hill, Betty 201
Hill, D.M. 141, 906, 1462
Hill, Ordelle 1291

Hill, Thomas D. 1292
Hilligoss, Susan Jane 409
Hilton, R.H. 803
Hinton, Norman Dexter 42,
  486
Hippeau, C. 936a
Hirsh, John C. 449, 852,
  924, 1407
Hissinger, P.F. 959
Hoe, Robert 1693a
Höltgen, Karl Joseph 304
Hoeper, Jeffrey David 142
Hoepffner, Ernest 374
Hoffman, Bonnie 555
Hoffman, Donald Lee 725,
  1533
Holland, William Edward 659,
  663
Hollis, Stephanie J. 1293
Hols, Edith Jones 907
Holt, J.C. 804-806
Holthausen, F. 722, 836, 1503
Homan, Delmar Charles 644
Hood, Edna Sue 1515
Hornstein, Lillian Herlands
  43, 410, 556, 1110, 1111
Horrall, Sarah M. 450, 451
Horstmann, C. 895, 1104,
  1105, 1122
Howard, Douglas Turner, Jr.
  428, 1022
Hudson, Harriet Elizabeth
  143, 452
Hülsmann, Friedrich 743, 746
Hume, Kathryn 144, 145, 146,
  429, 645, 646
Hunt, Tony 44, 45, 1634,
  1635
Hunter, Susan Marie 1294
Hurley, Margaret 147
Hurt, James R. 908
Hussey, S.S. 229
Huval, Barbara Jean 1295
Huws, Daniel 820
Hynes-Berry, Mary 909, 1534
Ikegami, M. 951
Ikegami, Tadahiro 876, 1296,

1297
Ingham, Muriel 1298
Irving, D. 732
Isaacs, Neil D. 3, 756
Ishkanian, Vahan 843
Izzard, E.R. 853
Jack, George B. 854
Jack, R.D.S. 818
Jackson, W.T.H. 20, 46, 47,
    148, 391
Jacobs, Nicolas 230, 616,
    709, 1023, 1174-1179, 1299
Jaech, Sharon L. Jansen 967
Jankowsky, Kurt R. 1530
Jansen, Hans 173
Janssen, Anke 1024
Jauss, Hans Robert 48, 149
Jeffrey, David Lyle 150, 1463
Jenkins, Elizabeth 305
Jennings, Margaret 1300
Johnson, Donald Dodge, Jr.
    680
Johnson, James D. 1025-1027
Johnson, Lynn Staley 1301
Johnston, Arthur 49
Johnston, Grahame 375, 376
Johnston, J. 926
Jones-Lee, Hazel 202
Jones, R.J. 306, 1203
Jordan, Robert M. 151
Joseph, Ruth Fairbanks 231
Jost, Jean E. 307
Kaeuper, Richard W. 781
Kahlert, Shirley Ann 377
Kahn-Blumstein, Andrée 50
Kaluza, Max 936b, 1397
Kaske, R.E. 1302
Kaufmann, Bruce Frank 487
Kealy, John Kiernan, Jr. 910
Kean, P.M. 51, 1303
Kean, Patricia 34
Keeble, N.H. 1464
Keen, M.H. 392
Keen, Maurice 511, 807
Keenan, Joan 1304
Keep, Ann E. 499
Keiser, George R. 453-456,

1028-1032, 1654
Kellogg, Robert 52
Kelly, C.S. 308
Kelly, Henry Ansgar 53
Kelly, Robert L. 1305
Kelly, Susan 309, 696
Kelton, Robert William 1525
Kempe, Dorothy 872a
Kemper, Viktor Robert 310
Kennedy, Beverly 350, 392a
Kennedy, Christopher B.
    1033, 1034
Kennedy, Edward D. 311, 968,
    1035, 1465
Ker, W.P. 152
Kevelson, Roberta 808
Kiernan, Kevin S. 681, 1562
Kikuchi, Kiyoaki 1306
Kimura, Takeo 1149
Kindrick, Robert LeRoy 1307,
    1371, 1516
Kinghorn, A.M. 1466
Kinney, Thomas L. 312
Kirk, Elizabeth J. 1286
Kirkpatrick, Hugh 557
Kirschten, Walther 877
Kiser, John E. 1586
Kissam, Margaret Denslow 153
Kitchel, Luann M. 203
Kittredge, George Lyman
    1391
Kjellmer, Goran 887
Klammer, Thomas P. 1467
Klausner, David Neal 558,
    697, 831
Knapp, James F. 1468
Knight, S.T. 1408, 1469,
    1470
Knobbe, Albert 715
Knopp, Sherron Elizabeth
    559, 969
Kobayashi, Atsuo 154
Kock, Ernst A. 953
Köhler, Erich 313
Kölbing, Eugen 436, 638,
    660, 706, 878, 1096, 1130,
    1388, 1526

Koenig, V. Frederic 1195
Kohl, Stephan 1150, 1150a
Kooper, Erik 1308, 1614
Kordecki, Lesley Catherine 512
Korrel, Peter G. 314, 970
Kossick, S.G. 1309
Kossick, Shirley 54, 232
Kozicki, Henry 1180
Kramer, Dale 647
Krappe, Edith Smith 1696
Kratins, Ojars 560, 648, 1636, 1637
Kratzmann, Gregory 929
Krause, F. 916
Kretzschmar, William A., Jr. 855
Krieg, Martha Fessler 1085
Krishna, Valerie 985, 1036-1038
Krzyzanowski, Julian 14
Kuhn, Ortwin 1638
Kurvinen, Auvo 600, 1706
Lacy, Norris J. 155
Lagorio, Valerie M. 315, 888-891
Laing, David 601, 602, 759, 814a, 1097, 1117, 1120, 1170
Lambert, Roy Eugene 430
Lane, Daryl F. Jr. 513, 1409
Lappert, Stephen Frederick 971, 1554
Lasater, Alice E. 55, 1471
Lasry, Anita Benaim 527
Lawlor, John 649
Lawrence, Harold Whitney 656
Lawrence, R.F. 233, 630, 631
Lawton, David A. 234-240, 632, 736, 885
Lawton, Lesley 1587, 1588
Leach, H.G. 698
Leach, MacEdward 56, 639, 1700
Lee, Anne Thompson 716, 719
Lee, Jennifer A. 1310
Lee, M. Owen 1472

Lee, S.L. 1690
Legge, M. Dominica 57, 156
Lehman, Anne Kernan 241
Lehman, David 1311
Leible, Arthur Bray 316
Lenaghan, R.T. 157
Lengert, O. 1118
Lenz, Joseph Martin 158
Leo, Diana Thomas 561
Leonardi, Phyllis 562
Lerer, Seth 1473
Levine, Robert 1312
Levy, Bernard S. 242
Lewes, Ülle Erika 317, 1535
Lewis, Janet E. 431
Lewis, R.E. 1655
Leyerle, John 385
Lippe, Karl 1039
Lipski, John Michael 58
Lister, W. 710
Littleton, C. Scott 318, 319
Lock, Richard Howard 59, 1313
Lodge, R.A. 300a
Lombardo, Stanley Daniel 1694
Long, Charles Edward, Jr. 1527
Long, Clarence Edward 159
Long, Richard A. 1087
Longsworth, Robert M. 1474
Loomis, Roger Sherman 320-325, 341, 1051
Loughman, Thomas Patrick 1615
Lovecy, Ian Charles 514, 1475
Lovell, Robert Earl 1138, 1371
Lowe, Virginia A.P. 699
Lucas, Peter J. 60, 1410, 1476
Lüdtke, Gustav 744
Luick, Karl 1185
Lumby, J. Rawson 603
Lumiansky, Robert M. 204, 488, 563, 933, 966, 972,

1040, 1041
Lupack, Alan C.   243
Luttrell, Claude   737, 938,
    939, 1314, 1315
Lyle, E.B.   1393, 1477, 1478,
    1593
McAlindon, T.   515, 516, 1042
McCallum, James Dow   1558
McCarthy, Terence   1043
McCausland, Elizabeth   920
McCobb, Lilian M.   1092, 1093
McCoy, Dorothy Schuchmann   664
    1112
McCreesh, Bernadine   856, 1411
McCroskery, Margaret S.   1536
MacCurdy, Marian Mesrobian
    528
McDiarmid, Matthew P.   1481
Macdonald, A.   721
MacDonald, Donald   244
McGee, Alan Van Keuren   1133
McGunnigle, Michael Gerard
    489
Machann, Clinton   326
McIntosh, Angus   245, 857,
    1044, 1124, 1134
Mackay, M.A.   246
McKnight, George H.   604, 1165
MacLaine, Allan H.   61
MaLaughlin, John   1479
McNeill, George P.   1528
Macrae, Suzanne Haynes   160
Macrae-Gibson, O.D.   457, 458
    661, 665, 954
McSparran, Frances   437, 1082
Madden, Sir Frederic   605,
    837, 1609
Maddicott, J.R.   809
Mätzner, Eduard   896
Magaw, Barbara L.   529
Magoun, Francis Peabody, Jr.
    624
Malone, Kemp   62
Mandel, Jerome   63
Manzalaoui, Mahmoud A.   973,
    1589
Marchalonis, Shirley   393,

530, 1382
Margeson, Robert Ward   974
Margetts, John   1638
Marino, James Gerard Americus   161
Markland, Murray Faulds   394
Markman, Alan Mouns   327
Markus, Manfred   1045
Marler, J.C.   1252
Marotta, Joseph Gerald   1151
Martin, B.K.   1412
Martin, J.E.
Martin, Jeanne Suzette   162
Martin, John Stanley   375
Masi, Michael   1480
Maslen, K.I.D.   476
Mason, Emma   832
Masters, George Mallary   1302
Mather, F.J., Jr.   1695
Matheson, Lister M.   666,
    1192
Mathew, Gervase   649
Mathewson, Jeanne T.   1316
Matonis, A.T.E.   247, 248
Matthews, William   328, 329,
    1046, 1606
Mead, Herman   1086
Mead, William Edward   1559
Mead, William Henry   1705
Meale, Carol M.   330, 883,
    884
Mehl, Dieter   64, 65, 163,
    164
Meletinsky, Elizar M.   66
Mendilow, A.A.   1642
Menkin, Edward Z.   782
Mennicken, M.   1013
Mercer, Mary Ellen   331
Merriman, James Douglas   332
Merritt, Karen Maxwell   1590
Metcalf, Allan   1317
Metlitzki, Dorothee   67
Meyer-Lindenberg, Herlint
    858
Meyer, Robert J.   165
Michel, Francisque   606
Michel, G.E.   1685

Mieszkowski, Gretchen 490
Milgrom, Robert Lee 249
Miller, B.D.H. 859
Miller, William E. 708
Mills, A.D. 20
Mills, Carol 1481
Mills, Maldwyn 607, 820, 860, 861, 936c, 940-942, 1413, 1639
Mitchell, Bruce 862, 1482
Mitchell, George Emil 1680, 1684
Mitchell, L.E. 565
Mitterman, Harald 566
Moe, Phyllis Gainfort 459, 1135, 1577
Montgomery, Robert L. 1674
Moore, Arthur K. 68
Moorman, Charles 250, 251, 333, 1204
Moran, Noreen Deane 166
Mordkoff, Judith E. Crounse 422, 460
Morgan, Alice B. 1685
Morgan, Gerald 1318, 1319
Morgan, H.E. 1047
Morgan, Hubert E. 461, 1320
Mōri, Yoshinobu 1483
Morley, Henry 1166, 1709
Morley, K.E. 531
Morris, Richard 608, 774, 1205
Morris, Rosemary 334
Morton, A.L. 335
Moseley, C.W.R.D. 252
Mudroch, Vaclav 46
Mueller, Janel M. 1656
Murphy, Christina J. 1484
Murphy, Gratia H. 1048
Murphy, Michael 532, 1321
Mustanoja, Tauno F. 738
Nash, D.W. 1705
Neaman, Judith Silverman 336
Neeson, Marjorie 1703
Nelson, Marie 1049
Newman, Barbara Florence

1322
Newstead, Helaine 167, 337, 1537-1541
Nicastro, Anthony Joseph 69
Nicholls, Jonathan 1323
Nichols, R.C. 1090
Nicholson, R.H. 1485
Nickel, Helmut 1324
Nimchinsky, Howard 1486, 1487
Nixon, Howard M. 1675
Noble, James Erwin 253
Nolan, Edward Peter 1640
Nolan, Robert 1698
Novak, James Ballaz 1325
Novelli, Cornelius 1379
Nuck, Richard 1106
Nygard, Holger Olof 168
Oates, J.C.T. 810
Oberempt, Kenneth 1686-1688
O'Brien, Timothy David 567, 911
Obst, Wolfgang 1050
Olmert, Michael 1326
O'Loughlin, J.L.N. 254, 1051
Olsen, Alexandra Hennessey 1113, 1488
Olshen, Barry N. 431
Olstead, Myra Mahlow 338
Onions, C.T. 1052
Orton, P.R. 1489
O'Sharkey, Eithne 1053
Osselton, N.E. 863
O'Sullivan, Mary Isabelle 609
Otlewksi, Eleanor 568
Ovitt, George Odell, Jr. 1054, 1490
Owen, A.E.B. 435, 462
Owen, D.D.R. 339, 340
Owen, Lewis J. 1491
Owens, Roger John 1641
Pace, George B. 1144
Painter, Sidney 70
Palmer, David Andrew 395
Panton, George A. 733
Parker, David 811

Parmisano, S.A.   71
Parr, Johnstone   1152
Partridge, A.C.   72
Paton, Florence Ann   688
Paton, Lucy Allen   341, 960
Patrick, Marietta Stafford
   1327
Patten, Clara Lucille   169
Patterson, Lee Willing   73,
   1055
Patton, Patricia Joan   1414
Payen, J. Ch.   126
Pearcy, Roy J.   1056
Pearsall, Derek   73a, 170-
   175, 255, 256, 438, 463, 464
   491-493, 789, 790, 1651
Peck, Russell A.   1057
Pelan, Margaret   765
Perry, G.G.   986
Perryman, Judith   917, 1328
Petricone, Ancilla Marie   378
Pettitt, T.   74
Phelan, Walter S.   1329
Phillips, Sir Thomas   821
Pickford, Cedric E.   300a,
   1542, 1543
Pickford, T.E.   657
Pickles, J.D.   783
Piehler, Paul   1330
Pietrkiewicz, C.F.E.B.   75
Pinkerton, John   610
Pollard, William F., Jr.
   1331
Pons, Émile   1206
Ponton, Thomas   961
Pope, Mildred K.   912
Popova, M.K.   76
Poppe, Nikolaus   205
Porter, Elizabeth   1058,
   1059
Pratt, John Harvey   569
Prior, Sandra Pierson   1332
Puhvel, Martin   1333-1336
Purdon, Liam Oliver   570
Puryear, Leslie C.   176
Quinn, Esther C.   342
Quinn, William Anthony   411,

412
Radcliffe-Umstead, Douglas
   1112
Radcliffe, Clara Jane   864
Raith, Josef   653
Rambo, Sharon M.   465
Ramsey, Lee C.   413
Ransom, James Fitzhugh   955
Raymo, Robert R.   9
Reagan, Christopher J.   10
Regan, Charles L.   1060, 1061
Reich, Rosalie   206
Reichardt, Paul F.   1337
Reid, Wendy M.   1338
Reilly, Robert   747
Reiss, Edmund   77, 177, 766,
   865, 1083
Renoir, Alain   494-497, 1153-
   1156
Rhŷs, John   343
Rice, Joanne Adrienne   178
Rice, Nancy Hall   1062
Richardson, Frances E.   1189
Richardson, Malcolm   1657
Richardson, Octavia   1693
Richmond, Velma E. Bourgeois
   78, 79, 80, 432, 833, 834
Rickert, Edith   753
Ricketts, P.T.   20
Riddy, Felicity   1492
Rigby, Marjory   1339
Rigsby, Roberta Kay   1699
Ringel, Faye Joyce   1340
Ringler, William, A., Jr.
   1658
Ritchie, R.L. Graeme   1121
Ritson, Joseph   611, 794,
   795, 1399
Ritzke-Rutherford Jean   1063,
   1064
Rivers, Bryan   1563
Robbins, Rossel Hope   1659
Roberts, Nanette McNiff   533
Roberts, Valerie Stewart
   Crozier   879
Robertson, M.J.   571
Robertson, Michael   1341

Robinson, Noel Petri 1342
Robinson, P.R. 437
Robson, C.A. 1415
Robson, John 612
Rodriquez, Marcia 1505
Rogers, Franklin R. 784
Rogers, G.E. 344
Rogers, H.L. 389
Rollow, Jack 1171
Rona, Eva 1564
Ronberg, Gert 633, 739, 740
Roney, L.Y. 1343
Ronquist, E.C. 1493
Rosenberg, Bruce A. 63, 179, 414, 1181
Ross, D.J.A. 197, 207
Ross, F.M. 819
Rosskopf, Karl 722
Rota, Felicina 1494
Rothwell, W. 1542
Rouillard, Zelda Jeanne 572
Rowland, Beryl 81, 91
Rubey, Daniel Robert 433
Rudnytsky, Peter L. 1344
Ruff, Joseph R. 396
Rumble, Thomas C. 613, 1544
Runde, Joseph 180
Russ, Jon Robin 1550, 1551
Ruthrof, Horst G. 785
Saito, Bishu 1297
Sajavaara, Kari 466, 1114, 1710
Salter, Elizabeth 82, 257, 258
Samuels, M.L. 538
Sanderlin, George 1345-1350
Sands, Donald B. 614
Sapora, Robert William, Jr. 259
Sarrazin, Gregor 1084
Scanlon, Paul 1660, 1661
Scattergood, John 1361
Scattergood, V.J. 83, 84, 812, 1351, 1648
Schelp, Hanspeter 181, 1065
Schendl, Herbert 711
Scheps, Walter 930
Scherer, Margaret R. 498

Schirmer, Walter F. 499
Schlauch, Margaret 85, 86, 87, 1157
Schleich, Gustav 822, 1172, 1186, 1190, 1385, 1621
Schlobin, Rober Clark 615
Schmelter, H.U. 208
Schmidt, A.V.C 616
Schmidt, Anna Johanna Erdman 1524
Schmolke-Hasselmann, Beate 88, 345
Schopf, Alfred 1352
Scott, Sir Walter 1529
Seaton, Ethel 89
Serjeantson, Mary S. 1201
Severs, J. Burke 43, 90, 91, 1495
Sevier, Marcus W. 723
Shackford, Martha Hale 1422
Shalvi, Alive 1642
Shaw, Ian 1353
Shaw, Margaret Jane 1354
Shenk, Robert 1607
Shepherd, Geoffrey 92, 260
Sherborne, J.W. 84
Shichtman, Martin Barry 346
Shimizu, Aya 347, 975
Shirt, David J. 1545
Shoaf, R.A. 1066, 1355
Shonk, Timothy Allen 467, 468
Shores, Doris 918
Shull, Donald Marshall 1116
Siciliano, Francis Xavier 835
Signer, Deborah A. 866
Silverstein, Theodore 1207
Simko, Jan 1067
Simms, Norman Toby 1355a, 1610, 1616, 1617
Simpson, J.A. 1356
Simpson, Jacqueline 1594
Singh, C. 261
Sisam, Celia 1423
Sisam, Kenneth 838, 1423, 1423a

Skeat, Walter W.   617, 618,
   625, 626, 775, 776, 839,
   927, 1115
Sklar, Elizabeth S.   469,
   667-669
Slater, David T.   573
Small, John   602
Smith, James A.   683
Smith, Kathleen L.   470
Smith, Majorie N.   1162
Smith, Sarah Stanbury   1357
Smithers, G.V.   581, 867,
   868, 944, 945, 947, 948
Smyser, H.M.   574
Smyth, Albert H.   654
So, Francis Kei-hong   182
Sommer, Carol   168
Sørensen, Preben Meulengracht
   52
Soucy, A. Francis   1358
Southgate, Minoo Sassoonian
   209
Spangehl, Stephen Douglas
   987
Spearing, A.C.   415, 700,
   701, 1158
Spector, Sheila Abbye   712
Speirs, John   93, 94
Spensley, Ronald M.   1094
Spring, Ian   1496
Srebnick, Walter   1359
Stainer, P.A.   500
Staines, David   869
Stanley, E.G.   225, 868
Stark, Marilynn Dianne   183
Steckmesser, Kent L.   813
Steffler, Gustav   1131
Steinberg, Theodore   1159
Stemmler, Theo   297, 379,
   1416
Stephany, William Alexander
   348
Stephens, Anthony   389
Stephens, George   1163
Stern, Karen   471
Stevens, David   1194
Stevens, John   184
Stevenson, George   619

Stevenson, Joseph   627, 928
Stevenson, Sharon Lynn   934
Stewart, Marion   1498
Stokes, Myra   1360, 1361
Stokoe, William C., Jr.
   1182
Stottlemyer, Ronald Steven
   1068
Stratmann, Gerd   297
Stratton, Russell Edgar   726,
   730
Strohm, Paul   95, 185, 186,
   187, 501
Stroud, Michael James   1069
Studer, John   1591
Stugrin, Michael   96
Sumner, Laura   1600
Sunderland, S.M.   349
Sundwall, McKay   741, 935
Sutherland, James   1662
Suzuki, Eiichi   262, 634,
   1070-1073, 1361a
Swanton, M.J.   786
Swanzey, Thomas Brian   575
Szarmach, Paul E.   242
Taglicht, J.   1622, 1642,
   1643
Taitt, Peter Stewart   517
Tajimi, Matsuji   1362
Takamiya, Toshiyuki   311
Tambling, Jeremy   1362a
Tamplin, Ronald   1546
Tarlinskaja, Marina   97
Tautscher, Eva Marie   952
Taylor, A.B.   760
Taylor, Anne Robb   1689
Taylor, Beverly   350, 351
Taylor, George   675
Taylor, J.   792
Taylor, Robert A.   88
Terrell, Natalie D.   708
Thomas, Ann C.   319
Thompson, John J.   472, 473
Thompson, Raymond H.   352,
   353, 534, 1517, 1595
Thoms, William J.   1679
Thomson, Derick S.   1481
Thorlby, Anthony   175

Thorpe, Lewis 1542
Thundy, Zacharias P. 386
Tilling, P.M. 1260
Tolkien, J.R.R. 1208
Tonguç, Sencer 518
Tonndorf, Max 1569
Tonsfeldt, Hugh Ward 1074
Torrini-Roblin, Gloria 1363
Torti, Anna 289
Trask, Richard 1364
Trautmann, Moritz 815
Treharne, R.F. 354
Treichel, A. 1167
Tripp, Raymond P., Jr. 1365
Trounce, A. McI. 676
Tsuchiya, Tadayuki 1209
Turley, Raymond V. 474
Turnbull, W.B.D.D. 620, 662, 707, 823, 1097
Turner, Jerry David 635
Turville-Petre, Gabriel 375
Turville-Petre, Thorlac 210, 263, 264, 475, 636, 637, 702, 1400, 1618
Tuve, Rosemond 98
Twomey, Michael 976
Urry, J. 777
Utley, Francis Lee 99, 355
Utterson, E. V. 621, 727, 1107, 1681
Vaghaiwalla, Feroza Rustom 1366
Vale, Juliet 1075
Van Buuren-Veenenbos, C.C. 476
Van Duzee, Mabel 751
Van Nuis, Hermine J. 1367
Van Os, Jaap 1611
Vantuono, William 1210
Varin, Amy 356
Varnhagen, Hermann 921
Varty, E.K.C. 300a
Varty, Kenneth 357
Várvaro, Alberto 48
Vasta, Edward 386
Vaughan, M.F. 1076
Vause, Deborah Noble 870
Veldhoen, N.H.G.E. 1518

Ven-Ten Bensel, Elise 358
Vicari, Patricia 1498
Viëtor, Wilhelm 717
Vinaver, Eugéne 188-190, 359
Visser, Elizabeth 949
Vitz, Evelyn Birge 100
Wadsworth, Rosalind 434
Wager, C.H.A. 1128
Waldman, Thomas G. 708
Waldron, Ronald A. 73a, 265, 1196, 1211
Wallace, Sylvia Crowell 1424
Wallner, Björn 670
Walpole, Ronald N. 1596
Walsh, Edward Michael 576
Walsh, Elizabeth 1570-1572, 1592
Ward, Margaret Charlotte 1368
Warden, John 1498
Wasserman, Julian N. 1235, 1246
Wasserman, Loretta 1369
Wattie, Margaret 922
Weber, Henry 622
Wehrli, Max 101
Weiss, Alexander 102
Weiss, Judith 477, 713, 871
Weiss, Victoria L. 1370
Wentersdorf, Karl P. 767
Wertime, Richard A. 977
West, Henry S. 913
Westlake, J.S. 1704
Wetherbee, Winthrop 1499
Wheatley, Henry B. 1705
Whitaker, Muriel Anna Isabel 360
White, Beatrice 103, 104, 703
White, Jack H. 1371
Whitebook, Budd Bergovoy 577
Whiting, Bartlett J. 1601
Wilgus, D.K. 168
Wilkin, Gregory J. 1372
Williams, E.G. 728
Williams, Edith W. 1373
Williams, Elizabeth 1394

Williams, M.E. 1506
Williams, Mary 361
Williems, D.J. 266
Wilson, A.D. 191
Wilson, Anne 105
Wilson, Edward 1374
Wilson, John Holmes 1575
Wilson, R.M. 1663
Wilson, Richard M. 106
Wilson, Robert H. 1077
Wimsatt, James 397
Wirtjes, Hanneke 173, 1375
Wissmann, Theodor 897-899
Wittig, Susan 192, 416, 578
Wolfzettal, Friedrich 362
Wolpers, Theodor 107
Woolf, Rosemary 108
Wrenn, C.L. 1044
Wright, Dorena Allen (see
   also Dorena Allen) 1500,
   1501
Wright, Michael J. 1417
Wright, Thomas 677, 778
Wright, W. Aldis 788
Wülfing, J. Ernst 932
Wülker, R. 1091
Wurster, Jutta 1078
Wurtele, Douglas 931
Yeager, Robert F. 109, 1677
Yoder, Emily 380, 1079
York, Ernest C. 1547-1549
Zaletel, Cora 1376
Zamora, Marcela C. 1080
Zanco, Aurelio 110
Zehringer, William Clark
   1555
Zellefrow, William Kenneth
   814
Zesmer, David A. 111
Zettersten, Arne 478
Ziegler, Georgianna 535,
   915
Zielcke, Oscar 1425
Zietsch, A. 1129
Zimbardo, Rose A. 3
Zimmerman, R. 1392
Zupitza, Julius 678, 824-826